# THE STORY OF AMERICA

# The Story of America

## ESSAYS ON ORIGINS

### Jill Lepore

PRINCETON UNIVERSITY PRESS

PRINCETON AND OXFORD

Copyright © 2012 by Jill Lepore
Requests for permission to reproduce material from this work should be sent to
    Permissions, Princeton University Press
Published by Princeton University Press, 41 William Street, Princeton, New Jersey 08540
In the United Kingdom: Princeton University Press, 6 Oxford Street, Woodstock,
    Oxfordshire OX20 1TW

press.princeton.edu

Parts of this book appeared originally in *The New Yorker*.
"Longfellow's Ride" is from *The American Scholar* 80, no. 1 (Winter 2011).
    Copyright © 2010 by Jill Lepore.

All Rights Reserved

Second printing, and first paperback printing, 2014
Paperback ISBN 978-0-691-15959-1

The Library of Congress has cataloged the cloth edition of this book as follows

Lepore, Jill, 1966–
        The story of America : essays on origins / Jill Lepore.
        p. cm.
        Includes bibliographical references and index.
        ISBN 978-0-691-15399-5 (alk. paper)
        1. United States—History—Sources. 2. United States—Politics and government—
Sources. I. Title.
        E173.L47 2012
        973—dc23          2012016854

British Library Cataloging-in-Publication Data is available

This book has been composed in Adobe Caslon Pro and Trade Gothic

Printed on acid-free paper. ∞

Printed in the United States of America

10 9 8 7 6 5 4 3 2

**What are the Great United States for, sir, if not for the regeneration of man?**

—Charles Dickens, *Martin Chuzzlewit*

# CONTENTS

# THE STORY OF AMERICA

# INTRODUCTION

In 1938, if you had a dollar and seventy-two cents, you could buy a copy of *The Rise of American Democracy*, a seven-hundred-page hardcover about the size of a biggish Bible or a Boy Scout Handbook. While a Bible's worth is hard to measure, the scout guide, at fifty cents, was an awfully good bargain and an excellent book to have on hand if you were shipwrecked on a desert island, not least because it included a chapter on How to Make Fire without Matches. But *The Rise of American Democracy* promised, invaluably, "to make clear how Americans have come to live and to believe as they do." It is also a very good read. "A Simple Book," its ad copy boasted. "Paragraphs average three to a page. Sentences are short." Better yet: "A Democracy Theme runs through the whole text."

*The Rise of American Democracy* was written by Mabel B. Casner, a Connecticut schoolteacher, and Ralph Henry Gabriel, a Yale professor of intellectual history, in 1937. In those dark days, with Fascism, not democracy, on the rise, Casner and Gabriel offered a wise and sober historian's creed: "We live today in perilous times; so did many of our forefathers. They sometimes made mistakes; let us strive to learn not to repeat these errors. The generations which lived before us left us a heritage of noble ideals; let us hold fast to these." Above all, they wanted students to understand the idea of democracy. But the book is also full of practical teaching tips and "Real life activities"—tested by Casner in her classroom in West

1

Haven, Connecticut—which, while "not to be followed slavishly," were supplied at the end of every chapter, and included instructions for an end-of-year finale, a class play, "The Rise of American Democracy: A Dramatization in Four Scenes," to be performed some cool June afternoon. It opens with a closed curtain:

> *Enter* COLUMBIA *from one side and* BOY *from Europe from the opposite side.*
> **Boy**. I am looking for Columbia. Do you know where I could find her?
> **Columbia**. I am she.
> **Boy** *(bowing).* I am happy and honored to make your acquaintance. I come from Europe. I have heard much of your democracy. I have come to you to find out what it is like. . . .
> **Columbia**. I shall be glad to show you. Perhaps the best way is to go on a journey through American history. (*Exit both together*)

The curtain rises on the Constitutional Convention, where Columbia and the earnest young European watch the delegates conclude their deliberations. Next, Columbia takes her awestruck European student of democracy to "the Western plains in the 1840's" to witness a shambles of bedraggled pioneers scuffle across the stage in the play's pitched climax, which combines singing, cowboy costumes, and even parts for pets, as per the sociable stage direction: "*dogs may be added.*"

"I understand that they are settling your great continent," the boy says, "but I do not understand what they have to do with democracy."

"They have only a few belongings and simple tools," Columbia points out, but "They are building a democratic nation. Men do not have to have possessions to do great things."[1]

No matter if the scenery toppled, if the pioneers tripped in their boots, if the dogs barked and bayed; everyone in the audience was treated to a concise restatement of the then-dominant interpretation of the rise of American democracy: that it was fueled by the settling of the frontier and that it chiefly involved the hardscrabble striving of the poor.

What accounts for the rise of American democracy? Casner and Gabriel tried to answer that question by staging a play, by telling a story. That was a good idea. The United States got its start as a story. It begins: "When in the course of human events . . . ." It has a moral: "All men are created equal." It even has a villain, George III, on whose machinations the plot turns: "The history of the present King of Great Britain is a history of repeated injuries and usurpations, all having in direct object the establishment of an absolute Tyranny over these States."

To say that the United States is a story is not to say that it is fiction; it is, instead, to suggest that it follows certain narrative conventions. All nations are places, but they are also acts of imagination. Who has a part in a nation's story, like who can become a citizen and who has a right to vote, isn't foreordained, or even stable. The story's plot, like the nation's borders and the nature of its electorate, is always shifting. Laws are passed and wars are fought to keep some people in and others out. Who tells the story, like who writes the laws and who wages the wars, is always part of that struggle.

Consider the Declaration of Independence. In March 1776, two months before John Adams was appointed to serve with Thomas Jefferson, Benjamin Franklin, Robert Livingston, and Roger Sherman, on a committee charged with drafting a declaration of independence, Abigail Adams wrote a letter to her husband. "I long to hear that you have declared an independency," she began.

> And, by the way, in the new code of laws which I suppose it will be necessary for you to make, I desire you would remember

the ladies and be more generous and favorable to them than your ancestors. Do not put such unlimited power into the hands of the husbands. Remember, all men would be tyrants if they could. If particular care and attention is not paid to the ladies, we are determined to foment a rebellion, and will not hold ourselves bound by any laws in which we have no voice or representation.[2]

Adams wrote back in April. "As to your extraordinary code of laws, I cannot but laugh," he began. "We have been told that our struggle has loosened the bonds of government everywhere; that children and apprentices were disobedient; that schools and colleges were grown turbulent; that Indians slighted their guardians, and negroes grew insolent to their masters. But your letter was the first intimation that another tribe, more numerous and powerful than all the rest, were grown discontented." He refused to take her story—about the rule of men over women—seriously. "Depend upon it," he resolved, "we know better than to repeal our masculine systems."[3]

The story of America isn't carved in stone, or even inked on parchment; it is, instead, told, and fought over, again and again. It could have gone a thousand other ways. Even the Declaration of Independence could have gone a thousand other ways. In June and into the first days of July, it went through draft after draft. In his original draft, Jefferson, a slave owner, included a breathless paragraph in which he blamed the king for slavery ("He has waged cruel war against human nature itself, violating its most sacred rights of life and liberty in the persons of a distant people who never offended him, captivating and carrying them into slavery"), for his thwarting of colonial efforts to abolish the slave trade ("determined to keep open a market where men should be bought and sold, he has prostituted his negative for suppressing every legislative attempt to prohibit or restrain this execrable commerce"), and for support for proclamations promising freedom to slaves who joined the British army ("he is now exciting those very people to rise in arms among us, and to purchase that liberty of which he had deprived them, by murdering the people upon whom he also obtruded them: thus paying off former crimes committed against the liberties of one people, with crimes which he urges them to commit against the lives of another").[4]

Jefferson's fellow delegates could not abide it. To some, it went too far; to others, it didn't go half far enough. It was struck out almost entirely.

If Adams had listened to his wife, if Jefferson had prevailed, if a thousand other things had gone a thousand other ways, the Declaration of Independence would have come out differently. Instead, the story told in the Declaration of Independence established the equality of all men (but not of women), decried tyranny (but not slavery), and chronicled the king's "long train of abuses and usurpations" to justify what was otherwise treason as necessary to the colonists' "future security." It used the past to make an argument about the future.

The Declaration of Independence is exceptionally beautiful as a piece of writing and as a statement of political philosophy, but using the past to make an argument about the future is far from exceptional; it is, instead, a feature of political rhetoric, always and everywhere. Politics involves elections and votes and money and power, but the heart of politics is describing how things came to be the way they are in such a way as to convince people that you know how to make things the way they ought to be.

This is curious, and worth pondering, because it reveals how much politics has in common with history. Politics is a story about the relationship between the past and the future; history is a story about the relationship between the past and the present. It's what history and politics share—a vantage on the past—that makes writing the history of politics fraught. And it's what they don't share that makes the study of history vital. Politics is accountable to opinion; history is accountable to evidence.

Consider the history of American democracy. Democracy in America was not established with the stroke of a pen, in 1776, when members of the Continental Congress signed the Declaration of Independence. Nor was it established in 1787, when delegates to the Constitutional Convention signed the Constitution. The rise of American democracy was neither inevitable nor swift. It countered prevailing political philosophy. If democracy is rule by the people and if the people are, as Federalists like John Adams believed, "the common Herd of Mankind"—the phrase was a commonplace—then democracy is the government of the worst, the tyranny of the idle, the ignorant, and the ill informed. Alexander Hamilton reasoned that there are but two types of men: "The first are rich and well-born, the other the mass of the people." The rich are wise, the masses fickle. "Give, therefore, to the first class a distinct, permanent share in the government," Hamilton recommended. "They will check the unsteadiness of the second."[5] These are the principles that informed the framers of the Constitution.

In the 1790s, Federalists kept on telling that same story, the story told in the Constitution, about well-born and well-educated men regulating the passions of the common herd; in that story, democracy was bad. Followers of Thomas Jefferson told a different story, much like that told in the Declaration of Independence, about the people rising up against tyranny: "He that is not a Democrat is an aristocrat," they said.[6] The election of 1800, the "revolution of 1800," was a battle between these two stories.

The "contest of opinion," as Jefferson called it, was waged in the pages of the nation's newspapers. (There were, at the time, no presidential debates and very few speeches. Americans considered politicians putting themselves so far forward to be unforgivably tacky. When Adams took a roundabout route, wending his way from Massachusetts to the nation's brand-new capital city through Pennsylvania and Maryland, a journey that looked suspiciously like campaigning, a Jeffersonian newspaper editor asked, "Why must the President go fifty miles out of his way to make a trip to Washington?")[7] In newspapers, Adams was generally caricatured as a monarch and Jefferson as an atheist. The Philadelphia *Aurora*, an organ of Jefferson's party, suggested that electing Adams, the incumbent, would mean keeping "Things As They Are":

> The principles and patriots of the *Revolution* condemned.
> The *Nation* in arms without a foe, and divided without a cause.
> The reign of terror created by false alarms, to promote domestic feud and foreign war.
> A Sedition Law.
> An established church, a religious test, and an order of Priesthood.

But electing Jefferson would lead to a different future, described as "Things As They Will Be":

> The Principles of the *Revolution* restored.
> The *Nation* at peace with the world and united in itself.
> *Republicanism* allaying the fever of domestic feuds, and subduing the opposition by the force of reason and rectitude.
> The Liberty of the Press.
> Religious liberty, the rights of conscience, no priesthood, truth, and Jefferson.[8]

The next day, a Federalist paper called the *Gazette of the United States* ran, on its front page, this piece:

> **THE GRAND QUESTION STATED**
>
> At the present solemn and momentous epoch, the only question to be asked by every American, laying his hand on his heart is: "Shall I continue in allegiance to
>
> GOD—AND A RELIGIOUS PRESIDENT:

Or impiously declare for

JEFFERSON—AND NO GOD!!!!"[9]

Jeffersonians described the choice as between war and peace; Federalists pit Jefferson against God.

Jefferson won, and Jeffersonianism prevailed. But what the election really did was establish two-party politics. Then came Jacksonianism. In the 1820s and 1830s, "democracy" was, for the first time, no longer a slur. New states entering the union adopted new and more democratic constitutions—and then old states revised their constitutions—calling for more direct and frequent elections, and eliminating property requirements for voting. By defining voters as white men, they defined women and black men as outside the electorate. A new kind of politics emerged, tied to party (candidates even began to campaign), arrayed against certain kinds of moneyed privilege (like the national bank), in the thrall of other kinds (like state banks), and with the questions of slavery, Indian sovereignty, and immigration entirely—and brutally—unresolved.

In the lifetime of an American born in 1760 and dead in 1860, the proportion of white men who were eligible to vote grew from less than half to nearly all. This sweeping redefinition of suffrage was unheard of, an astonishing political novelty; it seemed to call for a wholly new understanding of history.[10] Even as it was happening, people wondered what was driving it, and where it would lead. When Alexis de Tocqueville visited the United States in 1831—*"I wish to find out for myself what your American democracy is like," says the European to Columbia*—he concluded that American democracy followed from American equality. "The more I advanced in the study of American society," he wrote, "the more I perceived that this equality of condition is the fundamental fact from which all others seem to be derived." As Tocqueville saw it, a nation of men possessed of roughly equal estates and education must necessarily become a nation of men possessed of roughly equal political rights. "To conceive of men remaining forever unequal upon a single point, yet equal on all others, is impossible; they must come in the end to be equal upon all."[11]

In 1842, Charles Dickens traveled to the United States to discover American democracy, too. Unlike Tocqueville, he left bitterly disillusioned. "This is not the Republic I came to see," he wrote home. "This is not the Republic of my imagination."[12] Dickens found slavery sinister, the American people coarse, and American politics grotesque. He thought the story of America was a lie. By what his friend Thomas Carlyle called "Yankeedoodledum"—American bumptiousness—Dickens was amused but, more, offended.[13] He was especially disgusted by the party system, which he described as nothing so much as "the intrusion of the most pitiful, mean, malicious, creeping, crawling, sneaking party spirit into all transactions of life."[14]

There were more kinds of critics, too, including abolitionists, suffragists, and peace activists: people who pointed out the limits of American democracy. "What, to the American slave, is your 4th of July?" Frederick Douglass asked in 1852:

I answer; a day that reveals to him, more than all other days in the year, the gross injustice and cruelty to which he is the constant victim. To him, your celebration is a sham; your boasted liberty, an unholy license; your national greatness, swelling vanity; your sound of rejoicing are empty and heartless; your denunciation of tyrants brass fronted impudence; your shout of liberty and equality, hollow mockery; your prayers and hymns, your sermons and thanks-givings, with all your religious parade and solemnity, are to him, mere bombast, fraud, deception, impiety, and hypocrisy—a thin veil to cover up crimes which would disgrace a nation of savages.[15]

In 1879, a newspaperman named Henry George published a book called *Progress and Poverty*; it went on to become the most widely read American economic treatise of the nineteenth century. George saw himself as defending "the Republicanism of Jefferson and the Democracy of Jackson" and argued that both were under assault by speculative, industrial capitalism. The poor were getting poorer and the rich were getting richer. Agreeing with Tocqueville that equality of condition had made democracy possible, George argued that inequality of condition was making democracy impossible.[16]

The historian Frederick Jackson Turner thought that democracy was at risk, too, if for a different reason: the United States was running out of wilderness. In 1893, in an essay called "The Significance of the Frontier in American History," Turner argued that the frontier had made democracy possible. From colonial days onward, Turner argued, demands for fuller political participation—for local governance, more frequent elections, and broader suffrage—had come from scrappy, bull-headed frontier settlers bridling, and thumbing their noses, at the authority of eastern elites. "A fool can sometimes put on his coat better than a wise man can do it for him," they told royal governors and, later, state legislators and, most of all, the federal government. The Declaration of Independence and the Constitution may have been drafted on the shores of the Atlantic, Turner conceded, but they were tested in the foothills of the Alleghenies and beyond. "This, at least, is clear," Turner insisted, "American democracy is fundamentally the outcome of the experiences of the American people in dealing with the West."[17]

Turner's thesis influenced decades of American historical interpretation. Turner is why, in Gabriel and Casner's play, those Western settlers shuffle across the stage, dogs nipping at their heels. Turner saw American history as a battle between "savagery" and "civilization," and his thesis influenced, among other things, the founding of new university departments, as did the work of Charles Beard, whose best-selling 1927 book,

*The Rise of American Civilization*, written with his wife Mary Ritter Beard, located the origins of American politics in economic conflict.[18] In 1937, the year Casner and Gabriel finished writing *The Rise of American Democracy*, Harvard founded a graduate program called the "History of American Civilization." Brown University followed in 1945. That same year, in *The Age of Jackson*, Harvard historian Arthur Schlesinger, Jr., suggested that Turner's frontier thesis "is not perhaps so pat a case as some have thought." Following the Beards, Schlesinger believed that the rise of American democracy was the result of class struggle. For Schlesinger, this was a struggle of ideas, and even of stories.[19]

This debate went on and on. In 1948, Columbia historian Richard Hofstadter, then thirty-two, published twelve essays with the title *The American Political Tradition and the Men Who Made It*. Hofstadter thought Turner, the Beards, and Schlesinger were wrong. Telling the stories of American statesmen from Jefferson to FDR, Hofstadter argued that, for all their differences, these men shared a belief in the sanctity of private property, the value of economic opportunity, and the importance of competition.[20]

Hofstadter was groping to explain the origins of America. ("It is imperative in time of cultural crisis to gain fresh perspectives on the past," he insisted.)[21] So were very many other scholars. In 1946, Ralph Henry Gabriel founded a department at Yale called American Studies, whose purpose was "to achieve a broad understanding of American civilization—its origins, evolution and present world relationships." (Gabriel went on to found the American Studies Association.) A generation of historians attempted to define what made Americans American. Meanwhile, a generation of politicians tried to ferret out which Americans were un-American. Yale's American Studies program was utterly bound up with the politics of the Cold War. In 1950, the university accepted a $500,000 donation

stipulating that the American Studies department "provide
for more general understanding of the fact of American history and the fundamental principles of American freedom in
the field of politics, and of economics" in order to combat "the
menace of foreign philosophies." Gabriel resigned in protest.
The donor then demanded that the new chair be a professor
"who firmly believes in the preservation of our System of Free
Enterprise and is opposed to the system of State Socialism,
Communism and Totalitarianism."[22]

At mid-century, even as the Civil Rights movement offered
a searing critique of stories about the rise of American democracy, American historical writing was strikingly sweeping in
its claims about American origins. In 1965, Bernard Bailyn,
then forty-three, delivered three masterful lectures in which
he argued for the importance of institutions and ideas—not
land, or leaders—in shaping politics. The lectures were published with the title *The Origins of American Politics.*[23]

In the decades following the Second World War, graduate programs in American history, American civilization, and
American studies thrived. But by the end of the 1960s, more
and more students enrolling in these programs were interested
in studying the experiences of the vast number of people left
out of their advisers' work—women and children, slaves and
free blacks, servants and immigrants. These younger scholars produced a great deal of invaluable scholarship, but, in it,
they turned away from questions like "What are the origins
of American politics?" believing that even to ask that sort of
question was to participate in Cold War consensus-style intellectual conformity.

The study of neglected groups exploded. Black studies,
women's studies, and ethnic studies programs were founded.
By the 1970s, critics charged that scholars were writing more
and more about less and less for fewer and fewer. "The great
proliferation of historical writing has served not to illuminate

the central themes of Western history but to obscure them," Bailyn complained in 1981, in his presidential address to the American Historical Association. There followed similarly heartfelt laments by Eric Foner, Herbert Gutman, and Thomas Bender.[24] Schlesinger offered a jeremiad of his own in 1992 in *The Disuniting of America*, bemoaning "militant multiculturalism."[25] Meanwhile, during the very years that many historians within the academy were refusing to entertain questions about origins, a theory of constitutional interpretation called "originalism" gained sway among people outside of it; by the end of the twentieth century, originalism had come to dominate the jurisprudence of the U.S. Supreme Court, where it determined the outcome of landmark rulings on everything from the ownership of firearms to the funding of political campaigns.

In 1994, when I was in graduate school at Yale, in the American Studies Program that Ralph Henry Gabriel had founded half a century before, the ugliest battle of what came to be called the "history wars" took place in the nation's capital: after a team of academic historians prepared a set of national history standards, the U.S. Senate rejected them, condemning the proposed curriculum as nothing more than politics masquerading as history.[26] In the wake of this crisis, a great many scholars reflected on the future of the teaching and writing of history in the United States. The American Historical Association and the American Studies Association held forums. Speeches were made; opinion essays were published. Many fine articles and books were written, including *The Story of American Freedom*, a book of rare scope and subtlety, in which Columbia University historian Eric Foner traced the fitful and often bloody struggle over the meaning of freedom during the course of American history.[27] Princeton historian Sean Wilentz's answer to the call for synthesis was *The Rise of American Democracy: From Jefferson to Lincoln*. Wilentz rejected Turner's thesis about the wind of democracy blowing from the West ("In fact," Wilentz argued, "the West borrowed heavily from eastern examples"), but, more, he hoped to reaffirm "the importance of political events, ideas, and leaders to democracy's rise—once an all-too-prevalent assumption, now in need of some repair and rescue."[28]

There had been a drift. In the years between Casner and Gabriel's *Rise of American Democracy* in 1938 and Wilentz's *Rise of American Democracy* in 2005, American history books had changed. Their explanations had become more qualified, and their answers to questions like "What accounts for the rise of American democracy?" had grown vague, doubtful, and conflicted. More often, those questions were no longer asked, at first, because they were too big, and, later, because they were too small. At the beginning of the twenty-first century, advocates of global history dismissed the study of the nation-state as a variety of intellectual provincialism, leaving elementary and secondary school teachers to teach local, state, and national history without the benefit of a rigorous scholarship. Within the academic world, the study of American origins became remarkably unfashionable. Haunted by the knowledge of all that any single study leaves out—all the people, the conflict, the messiness, the obeisance to all the other scholarship— intimidated by ideological attacks, eager to disavow origins stories, and profoundly suspicious, as a matter of critical intelligence, of the rhetorical power of the storyteller, the ambit of academic writing kept getting smaller. So did its readership.

I began writing the essays in this book in 2005, not long after I started teaching at Harvard. All but one of these essays first appeared in *The New Yorker*. I wrote them because I wanted to learn how to tell stories better. But mostly I wrote them because I wanted to try to explain how history works, and how it's different from politics.

History is the art of making an argument about the past by telling a story accountable to evidence. In the writing of history, a story without an argument fades into antiquarianism; an argument without a story risks pedantry. Writing history requires empathy, inquiry, and debate. It requires forswearing condescension, cant, and nostalgia. The past isn't quaint. Much of it, in fact, is bleak. Also, what people will tell you about the past is very often malarkey. The essays in this book concern documents—things like travel narratives, the Constitution, ballots, the inaugural address, the presidential biography, the campaign biography, the I.O.U., and the dime novel. Historical inquiry relies on standards of evidence because documents aren't to be trusted. John Smith, the swashbuckling founder of Virginia, titled an account of his adventures *True Travels*, even though he made most of it up. One way to read this book, then, is as a study of the American tall tale. My advice is to keep one eyebrow cocked and watch out for shifty-looking characters with ink-stained hands and narrators who keep ducking into doorways, especially while reading about *The Life of Jackson*, the wildly fictitious campaign biography of Andrew Jackson; Edgar Allan Poe's "Philosophy of Composition," a pack of lies; and the hopelessly hyperbolic *Life and Adventures of Kit Carson . . . from Facts Narrated by Himself.*

I didn't write the essays in this book with an eye toward offering a novel interpretation of American history. Still, it strikes me that, taken together, they do make an argument, and it is this: the rise of American democracy is bound up with the history of reading and writing, which is one of the reasons the study of American history is inseparable from the study of American literature. In the early United States, literacy rates rose and the price of books and magazines and newspapers fell during the same decades that suffrage was being extended.

With everything from constitutions and ballots to almanacs and novels, Americans wrote and read their way into a political culture inked and stamped and pressed in print.

I've stitched all these essays together here, like the pieces of a quilt, and I've arranged them chronologically, from the sixteenth century to the twenty-first. They cover the length of American history; by no means do they cover its breadth. This book does not tell "the story of America." No one can write that story. This is, instead, a study of the story.

In *American Notes*, Charles Dickens's account of his travels in the United States, he explained that he regarded politics with a jaundiced eye: "I have seen elections for borough and county, and have never been impelled (no matter which party won) to damage my hat by throwing it up into the air in triumph, or to crack my voice by shouting forth any reference to our Glorious Constitution, to the noble purity of our independent voters, or, the unimpeachable integrity of our independent members." Perhaps, he admitted, he suffered "from some imperfect development of my organ of veneration."[29]

This defect is not uncommon. "I have no desire to add to a literature of hero worship and national self-congratulation which is already large," Richard Hofstadter explained in the introduction to *The American Political Tradition and the Men Who Made It*.[30] Neither do I. Instead, mindful of Casner and Gabriel's creed, I have tried to cherish ideas worth cherishing and to question ideas that need questioning. I have tried to do that, here, by studying stories, and by telling them.

# 1

# HERE HE LYES

Buried somewhere under the marble floor of the largest church in London lie the remains of Captain John Smith, who died in 1631, at the age of fifty-one. On a brass plaque, his epitaph reads,

> Here lyes one conquered, that hath conquered Kings,
> Subdu'd large Territories, and done Things
> Which to the world impossible would seem
> But that the Truth is held in more esteem.

In other words: he wasn't a liar. Ah, but don't believe it. The year before he died, Smith published *The True Travels, Adventures, and Observations of Captaine John Smith, in Europe, Asia, Africke, and America*, in which a discerning reader will learn to expect that when the captain, wearing full armor, has his stallion shot out from under him, he'll mount a dead man's horse before his own has hit the ground, and reload his musket while he's at it. Even his mishaps prove his valor: who could have survived so many sea-fights, shipwrecks, mutinies, deserted islands, musket wounds, betrayals, prisons, and gashes gotten while jousting, except a man whose coat-of-arms depicted the severed, turbaned heads of three Turkish army officers he defeated in back-to-back duels in Transylvania and whose motto—emblazoned on his shield—sounds like the title of a James Bond film set in Elizabethan England: *vincere est vivere*. To conquer is to live.[1]

In 1631, while Smith lay on his deathbed, a Welsh clergyman named David Lloyd published *The Legend of Captaine Jones*, a lampoon of Smith's *True Travels*. A later edition includes, by way of preface, a spoof of Smith's well-known epitaph:

Tread softly (mortalls) ore the bones
Of the worlds wonder Captaine Jones:
Who told his glorious deeds to many,
But never was believ'd of any:
Posterity let this suffice,
He swore all's true, yet here he lyes.[2]

That Captain John Smith, even before he died, was widely believed to be a liar is of more than passing interest, especially since he was also, arguably, America's first historian. In *True Travels*, Smith claimed to have defeated armies, outwitted heathens, escaped pirates, hunted treasure, and wooed princesses—and all this on four continents, no less, including a little island in North America that would one day be known as the birthplace of the United States: Jamestown, Virginia.

"I am no Compiler by hearsay, but have beene a reall Actor," John Smith wrote. He was an adventurer, and he was a historian. He recounted his adventures in Virginia not only in *True Travels*, but also, first, in a letter printed without his permission in 1608 as *A True Relation of Such Occurrences and Accidents of Noate as Hath Hapned in Virginia*; next, in an essay on the Virginia Indians published in 1612 as *A Map of Virginia* and bound with a longer account of the founding of Jamestown, *The Proceedings of the English Colonie in Virginia*; and, once more, in *The Generall Historie of Virginia*, printed in 1624.

John Smith was born in Alford, Lincolnshire, in 1580. He left England at the age of sixteen "to learne the life of a

Souldier." He fought the Spanish in France and in the Netherlands, sailed to Scotland, and returned to England to live
like a hermit in the woods, reading books and practicing to
be a knight: "His studie was Machiavills Art of warre, and
Marcus Aurelius; his exercise a good horse, with his lance and
Ring."[3] In 1600, he crossed the Channel again. After adventures in France, including a duel near Mont-St.-Michel, he
tried to sail from Marseilles to Italy but was thrown over-
board. Rescued by pirates, he sailed the Mediterranean and
learned to fight at sea. In 1601, he joined the Austrian army
to fight the Turks in Hungary, mainly because he regretted
having "seene so many Christians slaughter one another." He
was promoted to captain. Wounded in a battle near Bucharest,
in which thirty thousand men died, Smith and a handful of
survivors were captured and "sold for slaves, like beasts in a
market place." He was sent to Istanbul, to serve his owner's
mistress. But she fell in love with him. Eventually, he escaped.
After making his way through Russia and Poland, and fighting in Morocco, Smith returned to England in the winter of
1604–5.[4] In December 1606, when he was twenty-six, he sailed
to Virginia, with a fleet of three ships, the *Godspeed*, the *Susan
Constant*, and the *Discovery*.

Smith had three Turks' heads on his shield, but he wasn't
the only Jamestown adventurer to have traveled through the
Ottoman Empire.[5] William Strachey, who became secretary
of the colony in 1609, had been in Istanbul in 1607. George
Sandys, the colony's treasurer, had traveled, by camel, to Jerusalem and had written, at length, about the "Mahometan
Religion." To these men, the New World beckoned as but another battlefield for the Old World's religious wars; they went,
mainly, to hunt for gold to fund wars to defeat Muslims in
Europe.[6]

For much of the voyage to Virginia, Smith was confined
below decks, in chains, accused of plotting a mutiny to "make

himselfe king." In May 1607, Smith and 104 other colonists settled on the banks of a river they named the James, in honor of
their king, on land named after his predecessor, Elizabeth, the
Virgin Queen. On board ship they had carried a box containing a list of men appointed by the Virginia Company to govern
the colony, "not to be opened, nor the governours knowne until
they arrived in Virginia."[7] When at last the box was opened, it
was revealed that Smith, still a prisoner, was on that list. On
June 10, 1607, he was sworn as a member of the governing council.[8] In September 1608, he was elected its president, effectively,
Virginia's governor. By his telling, he was also its only hope.


Far from being the first Europeans to settle on land that
would one day become the United States, the English were
Johnny-come-latelies. The Spanish settled at San Augustine,
Florida, in 1565; by 1607, they were building Santa Fe. In 1975,
Yale historian Edmund Morgan famously dubbed Jamestown
a "fiasco": "Measured by any of the objectives announced for
it," Morgan reckoned, "the colony failed." The English landed,
and "for the next ten years they seem to have made nearly every
possible mistake and some that seem almost impossible." They
chose a poor site: on the banks of a brackish river. They had
a lousy plan: build a fort, and look for gold. They brought the
wrong kind of settlers: idle and indolent English gentlemen,
who spent their time bowling in the streets. (Smith counted
one carpenter, two blacksmiths, and a flock of footmen; the
rest of the settlers he wrote off as "Gentlemen, Tradesmen,
Servingmen, libertines, and such like, ten times more fit to
spoyle a Commonwealth, than either begin one, or but helpe
to maintaine one.") They made enemies easily: especially the
Powhatan Indians, even though they relied on them for food,
having harvested little of their own. Mostly, they died. Except
for the year Smith was in charge, from the fall of 1608 to the

fall of 1609, when he told its half-dead men, "he who does not worke, shall not eat," they starved.[9] It wasn't the land that was the problem. "Had we beene in Paradice it selfe (with those governours)," Smith complained, "it would not have beene much better."[10] After October 1609, when Smith returned to England (ostensibly, to recover from an injury but, really, he was more or less kicked out), Jamestown went to hell. In the winter of 1609–10 alone, five hundred colonists were reduced to sixty. A hair-raising account of those months, written by the colony's lieutenant governor, George Percy, the eighth son of the earl of Northumberland, paints this scene: "many, through extreme hunger, have run out of their naked beds being so lean that they looked like anatomies, crying out, we are starved, we are starved." In the end, they ate each other. Percy writes, "one of our Colline murdered his wife Ripped the Childe outt of her woambe and threwe it into the River and after Chopped the Mother in pieces and salted her for his food." Telling the story of the husband showering his wife with salt, another settler wondered: "Now whether shee was better roasted, boyled or carbonado'd, I know not, but of such a dish as powdered wife I never heard of."[11]

"An American dream was born on the banks of the James River," insisted Jamestown archaeologist, William M. Kelso, in *Jamestown: The Buried Truth*.[12] Kelso's book was published in 2007, Jamestown's four hundredth anniversary: America's birthday. Elizabeth the second turned up at Jamestown for the festivities—concerts, reenactments, exhibits, and more—and bookshops stocked up on confetti-laced books, including a Library of America edition of Smith's writings, wrapped in its signature red-white-and-blue ribbon.

Kelso was writing within a tradition of Jamestown boosters who triumph in the colony's eventual success. By the 1620s, in spite of a mortality rate that remained as high as 75 or 80 percent, the Virginia economy was booming. Hence, the American dream: arrive empty-handed, work hard, and get rich.

Just as cock-eyed, anachronistic, and overblown is a debunking tradition that damns Jamestown as the birthplace of the American nightmare: with corporate funding from wealthy investors (the Virginia Company), steal somebody else's land (the Powhatans') and reap huge profits by planting and harvesting an addictive drug (tobacco, whose sales were responsible for the boom), while exploiting your labor force (indigent Britons and, after 1619, enslaved Africans).

American dream or American nightmare, the bare facts about Jamestown can be dressed up and pressed into the service of either of these narratives. And they have been. One abolitionist, writing in 1857—Jamestown's 250th anniversary—argued that Americans ought to ignore 1607 and instead pay attention to the divided nation's twin, Cain-and-Abel, founding moments: the Pilgrims' 1620 landing in Plymouth and the arrival of the first Africans to Jamestown in 1619. "Here are the two ideas, Liberty and Slavery—planted at about the same time, in the virgin soil of the new continent; the one in the North, the other in the South. They are deadly foes. Which shall conquer?" To antebellum Northerners, Jamestown set in motion forces that would lead to Civil War. To organizers of Jamestown four hundredth anniversary, what started in their town was America itself.

For a very long time, the question that animated every history of Jamestown was the very one that most troubled John Smith: "howe it came to passe there was no better successe."[13] In other words, why did things go so badly? The debate over that question, in the 1970s and 1980s, in the shadow of Vietnam, was one of the most vigorous in all of early American

historical scholarship, at least as vigorous as, and more important than, the earlier and continuing argument over the causes
of the witchcraft outbreak in Salem in 1692, a debate that has
never really crawled out from under the shadow of McCarthy-
ism. The too-many-gentlemen theory is pretty compelling—in
Smith's shorthand, "miserable is that Land, where more are
idle then well imployed"—but for years historians marshaled
evidence in support of a range of provocative explanations,
from salt poisoning and contaminated wells to the Little Ice
Age and an epidemic of apathy and, finally, to the colonists'
sheer, stubborn preference for planting tobacco, to sell, instead
of corn, to eat.[14] But during Jamestown's four hundredth anniversary, historians turned this unanswered question upside
down, asking, not why Jamestown at first failed but why, in the
end, did it succeed? Thus did the Jamestown quadricentennial
snatch victory from the jaws of a man who ate his wife.

"To call Jamestown a failure, let alone a disaster," Kelso
wrote, "is to oversimplify."[15] Kelso's evidence for his claim was
what he'd found: Jamestown Fort. Before Kelso came along,
archaeologists had concluded that the remains of the fort the
settlers built in the spring of 1607 had long since been washed
away by the James River. Kelso was sure its foundation lay
under ground, and not under water. Beginning in 1994, when
he was hired as the head archaeologist of the Jamestown Recovery Project, Kelso oversaw the painstaking rediscovery
of the fort's footprint, one of the most exciting finds, ever,
in American historical archaeology. Within and around the
fort's footprint, Kelso's team dug up not only human remains,
palisade lines, and building foundations, but also a treasure of
artifacts: beads, armor, pottery, and tools, each with a story to
tell. The jawbone of a dog, with lead shot in it; a butchered
turtle; thimbles; a suit of armor, thrown down a well, piece by
piece; even a fancy silver "ear picker," a kind of combination
Q-Tip and toothpick. What story these artifacts tell is less

clear (wouldn't it have been better to pack a few more hoes for the voyage, and not so many ear pickers?). Kelso argued that the archaeological record tilts toward proving that Jamestown's first settlers weren't nearly as hapless as John Smith made them out to be; after all, they built a very good fort, very quickly: "There is evidence that some of the immigrants worked hard."[16]

"The truly remarkable thing about Jamestown is that it somehow survived," the historian Karen Kupperman argued in 2007, in *The Jamestown Project*. Kupperman mainly measured the colony against both earlier and later English settlement efforts in North America, including Roanoke, England's first attempt to establish a foothold in the New World, on the outer shoals of what is now North Carolina. Settled in 1584, Roanoke was deserted three years later, and it's anyone's guess what happened to the ninety men, seventeen women, and eleven children who were left behind when the governor, John White, sailed to England for help; when he returned, in 1590, they were gone. Compared to Roanoke, Kupperman pointed out, Jamestown is a stunner.

Kupperman's argument, that Jamestown wasn't really that bad, required her to explain why it *looks* so bad. Resolutely, she blamed the sources, "which consist largely of complaints, special pleading, and excuses sent by colonists back to their patrons in England."[17] They made everything sound worse than it was. And the devil of it is, some of these kvetchers were actually colorful writers, which, Kupperman warned, has led historians to make a fatal error: reading their accounts "to mine them for pithy quotes."[18] Again with the wife-eating man!

John Smith liked to blame whiners, too. "Ingenious verbalists," he called those who came to Virginia, while he was in charge, only to find themselves shocked by what they saw, "because they found not English Cities, nor such faire houses, nor at their owne wishes any of their accustomed dainties, with feather beds, and downe pillows, Tavernes and alehouses." Such men, he said, were those who would call Virginia, under his inspired leadership, "a misery, a ruine, a death, a hell."[19] But that was what Smith said about Virginia *before* he left. Only after he returned to England did he begin to see that what was going on in Jamestown was impossible to discover from so far away, investors having need of twisting the story this way and that, like so many corporate executives, in a world without a Securities and Exchange Commission (although by 1624 a royal commission had begun investigating the Virginia Company for mismanagement). No matter how many men ate their wives, Smith wearily concluded, reports in England would make "the Company here thinke all the world was Oatmeale there."[20]

The question of whether John Smith was a liar is inseparable from the question of whether Jamestown was a failure. They don't map onto one another exactly, but it usually works like this: if Smith told the truth, Jamestown was a disaster, except when he was in charge. It's possible to both believe Smith and see Jamestown as a success, but that requires quite a bit of squinting. Generally, if, like the Virginia Company, you'd like to think that everything in Jamestown was oatmeal, it helps if you are willing to say that Smith was either ill informed or stretching the truth, although, most often, those who discredit Smith aren't as gracious as that. Their assessments have a more of a liar-liar-pantaloons-on-fire quality. (As it happens, and for the record, they were: the injury that sent Smith back to England was a severe burn he sustained to his thighs and groin when his gunpowder bag, laying in his lap, caught the spark of a tobacco pipe and exploded.)[21]

This liar-disaster situation was a bind, and Smith knew it. He wrote, in 1616, that he fully expected to "live or die the slave of scorne and infamy."[22] And he did. As David Lloyd's *Legend of Captaine Jones* would have it, Smith made up most of what he wrote, or at least exaggerated, brazenly. Nevertheless, in the colonies, and especially in the early United States, *The Legend of Captaine Jones* was entirely forgotten and, despite lingering doubts about his credibility, Smith, no longer lampooned, became a romantic hero of the nineteenth-century American South, his exploits celebrated—and lavishly embroidered—in songs and on stage, in antebellum productions that implausibly but invariably paired him, romantically, with Pocahontas, who, only fourteen when Smith left Virginia, in 1609, had actually married a colonist named John Rolfe, in 1614.

This distortion of historical fact Henry Adams could not abide. Appalled by the myth of Smith's romance with Pocahontas, Adams earned his reputation as a historian by destroying the captain's. In an 1867 essay in the *North American Review*, Adams's very first piece of historical criticism (in 1870, he would be named professor of history at Harvard), he pointed out the discrepancies in Smith's different accounts of his rescue by Pocahontas, a story he told differently every time he told it and one that, after all, sounded not a little suspicious the first time. Worse, Smith didn't even mention the rescue until after Pocahontas's visit to London, in 1616, when she was received as a foreign dignitary. Only in 1617 did Smith boast that Pocahontas had once "hazarded the beating out of her owne braines to save mine," after her father, Powhatan, had ordered his men to kill him.[23] In his 1624 *Generall Historie*, Smith added still more detail: "being ready with their clubs, to beate out his braines, Pocahontas the Kings dearest daughter, when no intreaty could prevaile, got his head in her armes, and laid her owne upon his to save him from death." Smith's work, he concluded, contained "falsehoods of an effrontery seldom equaled in modern times."[24]

In offering this exposé, Adams claimed to have been motivated solely by his zeal to establish the "bald historical truth," but, privately, he confessed that he considered his essay "a rear attack on the Virginia aristocracy."[25] Writing in the immediate aftermath of the Civil War, Adams, who despised the South, delighted in defeating a founding father of the Old Dominion. Equally pleased was John Gorham Palfrey, a Harvard professor and New England booster who had persuaded Adams to write the essay in the first place, allegedly telling him that "a stone thrown at Smith would be as likely to break as much glass as a missile heaved in any other direction." He was right. Smith's reputation as a man of his word and, especially, as a historian, was shattered (and Palfrey's project, to promote New England as the birthplace of America, and 1620 as its birthday, greatly advanced). Smith had his defenders, to be sure, including Edward Arber, who edited an eleven-hundred-page compilation of his writings in 1884 and who argued, "wherever we *can* check Smith, we find him both modest and accurate." But far more common was the kind of dismissal offered by J. Franklin Jameson, in his 1891 *History of Historical Writing in America*, in which he concluded, after reading Smith, that "what was historical was not Smith's and what was his was not historical."[26] In effect, Adams and Jameson relegated John Smith's works to the (lowly) rank of literature and demoted Smith himself from historian to mere writer. After that, about the nicest thing any American historian was willing to say about John Smith was an aside offered by Samuel Eliot Morison, in 1930, who called him "a liar, if you will; but a thoroughly cheerful and generally harmless liar."[27]

After that, three things happened: it was discovered that much of what Smith wrote was actually true; historians began to care more about the art of lying, anyway; and Smith was rehabilitated as an astute, if biased, ethnographer.

In 1953, the historian Bradford Smith published a biography whose aim was to check John Smith's word against that of his contemporaries and, working both with newly discovered sources in England and, more importantly, with a Hungarian scholar named Laura Polanyi Striker, B. Smith concluded that J. Smith was a man of his word. A quixotic, self-aggrandizing Elizabethan gallant and knight-errant? Yes. But a fraud? No. Inspired by Bradford Smith's biography, Philip Barbour, a linguist and former intelligence officer, scoured archives across Eastern Europe, where he was able to corroborate an astonishing number of details in Smith's *True Travels*. All kinds of additional research—including a successful re-creation, by the Boy Scouts of Graz, Austria, of a mountaintop torch-message system that Smith had described but which had never before been tested—only further supported the captain's credibility.[28]

Meanwhile, many historians came to the generous assessment that Smith was, at heart, a man of letters, engaged in what the literary critic Stephen Greenblatt once labeled "self-fashioning." Then, too, scholars of a more anthropological cast of mind, and an interest in the Powhatans, claimed Smith as one of early America's best ethnographers. After all, compared to his contemporaries, Smith was a keen observer, although it's worth remembering that most of what he saw, in Transylvania as much as in Jamestown, was altogether new to him, stranger than strange, and he wasn't always able to make sense of it. Two historians, James West Davidson and Mark Hamilton Lytle, once tried to imagine how Smith might have reported what he could see from the pressroom at Yankee Stadium, some summer afternoon:

> Being assembled about a great field of open grass, a score of their greatest men ran out upon the field, adorned each in brightly

hued jackets and breeches, with letters cunningly woven upon their Chestes, and wearinge hats upon their heades, of a sort I know not what. One of their chiefs stood in the midst and would at his pleasure hurl a white ball at another chief, whose attire was of a different colour, and whether by chance or artifice I know not the ball flew exceeding close to the man yet never injured him, but sometimes he would strike att it with a wooden club and so giving it a hard blow would throw down his club and run away.[29]

In other words, you can count on Smith for abundant detail, and admirable accuracy, but he's fairly likely to leave out what you most want to know: "Yankees 10, Red Sox 3."

At the age of twenty-nine, John Smith returned to England. He spent most of the rest of his life, another twenty-two years, writing. "Envie hath taxed me to have writ too much, and done too little," he complained.[30] He never took up another profession. He never married, or had children (facts perhaps best explained by his pantaloons having once been set on fire; his wound has a decidedly Toby Shandy quality to it). He was restless. He wanted, urgently, to participate in more northern settlements—he gave "New England" its name—but the Puritans didn't want him along. Instead, he had to settle for giving them armchair advice, a role he hated: "it were more proper for mee, To be doing what I say, then writing what I knowe."[31] His last work, published posthumously, is an impassioned essay with a desperate title: *Advertisements for the unexperienced Planters of New-England, or any where.* Smith's advice—bring your women (just don't eat them), and don't forget to plant corn—was taken, and may well have saved New England from Jamestown's early misery, but Smith himself died poor and scorned. As Adams put it, using the very language so often used to describe early Virginia, Smith's career "turned out a failure, and his ventures ended disastrously."[32]


And Jamestown? Was it, too, a failure and a disaster? Or was it, instead, the birthplace of the American dream? This question outlived its usefulness a very long time ago. By considering the world that Jamestown made, and ignoring the world that made Jamestown, it hides more than it reveals. John Smith was more medieval than modern, closer to a Crusader than to a Founding Father. Neither he nor Jamestown can bear the burden of the national need for a tidy past. (Neither can Plymouth.) What happened in Jamestown is a story of vaunting ambition and staggering success in the face of surpassing cruelty and rank catastrophe. It is a story of some lessons painfully learned, and others not learned at all. Here are two. The world isn't made of oatmeal. And to conquer isn't the only way to live.

# 2

# A PILGRIM PASSED I

Samuel Eliot Morison, the last Harvard historian to ride his horse to work, liked to canter to Cambridge on his gray gelding, tie it to a tree in the Yard, stuff his saddlebags with papers to grade, and trot back home to his four-story brick house at the foot of Beacon Hill. "Ours was the horsey end of town," he once wrote, of the place where he was born, in 1887, and died, in 1976.[1] Morison has been called the greatest American historian of the twentieth century. With that, as these things go, not everyone agrees. He spent nearly all his career at Harvard; he entered as a freshman in 1904 and retired, an endowed professor, in 1955. Summers he spent sailing: he loved nothing so much as the ocean. "My feeling for the sea," Morison said, "is such that writing about it is about as embarrassing as making a confession of religious faith."[2]

Morison wrote more than fifty books and won two Pulitzer Prizes, but he is probably best remembered for his biography of Christopher Columbus, whose voyages he retraced, in 1939 and 1940, by yacht. When the resulting book was published in 1942, Franklin Delano Roosevelt was so impressed that he agreed to allow Morison to join the navy as a sailor-historian: for the remainder of the war, Lieutenant Commander Morison fought the battles about which he would later spend twenty years writing, in fifteen dense, salt-sprayed volumes, as the *History of United States Naval Operations in World War II*. He left the navy, in 1951, a rear admiral.

Besides the sea, Morison wrote about two things especially well: colonial New England and historical writing. In a 1931 essay called "Those Misunderstood Puritans," he fought hard against the notion that "the fathers of New England" were "somber kill-joys." For this myth, Morison blamed the Victorians, who cast the Puritans as prudes in order that they might feel, by comparison, broad-minded. As Morison pointed out, with characteristic clarity, relying on the nineteenth century to understand the seventeenth is a rather grave chronological error. Time moves forward, not backward. "The right approach to the Puritan founders of New England is historical, by way of the Middle Ages," he explained. "They were, broadly speaking, the Englishmen who had accepted the Reformation without the Renaissance."[3]

Reading Morison, you can almost hear yourself agree with him, even when you don't. That was Morison's gift. Except that it wasn't a gift. Morison cared about writing, but he had to work hard at it, and he railed against members of his profession unwilling to exert the same effort. In a twenty-five-cent pamphlet printed in 1946 as *History as a Literary Art: An Appeal to Young Historians*, Morison complained: "American historians, in their eagerness to present facts and their laudable concern to tell the truth, have neglected the literary aspects of their craft. They have forgotten that there is an art of writing history."[4]

They had forgotten, that is, an American literary tradition begun by "the earliest colonial historians," and, above all, by William Bradford, the governor and first chronicler of Plymouth plantation.[5] In 1620, Bradford crossed what he called "the vast and furious ocean" on board the *Mayflower*, a 180-ton, three-masted, square-rigged merchant vessel, its cramped berths filled with forty other religious dissenters who, like Bradford, wanted to separate from the Church of England, and some sixty rather less pious passengers who were in search of nothing so much as adventure. Bradford called these "profane" passengers "Strangers," but to modern sensibilities they can feel more familiar than, say, William Brewster, who brought along a son named "Wrestling," short for "wrestling with God."[6]

The colony William Bradford helped plant on the wind-swept western shore of Cape Cod bay was tiny, and it shrank before it grew; by 1650, its population had not yet reached a thousand. Plymouth colony was Bradford's colony. Between 1627 and 1656, he was elected governor every year.[7] Passionate, self-taught, and bold beyond measure, it was Bradford who called his people "pilgrims." He was also a poet, if not a very good one:

> From my years young in days of youth,
> God did make known to me his truth,
> And call'd me from my native place
> For to enjoy the means of grace.
> In wilderness he did me guide,
> and in strange lands for me provide.
> In fears and wants, through weal and woe,
> A Pilgrim passed I to and fro.[8]

Bradford wrote his history, he said, "in a plain style, with singular regard unto the simple truth in all things."[9] He might as well have been describing how he lived his life. But Bradford was more than plain and simple: he was contemplative. Cotton Mather once wrote of him, "He was a person for study as well as action," something that might equally be said of Samuel Eliot Morison who once, interrupted at his desk by the incessant barking of a neighbor's dog, went outside and shot it.[10]

Bradford began writing his history in 1630, the year the Englishman John Winthrop founded the Massachusetts Bay Colony, just to the north of Plymouth. Winthrop's colonists are more commonly called "Puritans," because they wanted to purify the Church of England, but the Pilgrims were Puritans, too—and "nobody more so," as Morison once put it.[11] The distinction between Pilgrims and Puritans is a nineteenth-century invention; in truth, their doctrinal differences were slight. Still, the rivalry between the two colonies was intense, and to Plymouth's disadvantage. By 1641, over twenty thousand colonists had settled in Massachusetts, entirely dwarfing the "Old Colony." (In 1691, Plymouth became part of Massachusetts.)

Governor Bradford, in other words, had more than barking dogs to distract him: not just Winthrop's colonists to the north, but Indians everywhere, pigs run amok, and Quakers in Rhode Island mocking ministers in the pulpit. Try as he might, Bradford just couldn't find the time to catch his past up with his present. He died in 1657, at the age of sixty-seven, his history unfinished.[12] Maybe because Bradford's history ends abruptly, in 1647, most Americans' sense of what happened to the Pilgrims vaguely trails off, too, sometime after the Wampanoag Indian Massasoit taught them to plant corn and joined them for the first Thanksgiving, but long before Plymouth and those same Indians went to war. Go to war they did. In 1675, Massasoit's son Metacom, known to the English as "King Philip," launched a war against Plymouth and, eventually, against Massachusetts and Rhode Island and Connecticut, too. The bloody carnage known as "King Philip's War" nearly put an end to the Puritan experiment.

In *Mayflower: A Story of Courage, Community, and War* (2006), a best-selling popular history, Nathaniel Philbrick called William Bradford's history "the greatest book written in seventeenth-century America."[13] (With that, as these things go, not everyone agrees.) Despite its title, Philbrick's book wasn't really about the Mayflower. The voyage is nearly over by the end of chapter 1, although not over soon enough for Bradford's distressed wife Dorothy, who had left her three-year-old son behind in Holland and who, in sight of land, fell—or more likely threw herself—over the gunwales, and drowned. And, unfortunately, by the time the Pilgrims go ashore, readers have learned more about things like the *Mayflower*'s sounding leads ("the deep-sea or 'dipsy' lead, which weighed between forty and one hundred pounds and was equipped with 600 feet of line, and the smaller 'hand-lead,' just seven to fourteen pounds with 120 feet of line") than about its passengers' religious convictions ("A Puritan believed that everything happened for a reason").[14] It's not that the ship doesn't matter. It does. But with every sway and pitch of its decks, readers are lulled into believing that the people on board, swaying and pitching in winds we can feel, clutching at ropes we can touch, were just like us. They were not.

Philbrick, a former all-American sailor and Sunfish-racing champion from Nantucket, seemed, at first glance, to be following in Morison's wake. Waves sloshed through all his earlier books, whose titles sound like the names of sea shanties: *The Sea of Glory, Away off Shore, Second Wind, In the Heart of the Sea*. Like Morison, Philbrick, who was trained as a journalist, found most history books written by professors a chore to read. Of his decision not to use footnotes or to refer to works of scholarship in his text he explained, "I wanted to remove the scholarly apparatus that so often gets in the way of the plot in academic history."[15]

Sam Morison never met a footnote he didn't like. Still, his relationship to academic history was a complicated one. At Harvard, he was neither a natural nor a beloved teacher. He never held office hours; he made his students come to class in coat and tie; he refused to teach Radcliffe girls (he considered them frivolous by which he meant, presumably, that they were not men). He liked to lecture, in his youth, in riding breeches and, in later years, in his navy uniform.[16] "Even before he became an admiral you felt as though he were one, and you were a midshipman," recalled his former student, Edmund Morgan.[17]

But Morison believed, ardently, that there was something about the hurly-burly of university life that made people more honest, and more accountable, and less likely to get things wrong. In a 1948 review in the *Atlantic Monthly* of a book by the historian Charles Beard, who had left Columbia thirty years before to live on a dairy farm, Morison suggested (terribly cruelly, since Beard was on his death bed at the time) that Beard's work had suffered from his isolation: "You get more back talk even from freshmen than from milch cows."[18]

Maybe if Nathaniel Philbrick had had to answer to freshmen, he would have learned to be a little bit more skeptical of his sources. The first half of Philbrick's book stars William Bradford and relies, appropriately, on Bradford's history or, rather, on Samuel Eliot Morison's invaluable edition of Bradford's history. So much did Morison admire Bradford, so much did he despise the myth of the Puritans, so much did he want Americans to read better history, that he spent five years meticulously preparing an edition of Bradford's history "that the ordinary reader might peruse with pleasure as well as profit."[19] Working closely with his lifelong secretary, Antha Card, to whom he read Bradford's every word aloud, Morison altered the original's antiquated spelling and cleared the text of notes and scribbles made by everyone from Bradford's biographers to his descendents, material that had been injudiciously included, and mistakenly attributed to Bradford himself, in earlier printed editions. To every trace of ink on the manuscript's pages, Morison applied his magnifying glass. Where earlier copyists had Bradford concluding, "the light here kindled hath shone to many," Morison pointed out that the light actually shone "unto" many; a splotch that looked as though Bradford had crossed out the "un" turned out to be, on closer inspection, "merely an inadvertent blot from the Governor's quill pen."[20] Published in 1952 as *Of Plymouth Plantation*, Morison's definitive edition of Bradford went through dozens of printings.

Not long after Bradford's death, Massasoit died, too; so ended an era of uneasy peace. Inheriting his father's position in 1662, Philip tried to halt English encroachment. When that failed, he began preparing for war. In January 1675, a Christian Indian named John Sassamon warned Plymouth's governor, Josiah Winslow, of Philip's plans. Sassamon was soon found dead. In June, Plymouth executed three of Philip's men for Sassamon's murder. Within days, Wampanoags began attacking English towns.

In proportion to population, King Philip's War was one of the most fatal wars in American history. Over half of all English settlements in New England were destroyed or abandoned. One in ten colonists was killed. Thousands of Indians died; those who survived, including Philip's nine-year-old son, were shipped out of the colonies and sold into slavery. Because it was, for both sides, a holy war, King Philip's War was waged with staggering brutality. New England's Indians fought to take their land back from Christians, mocking their praying victims: "Where is Your O God?" One, having killed a colonist, stuffed a Bible into his victim's gutted belly. Puritans read such acts as a sign of God's wrath, as punishment for their descent into sinfulness; not only had they become, over the years, less pious than the first generation of settlers, but they had also failed to convert the Indians to Christianity. Asked the Boston minister Increase Mather, "Why should we suppose that God is not offended with us, when his displeasure is written, in such visible and bloody Characters?"[21]

Reading those scarlet letters, Puritans concluded that God was commanding them to defeat their "heathen" enemies by any means necessary; for the English, all restraint in war, all notions of "just conduct" applied only to secular warfare; in a holy war, anything goes. Ministers urged their congregations to "take, kill, burn, sink, destroy all sin and Corruption, &C which are professed enemies to Christ Jesus, and not to pity or spare any of them."[22] Such a policy, as ever, breeds nothing if not merciless retaliation. As a Boston merchant reported to London, the Indians, in town after town, tortured and mutilated their victims, "either cutting off the Head, ripping open the Belly, or skulping the Head of Skin and Hair, and hanging them up as Trophies; wearing Mens [sic] Fingers as Bracelets about their Necks, and Stripes of their Skins which they dresse for Belts."[23]

In his recounting of the war, Philbrick placed at center stage a militia captain named Benjamin Church. Born in Plymouth in 1639, Church fought in many of King Philip's War's bloodiest engagements, including the "Great Swamp Fight" in December 1675, in which English forces killed thousands of Narragansett women, children, and old men hiding in a makeshift fort in the middle of a Rhode Island swamp. Most died after the English set the fort on fire. (Wrote one Boston poet: "Here might be heard an hideous Indian cry, / Of wounded ones who in the wigwams fry.")[24] In August 1676, after Philip was shot, it was Church who ordered the body drawn, quartered, and decapitated and had the head placed on a spike that Church marched to Plymouth, after which the colony declared a special day of Thanksgiving to give thanks to God for this signal victory. On top of a stake in the middle of town, Philip's head remained, rotting, for decades.[25]

Philbrick explained his choice of William Bradford and Benjamin Church as his two main characters this way: "Bradford and Church could not have been more different—one was pious and stalwart, the other was audacious and proud—but both wrote revealingly about their lives in the New World.

Together, they tell a fifty-six-year intergenerational saga of discovery, accommodation, community, and war."[26]

The problem is that Benjamin Church did not write revealingly about his life in the New World. In fact, he didn't write about it at all. In 1716, a Boston printer published a book called *Entertaining Passages relating to Philip's War . . . with some account of the Divine Providence towards Benjamin Church.* Its title page lists its author as Church's forty-two-year-old son, Thomas, who was just a baby at the time of the war. In the text, too, Thomas is named as the author, although a brief preface allows that, in drafting the manuscript, Thomas consulted his father's notes and that the elder Church "had the perusal of" his son's manuscript and found "nothing a-miss."[27] And why would he? *Entertaining Passages* paints Church not only as the hero of every battle he ever fought but as the Puritans' voice of reason and restraint, as the man of conscience who attempts, in vain, to halt every atrocity: when Mohegan Indians allied with his forces want to torment a captured Nipmuck with fire and knives, Church "interceded and prevailed for his escaping torture"; at the Great Swamp Fight, Church, badly injured, valiantly hobbles to his commanding officer and begs him to stop the attack, only to be rebuffed.[28]

This as-told-to, after-the-fact memoir is, hands down, the single most unreliable account of King Philip's War, one of the best-documented military conflicts of the colonial period. Over four hundred letters written by eyewitnesses in 1675 and 1676 survive in New England archives, along with at least twenty-one different printed accounts, written as the war was happening, or very shortly thereafter. There is, in other words, no shortage of better evidence.

Even though *Entertaining Passages* was compiled forty years after the war had ended and may well have been entirely written by Church's son (who, at the very least, edited his father's "notes" considerably), Philbrick used it without reservation or caution. Like footnotes, these facts apparently got in the way of Philbrick's plot. That Church is a "persona," Philbrick reluctantly conceded, on the second-to-last page of his book, where he insists: "that Church according to Church is too brave, too cunning, and too good to be true is beside the point."[29] This is about as reasonable, and as indefensible, as writing a history of the Vietnam War relying extensively and uncritically on an "autobiography" of John Kerry written in decades after the war's end by Kerry's daughter Vanessa. As Samuel Eliot Morison liked to say about such things, "Very suspicious!"[30]

If Morison cared about professional standards, he nonetheless held himself well above the academic fray. He was uninterested in historical debates; he hated academic fashions: "Somewhere along the assembly-line of their education, students have had inserted in them a bolt called 'points of view,' secured with a nut called 'trends,' and they imagine that the historian's problem is simply to compare points of view and describe trends. It is not."[31] Although he was once elected its president, and duly served, Morison almost never attended meetings of the American Historical Association. When he once did show up, he walked through a crowded hotel mezzanine, dazed academics parting before him like the Red Sea. Reaching the end of the room, he turned around and walked back, and back and forth again.

A friend came up to him and asked, "Sam, what are you doing?"

"Doing?" Morison replied. "*Doing*! Why, what do you think I'm doing? *Mixing*!"[32]

Morison also complained about what he called a "chain reaction of dullness": professors who write "dull, solid, valuable monographs" train graduate students to write dull, solid, valuable monographs, and, before you know it, the only history people read is written by journalists.[33] Morison didn't resent this—to the contrary, he urged his students to learn from the best journalists, and the best novelists, too—but it worried him. He at one time went so far as to support altogether Orwellian calls by members of the American Historical Association requiring that historians be licensed, like doctors, and subject to grand jury prosecution "if they misused the past."[34]

History isn't brain surgery. Even when it's done badly, it's not deadly. Still, it can knock you down. Philbrick rested his argument, or, rather, the arc of his plot, on his reading of Benjamin Church. "The great mystery of this story," Philbrick wrote, "is how America emerged from the terrible darkness of King Philip's War to become the United States." The answer? Church: "Out of the annealing flame of one of the most horrendous wars ever fought in North America, he forged an identity that was part Pilgrim, part mariner, part Indian, and altogether his own." Church, for Philbrick, is the ur-American, the ancestor of everyone "from Daniel Boone to Davy Crocket to Natty Bumppo to Rambo." He went further: by believing that "success in war was about coercion rather than slaughter," Philbrick argued, Church "anticipated the welcoming, transformative beast that eventually became—once the Declaration of Independence and the Constitution were in place—the United States."[35]

Huh? Is this the same Benjamin Church who, the year before he fell off his horse and died, a battle-weary "old soldier," had his son write a history recalling his glory days as a reluctant and principled Indian fighter by way of both enhancing his reputation and reconciling himself to a war that many Puritan New Englanders, like him, had since come to feel pretty badly about? In him we see the birth of a nation? The regret, in *Entertaining Passages*, breaks your heart. It was meant to. But it is evidence of remorse, not of restraint (and, even if it weren't, what restraint has to do with declaring

American independence is bewilderingly unclear). In one chapter, Thomas Church tells the story of his father finding an old Indian man in the woods, after the war's end:

> The Captain ask'd his name, who replyed, his name was *Conscience*; *Conscience*, said the Captain (smiling), then the War is over; for that was what they were searching for, it being much wanting.[36]

This, of course, is an allegory, not an experience. It is Church, father and son, abdicating the slaughter, four decades after it was all over. It reveals a great deal about how New Englanders remembered the war, but it's about the shoddiest evidence you can think of for telling the story of how they waged it, and a hopelessly leaky boat in which to try to sail to 1776 and 1787.

Those poor, misunderstood Puritans. Time still moves forward, not backward, and relying on the eighteenth century to understand the seventeenth is still a grave chronological error.

"The place of the Pilgrim Fathers in American history can best be stated by a paradox," Morison once wrote. "Of slight importance in their own time, they are of great and increasing significance in our time."[37] To them we look, in vain, to see ourselves. In this we are not alone: as Morison's colleague Perry Miller astutely observed, the Puritans, at the end of King Philip's War, made the same mistake: "They looked in vain to history for an explanation of themselves."[38]

The way Morison wrote about King Philip's War, and especially about Indians, is distressing at best. In his 1956 book, *The Story of the Old Colony*, Morison boasted, "whenever there was trouble with the Indians, Plymouth men were up in front, shooting!"[39] But even if he never fathomed New England's Algonquians, and never really tried to, Morison made close study of people like William Bradford, placing him, as best as he could, in his proper time and place. In preparing *Of Plymouth Plantation*, Morison crafted an edition that would be, as he put it, "modern (*not* modernized)."[40] It would not do, Morison knew, to try to update William Bradford. Better to understand him "by way of the Middle Ages." Of the vast gulf separating seventeenth-century New Englanders from himself, Morison wrote with grace and eloquence: "The ways of the puritans are not my ways, and their faith is not my faith," he confessed. "Nevertheless they appear to me a courageous, humane, brave, and significant people."[41]

For all his ambivalence about academic history, Morison was first and foremost a scholar. (During one of the nation's many bouts of anti-intellectual insanity, Morison—for God's sake, *Morison*—was targeted; in the early 1950s, just after he retired from the navy, he was labeled a "Harvard Red-ucator" and listed among Harvard's Communist-sympathizing "Egotistical, Arrogant, Eggheads.")[42] Yet, just after Morison's death, his colleague Bernard Bailyn observed, "There is no 'Morison school.'"[43] Because he wrote more for the public than for his fellow historians, Morison had few academic disciples, and if the chain reaction of dullness continues unbroken, decades after Morison's death, Morison is as much to blame as anybody.

In 1716, Benjamin Church, or at least his son Thomas, looked back at King Philip's War and decided that it was possible to be both victorious and virtuous in the kind of war the colonists had fought against the Indians—a people at a vast technological disadvantage, fighting a holy war, with almost nothing left to lose. But it wasn't possible. At least, nothing in the evidence from 1675 and 1676 suggests that it was. And pretending that Benjamin Church found "Conscience" in the woods of Plymouth in that winter of war, rather than understanding why, at the end of his life, he came to wish he had, doesn't make it any more possible centuries later.

The ways of the Puritans are not our ways. Their faith is not our faith. And their wars are not our wars.

# 3

# THE WAY TO WEALTH

Benjamin Franklin's genius gave him no rest. *A discontented man finds no easy chair*, Poor Richard says. On April 4, 1757, Franklin left Philadelphia by carriage, and reached New York just four days later, ready to sail for London. But one delay piled upon another, like so much ragged paper jamming a printing press, and he found himself stuck in the city for more than two months. In all his fifty-one years, he could barely remember having "spent Time so uselessly."[1] (From childhood, Franklin, the son of a chandler, had toiled dawn to dusk only to squander the tallow "reading the greatest Part of the Night.")[2] *Waste not life; in the grave will be sleeping enough.* He had some business to attend to—he wrote a new Will, and more letters than other men write in a lifetime—but it was scarcely enough. "This tedious State of Uncertainty and long Waiting, has almost worn out my Patience," he wrote to his wife at the end of May, asking her to send along some books, and a pair of spectacles he had left behind. *What signifies your Patience, if you can't find it when you want it.* He didn't board until June 5, and then the confounded ship lay anchored at Sandy Hook for two weeks more. In his cabin, maybe even before the ship finally sailed on June 20, he at last found something to do: he set about stringing together proverbs taken from twenty-five years of his *Poor Richard's Almanack*.

Franklin finished his little essay at sea, on July 7, 1757. When he reached England, he sent it back on the first eastbound vessel. It was published as the preface to *Poor Richard's Improved . . . 1758*, though it was reprinted, soon, often, and far and wide—in at least 145 editions and six languages even before the eighteenth century was over—usually with the title *The Way to Wealth*.[3] "It long ago passed from literature into the general human speech," Franklin's biographer Carl Van Doren wrote in 1938.[4] *The Way to Wealth* stands among the most famous pieces of American writing, ever, and one of the most willfully misunderstood. A lay sermon about how industry begets riches (*no Gains, without Pains*), *The Way to Wealth* has been taken for Benjamin Franklin's—and even America's—creed, and there's a line or two of truth in that, but not a whole page. *The Way to Wealth* is also a parody stitched and bound between the covers of a sham.

In 1767, when Franklin was sixty-one, long since famous the world over for his experiments with electricity but years before he signed the Declaration of Independence, the Treaty of Paris, and the Constitution, his sister Jane asked him for a copy of everything he had ever published. "I could as easily make a Collection for you of all the past Parings of my Nails," he answered.[5] *If you wou'd not be forgotten as soon as you are dead and rotten, either write things worth reading, or do things worth the writing.* Very few people have written more than Benjamin Franklin and you'd be hard pressed to think of anyone who has *done* more. And yet he remains as willfully, as woefully misunderstood as his *Way to Wealth. Let all Men know thee, but no man know thee thoroughly.*

Franklin, who had a rule for everything, had a rule for writing: "*no piece can properly be called good, and well written, which is void of any Tendency to benefit the Reader, either by improving his Virtue or his Knowledge.*"[6] But he only roped himself to this and so many other masts because he found himself so cast about by "the Force of perpetual Temptations." *He is a Governor that governs his Passions, and he a Servant that serves them.* He carried with him a book in which he kept track, day by day, of whether he had lived according to thirteen virtues, including Silence, which he hoped to cultivate "to break a Habit I was getting into of Prattling, Punning and Joking."[7] What made Franklin great was how nobly he strived for perfection; what makes him almost impossibly interesting is how far short he fell of it.

The tone of the vast bulk of Franklin's writing, and especially of his political pieces, is sober, stirring, and grave, as the occasion, and the times, all too often demanded. But he was also a sucker for a good joke or, really, even a lousy one. He loved hoaxes and counterfeits and had the sort of fondness for puns that, if he'd been much less charming and a lot less clever, would have been called a weakness, and not easily forgiven. As it was, Franklin's enemies damned his "trivial mirth." John Adams, who hated him, conceded that, "He had wit at will," and "talents for irony, allegory, and fable," but characterized his humor as "infantine simplicity."[8] Franklin's best satires are relentlessly scathing social and political commentary attacking tyranny, injustice, ignorance, and, at the end of his life, slavery. But reading his letters, you get the sense that he couldn't always govern his wit, as when, striving to collect himself, he began a new paragraph: "But to be serious."[9]

When Franklin was sixteen, and in the fourth year of a miserable apprenticeship to his brother, James, a Boston printer, because their father had no money to send any of the ten Franklin sons to college (there were seven more daughters), he pulled off his first stunt, or at least the first one that anyone knows about. Disguising his handwriting, he wrote an essay under the pen name "Silence Dogood" and slipped it under the printing house door. James, who, like many masters, beat his apprentice, had no idea his pest of a little brother was the author, and printed not only that first essay, but thirteen more, in his newspaper. As the sharp-tongued Widow Dogood, the well-drubbed Ben offered "a few gentle Reproofs on those who deserve them," including Harvard students, "Dunces and Blockheads," whose blindness to their good fortune left the poor apprentice all but speechless. Young Franklin then did his caustic widow one better. He invented for her a priggish critic, "Ephraim Censorious," who beseeched Mrs. Dogood to pardon young men their follies and save her scolding for the fair sex, since "Women are prime Causes of a great many Male Enormities."[10] Ahem.

Franklin wrote heaps of this kind of stuff. He got older, and a little less sophomoric—*At 20 years of age the Will reigns; at 30 the Wit; at 40 the Judgment*—but he never lost his appetite for satire and imposture. In 1732, when he was an aspiring twenty-six-year-old printer in Philadelphia, having run away from his apprenticeship, fathered an illegitimate child, and married a widow, he gave birth to the fictional Richard Saunders, a kindhearted but hapless astrologer with empty pockets. In the preface to the first *Poor Richard's Almanack*, Saunders addressed his "Courteous Reader": "I might in this place attempt to gain thy Favour, by declaring that I write Almanacks with no other View than that of the publick Good; but in this I should not be sincere; and Men are now a-days too wise to be deceiv'd by Pretences how specious soever. The plain Truth of the Matter is, I am excessive poor, and my Wife, good Woman, is, I tell her, excessive proud."[11] Sincerity and plain truth? Not a bit of it. Poor Richard was naught *but* pretense.

Almanacs, issued just before the New Year, were cheap page-a-month calendars, with tides, important dates, and the phases of the moon. They were handy. They were purchased, as Franklin pointed out, "by the common people, who bought scarcely any other books." Printers filled their blank space with poems, jokes, prophecies, and proverbs, which were, alas, almost never beautiful, funny, true, or wise. Then came Poor Richard.

Franklin didn't write Poor Richard's proverbs or, not most of them. By his own guess, he wrote one out of every ten; the rest he found in books, especially anthologies like Thomas Fuller's 1732, *Gnomologia: Adages and Proverbs; Wise Sentences and Witty Sayings Ancient and Modern, Foreign and Domestic.* But Franklin was the kind of literary alchemist who could turn drivel into haiku. Fuller had written, "A Man in Passion rides a horse that runs away with him"; Franklin outpaced him: *A Man in a Passion rides a mad Horse.* Where Titan Leeds, author of the deathless prose in *The American Almanack*, blathered, "Many things are wanting to them that desire many things," Poor Richard pegged it: *If you desire many things, many things will seem but a few.*[12]

What really set Franklin's almanacs apart was Poor Richard himself, who started out as an affectionate imitation of Jonathan Swift's 1708 satire of an imaginary almanac-maker, Isaac Bickerstaff. Like Bickerstaff, Saunders confidently, and of course wrongly, prophesied the death of his chief rival—in this case, the unfortunate Titan Leeds—reading the future by the stars badly to point out that it couldn't possibly be done well. Not everyone picked up on the homage to Swift, but Franklin's lampoon was hard to miss. (It helped that the word *poor* in the title of an almanac was an eighteenth-century term of art, a promise that a book would be silly and a warning that it might be vulgar.[13] Poor Richard's rivals included Poor Robin and Poor Will.) Almanacs forecast twelve months' worth of weather; Franklin knew this for nonsense: in 1741, Poor Richard predicted only sunshine, explaining to Courteous Reader, "To oblige thee the more, I have omitted all the bad Weather, being Thy Friend R.S."[14]

Franklin's brainchild was a blockhead: tenderhearted, henpecked, and witless. *Ever since Follies have pleas'd, Fools have been able to divert.* Poor Richard had picked up his pen because his wife had threatened to burn his books and star-gazing instruments if he didn't earn a few more farthings, and because (as a delighted Franklin winked at his readers) "The Printer has offer'd me some considerable share of the Profits." Saunders liked his privacy, and never told anyone where he lived—"I will eat my Nails first"—but everyone knew that Franklin kept his house and print shop on Market Street, and didn't split his earnings with anyone—at a time when the twenty-four-page almanac sold ten thousand copies a year, five pence each.[15] Franklin's wife, Deborah, who called the best-selling almanacs "Poor Dicks," could barely keep them in the shop.[16]

Saunders once complained that rumors had circulated "*That there is no such a Man as I am*; and have spread this Notion so thoroughly in the Country, that I have been frequently told it to my Face by those that don't know me." Some ill-natured fiends had even suggested that Benjamin Franklin was really Poor Richard. A pox on them. "My Printer, to whom my Enemies are pleased to ascribe my Productions," Saunders protested, "is as unwilling to father my Offspring as I am to lose the Credit for it."[17]

Poor Richard was Benjamin Franklin's most famous bastard, but by no means his last. Over the course of his long life, Franklin used more than a hundred pen names, from the high-minded "Americanus" to the humble "Homespun" to the farcical, and low, low, oh so very low, "FART-HING." Still, a pseudonym was too thin a veil for his most scandalous pieces, which he circulated only in manuscript. *Strange! That a Man who has wit enough to write a Satyr; should have folly enough to publish it.* In 1745, when Franklin was thirty-nine, he wrote a parody of a gentleman's conduct manual that his most exhaustive biographer, J. A. Leo Lemay, called "a small masterpiece of eighteenth-century bawdry."[18] Franklin, who had suffered much from "that hard-to-be-govern'd Passion of Youth," wrote a letter advising a young man suffering the same, but unwilling to seek marriage as a remedy for what ailed him, to take only older women for mistresses because "There is no hazard of Children." Also, older women are wiser, better talkers, better at intrigue, and better at other things, too, "every Knack being by Practice capable of Improvement"; not to mention, "They are *so grateful*!" And, lest Franklin miss any opportunity to use a pun or a proverb, he killed those two birds with one especially smutty stone: "in the dark all Cats are grey."[19]

Franklin counterfeited court documents, elegies, and even scripture. Some of his fakes are so cunning they weren't discovered to be fakes, or his, until long after he was dead, partly because he was remarkably discreet (*Three can keep a secret if two of them are dead*) and partly because he was a practiced mimic (*Write with the learned, pronounce with the vulgar*). The boy too poor to go to Harvard had taught himself to write by imitating the prose style he found in an English gentleman's magazine, the *Spectator*. "Extremely ambitious" to become a good writer, young Franklin made the *Spectator* the tutor he never had: he read an essay, abstracted it, and then rewrote the argument from the abstract, to see if he could improve on the original. To make his prose more lyrical, he then turned the essays into poetry, and back again.[20] In an essay he later wrote on literary style that reads like Strunk and White, he pledged himself to brevity ("a multitude of Words obscure the Sense"), clarity ("To write *clearly*, not only the most expressive, but the plainest Words should be chosen"), and simplicity: "If a Man would that his Writings have an Effect on the Generality of

Readers, he had better imitate that Gentleman, who would use no Word in his Works that was not well understood by his Cook-maid."[21]

About 1755, Franklin wrote a fake chapter of the Old Testament, a parable attacking religious persecution, in pitch-perfect King James. He had it printed and bound within the pages of his own Bible so that he could read it aloud, delivering its punch line with a straight face, to see who would fall for it. (Franklin's ideas about religion are hard to classify; it's an oversimplification to label him a Deist, though that comes close. Still, he usually kept his skepticism to himself. *Talking against Religion is unchaining a Tyger*.) In Franklin's Genesis Thirty-Nine, Abraham casts a bent and bowed old man out of his tent and into the wilderness when the stranger reveals himself an infidel. The next morning, a miffed and peevish God, finding the old man gone, thunders at Abraham, "Have I born with him these hundred ninety and eight Years, and nourished him, and cloathed him, notwithstanding his Rebellion against me, and couldst not thou, that art thyself a Sinner, bear with him one Night?"[22]

Benjamin Franklin took a great deal of pleasure in his wit, and maybe most of all in Richard Saunders. Even after he retired from business in 1748, to devote himself to reading, writing, scientific experiments, and what would turn out to be forty-two years of tireless public service, he kept on writing the prefaces to Poor Richard's almanacs, now printed by his partner, David Hall. But by 1757, on that voyage to London to lobby against the taxes Parliament was raising to pay for the French and Indian War, Franklin took up his favorite role for what he must have thought would be the last time. "The Way to Wealth," was Poor Richard's swan song, Franklin's farewell to a troubled America. (He did not return until 1764, and then only briefly. He spent most of the rest of his life in England and France.)

Saunders began by thanking his readers, "for they buy my Works; and besides, in my Rambles, where I am not personally known, I have frequently heard one or other of my Adages repeated, with, *as Poor Richard says*, at the End on't." This pleased him so much, he said, that, "I have sometimes *quoted myself with great Gravity*."[23] Then he told a story. He had recently stopped his horse at an auction, where one Father Abraham, "a plain clean old Man, with white Locks," stood before a crowd. (It's hard not to hear the echo of Franklin's biblical Abraham.) "*Pray, Father Abraham, what think you of the Times?*" the crowd asked the old man. "*Won't these heavy Taxes quite ruin the Country? How shall we be ever able to pay them?*" What followed, Father Abraham's harangue, was, of course, Franklin himself, quoting himself, just as he'd hinted, with counterfeit gravity, and with his characteristic charity, since the speech was his parting gift to countrymen bearing the cost of a war for which there was no end in sight (not for nothing did it come to be called the Seven Years' War):

> Friends, says he, and Neighbours, the Taxes are indeed very heavy, and if those laid on by the Government were the only Ones we had to pay, we might more easily discharge them; but we have many others, and much more grievous to some of us. We are taxed twice as much by our *Idleness*, three times as much by our *Pride*, and four times as much by our *Folly*, and from these Taxes the Commissioners cannot ease or deliver us by allowing an Abatement. However let us hearken to good Advice, and something may be done for us; *God helps them that help themselves*, as Poor Richard says.[24]

Much of the rest of the Father Abraham's speech, strung together from proverbs hoarded from earlier almanacs, endorsed thrift: "Here you are all got together at this vendue of fineries and knickknacks. You call them goods, but if you do not take care, they will prove evils to some of you. You expect they will be sold cheap, and perhaps they may for less than they cost; but if you have no occasion for them, they must be dear to you. Remember what Poor Richard says, *buy what thou hast no need of, and ere long thou shalt sell thy necessaries.*"

After the hoary old man finally finished, the people "approved the Doctrine and immediately practiced the contrary," Poor Richard smiled at his reader, "just as if it had been a common Sermon." The sale opened, and "they began to buy extravagantly."[25]

Franklin didn't mind Father Abraham's advice either. When he reached London, he sent his essay to his printing partner in Philadelphia. And then he went shopping, and shipped to his wife a huge collection of china ("there is something from all the china works in England"), along with melons, bowls, coffee cups, four silver salt ladles, "a little instrument to core apples," tea cloths ("for nobody here breakfasts on the naked table"), a carpet, tablecloths, napkins, sheets, fifty-six yards of cotton, seven yards of fabric for covering chairs, snuffers, a snuff-stand, silk blankets, and a gown made of sixteen yards of flowered tissue. To be fair, he did think about buying his daughter a harpsichord, but, thrifty man, he decided against it.[26]

The best-known proverb of *The Way to Wealth* is arguably the most witless. *Early to Bed, and early to rise, makes a Man healthy, wealthy and wise.* "The sorrow that that maxim has cost me through my parents' experimenting on me with it, tongue cannot tell," Mark Twain once wrote. By the time Twain was writing, in 1870, Benjamin Franklin had turned into Father Abraham in the American imagination. *The Way to Wealth*, so useful in the farming, boycotting, nonimporting, independence-loving eighteenth century came to be wor-shipped in the capitalizing, industrializing, Founders-revering nineteenth century. The joke fell flat. The parody within the sham became the man. Of the nineteenth century's thrifty, fru-gal, prudent, sober, homey, quaint, sexless, humorless, preachy Benjamin Franklin, loved (by Andrew Carnegie), hated (by D. H. Lawrence), and held up (by Max Weber) as the origi-nal American Puritan striver, the prophet of prosperity, Twain wrote, "He was a hard lot."[27]

Until Carl Van Doren's 1938 biography, Franklin was held hostage to this flawed, narrow, and pretty dim view of his character. Valiantly, Van Doren vowed "to rescue him from the dry, prim people who have claimed him as one of them. They praise his thrift. But he himself admitted that he could never learn frugality, and he practiced it no longer than his poverty forced him to. They praise his prudence. But at sev-enty he became the leader of a revolution." Van Doren, who had earlier written a biography of Swift, could hardly have tried harder to free Franklin from the shackles that bound him. "The dry, prim people seem to regard him as a treasure shut up in a savings bank, to which they have the lawful key. I herewith give him back, in grand dimensions, to his nation and the world."[28]

Bad biographies make small men great; with the excep-tion of Van Doren, most of Franklin's biographers have had the opposite problem. It's hard to fit Franklin between the covers of a book. His polymath contributions to statesman-ship, science, philanthropy, and literature were unrivalled both in his time and in ours. Even though Van Doren's *Benjamin Franklin* was "cut with hard labour to the bone," it still runs well past eight hundred pages. People who fall for Franklin fall hard. William Strahan, the London printer who brought out Samuel Johnson's dictionary, wrote in 1757, on meeting Franklin, "I never saw a man who was, in every respect, so perfectly agreeable to me. Some are amiable in one view, some in another, he in all."[29] Van Doren felt the same way.

For all that Van Doren did, he failed. Nearly every biographer to follow Van Doren has had to try to unfetter Franklin from his myth. But Benjamin Franklin is still good and stuck, a walking, talking, page-a-day desk calendar. To his twee reputation, the man's breathtakingly vast, cosmopolitan, enlightened, revolutionary life, and volume after volume of his *Papers*, seem to matter not at all. As Poor Richard once said, sometimes *Force shites upon Reason's back.*

But maybe the blame ought to be laid at Franklin's own desk. On board that ship to London in 1757, he looked at twenty-five years' worth of Poor Dicks and chose ninety-odd proverbs to put in *The Way to Wealth*, a set that, by any measure, is no fair sample of Poor Richard's wisdom, which was not mostly or even very much about money and how to get it. If Franklin hadn't been so worried about taxes, he might instead have pulled together some of Poor Richard's many proverbs about equality: *The greatest monarch on the proudest throne, is oblig'd to sit upon his own arse.* Or hypocrisy: *He that is conscious of a Stink in his Breeches, is jealous of every Wrinkle in another's Nose.* Or courtship: *Neither a Fortress nor a Maidenhead will hold out long after they begin to parly.* Or religion: *Serving God is Doing good to Man, but Praying is thought an easier Service, and therefore more generally chosen.* Or delusion: *He that lives upon Hope, dies farting.* (Scholars have suggested that that last one was a printer's error, and should have read "fasting," but, I ask you, who was the printer?) Or, he might have chosen to collect the dozens of Poor Richard's proverbs advising *against* the accumulation of wealth: *The Poor have little, Beggars none; the Rich too much, enough not one.*

Franklin didn't live by Poor Richard's proverbs, nor did he agree with all of them. *He that best understands the World, least likes it* could hardly be farther from Franklin's philosophy. And *Nothing dries sooner than a Tear* is not the sentiment of a man who, thirty-six years after the death of his four-year-old son, Francis, was still felled by grief at the thought of the boy.

But he did believe, earnestly and passionately, in hard work and sacrifice. The man behind Silence Dogood was committed to nothing so much as the principle of silently doing good. And he had boundless sympathy for the common people who bought his almanacs, people the likes of John Adams disdained as "rabble," people as poor and humble as the tenth son of a second-rate chandler. In 1757, when Franklin finally set sail on that ship to England, he picked proverbs that might help struggling Americans bear the cost of the war. "I would rather have it said, *He lived usefully*, than, *He died rich*," Franklin once wrote, and he meant it.

In 1764, briefly back in Philadelphia, Franklin reprised Poor Richard, and wrote one last preface to his almanac. The war had ended in 1763, but half of Britain's revenues were now going to pay interest on its debt and Parliament, which had just passed the Sugar and Currency Acts, was debating a new stamp tax. Once again, Poor Richard urged frugality. "Taxes are of late Years greatly encreased among us, and now it is said we are to be burthened with the Payment of new Duties," a distressingly sober and spiritless Saunders observed. "What are we to do, but, like honest and prudent Men, endeavour to do without the Things we shall, perhaps, never be able to pay for; or if we cannot do without them or something like them, to supply ourselves from our own Produce at home." In these dire times, Poor Richard offered not earthy proverbs but homegrown recipes, to help Americans get by without imported sugar: recipes for wine made from grapes, rum made with corn, and sugar made from beets.[30] Later that year, back in London, Franklin was questioned before the House of Commons during its deliberations on the Stamp Act: "What used to be the pride of Americans?" he was asked. "To indulge in the fashions and manufactures of Great-Britain. Q. What now is their pride? A. To wear their old cloaths over again, till they can make new ones." Asked how soldiers sent to enforce the new taxes would be received, Franklin answered, "They will not find a rebellion; they may indeed make one."[31]

The king and Parliament heeded Franklin's advice just about as much "as if it had been a common Sermon." They sent the soldiers. They made a rebellion. In 1771, not long after the Boston Massacre, in which British troops fired into a crowd of civilians, Franklin began writing his autobiography. He never finished it; it breaks off in 1758, just after he tells the story of sailing to London. By 1771, *The Way to Wealth* had already risen to its unexpected status as his most celebrated piece of writing. "The Piece being universally approved was copied in all the Newspapers of the Continent," Franklin noted.[32] It had proven useful. Franklin's *Autobiography*, as carefully crafted a piece of prose as anything else he ever wrote, is, in some ways, *The Way to Wealth* writ large; it was, as he must have judged it, the useful thing he could offer to his son, to whom he addressed it, or to the American people, into whose service he had long since pressed his very self. *The Master-piece of Man is to live to the purpose.*

In short, Benjamin Franklin abridged himself. But he reads better, unabridged. And *The Way to Wealth* makes a poor epitaph. Wiser to repay his wit with irreverence, and remember him by the epitaph he wrote for himself, in 1728:

The Body of
B Franklin Printer,
(Like the cover of an old Book
Its Contents torn out
And stript of its Lettering & Gilding)
Lies here, Food for Worms.
But the Work shall not be lost;
For it will, (as he believ'd) appear once more,
In a new and more elegant Edition
Revised and corrected,
By the Author.[33]

And sweet, tenderhearted Poor Richard? Maybe he's best remembered by his annual farewell: "May this Year prove a happy One to Thee and Thine, is the hearty Wish of, Kind Reader, Thy obliged Friend, R. SAUNDERS."

# 4

# THE AGE OF PAINE

In the winter of 1776, John Adams read *Common Sense*, an anonymous, fanatical, and brilliant forty-six-page pamphlet that would convince the American people of what more than a decade of taxes and nearly a year of war had not: that it was nothing less than their destiny to declare independence from Britain. "The cause of America is in a great measure the cause of all mankind" was *Common Sense*'s astonishing and inspiring claim about the fate of thirteen infant colonies on the edge of the world. "The sun never shone on a cause of greater worth. 'Tis not the affair of a city, a county, a province, or a kingdom; but of a continent—of at least one-eighth part of the habitable globe. 'Tis not the concern of a day, a year, or an age; posterity are virtually involved in the contest, and will be more or less affected even to the end of time, by the proceedings now."[1] Whether these words were preposterous or prophetic only time would tell, but, meanwhile, everyone wondered: who could have written such stirring stuff?

"People Speak of it in rapturous praise," a friend wrote Adams. "Some make Dr. Franklin the Author," hinted another. "I think I see strong marks of your pen in it," speculated a third. More miffed than flattered, Adams admitted to his wife, Abigail, "I could not have written any Thing in so

manly and striking a style." Who, then? Adams found out:
"His Name is Paine."[2]

Thomas Pain was born in Thetford, England, in 1737 (he
added the "e" later, and was only called "Tom" by his enemies),
the son of a Quaker journeyman who sewed the bones of
whales into stays for ladies' corsets. He left the local grammar
school at the age of twelve, to serve as his father's apprentice.
At twenty, he went to sea, on a privateer. In 1759 he opened
his own stay-making shop and married a servant girl but the
next year both she and their child died in childbirth. For a
decade, Pain struggled to make a life for himself. He taught
school, collected taxes, and, in 1771, married a grocer's daughter. Three years later, he was fired from his job with the excise
office; his unhappy and childless second marriage fell apart;
and everything he owned was sold at auction to pay off his
debts. At the age of thirty-seven, Thomas Pain was ruined. He
therefore did what every ruined Englishman did, if he possibly could: he sailed to America. Sickened with typhus during
the journey, Pain arrived in Philadelphia in December 1774 so
weak he had to be carried off the ship. What saved his life was
a letter found in his pocket: "The bearer Mr Thomas Pain is
very well recommended to me as an ingenious worthy young
man."[3] It was signed by Benjamin Franklin. It was better than
a bag of gold.

How an unknown Englishman who had been in the colonies for little more than a year came to write the most influential essay of the American Revolution—no matter that he had
once caught Franklin's eye during a chance meeting in London—is a mystery not easily solved. Paine is a puzzle. Lock-
ean liberalism, classical republicanism, and Leveller radicalism
all can be found in his work, though whether he ever read
Locke, or any one else, is probably impossible to discover. His
love for equality has been traced to Quakerism, his hatred of

injustice to growing up next door to a gallows. Good guesses, but guesses all the same.

"I offer nothing more than simple facts, plain arguments, and common sense," Paine wrote, but this was coyness itself: *Common Sense* stood every argument against American independence on its head. "There is something absurd in supposing a continent to be perpetually governed by an island," he insisted. As to the colonies' dependence on England, "We may as well assert that because a child has thrived upon milk, that it is never to have meat." And hereditary monarchy? "Nature disapproves it, otherwise she would not so frequently turn it into ridicule by giving mankind an ass for a lion."[4]

Adams, who had been the colonies' most ardent advocate for independence, refused to accept that Paine deserved any credit for *Common Sense*. "He is a keen Writer," Adams granted, but he'd offered nothing more than "a tolerable summary of the argument which I had been repeating again and again in Congress for nine months." The longer John Adams lived, the more he hated Thomas Paine, and the more worthless he considered that forty-six-page pamphlet. Adams believed, with many of his contemporaries, that the democracy was dangerous, that the rule of the mob was one step away from anarchy; the rabble must be checked. Paine's notion of common sense, he believed, was "democratical without any restraint." By the end of his life, the aging and ill-tempered ex-president would call *Common Sense* "a poor, ignorant, Malicious, short-sighted, Crapulous Mass."[5]


Thomas Paine is, at best, a lesser Founder. In the comic book version of history that serves as America's national heritage, where the Founding Fathers are like the Hanna-Barbera SuperFriends, Paine is Aquaman to Washington's Superman and

Jefferson's Batman; we never find out how he got his super powers and he only shows up when they need someone who can swim. That this should be the case—that Americans have proven ambivalent about Paine—seems, at first, surprising, since Paine's contributions to the nation's founding would be hard to overstate. *Common Sense* made declaring independence possible. "Without the pen of the author of Common Sense, the sword of Washington would have been raised in vain," Adams wrote.[6] But Paine lifted his sword, too, and emptied his purse. Despite his poverty—he was by far the poorest of the Founders—he donated his share of the profits from *Common Sense* to buy supplies for the Continental Army, in which he also served. His chief contribution to the war was a series of essays known as the *American Crisis*. He wrote the first of these essays by the light of a campfire during Washington's desperate retreat across New Jersey, in December 1776. Making ready to cross the frozen Delaware River—at night, in a blizzard—to launch a surprise attack on Trenton, Washington ordered Paine's words read to his exhausted, frostbitten troops: "These are the times that try men's souls. The summer soldier and the sunshine patriot will, in this crisis, shrink from the service of their country; but he that stands it now, deserves the love and thanks of man and woman. Tyranny, like hell, is not easily conquered; yet we have this consolation with us, that the harder the conflict, the more glorious the triumph."[7] The next morning, the Continentals fought to a stunning, pivotal victory.

It's hard to believe anyone thought Adams could have written lines like these; Paine wrote like no one else: he wrote for everyone. "As it is my design to make those that can scarcely read understand," he explained, "I shall therefore avoid every literary ornament and put it in language as plain as the alphabet."[8] So gripping was Paine's prose, and so vast was its reach, that Adams once complained to Jefferson, "History is to ascribe the American Revolution to Thomas Paine."⁹ But history has not been kind to Paine, who forfeited his chance to glorify his role, or at least to document it: at the end of the war, Congress asked him to write the history of the Revolution, but he declined. And the person who did write that history, John and Abigail Adams's close friend, the Massachusetts poet and playwright Mercy Otis Warren, relegated Paine to a footnote—literally—in her magisterial two-volume 1805 *History of the Rise, Progress, and Termination of the American Revolution*.¹⁰ By the time Paine died in 1809, all of the surviving Founders had renounced him. (Jefferson even refused to allow his correspondence with Paine to be printed. "No, my dear sir, not for this world," he told an inquirer. "Into what a hornet's nest would it thrust my head!")¹¹ And nearly no one showed up to see him buried. As Paul Collins observed in *The Trouble with Tom: The Strange Afterlife and Times of Thomas Paine*, "There were twenty thousand mourners at Franklin's funeral. Tom Paine's had six."¹²

Disavowed by his contemporaries, Paine left little behind in his own defense; the bulk of his papers, including notes for an autobiography, were destroyed in a fire. (Even his bones have been lost; they were stolen, stashed, smashed, and finally probably thrown out with the rubbish.) Paine enjoyed a brief revival in the 1940s, after FDR quoted the *American Crisis*— "these are the times that tried men's souls"—in a fireside chat in 1942, three months after the attack on Pearl Harbor; and an excellent two-volume set, *The Complete Writings of Thomas Paine*, was published in 1945, edited by Philip Foner. But Paine has never much enjoyed the esteem of academics who, on the whole, have shared John Adams's view of him, whatever the rest of America might think. Perry Miller believed that Paine's obscurity was well deserved. In a review of *The Complete Writings* in *The Nation* in 1945, Miller sneered, "The price of popularizing for contemporaries is temporary popularity." In 1980,

Ronald Reagan inaugurated a second Paine revival when, accepting the Republican Party nomination for president, he quoted *Common Sense*: "We have it in our power to begin the world over again." But Paine emerges in most academic accounts as a kind of idiot savant; savvy about adjectives but idiotic about politics. *Common Sense* is "a work of genius," Bernard Bailyn concluded in 1990, but, next to men like Adams, Jefferson, and Madison, Paine was "an ignoramus."[13]

Thomas Paine left the United States in 1787. "Where liberty is, there is my country," Franklin once said, to which Paine replied, "Wherever liberty is not, there is my country."[14] In England in 1791, he wrote the first part of *Rights of Man*, a work he considered an English version of *Common Sense*. Defending the French Revolution from English critics, he argued that France had "outgrown the baby clothes of count and duke, and breeched itself in manhood." Americans had weaned themselves of milk and the French had put on pants, now it was time for the British to grow beards. "It is an age of revolutions, in which every thing may be looked for." The next year Paine wrote *Rights of Man, Part the Second*, his most important statement of political principles, in which he explained and insisted on natural rights, equality, and popular sovereignty. He went further: "When, in countries that are called civilized, we see age going to the work-house and youth to the gallows, something must be wrong in the system of government."[15] By way of remedy, Paine proposed the framework for a welfare state, providing tax tables calculated down to the last shilling.

The first part of *Rights of Man* sold fifty thousand copies in just three months. The second part was outsold only by the Bible. But British conservatives didn't want to follow France, especially as the news from Paris grew more gruesome. Paine was charged with seditious libel, and, everywhere, his ideas were suppressed and his followers persecuted. "I am for equality. Why, no kings!" one Londoner shouted in a coffeehouse, and was promptly sent to prison for a year and a half.[16] Meanwhile, William Pitt's government hired hack writers to conduct a smear campaign in which it was asserted, among other things, that Paine—horribly ugly, smelly, rude and relentlessly cruel, even as a child—had committed fraud, defrauded his creditors, caused his first wife's death by beating her while she was pregnant and abused his second wife almost as badly, except that she wasn't really his wife because he never consummated that marriage, preferring, instead, to have sex with cats.

"It is earnestly recommended to Mad Tom that he should embark for France and there be naturalized into the regular confusion of democracy," the London *Times* urged.[17] In September 1792, that's just what Paine did, fleeing to Paris, where he had already been elected a member of the National Assembly, in honor of his authorship of *Rights of Man*. In France, he faltered and fell, not least because he spoke almost no French but mostly because he argued against executing Louis XVI, suggesting, instead, that he be exiled to the United States where, "far removed from the miseries and crimes of royalty, he may learn, from the constant public prosperity, that the true system of government consists not in kings, but in fair, equal, and honourable representation."[18]

Back in England, Paine's trial for *Rights of Man* went on without him; he was found guilty, and outlawed. "If the French kill their King, it will be a signal for my departure," Paine had pledged before he left for France, but now he had no choice: not only could he not return to England, he couldn't venture an Atlantic crossing to the United States, for fear of being captured by a British warship. Instead, he stayed in his rooms in Paris, and waited for the worst. As the Reign of Terror unfolded, he drafted the first part of *The Age of Reason*. In December 1793, when the police knocked at his door, he handed a stash of papers to his friend, the American poet and statesman Joel Barlow. Barlow carried the manuscript to the printers; the police carried Paine to an eight-by-ten cell on the ground floor of a prison that had once been a palace. There, he would write most of the second part of *The Age of Reason* as he watched his fellow inmates go daily to their deaths. (In six weeks in the summer of 1794, more than thirteen hundred people were executed.)[19]

When the U.S. government failed to secure his release, Paine at first despaired. Then he raged, writing to the American ambassador, James Monroe, "I should be tempted to curse the day I knew America. By contributing to her liberty I have lost my own."[20] Finally, after ten months, he was freed. But he left prison an invalid. Ravaged by typhus, gout, recurring fevers, and a suppurating wound on his belly, he would never really recover. He convalesced at Monroe's home in Paris and, for years, at the homes of a succession of supporters. After Jefferson defeated Adams in the election of 1800, the new president invited Paine to return to the United States. He sailed in 1802.

"The questions central to an understanding of Paine's career do not lend themselves to exploration within the confines of conventional biography," Eric Foner argued in 1976, in *Tom Paine and Revolutionary America*.[21] You can say that again. What with the burned papers, the lost bones, and Paine's role in three revolutions, not to mention tabloid allegations of wife-beating, it's hard to know how to write about Paine. What Foner called "The Problem with Paine" has a lot to do with the very thing about him that contributed most to his obscurity in the first place: his uncompromising condemnation of all of the world's religions. In *The Age of Reason*, published in 1794 and 1795, Paine wrote: "All national institutions of churches, whether Jewish, Christian, or Turkish, appear to me no other than human inventions, set up to terrify and enslave mankind, and monopolize power and profit. Each of those churches accuses the other of unbelief; and for my own part, I disbelieve them all." Theodore Roosevelt once called Paine a "filthy little atheist," but, as Paine was at pains to point out, he did believe in God; he just didn't believe in the Bible, or the Koran, or the Torah; these he considered hearsay, lies, fables, and frauds that served to wreak havoc with humanity while hiding the beauty of God's creation, the evidence for which was everywhere obvious in "the universe we behold." In *The Age of Reason*, Paine offered his own creed:

> I believe in one God, and no more; and I hope for happiness beyond this life. I believe in the equality of man; and I believe that religious duties consist in doing justice, loving mercy, and endeavoring to make our fellow creatures happy. But . . . I do not believe in the creed professed by the Jewish Church, by the Roman Church, by the Greek Church, by the Turkish Church, by the Protestant Church, nor by any church that I know of. My own mind is my own church.[22]

"Paine's religious opinions were those of three-fourths of the men of letters of the last age," Joel Barlow observed, probably overstating the case only slightly.[23] Paine's views were hardly original; what was new was his audience. Not for nothing did Sean Wilentz call *The Age of Reason* a "Reader's Digest rendering" of the Enlightenment.[24] But, while other Enlightenment writers wrote for one another, Paine wrote, as always, for everyone. To say that Paine was vilified for doing this is to miss the point. He was destroyed.

Mark Twain once said, "It took a brave man before the Civil War to confess he had read the *Age of Reason*."[25] But that didn't mean it wasn't read. In Britain, sales of *The Age of Reason* outpaced even those of *Rights of Man*, though, since it was banned as blasphemous, it's impossible to know how many copies were actually sold. London printer Richard Carlisle, who called his bookstore The Temple of Reason, was fined a thousand pounds for selling it, and sentenced to two years in jail. (During an earlier trial on similar charges, Carlisle had read aloud from *Rights of Man*, a ploy that allowed him to publish it again, as a courtroom transcript.) After Carlisle's wife fell into the trap of selling *The Age of Reason* to a government agent posing as a bookstore browser, she—and her newborn baby—followed her husband to prison. Eventually, in order to avoid exposing anyone inside the bookstore to further prosecution, there appeared outside The Temple of Reason an "invisible shopman," a machine into which customers could drop coins and take out a book.[26]

But *The Age of Reason* cost Paine dearly. He lost, among other things, the friendship of Samuel Adams, who seethed, "Do you think that your pen, or the pen of any other man, can unchristianize the mass of our citizens?" Even before Paine returned to the United States in 1802, Federalists used him as a weapon against Jefferson, damning the "two Toms" as infidels while calling Paine "a loathsome reptile." Ministers and their congregants, caught up in the early stages of a religious revival now known as the Second Great Awakening, gloried in news of Paine's physical and mental decline, conjuring up a drunk, unshaven, and decrepit Paine, writhing in pain, begging, "Oh Lord help me! Oh, Christ help me!"[27]

Some of that fantasy was founded in fact. Even at his best, Paine was rough and unpolished—and a mean drunk. In his tortured final years, living in New Rochelle and New York City, he displayed signs of dementia. (Scurrilous rumors about cats aside, Paine's behavior throughout his life appears erratic enough that Eric Foner wondered if he suffered from crippling bouts of depression.) At home, he was besieged by

visitors who came either to save his soul or to damn it. He told
all of them to go to hell. When an old woman announced, "I
come from Almighty God to tell you that if you do not repent
of your sins and believe in our blessed Savior Jesus Christ, you
will be damned," Paine replied, "Pshaw. God would not send
such a foolish ugly old woman as you."[28]

Admirers of Paine's political pamphlets have long tried to
ignore his religious convictions. In 1800, a New York Republican Society resolved: "May his *Rights of Man* be handed down
to our latest posterity, but may his *Age of Reason* never live to
see the rising generation."[29] That's more or less how things
have turned out. So wholly has *The Age of Reason* been forgotten that Paine's mantle has been claimed not only by Ronald
Reagan but also by North Carolina Senator Jesse Helms, who
in 1992 supported a proposal to erect a Paine monument in
Washington, DC. Nor have liberals who have embraced Paine
had much interest in the latter years of his career. Maybe that's
what it means to be a lesser SuperFriend: no one cares about
your secret identity. They just like your costume.

Historians, too, have tried to dismiss *The Age of Reason*,
writing it off as simplistic and suggesting either that Paine
wrote it to please his French jailers or that, in prison, he went
mad. This interpretation began with Mercy Otis Warren, who
called *The Age of Reason* "jejune," explained that Paine wrote
it while "trembling under the terrors of the guillotine," and
concluded that, "imprisoned, he endeavoured to ingratiate
himself."[30] But Paine himself considered his lifelong views on
religion inseparable from his thoughts on government. "It has
been the scheme of the Christian Church, and of all other
invented systems of religion, to hold man in ignorance of the
Creator, as it is of Governments to hold man in ignorance of
his rights." Writing about kings and lords in Common Sense,
he wondered "how a race of men came into the world so

exalted above the rest, and distinguished like some new species." In *The Age of Reason*, he used much the same language
to write about priests and prophets: "The Jews have their
Moses; the Christians have their Jesus Christ, their apostles
and saints; and the Turks their Mahomet, as if the way to God
was not open to every man alike." He wrote *Common Sense*,
*Rights of Man*, and *Age of Reason* as a trilogy. "Soon after I
had published the pamphlet 'Common Sense,' in America," he
explained, "I saw the exceeding probability that a revolution in
the system of government would be followed by a revolution
in the system of religion."[31]

That Paine was wrong about the coming of that revolution
doesn't mean that anyone ought to forget that he yearned for
it. In 1806, John Adams railed that the latter part of the eighteenth century had come to be called "The Age of Reason": "I
am willing you should call this the Age of Frivolity, and would
not object if you had named it the Age of Folly, Vice, Frenzy,
Brutality, Daemons, Buonaparte, Tom Paine, or the Age of the
Burning Brand from the Bottomless Pit, or anything but the
Age of Reason." But even Adams would not have wished that
so much of Paine's work—however much he disagreed with
it—would be so willfully excised from memory. "I know not
whether any man in the world has had more influence on its
inhabitants or affairs for the last thirty years than Tom Paine,"
Adams admitted, adding, with irony worthy of the author of
*Common Sense*, "Call it then the Age of Paine."[32]

Adams wrote those words, in 1806, as if Paine were already
dead. He was not. That year, a neighbor of Paine's came across
the old man himself, in a tavern in New York, so drunk and
disoriented and unwashed and unkempt that his toenails had
grown over his toes, like bird's claws. While Adams, at his
home in Quincy, busied himself reflecting on the Age of Paine,
Paine hobbled to the polls in New Rochelle to cast his vote
in a local election. He was told that he was not an American

citizen, and turned away. So much for the rights of man. Three years later, as the seventy-two-year-old Paine lay dying in a house in Greenwich Village, his doctor pressed him, "Do you wish to believe that Jesus Christ is the Son of God?" Paine paused, then whispered, "I have no wish to believe on that subject."

# 5

# WE THE PARCHMENT

It is written in elegant, clerical hand, on four sheets of parchment, each two feet wide and a bit more than two feet high, about the size of an eighteenth-century newspaper but finer, and made not from the pulp of plants but from the hide of an animal. Some of the ideas it contains reach across ages and oceans, to antiquity; more were, at the time, newfangled. "We the People," the first three words of the preamble, are giant and Gothic: they slant left, and, because most of the rest of the words slant right, the writing zigzags. It had taken four months to debate and to draft, including two weeks to polish the prose, neat work, done by a committee of style. By Monday, September 17, 1787, it was ready. That afternoon, the Constitution of the United States of America was read out loud in a chamber on the first floor of Pennsylvania's State House, where the delegates to the Federal Convention had assembled to subscribe their names to a wholly new system of government, "to form a more perfect Union, establish Justice, insure domestic Tranquility, provide for the common Defence, promote the general Welfare, and secure the Blessings of Liberty to ourselves and our Posterity."

Benjamin Franklin rose from his chair, and wished to be heard, but, at eighty-one, he was too tired to make another speech. He had written down what he wanted to say, though, so James Wilson, a Pennsylvania delegate decades Franklin's junior, read his remarks, addressed to George Washington, presiding. "Mr. President," he began, "I confess that there are several parts of this constitution which I do not at present approve, but I am not sure I shall never approve them." Franklin liked to swaddle argument with affability, as if an argument were a colicky baby; the more forceful his point, the more tightly he swaddled it. What he offered that day was a well-bundled statement about changeability. I find that there are errors here, he explained, but, who knows, some day I might change my mind; I often do. "For having lived long, I have experienced many instances of being obliged by better Information, or fuller Consideration, to change Opinions even on important Subjects, which I once thought right, but found to be otherwise." That people so often believe themselves to be right is no proof that they are. "Most men indeed as well as most sects in Religion, think themselves in possession of all truth, and that wherever others differ from them it is so far error." The only difference between the Church of Rome and the Church of England, he said, is that the former is infallible while the latter is never in the wrong. He closed with a plea: "I can not help expressing a wish that every member of the Convention who may still have Objections to it, would with me, on this occasion doubt a little of his own Infallibility, and to make manifest our Unanimity, put his name to this Instrument." He doubted that any other assembly would, at just that moment, have been able to draft a better one. "Thus I consent, Sir, to this Constitution because I expect no better, and because I am not sure, that it is not the best."[1]

Three delegates still refused to sign but at the bottom of the fourth page of the Constitution appear the signatures of the rest, in two columns. What was written on parchment was then made public, printed in newspapers and on broadsheets, often with "We the People" set off in extra-large type. Meanwhile, the secretary of the Federal Convention carried the original to New York to present it to Congress, which met, at the time, at City Hall. There it was simply filed away and, later, shuffled from one place to another. When City Hall underwent renovations, the Constitution was transferred to the Department of State. The next year, it moved with Congress to Philadelphia, and, in 1800, to Washington, where it was stored at the Treasury Department until it was shifted over to the War Office. In 1814, three clerks stuffed it into a linen sack and carried it to a gristmill in Virginia, which was a good idea, because the British burned the city down. In the 1820s, when someone asked James Madison where it was, he had no idea.

In 1875, the Constitution found a home in a tin box in the bottom of a closet in a new building housing the Departments of State, War, and Navy. In 1894, it was sealed between glass plates and locked in a steel safe in the basement. In 1921, Herbert Putnam, a librarian, drove it across town in his Model T. In 1924, it was put on display in the Library of Congress, for the first time ever. Before then, no one had thought of that. In 1941, the Constitution was carried to Fort Knox. At the end of the war, it was brought back to the Library of Congress and, in 1952, it was driven, in an armored tank, under military guard, to the National Archives, where it remains, in a shrine in the rotunda, alongside the Declaration of Independence and the Bill of Rights.[2]

The United States Constitution is one of the oldest written constitutions in the world and the first, anywhere, submitted to the people for their approval.[3] As Madison explained, the Constitution is "of no more consequence than the paper on which it is written, unless it be stamped with the approbation of those to whom it is addressed . . . THE PEOPLE THEMSELVES."[4] By the beginning of the twenty-first century, some people said, it had been thrown in the trash. A political movement, the Tea Party, rallied around the cause of rescuing it. "Stop Shredding Our Constitution!" read the Tea Party rally signs in 2009. "FOUND IN A DUMPSTER behind the Capitol," read one poster, on which was pasted the kind of faux parchment Constitution you could buy in the souvenir shop at any history-for-profit heritage site. I once bought one at Bunker Hill. All four pages are printed on a single sheet of foolscap and the writing is so small that it's illegible; then again, the knick-knack Constitution's not meant to be read.[5]

Parchment is beautiful. As an object, the Constitution has more in common with the Dead Sea Scrolls than with what Americans, at the beginning of the twenty-first century, thought of as writing: pixels floating on a screen, words suspended in a digital cloud, bubbles of text. R we the ppl? Words, in the digital age, are vaporous. Not the Constitution. "I have this crazy idea that the Constitution *actually means something*," read one bumper sticker. Ye olde parchment had come to serve as shorthand for everything old, real, durable, American, and true, a talisman held up against the uncertainties and abstractions of a meaningless, changeable, paperless age.

You can keep a copy of the Constitution in your pocket, as Thomas Paine once pointed out.[6] Pocket constitutions have been around since the 1790s, usually bound with the Declaration of Independence.[7] Andrew Johnson, our first impeached president, was said to have so often waved around his pocket constitution that he resembled a newsboy hawking the daily paper.[8] Crying constitution is a minor American art form. "This is my copy of the Constitution," Congressman John Boehner said at a rally in 2009, waving a pocket-sized pamphlet at the crowd. "And I'm going to stand here with our Founding Fathers, who wrote in the preamble: 'We hold these truths to be self-evident, that all men are created equal, that they are endowed by their creator with certain unalienable rights including life, liberty and the pursuit of happiness.'" Not to nitpick, but this is not the preamble to the Constitution. It is the second sentence of the Declaration of Independence.

At 4,400 words, not counting amendments, the U.S. Constitution is one of the shortest in the world, quite a bit shorter than, say, this essay. Nevertheless, few Americans read the whole of it. A national survey conducted in 2010 reported that 72 percent of about a thousand people polled had never once read all 4,400 words. Not having read the Constitution has generally proven no bar to cherishing it; 86 percent of respondents said the Constitution had "an impact on their daily lives."[9] The point of such surveys is that if more of Americans read the Constitution, all Americans would be better off, because we would demand that our elected officials abide it and we'd be able to tell when they weren't, and to punish them accordingly.[10]

If you haven't read the Constitution lately, do. Chances are that you'll find that it doesn't exactly explain itself. Consider Article 3, Section 3: "The Congress shall have Power to declare the Punishment of Treason, but no Attainder of Treason shall work Corruption of Blood, or Forfeiture except during the Life of the Person attained." This is simply put—hats off to the committee of style—but what does it mean? A legal education helps. Lawyers won't stumble over "attainder," even if the rest of us will. Part of the problem would appear to be the distance between our locution and theirs.[11] "Corruption of blood"? The document's learnedness and the changing meaning of words isn't the whole problem, though, because the charge that the Constitution is too difficult for ordinary people to understand—not because of its vocabulary but because of the complexity of the ideas it contains—was made nearly the minute it was made public. Anti-federalists charged that the Constitution was so difficult to read that it amounted to a conspiracy against the understanding of a plain man, as if it were *willfully* incomprehensible. "The constitution of a wise and free people, ought to be as evident to simple reason, as the letters of our alphabet," wrote one Anti-federalist.[12] "A constitution ought to be, like a beacon, held up to the public eye, so as to be understood by every man," Patrick Henry argued. He believed that what was drafted in Philadelphia was "of such an intricate and complicated nature, that no man on this earth can know its real operation."[13] Anti-federalists had more complaints, too, which is why ratification was touch and go. Rhode Island, the only state to hold a popular referendum on the Constitution, rejected it. Elsewhere, in state ratifying conventions, the Constitution passed only by the narrowest of margins: 89 to 79 in Virginia; 30 to 27 in New York; 187 to 168 in Massachusetts.

Nor were complaints that the Constitution is obscure silenced by ratification. In a 1798 essay called "The Key to Libberty," William Manning, the plainest of men—a New England farmer, Revolutionary War veteran, and father of thirteen children—expressed a view widely held by Jeffersonian Republicans. "The Federal Constitution by a fair construction is a good one prinsapaly," Manning wrote, "but I have no dout but that the Convention who made it intended to destroy our free governments by it, or they neaver would have spent 4 Months in making such an inexpliset thing." Franklin had called the Constitution an "instrument"; he meant that it was a *legal* instrument, like a will. Manning thought the Constitution was an instrument, too, but of a different sort. "It is made like a Fiddle, with but few Strings, but so that the ruling Majority could play any tune upon it they pleased."[14]

For all the charges that the Constitution is difficult to understand, it wasn't much taught. Between 1789 and 1860, only one state, California, had required that the Constitution be taught in school.[15] The first textbooks examining the

Constitution weren't printed until the 1820s, and they were for law students. Three volumes of *Commentaries on the Constitution*, written by Supreme Court justice Joseph Story, appeared in 1833.[16] The next year, Story published an abridgement for common schools. In it, he explained that the Constitution "is the language of the People, to be judged of according to the common sense, and not by mere theoretical reasoning."[17] That may be, but Story's abridgement is 166 pages of closely argued legal argument.

You can't explain a thing without interpreting it. Story, a northerner and a nationalist, emphasized the Supreme Court's role in arbitrating disputes between the federal government and the states, disputes which, in those years, mainly had to do with slavery; southerners who glossed the Constitution stressed state sovereignty. In 1846, William Hickey published a constitutional concordance.[18] He got the idea from James K. Polk's vice president, George Dallas, an expansionist who favored the annexation of Texas and who believed the Constitution prohibited Congress from interfering with the extension of slavery into western territories. The U.S. Senate, over which Dallas presided, ordered twelve thousand copies of Hickey's proslavery *vade mecum*. It does not appear to have elevated congressional conversation. New York governor Silas Wright observed, in 1847: "No one familiar with the affairs of our government, can have failed to notice how large a proportion of our statesmen appear never to have read the Constitution of the United States with a careful reference to its precise language and exact provisions, but rather, as occasion presents, seem to exercise their ingenuity . . . to stretch both to the line of what they, at the moment, consider expedient."[19]

By the middle of the nineteenth century, nearly all white men could vote. Not all of them could read and not all of them owned a copy of the Constitution, but Daniel Webster insisted, "Almost every man in the country is capable of reading it."[20] Whether they did or not is hard to say. Some men did more than read it. William Lloyd Garrison burned the Constitution at an antislavery rally in Massachusetts, calling it a "covenant with death, an agreement with hell." As the crowd cried, "Amen," Garrison ground the ashes of the Constitution beneath the heel of his shoe.[21] John Brown wrote his own constitution, replacing "we the people" with "we, citizens of the United States and the Oppressed People, who . . . have no rights." It was found on Brown's body when he was captured at Harper's Ferry.[22] William Grimes, a fugitive slave, had a different idea about what to do with the Constitution: "If it were not for the stripes on my back which were made while I was a slave, I would in my will, leave my skin a legacy to the government, desiring that it might be taken off and made into parchment and then bind the constitution of glorious happy *and free* America."[23] And then, the American people went to war, over their different ways of reading letters inked on parchment and wounds cut into the skin of a black man's back.

"FIND IT IN THE CONSTITUTION" read the Tea Party rally signs, in 2010, during a debate over the federal government's reform of health care. Forty-four hundred words and "God" is not one of them. Benjamin Rush complained to John Adams, hoping that this error might be corrected: "perhaps acknowledgement might be made of his goodness or of his providence in the proposed amendments."[24] It was not. The word "white" isn't in the Constitution, but Illinois senator Stephen Douglas was still sure that the government established by the Constitution was "made by white men for the benefit of white men and their posterity forever." What about black men? "They are not included, and were not intended to be included," the Supreme Court ruled, in 1857. Railroads, banks, women, education, free markets, privacy, health care, wiretapping: not there.

"There is nothing in the United States Constitution that gives the Congress, the President, or the Supreme Court the right to declare that white and colored children must attend the same public schools," said Mississippi senator James Eastland, after *Brown v. Board of Education*.[25] "Have You Ever Seen the Words Forced Busing in the Constitution?" read a sign carried in Boston in 1975.[26] "Where in the Constitution is the separation of church and state?" Tea Party Senate candidate Christine O'Donnell asked her Democratic opponent Chris Coons during a debate in 2010. When Coons quoted the First Amendment, O'Donnell was flabbergasted. "That's in the First Amendment?" Left-wing bloggers slapped their thighs; Coons won the election in a landslide. But the phrase "separation of church and state" really isn't in the Constitution.[27]

A great deal of what many Americans hold dear is nowhere inked on those four pages of parchment, nor in any of the twenty-seven amendments to the Constitution. What makes the Constitution durable is the same as what makes it so demanding: so much was left out of it. Felix Frankfurter once wrote that the Constitution "is most significantly not a document but a stream of history."[28] The difference between forty-four hundred words and a stream of history goes a long way toward accounting for the panics that plague American politics, every few decades or so, that the Constitution is in crisis, that the American people have forsaken the Constitution, and that what is necessary, to renew America, is a return to constitutional principles through constitutional education.[29] One side is always charging the other with not knowing the Constitution but they are talking about different kinds of knowledge.[30]

"We'll keep clinging to our Constitution, our guns, and our religion," former Alaska governor Sarah Palin said in 2010, "and you can keep the change." Behind the word "change" is the word "evolution." In 1913, Woodrow Wilson insisted, "All that progressives ask or desire is permission—in an era when 'development,' 'evolution,' is the scientific word—to interpret the Constitution according to the Darwinian principle; all they ask is a recognition of the fact that a nation is a living thing and not a machine."[31] Conservatives called for a rejection of this nonsense about a "living constitution." In 1916, the Sons of the American Revolution launched a campaign to celebrate the seventeenth of September as Constitution Day. In 1919, the National Association for Constitutional Government published fifty thousand copies of *A Pocket Edition of the Constitution of the United States* (the association's other publications included an investigation into the influence of socialists in American colleges).[32] In 1921, Warren Harding called the Constitution divinely inspired, and it was Harding who ordered the librarian of Congress to take the parchment out of storage and put it into a shrine. Soon the National Security League was distributing free copies of lectures written by "Mr. Constitution," James Montgomery Beck, Harding's solicitor general, who wrote a series of phenomenally popular books about the Constitution.[33] "No student of our institutions can question that the Constitution is in graver danger today than at any other time in the history of America," Beck warned.[34] By 1923, twenty-three states required constitutional instruction and, by 1931, forty-three.[35] Studying Middletown high school in 1929, the Lynds found this kind of instruction concerning: "70 percent of the boys and 75 percent of the girls answered 'false' to the statement 'A citizen of the United States should be allowed to say anything he pleases, even to advocate violent revolution, if he does no violent act himself.'"[36] Still, the texts published for these courses were by no means uniformly conservative.[37] Wrote the author of an elementary school textbook published in 1930: "This Constitution is yours, boys and girls of America, to cherish and to obey, to preserve and, if need be, to better."[38]

The New Deal broadened and intensified a long-standing debate over the nature of the Constitution, a debate whose cramped terms later generations inherited.[39] "Hopeful people today wave the flag," as FDR's future assistant attorney general Thurman Arnold saw it in 1935; "Timid people wave the Constitution . . . the only bulwark against change."[40] In 2008, supporters of the presidential campaign of Barack Obama carried placards with a single word: CHANGE; two years later, Tea Partiers carried copies of the Constitution.[41] Liberals argued for progress; conservatives argued for a return to the nation's founding principles. Change is a founding principle, too, but people divided by schism are blind to what they share: one half, infallible; the other, never wrong.

Pop quiz, from a test administered by the Hearst Corporation in 1987, during the Constitution's bicentennial:

> *True or False: The following phrases are found in the U.S. Constitution:*
>
> "From each according to his ability, to each according to his need."
> "The consent of the governed."
> "Life, liberty, and the pursuit of happiness."
> "All men are created equal"
> "Of the people, by the people, for the people."[42]

This is what's known as a trick question. None of these phrases are in the Constitution. Eight in ten Americans believed "all men are created equal" to be in the Constitution. Even more thought that "of the people, by the people, for the people" was in the Constitution. Abraham Lincoln, Gettysburg, 1863.

Nearly five in ten thought "from each according to his ability, to each according to his need," was written in Philadelphia in 1787. Karl Marx, 1875.[43]

Something between a quarter and a third of American voters are what political scientists call, impoliticly, "know nothings," meaning that they possess almost no general knowledge of the workings of government, at least according to studies conducted by the American National Election Survey (ANES).[44] This problem is said to be intractable. The know-nothing rate just won't budge; it's been about the same since the Second World War. Critics have charged that these studies systemically overestimate political ignorance. A 2000 ANES survey asked interviewees to identify William Rehnquist's job. The only correct answer was "the Chief Justice of the United States Supreme Court." Answers like "Chief Justice," "Justice," "Chief Justice of the Court," and anything breezier ("a Supreme Court judge who is the head honcho") were all marked as incorrect. (And the ANES people were wrong, too. Technically, the chief justice is "the Chief Justice of the United States.")[45]

Even if the know-nothing rate is inflated, that a substantial number Americans lack basic knowledge of the workings of government is, needless to say, terribly troubling. But so are surveys conducted during the Cold War that appear to have been designed to elicit the headline-generating news that Americans are so ignorant of the Constitution that they can be gulled into believing a piece of it was written by the founding father of communism. To know the Constitution, the Hearst survey report concluded, is to love the original: "those Americans who are *most* knowledgeable about the Constitution are the *least* likely to support changes."[46] (This runs counter to the judgment of historian Michael Kammen. "Americans have known the Constitution best when they have revered it least," Kammen wrote, in an extraordinary and an exhaustively researched account of the history of the Constitution, published in 1986.)[47] In 1985 and 1986, Reagan's attorney general, Edwin Meese III, made a series of speeches advocating originalism.[48] Reagan nominated Antonin Scalia to the Supreme Court in August 1986. The Hearst survey was conducted in October and November of that year. It was released in February 1987. That May, Thurgood Marshall gave a speech about the Constitution, in which he said, "I do not believe that the meaning of the Constitution was forever 'fixed' at the Philadelphia Convention."[49] That July, Reagan nominated Robert Bork to the Court, and, despite the failure of Bork's nomination, originalism never looked back.

In February 2010, a coalition of prominent conservatives, including Meese, Grover Norquist, and leaders of the Heritage Foundation, the *National Review*, and the Federalist Society, met in Virginia to sign "The Mount Vernon Statement." It called for a coalition of social, economic, and national security conservatives to lead the way in returning the nation to its founding principles, as stated in the Declaration of Independence and the Constitution, and which are "presently under sustained attack": "In recent decades, America's principles have been undermined and redefined in our culture, our universities and our politics. The self-evident truths of 1776 have been supplanted by the notion that no such truths exist. The federal government today ignores the limits of the Constitution, which is increasingly dismissed as obsolete and irrelevant."

The Mount Vernon Statement was modeled on the Sharon Statement, written by William F. Buckley, Jr., and signed in 1960.[50] The threat to the Constitution, in the Sharon Statement, was a "menace," and it came from "the forces of international Communism." In the Mount Vernon version, the threat to the Constitution was "change": change is "an empty promise" and "a dangerous deception," and it comes from no being original, in the sense of being the same age as those four sheets of parchment in the National Archives, is a pastiche. Consider the Second Amendment: "A well regulated Militia, being necessary to the security of a free State, the right of the people to keep and bear Arms, shall not be infringed." Before the 1960s, as Yale Law School's Reva Siegel argued, legal scholars had commonly understood the Second Amendment as protecting the right of citizens to form militias—as narrow a right as the protection provided by the Third Amendment against the federal government forcing you to quarter troops in your house. As late as 1989, even Bork could write that the Second Amendment works "to guarantee the right of states to form militia, not for individuals to bear arms." Beginning in the early 1970s, lawyers employed by the National Rifle Association, eager to overturn gun-control laws passed in the wake of the assassinations of Martin Luther King, Jr., and Robert F. Kennedy, began arguing that the Second Amendment protects the right of individuals to bear arms. In the 1970s and especially the 1980s, politicians who advanced this interpretation of the Second Amendment claimed that it represented a restoration of its original meaning. The NRA, which had never before backed a presidential candidate, backed Ronald Reagan in 1980. In an interview in 1991, former chief justice Warren Burger said the NRA's interpretation of the Second Amendment was "one of the greatest pieces of fraud, I repeat the word 'fraud,' on the American public by special interest groups that I have ever seen in my lifetime." People who disagreed with it were accused of failing to respect the Constitution, or being too stupid to understand it. Newt Gingrich wrote, in *To Renew America*, in 1994: "Liberals neither understand nor believe in the constitutional right to bear arms." In 2005, Mark Levin, a talk radio host who worked under Meese in the Reagan Justice Department, wrote that Thurgood Marshall "couldn't have had a weaker grasp of the Constitution."[55]

In 2008, the NRA's argument about the Second Amendment was made law in *The District of Columbia v. Heller*, which ruled as unconstitutional a gun-control law passed in DC decades before.[56]

A different approach was taken by Larry D. Kramer, dean of Stanford Law School, who, in 2004, offered a rival, another jurisprudence based on different historical claims, something called popular constitutionalism.[57] Popular constitutionalism is original, Kramer argued, but judicial review is not. (Kramer was arguing not against originalism but against judicial review, a power wielded, in recent years, by an originalist Court.) "The Supreme Court is not the highest authority in the land on constitutional law," Kramer wrote. "We are."[58] It's not altogether clear how popular constitutionalism works, but activists' opposition to forced busing, the NRA's interpretation of the Second Amendment, and Iowans voting out of office judges who supported same-sex marriage would all seem to fit into this category. Whenever legislation is overturned by an incoming Congress elected by people who believe that legislation to be unconstitutional, that is popular constitutionalism, too.

Originalism grew popular. In 2010, four in ten Americans favored it. Originalism, which has no purchase anywhere but the United States, has a natural affinity with certain types of Protestantism, and the United States differs from all other Western democracies in the sizable proportion of its citizens who believe in the literal truth of the Bible. Although originalism is a serious and important mode of constitutional interpretation, Greene argued that it should also be understood as a political product manufactured by the New Right and marketed to the public by direct mail, talk radio, cable television, and the Internet. In that market, it enjoyed a competitive advantage over other varieties of constitutional interpretation, partly because it's the easiest.[59] Originalism's populist appeal

is identical to that of heritage tourism: both work by collaps-
ing the distance between past and present and by opposing
change: change is decay; virtue lies in a faux eighteenth century wherein are to be found unity of purpose and, between
"the people" and "the elite," no difference or disagreement
whatsoever.[60]

An unexamined question at the heart of this debate, then,
was how people, rather than judges, actually read the Constitution. In 2009 and 2010, the Tea Party Express endorsed
a guide called *The Constitution Made Easy*, a translation into
colloquial English made by Michael Holler. Holler studied at
Biola University, a Christian college offering a biblically centered education. Much of his translation, which appears side
by side with the original, is forthright. His Article 3, Section
2, reads, "Congress will have Power to declare the punishment
for treason, but the penalty may not include confiscating a
person's property after that person is executed," and, in a footnote, he supplies the helpful information that "Corruption of
Blood" refers to the common-law confiscation of the property
of executed traitors, which "had the effect of punishing the
traitor's heirs, or bloodline." Less straightforward is Holler's
Second Amendment, which inverts the language of the original, so to read: "The people have the right to own and carry
firearms, and it may not be violated because a well-equipped
Militia is necessary for a State to remain secure and free."
Holler was an NRA-certified handgun instructor who, in ad-
dition to offering courses on the Constitution, sold classes on
how to obtain a concealed handgun permit.[61]

*U.S. Constitution for Dummies*, published in 2009, was written by Michael Arnheim, an English barrister originally from
South Africa. The book includes a foreword by Ted Cruz, a
nationally prominent defender of the death penalty and former solicitor general of Texas who had successfully defended
a monument to the Ten Commandments at the Texas State

Capitol. In 2008, Cruz argued the progun case before the Supreme Court, in *Heller*. Arnheim's "plain-English guide" translates portions of the Constitution (e.g., "*Due process* is really just an old-fashioned way of saying 'proper procedure'"), with an emphasis on contemporary controversies, which he frames as battles between "judge-made law" and the proper workings of democracy: the right to privacy, for instance, is an example of judge-made law, beginning with *Griswold v. Connecticut*. Arnheim was not stinting with his views. "In my opinion," he wrote, "same-sex marriage in Massachusetts is unconstitutional, and the other states therefore don't have to recognize such unions. I am available if anyone wants to take this issue to the U.S. Supreme Court!"[62]

"I never knew what the Constitution really is until I read Mr. Beck's book," a sly critic of James Montgomery Beck's account of the Constitution once wrote. "You can read it without thinking."[63]

When ideas are reduced to icons, constitutionalism and originalism look exactly the same: the faux parchment stands for both. But originalism and constitutionalism are not the same, and the opposite of original is not unconstitutional. Originalism is one method of constitutional interpretation. Popular originalism is originalism scrawled with Magic Markers, on poster board. Beginning in the 1970s, the NRA opposed gun-control laws. It argued, at length, and over years, that those laws violated the Second Amendment. Eventually, in 2008, the Supreme Court agreed. In 2009, the Tea Party's passions ignited faster and were stated more simply. A sign at a Tea Party rally in Temecula, California, read: "Impeach Obama: He's Unconstitutional."

The Constitution is ink on parchment. It is forty-four hundred words. And it is, too, the accreted set of meanings

# 6

# I.O.U.

John Pintard, a man of steady habits, made profitable use of his year and change in debtors' prison. Locked up from July 1797 to August 1798 in a two-story stone jail in Newark that loomed like a tombstone over the town's burying ground, he walked more than a thousand miles, 113,984 lengths of the hall, and read more than a hundred books.[1] He read everything he could get his hands on, from *Don Quixote* ("exquisite performance") to a pamphlet called *National Debt Productive of National Prosperity* ("exhibits considerable ingenuity") to Samuel Johnson's dictionary, which he digested at a rate of nine minutes per page, which meant that, between the time he spent pacing like a caged animal and the hours he whiled away drafting letters to his creditors, begging them to forgive his debts, it took him 157 days, and some not small number of candles, to get from ABACUS to ZOOTOMY.[2] Reading the dictionary was a way to mark time, like making hash marks on the wall of a cell with a lump of coal. But it was more, too. "I am more indebted to him than to any other writer," Pintard wrote of Johnson, aptly.[3] Johnson himself had spent time in debtors' prison—he was imprisoned twice, once for a debt of £5—and had pointed out the senselessness of it. "We have now imprisoned one generation of Debtors after another,"

Johnson observed in 1758, the year after Pintard was born, "but we do not find that their numbers lessen."[4]

What's a society to do with people who can't pay what they owe? If a man has already handed over to his creditors everything he owns, asked the author of *The Ill Policy and Inhumanity of Imprisoning Insolvent Debtors*, printed in Rhode Island in 1754, what's the point of chucking him in the chokey? "Can his Creditors, with all their Wisdom, have more than All? Will his Imprisonment increase his Estate? Will his Confinement pay or diminish his Debts? or the Punishment of his Body be any Kind of Advantage to them, or to Society?"[5]

It isn't hard to make the argument against debtors' prison. But it took much more than an argument—and two centuries—to abolish it, mainly because, its seeming preposterousness notwithstanding, it was just so gruesome that it worked, if, mainly, as a threat: few things motivate prompt repayment of money owed better than the prospect of a dark, dank dungeon where rats and smallpox thrive while men and women shrink and shrivel and starve and die.[6] (Jailers provided food, bedding and fuel for felons; debtors were left to fend for themselves.) Parliament didn't ban the imprisonment of debtors until 1869. The practice met its end much sooner in the United States. Imprisonment for debt was abolished in New York in 1831; the rest of the country soon followed.[7]

What replaced it, what was already replacing it, in John Pintard's lifetime, was bankruptcy. Pintard escaped debtors' prison by availing himself of a 1798 New Jersey insolvency law and then filed for bankruptcy under the terms of the first U.S. bankruptcy law, passed in 1800. His debts were discharged—he was legally relieved of the obligation ever to repay them—his ledger erased, his slate wiped clean, and his past, eventually, forgotten.[8]

Americans have discharged one generation of debtors after another, but, as Johnson put it, we do not find that their numbers lessen. We only find that we forget, when times are good, that times were ever bad. The colonies were settled, the nation founded, the country built, by debtors. Americans have forgotten that; debtors like to forget. "The present generation is bankrupt of principles and hope, as of property," Ralph Waldo Emerson wrote during the Panic of 1837. Mostly, though, we're bankrupt of history.

The state has long arbitrated insolvency. Under ancient Roman law, the body of a debtor could be cut up and disbursed to his creditors: your money or your life. That probably never happened, but debtors did commonly end up as slaves.[9] Debt and slavery, historically, and conceptually, too, are always tangled together. In England, statutes decreeing imprisonment for debt date to the thirteenth century.[10] The practice prevailed in most parts of the early modern world, and, in the seventeenth century, it traveled, with English common law, to America. A 1641 Massachusetts law known as the "Body of Liberties" spelled out a rule of thumb that closely followed English practice: "No mans person shall be Arrested, or imprisoned upon execution or judgment for any debt or fine, If the law can finde competent meanes of satisfaction otherwise from his estaite, and if not his person may be arrested and imprisoned where he shall be kept at his owne charge, not the platife's till satisfaction be made." You're free, that is, unless you can't afford to pay what you owe, and if you end up in prison, it's on your penny. The logic behind this bring-your-own-mutton-and-tallow clause was that you might be hiding your money, and if you weren't, and were truly broke, your friends and family would pony up, either to keep you in food and firewood or, better still, to pay your debts and get you out. The point wasn't to lock you up—as the proverb had it, "A prison pays no debts"—it was to terrify you.[11]

Alas, it didn't work as well in the colonies. As many as two out of every three Europeans who came to the colonies were debtors: they paid for their passage by becoming indentured servants. Early on, labor was so scarce that colonists who fell into debt after they arrived paid with work; there was much to be done, and there weren't many prisons, anyway. In 1674, the Massachusetts court ordered Joseph Armitage, who owed John Ruck twenty-two pounds, to serve as Ruck's servant for seven years.[12] (What relieved the colonies' labor scarcity and spelled the end of debtor servitude was the rise of the African slave trade.)[13] The New World was also a good place to go to run away from your debts. Some colonies were, basically, debtors' asylums. In 1642, Virginia, eager to lure settlers, promised five years' protection from any debts contracted in the Old World. North Carolina did the same in 1669. Creditors, in any case, found it all but impossible to pursue fugitive debtors across the Atlantic. (Not for nothing did Defoe's Moll Flanders, born in London's Newgate prison, sail to Virginia.)[14] Then there was an early version of a farm subsidy: Connecticut and Maryland forbade the prosecution of debtors between May and October and released prisoners to plant and harvest on the unassailable argument that "the Porest sort of the Inhabitants" were often "undone in that they cannot be at Liberty to make their Cropps."[15]

As early as 1680 one colonist could observe, "it is every dayes way in every trading towne, for merchants upon neglect of payment, for to arrest theire debtors."[16] Debt grew both more common and more complicated. As the colonial economy grew and, like England's, commercialized, it depended, more and more, on pieces of paper, whose value can and nearly always does fluctuate and, of course, is meant to; that's what makes gains. On this side of the ocean, where there was never much cash and where funds had to travel for miles, this was a more treacherous arrangement. At first, only merchants relied on paper credit, not so much currency as notes of hand, bills of exchange, and I.O.U.s. (the I.O.U., as parlance, dates to the 1610s). Soon, though, tradesmen and artisans and even people of decidedly modest means were using credit. Debt might be a crime, and, worse, a sin, Cotton Mather preached in a 1716 sermon titled "Fair Dealing between Debtor and Creditor," but if the colonists, cash poor and on the edge of the world, couldn't live with it, they certainly couldn't live without it: "Yea, without some *Debt*, there could be no *Trade* be carried on."[17] Some debt, yeah. But how much is too much?

In London, debtors' prisons filled. And then they teemed. In 1728, an architect named Robert Castell died of smallpox in Fleet Street prison. Castell happened to be a friend of a member of Parliament named James Oglethorpe, who urged an investigation, which led, in turn, to legislative reform, including An Act for the Relief of Insolvent Debtors, outlawing the imprisonment of debtors who owed very small sums and resulting in the immediate release of as many as ten thousand debtors.[18] Then Oglethorpe had another idea: what about just shipping the miserable wretches across the ocean? In 1732, he founded and became the first governor of Georgia, intended as a refuge for debtors released from English prisons.[19]

Flushing debtors out of the system by whisking them across the Atlantic didn't quite solve the problem. In 1750, an infection at the Old Bailey spread and led to the death of more than twenty people who weren't even prisoners, including lawyers, and four out of the six judges on the bench. That, too, led to an investigation.[20] Further impassioned calls for reform came from writers, including novelists, who, it turns out, were very likely to run into debt, get arrested for it, and write about it, writing, even, while *in* prison, to write themselves out.

That writers were forever going broke might not be surprising, but it's important. Eighteenth-century writers, as much as stock-jobbers, were in the business of producing paper whose value tended to fluctuate wildly; that made them especially prone to falling, even irretrievably, into debt. (So were artists, for the same reason. Hogarth, another jailbird, made debtors' prison a stop on the "Rake's Progress".) Eighteenth-century novels are chock-a-block with scenes set in debtors' prison; Henry Fielding's 1751 *Amelia* is a good example. (Fielding went to debtors' prison in 1741; he died insolvent in 1754.)[21] Cleland (Fleet Street) Smollett (King's Bench) went to prison, too, and Goldsmith only narrowly averted it when Johnson rescued him by rushing the manuscript of a novel Goldsmith had just finished writing to a publisher, selling it for sixty pounds, and using the money to make good Goldsmith's debt (that novel, *The Vicar of Wakefield*, published in 1764, is the story of a man of virtue who ends up, of course, in debtors' prison). English literary scholars have argued, not without cause, that debt lies behind the plot of nearly every eighteenth-century novel.[22]

What fueled fiction—tear-jerking tales of people locked up, for years, for owing tuppence—galled reformers, too. In 1773, a London goldsmith named James Neild founded the Society for the Discharge and Relief of Persons Imprisoned for Small Debts. Neild's own story sounds like it came straight out of a novel: as a young man, he had seen a fellow apprentice locked up in King's Bench— his life ruined, for a pittance. When Neild inherited a fortune, he decided to use it to buy debtors out of Britain's prison, one by one, shilling by shilling. He eventually bought the liberty of twenty-five thousand debtors; they owed, on average, less than three pounds.[23]

The same year that Neild began his work, an English sheriff, John Howard, began a tour of prisons in England and Wales; in 1777, his report painted an unrelieved picture of filth, squalor, pestilence, and want. He called attention, too, to a particular injustice: "debtors have no bread; although it is granted to the highwayman, the house-breaker, and the murderer."[24]

The work of Neild and Howard exerted considerable influence in the rebelling colonies, where sympathy for debtors was long-standing, and growing, and, increasingly, attached to the patriot cause. Beginning in the 1760s, whenever New York's Sons of Liberty held a banquet, they made a show of sending the leftovers to the city's imprisoned debtors.[25] There was a principle at stake. Weren't all the Sons of Liberty debtors, too? A creditor was "lord of another man's purse"; hadn't British creditors swindled all American debtors of their purses? Virginia planters like Jefferson, Madison, and Washington were monstrously in debt to factors in London. Hadn't they been reduced to little more than the slaves of avaricious English merchants? This, anyway, is how many colonists came to understand their economic dependence on Britain. Declaring independence was a way to sever those ties, to cancel those debts. The American Revolution, some historians have argued, was itself a form of debt relief.[26]

In 1776, just a few months before the Declaration of Independence, Philadelphians formed the Society for Assisting Distressed Prisoners, modeled after Neild's society.[27] In 1787, just before the Constitution was drafted, New Yorkers formed the Society for the Relief of Distressed Debtors and began inspecting the city's debtors' prison.[28] This is what they discovered: of 1,162 debtors committed to debtors' prison in New York in 1787 and 1788, 716 of them owed less than twenty shillings.[29]

Debtors in New York used to be locked up in the garret of City Hall, at the corner of Wall Street, in a cramped nook under the roof. From its dormers, they would lower shoes, tied to a string, to collect alms from passers-by.[30] (Debtors' prisons in other cities and towns had what were called "beggars' grates," iron bars through which prisoners in cellar dungeons could extend outstretched palms.) In 1759, New York's debtors were moved to the New Gaol, near what was then called the Commons. After 1775, when the city's criminals were relocated to a new prison, Bridewell, the debtors were left behind. They had the New Gaol, such as it was, to themselves. Three floors, fourteen rooms.[31] Toffs, merchants and the like, shared rooms on the second and third floors; artisans on the first. In the 1780s, the Connecticut-born painter Ralph Earl must have occupied rooms on an upper floor, where he had light enough to paint, because the members of the Society for the Relief of Distressed Debtors came up with an ingenious plan to save him: they hired him to paint their portraits. (Earl painted more than a dozen portraits during his two years in prison.)[32] But New York's poorest debtors sat in darkness, day and night. They had no windows because they had no rooms at all; they slept on the floor in the ground floor hall. And the wretched, the truly wretched and the doomed, were shut up in the cellar.[33]

New York's debtors' prison was a ship of misery in a sea of anarchy. In 1794, the debtors on the two top floors drafted their own constitution, established their own courts, and elected their own sheriffs, to enforce the laws. (Debtors in Philadelphia printed their own newspaper.)[34] The wife of one debtor, who lived in the prison with her husband (as did many wives, and children, too, though almost all imprisoned debtors were men),[35] was fined, for instance, for "not cleaning herself and becoming lousey."[36]

John Pintard, a consummate New Yorker, ended up in debtors' prison in Newark only because he was trying so desperately to stay out of the lice-ridden debtors' prison in New

York.[37] Pintard knew a fair bit about incarceration. From 1777 to 1780 he had served on a commission to relieve the distress of Americans held in New York City as prisoners of war. He changed bandages, brought blankets, and consoled the dying, many of whom were starving to death.[38]

After the war, Pintard had opened offices at 12 Wall Street and became one of the city's most prosperous importers, specializing in the China and Indies trades.[39] In 1790, he was elected to the state legislature; he also helped found the American Museum, the nation's first, "to perpetuate the Memorial of national events and history," and contributed a column called "American Chronology" to *New York Magazine*. He opened a stockbroker's office, on King Street. In 1791, he became a partner of Leonard Bleecker (who happened to be the secretary of the Society for the Relief of Distressed Debtors); they auctioned stock at the Tontine Coffee House, and they appeared to be making a fortune. ("What magic this among the people, / That swells a may-pole to a steeple?" asked one newspaper, in a poem titled "Speculation.") Here was a new thing under the sun: Pintard was one of America's very first specialized securities brokers.[40] Pintard befriended Alexander Hamilton and supported the treasury secretary's scheme to fund the national debt. Bleecker, worried about speculative risk, dissolved the partnership and Pintard began dealing with New York speculator and assistant secretary of the treasury William Duer, who was attempting to corner the market on stock in the Bank of the United States. Duer was a swindler; Pintard fell for him. Duer borrowed, with Pintard as his agent, the life savings of "shopkeepers, widows, orphans, Butchers, Carmen, Gardners, market women." Pintard signed over a million dollars' worth of bank notes. In 1792, when Duer's scheme fell apart and it was revealed that all those bank notes were worthless, Duer landed in the New Gaol (or, rather he was chased there, by a mob that was attempting to stone him to death; another New Yorker broke in, and challenged Duer to a duel).[41] Pintard's friends couldn't decide whether to "pity his want of prudence" or condemn him as a "perfect swindler."[42] Pintard tried, for a while, to hide out in his Manhattan townhouse. "Would it not be prudent for him to remove to a State where there is a Bankrupt Act?" one friend wondered.[43] Pintard sold everything he owned—his ships, their cargoes; his houses, their libraries[44]—and fled to New Jersey, where he endured five years of exile before his creditors finally managed to catch up with him. (Hiding out in just this way was not uncommon; Fielding wrote *Joseph Andrews*, yet another novel plotted by debt, while hiding from his creditors in Charing Cross.[45] The practice was known as "keeping house"; if you never left your house, you couldn't be served with a writ, and you could avoid debtors' prison; this was usually easier to do if you were also out of town. Happily, you could count on getting out of the house at least once a week, since a writ for debt couldn't be served on a Sunday.)[46]

The insolvency of Duer and Pintard triggered the Panic of 1792, the nation's first stock market crash. It ruined lives. Losses were estimated at about five million dollars, about the value of New York City.[47] Recovery came quickly.[48] But the panic spurred New York brokers to sign an agreement banning private bidding on stocks, so that no one, ever again, could do what Duer had done; that agreement marks the founding of what would become the New York Stock Exchange. All of which is to say: John Pintard was no ordinary debtor. Ordinary debtors weren't just insolvent—owing more than they owned—they were indigent. That was most of them. Generally, it's better to be rich and owe a fortune than to be poor and owe a pittance. The first thing John Pintard did, when he got to debtors' prison, was to decorate. "The necessary repairs of the apartment allotted to me in this abode of human wretchedness has so engrossed my attention that I have not looked into a book scarcely the last week," he had complained in his diary, just after he was arrested, in July 1797. He *wallpapered*.[49] He also didn't stay there all that long. Pintard managed to avail himself of an insolvency law passed in New Jersey in January 1798. "My week has been broken & interrupted," he complained in March, "with the disagreeable tho' necessary review of my accounts & transactions, to be laid before the Court in order to obtain my release from confinement."[50]

The paperwork that interfered with Pintard's reading would take months to make its way through the courts. Meanwhile, he returned to his books. On April 25, 1798, five days after Pintard finished reading Johnson's dictionary in Newark, twenty-four debtors imprisoned in New York's New Gaol staged a jailbreak.[51] Reported one newspaper, "Desperate Laws occasion desperate means."[52] The week all but seven of those fugitives were caught, Pintard moved on to reading *Thoughts in Prison*, poems written from Newgate in 1777 by an English clergyman named William Dodd while awaiting execution for having forged a bill of exchange—he had signed as Lord Chesterfield—to bail himself out of debt. (Dodd had earlier helped Neild found the Society for the Discharge and Relief of Persons Imprisoned for Small Debts.) Johnson had tried to rescue Dodd and, when he failed, had written a speech for Dodd to deliver on the gallows, perhaps cringing at the prospect of what Dodd would say, if left to his own talents. Pintard, like most critics, found Dodd a terrible writer ("Blank verse, no peculiar excellence"), but he nevertheless copied Dodd's lines into his diary:

> Alas! The worthiest may incur the stroke
> Of worldly infelicity! What man,
> How high so'er he builds his earthly nest,
> Can claim security from Fortune's change?[53]

Three months later, Pintard and his fellow debtors celebrated the Fourth of July. To the United States, they proposed
a toast: "May its next revolution no longer find imprisonment
for debt & personal slavery, solecisms, in the chapter of American rights & privileges." Then Pintard, who had been on a
Shakespeare kick ever since finishing Dodd, rang in the day
with his version of Henry V's St. Crispen's speech:

> We few, we wretched few, we band of brothers,
> For he to day that is confined with us
> Shall be our brother, be he ne'er so vile
> This day shall gentle his condition.[54]

Pintard's condition soon did gentle. That 1798 New Jersey insolvency law was meant to discourage creditors from imprisoning people for small sums and to save poor debtors from
starvation by requiring a creditor to pay four shillings a week
for his debtor's keep. When Pintard's creditor missed a payment, Pintard—whose prison syllabus included law books—
seized upon this technicality.[55] That got him out of jail, a
month later.[56] There remained, however, the small matter of
discharging his debts, and forgetting his past.

The Constitution grants to Congress the power "to establish
uniform Laws on the subject of Bankruptcies." What the framers did not make clear, and what led to decades of debate, was
who those laws were for. Bankruptcy for some or bankruptcy
for all?[57] There seemed to be two kinds of debt: debts incurred
by "traders" (stock brokers, bankers, and merchants) and debts
incurred by everyone else. The first kind could be forgiven, for
the sake of commerce; the second kind had to be enforced, for
the sake of creditors, not to mention, public morality. Traders
take on financial risks, and society benefits; for commerce to
thrive, a trader's liability has to have a bottom. Bankruptcy

laws had existed in England for centuries, but only traders could avail themselves of those laws; other debtors were left to tangle with insolvency laws, or, more likely, to go to jail.

The idea that debt is necessary for trade, and has to be forgiven, is consequent to the rise of a market economy, while the idea that debt is wrong and should be punished is a feature of a moral economy, with this American adjustment: in the United States, sorting debtors into two systems (bankruptcy for wheelers-and-dealers; debtors' prison for chumps) was considered not only immoral but, finally, undemocratic.

In 1788, delegates to the New York ratifying convention proposed an amendment to the Constitution: bankruptcy laws passed by Congress "shall only extend to merchants and other traders," but states should have the power "to pass laws for the relief of other insolvent debtors."[58] That amendment didn't pass. When Congress passed the first federal bankruptcy act in 1800, it followed English precedent and applied only to traders, which is why enterprising John Pintard crossed the Hudson to New York, took out an ad in the newspaper, announcing that he was doing business as a broker, went to a coffee shop and traded a single stock, at a profit of fifty-eight cents (which he, expiating, donated to charity), and promptly filed for bankruptcy. On September 10, 1800, seven days before his bankruptcy was finally declared, he wrote in his diary, "Should prosperity smile, let me never forget the suffering I have endured to serve as a check against presumptuous hopes."[59]

In 1802, New York's Society for the Relief of Distressed Debtors opened the nation's first soup house, near the jail.[60] The next year, the federal bankruptcy law was repealed. It seemed, by forgiving speculative failure, to reward incaution; the House committee on repeal concluded that the law promoted "fraud, speculation, and extravagance."[61] It also helped the people who least needed it. Wrote one observer, "We saw rich men today, bankrupt tomorrow, and next day in full business and great style, while the poor farmer or manufacturer who had been ruined by their extravagance must suffer the penalties of the law in a jail."[62]

Pintard floundered. In 1802, he served, briefly, as a newspaper editor; the next year, his only surviving son was lost at sea (another son had died at thirteen, while living with his father in debtors' prison).[63] But then, in 1804, DeWitt Clinton, the mayor, appointed Pintard the city's first inspector. Pintard became, in effect, the city's statistician. (Between 1790 and 1830, the population of New York grew more than five hundred percent.)[64] He counted things, especially things having to do with public health: taverns, streets, people, cellars, births, deaths, firemen, dog licenses.[65] He also founded, in 1804, the New-York Historical Society. All those books he read while in debtors' prison: they formed the core of the Society's library.[66] In a broadside addressed to the public, Pintard, engaged in "the humble task of collecting and preserving whatever may be useful to others in the different branches of historical inquiry," begged for donations of papers—letters, books, tracts, magazines, anything—all this, he hoped, to rescue from "dust and obscurity."[67]

Pintard collected and catalogued and counted and reported. He wanted to bring order to New York, past and present. He shared an office with the street commissioner, who was turning the city's streets into a grid. "It was proposed to call the longitudinal Roads Avenues," Pintard wrote in his diary, after a meeting in 1806.[68] That year, the Humane Society ladled out, to debtors, nine thousand quarts of soup.[69] The number of debtors in the city, like just about everything else, grew. In 1808, thirteen hundred New Yorkers were jailed for debt.[70] During the Panic of 1809, the Humane Society petitioned the New York legislature to pass a law prohibiting imprisonment for debts less than twenty-five dollars. The bill, which had Clinton's support, failed.[71] Pintard, meanwhile, came to believe that the city's working poor frittered their wages: "The whole is therefore generally spent in the purchase of frippery among the females, & in the indulgence of vicious habits among the males." He wondered about the possibility of getting their money, and investing it on their behalf, and drafted "A Plan for forming a Savings Association."[72]

In 1811, a New York lawyer named Joseph Dewey Fay, using a pseudonym recalling the English reformer, John Howard, published *Essays of Howard, or, Tales of the Prison*, exposing the evils of the institution with an abolitionist's zeal. Fay claimed to have spent sixteen years in debtors' prison; it's not clear that he did. But he wrote with passion and conviction. He estimated that in 1810 fully ten perfect of New York's free adult men had been arrested for debt and that, between 1800 and 1810, fifty debtors had died in jail. "Americans boast that they have done away with torture," Fay wrote, "but the debtors' prison is torture."[73] Fay went to Albany and lobbied the legislature to pass an expanded insolvency law for imprisoned debtors. The day the bill became law, Fay advertised his legal services in the newspaper: who better to help you clear your debts than Joseph Fay, Esq.?[74] Six hundred and twenty-five hundred debtors availed themselves of discharge in the law's first ten months. The law was so generous that people had themselves arrested for debt, merely to take advantage of it.[75]

"We all owe a debt to Society as well as to God," John Pintard wrote in 1816, "and I wish to discharge my share."[76] That year, John Pintard found a home for the New-York Historical Society: the abandoned almshouse, next door to the debtors' prison.[77] An active philanthropist, he had by now become involved in a dozen causes.[78] His bankruptcy had changed him, for good, and for better.

A state law passed in 1817 prohibited imprisoning debtors who owed less than twenty-five dollars. The debtors' prison emptied, but the streets filled with beggars; the Humane Society turned to pouring soup for the poor.[79] That year, Pintard and two other men founded the Society for the Prevention of Pauperism (the SPP): "the intention of this Society is not to afford alms but labour," Pintard wrote, "so that there shall be no pretext for idleness."[80] During the Panic of 1819, Pintard founded another library, the Mechanics and Apprentices Library, and his idea about investing the money of the working poor finally came to fruition.[81] "Americans are an active restless people impatient of slow profits," he wrote. "Their habits," he believed, "must undergo, not a reformation, but a complete revolution. A new race must arise on the broken fortunes of the present." That new race had to learn "to plod and earn an honest living, to accumulate by slow degrees."[82] That year, Pintard started the country's first savings bank, the New York Bank for Savings, and served as its first president (the bank was sponsored by the SPP).[83] The poor, Pintard believed, "are like the Indians, who think when Spring comes that there will be no more winter."[84] A savings bank could help them weather all seasons.

The nineteenth century was an age of panics, an age of speculation, and an age, for New York especially, of vast capital accumulation. In this swirl of economic activity, Pintard's savings bank had a place, but not much of one.[85] "Many who have calculated upon fortunes will turn out Bankrupts," Pintard predicted, during the Panic of 1819.[86] Americans liked to get rich fast. That this meant that they went broke fast, too, they tried to forget. In 1935, a good time to take a close look at economic failure, Charles Warren, the first historian to make a careful study of bankruptcy ("Bankruptcy is a gloomy and depressing subject," Warren explained), found that every major American bankruptcy law has been the product of a financial crisis or depression—and that nearly every major American bankruptcy law was subsequently repealed when the economy revived.[87] The 1800 law that discharged Pintard's debts was passed to help the nation recover from the Panic of 1792, which Pintard, of course, had started; it was repealed in 1803. Between 1800 and 1898, every American bankruptcy law, passed in the wake of panic, was diluted or repealed when the panic passed.[88] The same is true for the laws passed in the state of New York. The 1811 insolvency law, a response to the panic of 1809, was repealed in just ten months. (And, in 1819, the Supreme Court ruled it unconstitutional, anyway; only Congress can pass bankruptcy laws.)[89] The 1841 U.S. bankruptcy law (passed the year Pintard retired from the New York Bank for Savings, when he eighty-two, and blind) was a response to the Panic of 1837. It set a precedent: it was the first national bankruptcy law, anywhere, to offer bankruptcy to everyone.[90] New Yorker Henry Anstice, who kept a stationary shop on Nassau Street where he mostly sold blank forms, printed, in 1843, a directory of everyone who had declared bankruptcy under the 1841 Act: *An Alphabetical List of Applicants for the Benefit of the Bankrupt Act . . . for Their More Certain Identity.* The point of the directory was to warn shopkeepers off extending any of these failures further credit, but it's a testament, too, to the democratization of bankruptcy. The list ran from "ABBEY, DAVID, jr., weigh-master, Rondout, Ulster county," to "Zeregher, Augustus, merchant, New-York." There are carpet-dealers, grocers, stove-makers, merchants, clerks, dentists, tin workers, even a towboat captain.[91] By the time Anstice published his directory, the economy had begun to improve and the law, predictably, had already been repealed. But bankruptcy protection would never again be restricted to brokers. It would be for everyone.

but surely, did the rest of the union.[97] The last debtors in the New Gaol left on March 1, 1832.[98] The building, whose twenty-two-inch thick stone walls made it fireproof, was turned to another use: housing the city's archives.[99]

William Duer died, in the "limits" of New York's New Gaol, in 1799, just months before that first federal bankruptcy law was passed.[100] John Pintard got off nearly scot-free. He led a life of public service. "Monday 4 P.M. Committee of the pauperism Society on the subject of a Savings Bank," he wrote, during a typical week, "Tuesday 4P.M. Committee of the Historical Society on the Library, on the propriety of establishing a reading room."[101] Among the very many fine things Pintard did with his fresh start was to promote the Erie Canal, which spurred manufacturing and created thousands of jobs.[102] If his descendants are to be believed, Pintard's strategic support of the canal project was, at a crucial moment, when public support was floundering, instrumental. They might just be right: when the canal was opened, it was Pintard who was charged with carrying the bottle of water from the Atlantic, to pour into it, an honor not granted to just anyone.[103]

It's good, then, that Pintard didn't die in Newark's jail, a stone's throw from the town's burying ground. Forgiveness of debts, of everyone's debts, lay behind some large part of American prosperity, when times were prosperous. While nineteenth-century British writers—Dickens, Thackeray, and Trollope, among them—kept writing gloomy novels with scenes set in debtors' prisons (Dickens's father went to debtors' prison; Thackeray was arrested for debt; and Trollope fled the country to avoid it), American writers turned to shiny, bright-eyed new plots, rags-to-riches, the hazards of new fortunes. In the United States, debtors' prison was abolished, and bankruptcy law was liberalized, because Americans came to see that most people who fall into debt are victims of the business cycle, and not of fate, or divine retribution, or the wheel of fortune.

As John Pintard put it on the motto he chose for his family's coat-of arms: NEVER DESPAIR.[104]

# 7

# A NUE MERRYKIN DIKSHUNARY

On June 4, 1800, Noah Webster, a sometime schoolteacher, failed lawyer, and staggeringly successful spelling-book author, took out an ad in the back pages of a Connecticut newspaper, just above notices of a sailor's death, a shoe sale, and a farmer's reward for a stray cow. The sailor had drowned; the cheap shoes were "Ladies Morocco"; the cow was red with a white face. Webster, who was forty-two, had this to say: he was busy writing a "Dictionary of the American Language," and he wanted the world to know it.

"It is found that a work of this kind is absolutely necessary," Webster announced, "on account of considerable differences between the American and English language." The American people had declared independence and constituted their own government. Now they needed their own dictionary, a place to put all the new words they had coined—Americanisms like *lengthy*, a good word to describe both the dictionary and the amount of time it would take Webster to finish it. Seventy thousand entries and a quarter century later, he would write his last definition, much to the relief of his wife and seven children and, toward the end, the tumbles of grandchildren who stomped up and down the stairs while Dear Pa toiled away, *A* to *Z*, in a study whose walls had been packed with sand to keep out the noise of even their whispers. ("RACKET, *n*. A confused, clattering noise . . . . We say, the children make a *racket*.") Although, for those brave enough to open his study door, Webster stocked a desk drawer with raisins and peppermints.[1]

Webster's epic, monumental *American Dictionary of the English Language* was published in 1828. It rivaled—and dwarfed—Samuel Johnson's 1755 *Dictionary of the English Language*: Johnson's listed some 43,000 words, Webster defined more than 70,000, and Webster, unlike Johnson, had written his dictionary himself, without so much as an amanuensis.

Johnson was a stylist, a wit, and a poet. Webster was a different sort of man altogether: a pedant, a pedagogue, and, above all, a politician. Johnson famously—and disingenuously—defined a lexicographer as a "harmless drudge." Webster may have been a drudge, but, if his critics are to be believed, he was far from harmless.

Webster's proposal made national news. No news might have been better. Within a week, a Philadelphia newspaper editor called Webster's idea preposterous (it is "perfectly absurd to talk of the *American* language") and his motives mercenary ("the plain truth is that he means to *make money*").[2]

To be fair, much the same scorn had greeted two American dictionaries, published just months earlier. A pair of Connecticut men, including the aptly-named-but-no-relation Samuel Johnson, Jr., offered a work promising "a number of words in vogue not included in any dictionary." Reviewers agreed that most of them didn't *belong* in any dictionary: *sans culottes* (no: French!), *tomahawk* (axe it: Indian!), and *lengthy* (good grief: what's next, *strengthy*?). "At best, useless," was one critic's three-word verdict on the first American dictionary. No better were notices of Massachusetts minister Caleb Alexander's

*Columbian Dictionary,* containing *"Many NEW WORDS, peculiar to the United States."* "A disgusting collection" of idiotic words "coined by presumptuous ignorance," wrote one reviewer, referring to Alexander's inclusion of Americanisms like *rateability* and *caucus.* His final ruling on *The Columbian Dictionary?* "A record of our imbecility."[3]

For rancorous contempt in a literary review, it's hard to think of much worse than "at best, useless" and "a record of our imbecility," at least not without thumbing through a thesaurus for synonyms for *worthless* and *tripe.* But Webster's critics were pretty resourceful. Joseph Dennie, editor of the *Gazette of the United States,* began his reply to Webster's announcement by sneering, "If, as Mr. Webster asserts, it is true that many new words have already crept into the language of the United States, he would be much better employed in rooting out those anxious weeds, than in mingling them with the flowers." He then printed a pile of (fake) letters from readers, addressed to Webster, and atrociously spelled:

Sur,
I find you are after meaking a nue Merrykin Dikshunary; your rite, Sir; for ofter lookin all over the anglish Books, you wont find a bit of SHILLALY big enuf to beat a dog wid.

PAT O'DOGERTY

As I find der ish no DONDER and BLIXSUM in de English Dikshonere I hope you put both in yours.

HANS BUBBLEBLOWER

Massa Webser plese put sum HOMMANY and sum GOOD POSSUM fat and sum two tree good BANJOE in your new what-you-call-um Book for your fello Cytzen.

CUFFEE

Mr. Webster,
tother day as Jack Trotter and I were twigging an Old
Codger with our Puns & Jokes. out came a develish keen
thing from Jack—dang it, Thats a dagger says I.

Jack says this is a new application of the word Dagger;
if so, it is at your servis.

DICK SPLASHAWAY

Mistur Webstur
please to let me know whether you buy words by the
hundred or by the dozen, &c your price, I unclose your a
certificat from my husband of my billyties

MARTHA O'GABBLE

I hereby certify that my wife martha has the best knack at
coining new words of any I ever knew—& with the aid of
a comforting drop she'll <u>fill you two dictonerys in an hour
if you please</u>

DERMOT O'GABBLE[4]

This kind of ranting is so drearily familiar that it's easy to assume that editors like Dennie, mocking Pat, Hans, and Cuffee,
drank from the same political well water as pundits who, two
centuries later, railed against bilingual education. Or to imagine that early American literati who objected to the clunky
*rateability* and the ill-gotten *lengthy* were just the kind of language purists who would later scorn every "thru" and mistaken
"hopefully" as just so many weeds in the garden of good English. It would make sense if Webster's critics were political and
cultural conservatives. But they weren't or, at least, they were
only that. Webster's Nue Merrykin Dikshunary was conceived
in the era in which modern political parties were born. He announced his plan during a presidential election year, the bitterly
fought battle between the Republican, Thomas Jefferson, and

the Federalist, John Adams. In a year of polarizing political rhetoric, Webster's plan for an American dictionary had the very bad bipartisan luck of offending nearly everybody.

The snootiest opposition came from members of Webster's own Federalist Party. Webster himself was so ardent a conservative that even fellow Federalists called him "The Monarch." In January 1800, six months before he announced his plan to compile a dictionary, Webster had elaborated on his political views in a series of lengthy public letters in which he held firm to conservative Federalist ideals. "Whatever may be thought of the position, I am persuaded from extensive reading and twenty years' observation that no truth is more certain than that a republican government can be rendered durable in no other way than by excluding from elections men who have so little property, education, or principle, that they are liable to yield their own opinions to the guidance of unprincipled leaders." In August, Republican editor William Duane replied in the Philadelphia newspaper the *Aurora*, "*Noah Webster* says that, in order to give republicanism a permanent existence, the poorer class of people should be excluded from elections. . . . If excluding a portion of the people from elections constitute the only durable basis of republicanism, then we might truly say that republicanism may *mean any thing*."[5]

As the months passed, and more and more Republicans were elected to legislative office, Webster only became more committed to voting restrictions. In December 1800—before Jefferson's victory was assured (an Electoral College tie between Jefferson and his running-mate, Aaron Burr, would not be broken by the House of Representatives until February 1801)—the forty-three-year-old Webster wrote to Benjamin Rush with dismay, "It would be better for the people; they would be more free and more happy, if all were deprived of the right of suffrage until they were 45 years of age, and if no man was eligible to an important office until he is 50."[6]

But when it came to his dictionary, Webster was a democrat. He believed, extraordinarily for his time, that the mass of common people, not a select few, form language and establish its rules. Their judgment, not the judgment of better-educated men, holds sway: "The man who undertakes to censure others for the use of certain words and to decide what is or is not correct in language seems to arrogate to himself a dictatorial authority, the legitimacy of which will always be denied."[7]

Born in 1758 in Hartford, Connecticut, Webster graduated from Yale in 1778. In 1783 he published his first book, a spelling book, an *American* spelling book. "A national language is a national tie," he insisted, "and what country wants it more than America?"[8] While lecturing in Philadelphia, he met Benjamin Franklin, who proposed simplifying spelling by deleting the letters *c, w, y,* and *j* from the alphabet, and adding six new letters. In 1789, Webster announced his own plan for a reformed orthography, insisting, "*NOW* is the time, and *this* is the country." He concluded, "There iz no alternativ."[9]

When, in 1800, Webster announced that his proposed "Dictionary of the American Language" would surpass the work of Samuel Johnson, an Englishman named Jonathan Boucher set about compiling his own American dictionary or, really, an anti-American anti-dictionary, a list of words so useless and imbecilic that he could hardly believe that anyone, even uncouth Americans, had ever used them. Americans, he scoffed, were "addicted to innovation," no less in language than in everything else: "The United States of America, too proud, as it would seem, to acknowledge themselves indebted to this country, for their existence, their power, or their language, denying and revolting against the two first," are now making haste "to rid themselves of the last."[10]

This, after all, was exactly what Webster intended. But with Boucher's criticism of Americans' addiction to innovation, Webster agreed. Attacking innovation, on principle, as heedless and rash and, worse, vaguely French, was not just an English fashion; during the 1790s, it was also a prominent feature of the rhetoric of American Federalists, especially during the bloodiest years of the French Revolution—a revolution that had gone too far, had experimented, had *innovated* too much, had not known when to stop. Federalists believed, urgently, that Americans must either stifle their impulse to innovate or risk their own Reign of Terror. Having ratified the U.S. Constitution and established an orderly government, the time had come to forswear novelty. Wasn't the Bill of Rights enough already? Webster wholly shared this aversion to innovation: "I do *not* innovate, but *reject innovation*."[11]

Federalist critics of Webster's proposed dictionary attacked it by calling it innovative. Federalist editor Joseph Dennie, signing himself "An Enemy to Innovation," wrote, "These innovations in literature are precisely what Jacobinism is in Politics. They are both owing to the stupid vanity of the present day, which induces mankind to despise the well-tried principles of their Ancestors." It was just this kind of thing that led to anarchy. "If we once sanction the impertinence of individuals, who think themselves authorized to coin new words on every occasion," Dennie warned, "our language will soon become a confused jargon, which will require a new Dictionary every year."[12] Another Federalist critic, lampooning Webster's lexicographical republicanism, wrote, "To coin new words, or to use them in a new sense, is, incontrovertibly, one of the unalienable rights of freemen, and whoever disputes this right, is the friend of civil tyranny, and an enemy to liberty and equality."[13]

It's hardly surprising that Webster's fellow Federalists wanted nothing to do with his dictionary. More difficult to explain is why his proposal was so fiercely attacked by Republicans, who billed themselves as champions of innovation. Led by Jefferson, Republicans believed that the American Revolution had not gone far enough, and blamed the Federalists for halting it. They embraced novelty, pointing to corrupt and decayed England as a place where, as Jefferson put it, "the dread of innovation and especially of any example set by France, has palsied the spirit of improvement." They supported the French Revolution, even as they decried the violence of Robespierre. And they admired the way France's revolution had revitalized the French language, spawning hundreds of new words—*les materialistes, les demagogues, Monsieur Veto, les sans culottes*. As Jefferson exulted, "What a language has the French become since the date of their revolution, by the free introduction of new words!"[14]

Mocking Federalist criticism of his dictionary, Webster wrote, "An American Dictionary! Impossible! . . . Ridiculous!" he quipped. "None but a blockhead would ever think of such a project! . . . I turn from the wretch with disgust and contempt! . . . New words! New ideas! What, Americans have *new* ideas! Why the man is mad!"

Republicans, with their love of innovation, might have been sympathetic. But they weren't. They really *did* think Webster was mad. A "mortal and incurable lunatic," one Republican called him. And worse: a "pusillanimous, half-begotten, self-dubbed patriot," a "mortal and incurable lunatic," a writer of "nonsense pseudo political and pseudo philosophical," and, most memorably, a "dunghill cock of faction."[15] Republicans didn't exactly object to Webster's dictionary, they objected to *him*. In the 1790s Webster had been an immensely prolific and partisan political pamphleteer and newspaper editor. He had cursed the French, derided Republicans, and supported every curb of liberty imposed by the Washington and Adams administrations, including the notorious 1798 Alien and Sedition

Acts, restricting foreign immigration and banning political opposition, under which Republican newspaper editors were jailed for calling John Adams's judgment into question. "Jacobinism must prevail," Webster warned, "unless more pains are taken to *keep public opinion correct.*"[16]

Jefferson was inaugurated on March 4, 1801. Six months later, Webster sent him a letter—an unsparing and vicious critique of his administration—beginning, "I candidly acknowledge that I was one who regretted your elevation to the Presidency of our empire." He then offered an exegesis of the president's inaugural address (on the ground that "surely every sentence of the philosophical Jefferson must carry with it *meaning*"). In his inaugural, Jefferson had declared, "Sometimes it is said that man can not be trusted with the government of himself. Can he, then, be trusted with the government of others? Or have we found angels in the form of kings to govern him? Let history answer this question." As for history, Webster had this answer: "If there ever was a government, which under the *name* of a republic or democracy, was generally guided by eminent wisdom, virtue and talents, it was a government of a mixed kind, in which an *aristocratic* branch existed independent of popular suffrage. After all, Webster asked, "what do men gain by elective governments, if fools and knaves have the same chance to obtain the highest offices, as honest men?"[17]

Noah Webster lacked for tact. Jefferson, who considered Webster "a mere pedagogue, of very limited understanding," never replied to his letter.[18] Webster added the slight to his list of grievances.


The election that carried Thomas Jefferson to the White House sent Noah Webster to the state house. In 1800, Webster was elected to the Connecticut legislature. He served until

1807. As a legislator, he chiefly occupied himself with attempting to block bills eliminating the property qualification for voting—in the hope that no more knaves like Jefferson would ever be elected again. He called men without property "porpoises" (by which he meant that they would swim in a school, and not think for themselves). He himself had earned the right to vote, he was keen to point out, by writing his spelling books. "I am a farmer's son and have collected all the small portion of property which I possess by untiring efforts and labors to promote the literary improvements of my fellow citizens." And he would not have political decisions made for him by men who had no similar stake in the world. "If all men have an equal right of suffrage, those who have *little* and those who have *no* property, have the power of making regulations respecting the property of others," he reasoned. "In truth, this principle of *equal suffrage* operates to produce extreme *inequality of rights*, a monstrous inversion of the natural order of society."[19]

Despite Webster's best efforts, more and more states lifted property restrictions on voting and declaimed in favor of universal suffrage. Webster complained, "The men who have preached these doctrines have never defined what they mean by the *people*, or what they mean by *democracy*, nor how the *people* are to govern themselves."[20]

After his home state grew more democratic, Webster insisted that he "wished to be forever delivered from the *democracy* of Connecticut." He'd even be willing to make the great sacrifice of moving to Vermont, if that state could be "freed from our *democracy*," adding, "as to the cold winters, I would, if necessary, become a troglodyte, and live in a cave."[21]

Webster's work as a member of the Connecticut legislature delayed progress on the dictionary. He had more distractions, too: the births of his first son, William, in 1801, and of his fifth daughter, Eliza, two years later. If he were ever going to finish his magnum opus, he'd need to find a better way to feed his family.

In 1806, strapped for cash, Webster published a little dictionary, aimed at merchants, students, and travelers, a *Compendious Dictionary*, containing no etymologies or quotations and only pithy definitions. ("COMPENDIOUS, *a.* short, brief, concise, summary.") Reviews were brutal. "Believing that this Dictionary was intended by its author to promote his favorite project, *an American language*," one critic wrote, "I cannot but hope that it will be excluded from all Colleges, schools and seminaries of learning; that it will be opposed by all that is correct in taste, and respectable in literature; by the acuteness of criticism, and the poignancy of ridicule." Another, much later critic cobbled together an intentionally alarming "specimen of Webster's orthography," placing in italics words whose spelling he found in the *Compendious Dictionary*: "A *groop* of *Neger wimmen* black as *sut* were told to *soe* and hold their *tungs*; but *insted* of *soing* they left their *thred*, regardless of *threts*, and went to the *theater*."[22] (About Webster's spelling, even his supporters had their doubts: "I ain't yet quite ripe for your *Orthography*," his brother-in-law admitted.)[23] Other readers took issue with Webster's inclusion of particular words. John Quincy Adams, who admired Webster's doggedness, chided him for his "liberality of admission" in allowing in so many new words.[24] But, frankly, few people gave the dictionary much attention. One correspondent, who wrote to complain about words Webster had *left out—papoose, stall,* and *catbird*—confessed that he had written mostly "To convince you that one of your Readers, at least, has proceeded beyond the Preface."[25]

But Webster's severest critics marshaled the evidence of his hypocrisy. In the *Monthly Anthology*, James Savage attacked Webster without mercy, sparing not his "suspicions of the definitions of Johnson," his "ridiculous violations of grammar," nor his "hurtful innovations in orthography." "But the fault of most alarming enormity in this work," Savage concluded, "is the approbation given to the vulgarisms" (like *congressional, presidential, departmental, crock, spry, tote, whop,* and, of course, the inevitable *lengthy*). Gleefully, Savage pointed out that Webster hated the common people and admired only their words. In Connecticut, Savage reported,

> in the midst of a people grave, stable and just, the foes to jaco-
> bins and disorder, no individual presents a bolder front against
> the demon of innovation than Mr. Webster. No contemptible
> epithet is in his estimation too severe for the common people.
> He characterizes them as "porpoises," the most senseless ob-
> jects of creation. After making this comparison in a legislative
> body, Mr. W. could retire to his closet to write grammars and
> dictionaries, and declare in them that the common people alone
> are the lawful sovereigns over the realms of language; and that
> scholars and learned men ought to bend to their supremacy.[26]

Webster, no fainter, battled back. "I am accused of introducing into my Dictionary *Americanisms and vulgarisms,*" he wrote. But what is a lexicographer to do when the people of Connecticut use *fourfold* as a verb? "Is this *my* fault?"[27]

He fought in vain. The first "Webster's" was a flop. It failed because of who Webster was, a political conservative with liberal ideas about language, living in a democratizing nation. Only after what Noah Webster stood for no longer mattered, only after Americans had begun to forget who he was, would his dictionaries succeed.

Meanwhile, Webster's domestic life darkened: in 1806, his second son, Henry Bradford, died within weeks of his birth. In April 1808, his wife, now aged forty-two, gave birth to her last child, a girl named Louisa, whose life would be blighted by severe mental and physical infirmities. Webster was at his lowest. That month, he found Jesus, in his study: "a sudden impulse upon my mind arrested me, and subdued my will. I instantly fell on my knees and confessed my sins to God, implored his pardon, and made my vows to him that from that time I would live in entire obedience to his commands, and be devoted to his service."[28]

When he first proposed his dictionary, in June 1800, Webster had guessed it might take him five years, or eight, to finish it. Ten at the outside. But the work was much more painstaking than he had expected, and the scope of the project only grew. In 1807, he published a circular letter addressed "To the Friends of Literature," detailing his ambition for the great dictionary, and seeking advance subscriptions at ten dollars each.[29] A friend in New York warned, "My experience of the world has satisfied me that it is in vain to reason with the greatest part of mankind, if they have to pay Ten Dollars, in consequence of being convinced."[30] From Albany, James Kent weighed in, "I am sorry to say that there is no Prospect of encouragement here," though the fault lay not with Webster's plan but with a lack of interest in literature; "if *Samuel Johnson* was here on the spot, it would be the same thing."[31]

There was nothing left to do but to set about collecting subscriptions in person, traveling from town to town. In September 1809, he found himself in Salem, north of Boston, where, as elsewhere, he met with little success. Webster had a knack for making enemies everywhere he went. He struggled, to be sure, but much of his struggle was of his own making. Maybe if Webster hadn't been so interested in calling Jefferson a fool, he might have found in the sage of Monticello a supporter. "I am a friend to *neology*," Jefferson wrote John Adams in 1820. "And give the word neologism to our language, as a root, and it should give us it's [*sic*] fellow substantives, neology, neologist, neologisation; it's adjectives neologous, neological, neologistical, it's verb neologise, and adverb neologically."[32] But Webster was way ahead of him: he had included *neology*, *neological*, and even *neologist* in his *Compendious Dictionary*, years before. In 1806, Webster had sent Jefferson a copy, but the former president probably never cracked its spine.

What saved Noah Webster's American dictionary was how long it took him to finish it. Much of this delay was the result of his decision to investigate the origins of words. Even before he was born again, Webster had determined to study etymology. But, after 1809, he brought to this work the zeal of a convert. He decided, in his dictionary, to offer proof that the Old Testament contained the literal truth: that all languages derive from a single, original, pre-Babel language, the language of Eden. While he quested this grail, he stopped working on definitions altogether, a detour he could ill afford. "I shall sell my house to get bread for my children," Webster wrote in 1811. The next year, he moved to Amherst, Massachusetts, where he could live more cheaply.[33]

In his new house, he installed a custom-made desk, "two foot wide, built in the form of a hollow circle," on which he placed dictionaries of twenty languages. Standing in the opening at the center of the table, Webster spent his days turning around in the circle, following the roots of words from one language to the next, his heart racing at the pursuit. (He liked to take his pulse: when he was working, it rose from sixty to eighty or eighty-five beats a minute.) For the ten years he lived in Amherst, Webster chased etymologies, round and round.[34]

In 1822, Webster and his family returned to New Haven. Two years later, he sailed to Europe on a research trip underwritten by a thousand-dollar loan from his daughter Harriet. He spent a year in France and England, continuing his studies at the world's best libraries. He was homesick. "I cannot endure most of the dishes of French Cookery," he wrote to his wife, though he did enjoy the *very good* coffee" to be had in Paris.[35]

In January 1825, in a boarding house in Cambridge, England, Webster finally finished the dictionary. "When I had come to the last word," he later recalled, "I was seized with a trembling which made it somewhat difficult to hold my pen steady for writing."[36] The manuscript his wife called "the babe which he had dandled twenty years and more" finally left his lap, to toddle off into history.

It took three years to set and proof the type. Webster boasted to James Madison that "types of the oriental languages" would come from Germany but "everything else about the work will be *American*."[37] The massive, two-volume *American Dictionary of the English Language* was printed in November 1828. It had taken its compiler not five years, or ten, but twenty-eight.

By then, the Federalist Party was dead. So was almost everyone Webster had known in his youth, or even his middle age. Republicans from Virginia—Jefferson, Madison, and Monroe—had filled the White House for a quarter century. So far had republicanism prevailed that Andrew Jackson, who was not only a champion of the common man—a democrat—but also a notoriously bad speller (he spelled *government* without an *r*), had just been elected president. With populism on the rise, no one now disputed the dictionary's republicanism, its embrace of lowly words like *crock*. And no one gave a fig about Webster's quaint Federalism. At seventy, Webster had outlived most of his enemies and aged into an anachronism, an elder statesman whose feebleness was mistaken for harmlessness.

It also helped that he had abandoned simplified spelling. He did spell *hore* without the *w*, and *goom* without the *r* (*whore* and *groom* he considered corruptions), and in his definition for SPELL ("*v.i.* To form words with the proper letters"), he offered this example of how to use the word in a sentence:

"Our orthography is so irregular that most persons never learn to *spell*." But, other than these, and except for dropping the *k* in words like *mimic* and the *u* in words like *favor*, he largely left spelling alone.

He had also quieted his nationalism: the proposed "Dictionary of the American Language" turned out to be *An American Dictionary of the English Language*. Webster would be an American Johnson, not the Johnson of an American language. Nevertheless, many of his entries display his fascination with fine, local distinctions:

> BUTTER-MILK, *n*. The milk that remains after the butter is separated from it. Johnson calls this *whey*; but whey is the thin part of the milk after the curd or cheese is separated. Butter-milk in America is not called *whey*.

And he enjoyed explaining words with reference to American people and places:

> OPPOSITE, *a*. Standing or situated in front; facing; as an edifice *opposite* to the Exchange. Brooklyn lies *opposite* to New York, or on the opposite side of the river.

But he now doubted whether any Americanisms even existed. In the dictionary's preface he wrote, "As to Americanisms, so called, I have not been able to find many words, in respectable use, which can be so denominated. These, I have admitted and, noted as peculiar to this country." These include words we still use, *lengthy*, *skunk*, *caucus*, and words that were already dying out in Webster's lifetime:

> SHAVER, *n*. A boy or young man. This word is still in common use in New England. It must be numbered among our original words.

But, as to the rest, Webster wrote, "I have fully ascertained that most of the new words charged to the coinage of this country, were first used in England."

What most made Webster's dictionary American was his commitment to quoting American authors to illustrate the meanings of words. Of these men, he wrote, "It is with pride and satisfaction that I can place them, as authorities, on the same page with those of Boyle, Hooker, Milton, Dryden, Addison." On proverbs suitable for guiding daily living, Webster loved, best, to quote Franklin:

> DEBT. When you run in *debt* you give to another power over your liberty.

He never quoted Jefferson—not once.

But George Washington's place in the *American Dictionary* is so prominent that it could be argued that the two-volume set is a monument to the nation's first president. Consider, for example, SURPASS, whose meaning Webster illustrated with the sentence: "Perhaps no man ever *surpassed* Washington in genuine patriotism and integrity of life." Or look at MODEL, "take Washington as a *model* of prudence, integrity and patience," or "CELEBRATE, *v.t.* To honor or distinguish by ceremonies and marks of joy and respect; as, to *celebrate* the birthday of Washington," or FATHER, "Washington, as a defender and an affectionate and wise counselor, is called the *father* of his country."

The dictionary was, equally, a celebration of the United States. At GAIN, Webster used this illustration: "Any industrious person may *gain* a good living in America." Or consider: "INESTIMABLE, *a.* . . . . The privileges of American citizens, civil and religious, are *inestimable.*" At GUARANTY, Webster quoted from the Constitution: "The United States shall *guaranty* to every state in the Union a republican form of government." Often, the encomiums to Washington and to his nation intersect, as at CITIZEN: "If the citizens of the U. States should not be free and happy, the fault will be entirely their own. *Washington.*"

Webster also added plenty of his own political opinions ("PREPOSTEROUS, *a.* a republican government in the hands of females, is *preposterous*"), especially his views on slavery, which he expressed both in predictable places ("SLAVE-TRADE, *n.* The barbarous and wicked business of purchasing men and women, transporting them to a distant country, and selling them for slaves") and in unexpected entries, including FORMERLY, whose use he illustrated with the sentence, "We *formerly* imported slaves from Africa."

At twenty dollars a copy, the *American Dictionary* didn't exactly fly from the shelves. But it was respected and, soon enough, revered. Webster's definitions could be spot-on: "DANDY. *n.* A fop, a coxcomb; one who dresses himself like a doll, and who carries his character on his back." Sir James Murray, first editor of the *Oxford English Dictionary*, called Webster "a born definer of words." At definitions, Webster was better than Johnson: less literary, less witty, but more exact. Johnson defined *admiration* as "wonder, the act of admiring or wondering"; to Webster it was "wonder mingled with pleasing emotions, as approbation, esteem, love, or veneration; a compound emotion excited by something novel, rare, great, or excellent; applied to persons and their works. It often includes a slight degree of surprise."

The ridicule to which Webster had once been exposed now only bolstered his claim to greatness. In the *North American Review*, Yale scholar James Luce Kingsley wrote, "The author, it is well known, met with much opposition at the commencement of his labors; and it is equally notorious, that as he proceeded in the accomplishment of his design, he was seldom cheered with the voice of encouragement and approbation."[38] That over the labor of so many years, one man, so unrewarded, so alone, had been so undeterred, formed no small part of the dictionary's vaunted merit.

But what contributed most to the dictionary's success was its auspicious timing: it was published at the height of America's greatest religious revival, the Second Great Awakening.

Webster's own conversion came at the movement's very beginning. Webster's dictionary was a Christian dictionary, almost a
catechism. It wasn't only the just-so, evangelical etymologies.
Webster's faith shines through on every page, even under the
most unlikely bushels:

> INSTRUMENT, *n.* 2. . . . The distribution of the Scriptures may be
> the instrument of a vastly extensive reformation in morals
> and religion.
>
> MERITORIOUS, *a.* . . . We rely for salvation on the *meritorious*
> obedience and sufferings of Christ.
>
> LOVE, *n.* 1. The *love* of God is the first duty of man . . . *v.t.* 1. . . .
> The Christian *loves* his Bible.

Born-again Americans applauded it; they loved it as they
loved their Bibles. (Webster's next project was an emendation
of the King James Bible.)[39] Webster's Federalist views on politics, his republican opinions about language, his crustiness, the
political turmoil that had swallowed up his 1806 dictionary—
all these were forgotten. Webster began writing for his country; he ended up writing for Christ.

# 8

# HIS HIGHNESS

Jared Sparks, thirty-seven, and known for his editorial eye, reached Mount Vernon by carriage just before sunset on March 14, 1827. He made no note of the grounds, the house, the stables, the slope of the hill. He sought only George Washington's papers; it had taken him nearly a decade to get permission to see them, finally securing it, from Washington's nephew and literary executor, Supreme Court justice Bushrod Washington, only by pledging discretion, and, not less importantly, agreeing to split the profits from publishing an edition of Washington's writings.[1] Sparks, former chaplain of Congress, was editor and owner of the United States' first literary magazine, the *North American Review*, which, under his direction, was distinguished for its judiciousness.[2] A man better suited to the work of editing Washington's papers and writing his biography would have been hard to find, which makes it all the stranger that what Sparks did to those papers would, in his lifetime, be called "one of the most flagrant injuries" ever done by an editor to a writer or by a biographer to his subject— some swipe, even making allowances for hyperbole.[3]

No one could have seen that coming, in 1827, when Sparks climbed out of that carriage, up those steps, and into the house in which he would cloister himself for more than a month.

Diaries, notebooks, drawings, scraps, and more than forty thousand letters: a biographer's harem. He was, he wrote to a friend, in Paradise.[4] No one bothered him. "I have been here entirely alone," he wrote in his own diary, and you can almost hear his heart beating. In a garret, he pried open a chest: "Discovered some new and valuable papers to-day, particularly a small manuscript book containing an original journal of Washington, written in the year 1748, March and April, when he was barely sixteen years old." Everything was a find. "It is quite certain that no writer of Washington's biography has seen this book."[5] Maybe, at long last, Washington's secrets would be revealed.

No biographer of George Washington has failed to remark on his inscrutability. Bestselling biographer Ron Chernow once called Washington "the most famously elusive figure in American history."[6] Sparks eventually published eleven volumes of Washington's writings, along with a one-volume biography.[7] In 1893, Worthington C. Ford published the last installment of a fourteen-volume set. An edition of thirty-nine volumes was completed in 1940. Of the University of Virginia Press's magnificent *Papers of George Washington*, begun in 1968, sixty-two volumes have been published so far.[8] But for all those papers, Washington rarely revealed himself on the page. Even his few surviving letters to his wife are formal and strained. Those diaries? Here is Washington's *entire* diary entry for October 24, 1774, a day he was in Philadelphia, as a delegate to the Continental Congress, debating, among other things, a petition to be sent to the king: "Dined with Mr. Mease & Spent the Evening at the New Tavern."[9] Here is how John Adams's diary entry for that same day *begins*:

> In Congress, nibbling and quibbling, as usual.
> There is no greater Mortification than to sit with half a dozen Witts, deliberating upon a Petition, Address, or

Memorial. These great Witts, these subtle Criticks, these re-
fined Genius's, these learned Lawyers, these wise Statesmen,
are so fond of shewing their Parts and Powers, as to make their
Consultations very tedius.

Young Ned Rutledge is a perfect Bob 'o Lincoln—a
Swallow—a Sparrow—a Peacock—excessively vain, excessively
weak, and excessively variable and unsteady—jejune, inane, and
puerile.

Mr. Dickinson is very modest, delicate, and timid . . . .[10]

Aside from chucking Washington in favor of writing about
Adams, what's a biographer to do?

Washington's contemporaries saw in him what they
wanted to see. So have his biographers, of whom there have
been many, including a delegate to the Continental Congress
(David Ramsay), a U.S. senator (Henry Cabot Lodge), a chief
justice of the Supreme Court (John Marshall), and an American president (Woodrow Wilson). Novelists from Washington
Irving to Gore Vidal have written Washington's life, and, although William Faulkner never did, that would have been interesting. There have always been Washington killjoys. Abigail
Adams was troubled by the beatification of Washington: "To
no one Man in America," she believed, "belongs the Epithet
of *Saviour*."[11] In 1858, Confederate Edmund Ruffin expressed
his view that Washington had never "originated an important
idea, or was the first or even among the first, in any new &
important political movement, or devised any policy conduc-
ing greatly to the welfare of the people or the government."[12]
Mark Twain once said that while Washington couldn't tell
a lie, Twain could, and didn't, which made Twain the better
man. The first Washington-was-a-fraud biography was published in 1926. Its author, William E. Woodward, had, in his
1923 novel, *Bunk*, coined the word "debunk." (In the 1920s, a
"debunker" was, quite specifically, someone who assaulted the

memory of Washington.) Woodward argued, mostly, that the father of the country was dim-witted: "Washington possessed the superb self-confidence that comes only to those men whose inner life is faint." The *Times* called it tittle-tattle.[13]

Every generation must have its Washington, but some generations have more Washingtons than others. Ronald Reagan, in his first inaugural address, looked at the obelisk across the Mall and spoke about "the monument to a monumental man."[14] Between 1990 and 2010, major American publishing houses brought out no fewer than eighteen Washington biographies, a couple of them very fine, to say nothing of the slew of boutique-y books about the man's military career, his moral fortitude, his friendship with Lafayette, his faith in God, his betrayal by Benedict Arnold, his "secret navy," his inspiring words, his leadership skills, his business tips, and his kindness to General William Howe's dog.[15] It was a Georgian revival.

George Washington was born in Westmoreland County, Virginia, in 1732. His father died when he was eleven. When he was sixteen, he went on a surveying trip in the Shenandoah Valley—and wrote that diary Sparks found—and, three years later, traveled to the West Indies. At twenty, he assumed his first military command; his reckless and often failed but indisputably bold campaigns, in the 1750s, gained him a reputation for invincibility. He was tall and imposing, at once powerful and graceful, and he rode a horse exceptionally well. "Well turned" is what people said in the eighteenth century about a man like that. More recent descriptions range from the fabulous to the enthralled. Woodrow Wilson, in his 1896 biography, made it sound as if Washington grew up in Sherwood Forest: "All the land knew him and loved him for gallantry and brave capacity; he carried himself like a prince."[16] Ron Chernow, in *Washington: A Life*, dwelled on Washington's manliness, describing him, every few pages or so, as "a superb physical specimen, with a magnificent physique," "an exceptionally muscular and vigorous young man," with an "imposing face and virile form," "powerfully rough-hewn and endowed with matchless strength," not excepting his "wide, flaring hips with muscular thighs."[17] The mar to his beauty was his terrible teeth, which were replaced by failed transplant surgery and by dentures made from ivory and from teeth pulled from the mouths of his slaves.[18]

Washington married in 1758 and was elected to the Virginia Assembly the next year. He occupied himself managing his vast tobacco estate and wasn't much animated by the colonies' growing struggle with Parliamentary authority until the passage of the Intolerable Acts, but then he threw himself into it, beginning by serving as a delegate to the First Continental Congress in 1774. The next year, he was appointed commander-in-chief of the Continental Army and rode to Cambridge to take command. Over the course of the war, and, even more, after it, Washington came to embody the new nation's vision of itself: virtuous, undaunted, and incorruptible.[19] Nothing earned him more or better deserved admiration than surrendering his command at the end of the war. That resignation—relinquishing power when he could so easily have seized it—saved the republic. He returned to public life in 1787, to preside over the Constitutional Convention, where he played a largely ceremonial but nonetheless crucial role, as was often the case. Washington knew the difference between ceremony and pomposity, and kept to one side of it. He was elected president by a unanimous vote of the Electoral College. In his inaugural address (written by James Madison), he said that "the preservation of the sacred fire of liberty and the destiny of the republican model of government" were fated by "the eternal rules of order and right which Heaven itself has ordained" and staked deeply, finally, "on the experiment

entrusted to the hands of the American people." Charged
with leading a wholly new form of government, wherein
his every decision set a precedent, he began holding, in 1791,
what came to be called cabinet meetings. His presidency was
marked by much debate about how he ought to be treated, and
even how he should be addressed. (Adams had wanted to call
him His Most Benign Highness and Washington was fond of
His High Mightiness.)[20] Owen Wister began his biography
of Washington with this story: "On the 22d of February, 1792,
Congress was sitting in Philadelphia, and to many came the
impulse to congratulate the President upon this,"—his sixti-
eth birthday—"therefore a motion was made to adjourn for
half an hour, that this civility might be paid. The motion was
bitterly opposed, as smacking of idolatry and as leaning toward monarchy."[21]

Washington was a very good president, and an unhappy
one. Distraught by growing factionalism within and outside
his administration, especially by the squabbling of Hamilton,
Jefferson, and Adams and the rise of a Jeffersonian opposition,
he served another term only reluctantly. His second inaugural
address was only 135 words long; he said, more or less, Please,
I'm doing my best. In 1796, in his enduringly eloquent Farewell
Address (written by Madison and Hamilton), he cautioned
the American people about party rancor: "The alternate domination of one faction over another, sharpened by the spirit of
revenge, natural to party dissention, which in different ages &
countries has perpetrated the most horrid enormities, is itself
a frightful despotism."[22] And then he went back to Mount
Vernon. He freed his slaves in his will, hoping that this, too,
would set a precedent. It did not.

Washington isn't like Adams, effusively cantankerous; he's
not like Jefferson, a cabinet of contradictions. He's not funny
like Franklin or capacious like Madison. Washington wasn't
a tortured man; nor was he enigmatic. He was a staged man,

shrewd, purposeful, and effective.[23] Not surprisingly for an eighteenth-century military man, he held himself at a considerable remove from his men. But he also held himself at this remove from just about everyone else. He played a role, surpassingly well. He dressed for the part (he was obsessed with his clothes), and studied for it (he copied out, as a boy, a set of sixteenth-century Italian "Rules of Civility" that read like stage directions: "Bedew no man's face with your Spittle by approaching too near to him when you Speak"). Washington's theatrical reserve can look, now, like mysteriousness, which wasn't what he was going for, which was an imperturbability to do with eighteenth-century notions of honor, gentility, and manliness, and whose closest surviving kin, today, is what's called military bearing.[24] Making Washington less stiff and more human has been the aim of every Washington biographer, from the start, and not a one of them has done it.[25] Sparks, so far from doing it, only made things worse. "Setting Washington on stilts" is what Sparks was charged with, although, really, Washington was already up there, leaning on legs of wood.[26]

Washington retired from public life just when biography was becoming a popular middlebrow genre.[27] Lives have been written since before Plutarch, but the word "biography" wasn't coined until the seventeenth century, and the modern genre only really began to take shape, in 1791, with the publication of Boswell's *Life of Johnson*. The United States was new; the presidency was new; biography was new. How Washington's life was written would set a precedent. What would biography be, in a republic?

In June 1799, Mason Weems, an itinerant preacher and bookseller, wrote to the Philadelphia printer Matthew Carey to tell him he had begun writing a life of Washington: "'Tis artfully drawn up, enliven'd with anecdotes, and in my humble opinion, marvelously fitted"; it "will sell like flax seed." That December, Washington died, quite suddenly. The nation mourned, but the timing, so far as Weems was concerned, could hardly have been better. "Washington, you know is gone!" Weems wrote Carey. "Millions are gaping to read something about him. I am very nearly prim'd and cock'd for 'em." Weems's chatty and exuberant *Life and Memorable Actions of George Washington* was first published in 1800. It sold like flax seed.[28]

By then, Weems was already soliciting advance subscriptions for a quite different sort of biography, a wildly hyped but stuffy, ponderous, and ultimately commercially disastrous five-volume set, written by John Marshall. Adams, Washington's successor, had nominated Marshall as chief justice in 1801, in the last months of his presidency; Marshall's *Life of Washington*, a defense of Federalism and an attack on Jeffersonianism, is a testament to the party rancor Washington despised. Its first two volumes came out in 1804, while Jefferson was running for reelection. Federalists were disappointed in it; Republicans were disgusted by it.[29] It was a spectacular flop.[30]

In writing it, Marshall claimed to have relied "chiefly on the manuscript papers of George Washington"—those papers at Mount Vernon in the possession of Bushrod Washington, who was also an Adams appointee to the Supreme Court, and who gave Marshall permission to write an authorized biography—but it has since been discovered that Marshall actually copied a great deal from published sources, without attribution, and Jefferson liked to say that Marshall made most of it up.[31] At the time, rules about evidence were changing. What Marshall ought to have put in quotes, by modern standards, he sometimes did, and sometimes didn't. How much a biographer ought to rely on anecdotes was unclear. The story about young George chopping down a cherry tree—"*I can't tell*

*a lie, Pa; you know I can't tell a lie. I did cut it with my hatchet"*—
comes from Weems and is generally thought to be Weems's
invention (which makes a nice riddle: if "I can't tell a lie" is a
lie, what's true?). But the story, Weems said, was "related to me
twenty years ago by an aged lady, who was a distant relative."[32]
And maybe it was.

Sparks believed that the aim of biography was "to bring
together a series of facts which should do justice to the fame
and character of a man, who possessed qualities, and performed deeds, that rendered him remarkable."[33] He first wrote
to Mount Vernon in 1816, a year after he graduated from Harvard, begging for "a scrap of General Washington's handwriting."[34] He got one. But it scarcely satisfied him. Beginning in
the 1820s, Sparks traveled all over the United States and across
Europe, gathering the lost, scattered, and junked papers of the
Revolutionary generation. Sheaves of Benjamin Franklin's papers had wound up in a tailor's shop on St. James Street in
London; some of them had been cut into sleeve patterns.[35]
"Those who established our liberty and our government are
daily dropping from among us," Daniel Webster said, at the
dedication of the Bunker Hill monument, at the battle's fiftieth anniversary, on June 17, 1825.[36] Adams and Jefferson died on
the fiftieth anniversary of the Declaration of Independence,
July 4, 1826. Six months later, Sparks set out for Virginia, in-
tending to satisfy himself about Marshall's and Weems's reli-
ability by talking to people who knew Washington well, before the last of them died. A nephew of Washington's told
him that Weems really had talked to a lot of old people, that
his biography was "generally accurate as to facts," and that his
use of anecdote, while embellished, "seldom misleads." Sparks
went to visit Madison, who was seventy-six. Madison said that
he found Marshall's volumes "highly respectable" but riddled
with "the bias of party feeling."[37]

Most of the time, though, Sparks stayed at Mount Vernon, shut up with Washington's papers. He guessed it would take him a year just to *read* them. He wrote to Bushrod Washington, begging permission to bring them back home, to Boston. He planned the removal down to the last detail. He would build boxes. He would buy insurance. He would build a fireproof safe, and have it installed in his study, or else he would lock the papers in a vault in a bank. The judge agreed. Washington's papers left Mount Vernon.[38] Back in Massachusetts, Sparks moved, with his eight boxes, into a house in Cambridge that had briefly served as Washington's headquarters, so that he could edit the papers where the great man himself once wrote them.[39]

Sparks adored Washington, his courage, his character, his poise, even his handwriting, which he found "close and handsome."[40] He did not, however, adore his literary style. "That Washington was not a scholar is certain," Adams wrote. "That he was too illiterate, unlearned, unread for his station and reputation is equally past dispute."[41] Washington was poorly educated and, at least compared to writers like Adams, Franklin, Jefferson, and Madison, a charming fluency on the page was not among his talents. On paper, he could be clumsy and awkward, exactly the opposite of what he was in person. Sparks wanted to fix that, and did. His ideas about editing came from the world of magazines, where he had a very heavy hand.[42] One of his *North American Review* writers, the historian George Bancroft, was forever warning him, "You must not make any alterations or omissions without consulting me," and Sparks was forever ignoring him.[43] (Late in 1826, while Sparks was preparing for his trip to Mount Vernon, Bancroft threatened legal action.)[44] Sparks corrected Washington's spelling and punctuation. What he found badly expressed, he rewrote. Where Washington called Israel Putnam "Old Put," Sparks had him call him "General Putnam." (Putnam was the general who is supposed to have told the Americans facing the British at the Battle of Bunker Hill not to fire till they saw "the whites of their eyes.") When Washington called too little money a "flea-bite," Sparks changed this to a sum "totally inadequate to our demands."[45] Passages in which Washington criticized New England men, as when he remarked on the "unaccountable kind of stupidity in the lower class of these people," Sparks simply struck out—silently—despite having been advised that if he must make emendations he ought to at least mark an omission with an asterisk.[46]

The work of selecting, copying, and editing took ten years; Sparks's *Writings of Washington* was completed in 1837.[47] The next year, Sparks joined the faculty at Harvard, the first professor of American history. In 1849, a year after the cornerstone was laid for the Washington Monument, Sparks became president of Harvard. He had also published Franklin's papers, written a life of Franklin, and launched a popular book series, the Library of American Biography. People called him the American Plutarch.

No one noticed Sparks's changes to Washington's prose until 1851, when several of them were separately observed by a British historian and by a contributor to the New York *Evening Post*. In a flurry of charges and rebuttals, Sparks was accused of painting the president with "patriotic rouge."[48] The *Democratic Review* called him an "Old Fogy" and concluded, "Mr. Jared Sparks has made biography what it never was before—the lie to history."[49] (It was certainly bad, but was it that bad? The fuss had less to do with fleabites than with the stature of the man whose words had been messed with.) As to the specifics, Sparks defended himself by pointing out that he had, after all, supplied a preface, describing, at least in part, his editorial methods. And, as to the principle, he invoked "the dignity of history": Washington would not have wanted to be seen, exposed (which is doubtless true); these were his private writings, and if he had intended them to be published, he would have hired someone just like Sparks to fix them up first (also true). The *Literary World* answered back that what Washington wanted wasn't the point. The point was what the reading public wanted:

> Washington, we may be sure, will bear to be looked at in undress. His figure is a good one without the tailor. The public has seen him too exclusively on horseback and in his regimentals. We want to be nearer to the man. Every reader has felt this—and the biographer who will best supply this by personal anecdotes, even if they fall below that excessive bugbear, the dignity of history, will be the truest and best biographer.[50]

This, of course, is exactly what the public has gotten: celebrity intimacy. *We want to be nearer the great.* It sells like flax seed.

The great used to be revered from afar; lately, they're revered up close. Aside from Weems, Washington's early biographers barely mentioned his childhood. Even the gossipy Weems ignored Washington's mother, Mary, about whom little was then, or is now, known, calling her only a "charming girl."[51] Marshall dispensed with Washington's childhood in a page and a half.[52] Ramsay covered the first nineteen years of the man's life in a sentence of twelve words.[53] When Sparks was in Virginia, he rummaged around but didn't find out much, except that Mary Washington was "little polished by education," and "remarkable for taking good care of her ducks and chickens." In print, he was circumspect: "Her good sense, assiduity, tenderness, and vigilance overcame every obstacle."[54] But Ron Chernow, in his 2010 biography, having almost nothing more to go on, built a character out of a stack of adjectives. On page five his Mary Washington is "pious," "headstrong," "feisty," "indomitable," and "illiterate." On the next, she is "crusty," "anxious," "stubborn," "flinty," "thrifty," "plain," "homespun," and "unlettered." Four pages later, she is "strong-willed" and "unbending, even shrewish," as well as "frugal," "demanding," "forbidding," and, in sum if not conclusion, a "trying woman." One page further along, she persists in being "crude and il-literate," and is now "slovenly." In chapter 2, we are reminded that George suffered from a "difficult mother," alerted about "his mother's domination," and alarmed to hear that she was not only "self-interested," surely a sign of wickedness in the female sex, but also "strangely indifferent" toward her eldest son's towering ambition. Finally comes, in lieu of evidence, this:

> The hypercritical mother produced a son who was overly sensi-tive to criticism and suffered from a lifelong need for approval. One suspects that, in dealing with this querulous woman, George became an overly controlled personality and learned to master his temper and curb his tongue. It was the extreme self-control of a deeply emotional young man who feared the fatal vehemence of his own feelings, if left unchecked. Anything pertaining to Mary Ball Washington stirred up an emotional tempest that George quelled only with difficulty. Never able to express these forbidden feelings of rage, he learned to equate silence and a certain manly stolidity with strength. This boy-hood struggle was, in all likelihood, the genesis of the stoical personality that would later define him so indelibly.[55]

The diagnosis had supplanted the document. Sparks thought he knew how Washington wanted to be remembered, but he never pretended to know what it felt like to *be* Washington. Chernow's was a prodigious biography, expertly narrated and full of remarkable detail. But it was a psychological profile of a man who lived and died long before a psychological age, a ro-mantic portrait of a man who was not a Romantic: Washington lies upon the analyst's couch, teeth clenched, tormented by his mother, the madwoman in Mount Vernon's cobwebby attic. All Sparks ever found up there was a diary.

In the end, "Mr. Jared Sparks's Liberties with George Washington," as one critic dubbed the affair, had less to do with gussying up the president's prose than with editorial presumption set loose in an archive. Sparks believed that "The machinery of society and government is kept in motion by the agency of a few powerful minds." He kept only what he valued: the worthy political writings of great men. Letters he didn't find interesting he cut up, handing the scraps out as mementos.[56] In the margin of a seventy-three-page draft of Washington's first inaugural address, he wrote, "Washington's handwriting but not his composition," and then cut it up, and gave the cuttings to friends.[57] Correspondence with nobodies he threw away.[58]

Are the papers of the obscure garbage? About the time that Sparks was defending himself against charges of bowdlerizing Washington's letters, Herman Melville was reading a "tattered copy, rescued by the merest chance from the rag-pickers," of an out-of-print book called the *Life and Remarkable Adventures of Israel R. Potter*, the memoir of a poor Rhode Island farmer who claimed to have been wounded at Bunker Hill and taken to England as a prisoner of war, where, a beggar on the streets of London, he scraped by, mending broken chairs.[59] The *Life of Potter* is a cheap, tiny book, "forlornly published on sleazy gray paper," about a very unimportant person—just the kind of book Sparks hated. "The present unfortunate propensity of filling tomes of quartos and octavos with marvellous accounts of the lives of men and women, who, during their existence, produced no impression on the publick mind, and who were not known beyond the circle of their immediate friends, or the mountains, which bounded the horizon of their native villages, is preposterous and absurd," Sparks wrote. "Why should the world be called off from its busy occupations to listen to an ill told story of their little concerns?"[60]

Melville knew what it meant to watch one's writing reduced to wastepaper. "Though I wrote the Gospels in this century, I should die in the gutter," he wrote to Hawthorne in 1851, predicting, rightly, that *Moby Dick* would be a disaster. (The *North American* didn't even run a review.) The next year, a Boston newspaper called *Pierre*, Melville's bitterly satirical novel about the literary marketplace, "utter trash."[61] In 1854, Melville produced a difficult and messy comic novel based on Potter's failed, forgotten, and pathetic memoir, thereby willfully defying popular taste. Melville's *Israel Potter* is a parody of biography; it upends every convention of Sparks's Library of American Biography. The glory of war? Melville skips over the Battle of Bunker Hill as a story too boring to tell: "Suffice it, that Israel was one of those marksmen whom Putnam harangued as touching the enemy's eyes." The rewards of patriotic virtue? After fifty years of indigence in England, Potter, a poor and pitiful old man, returns to Boston on the Fourth of July, 1826, and a parade, passing by Faneuil Hall, nearly runs him over.

Melville, signing himself, "THE EDITOR," dedicated his bizarre and doomed novel about the Revolution and the American biographical tradition,

TO

His Highness

The

Bunker-Hill Monument

and, in that dedication, apologized—to 221 feet of granite— that Israel Potter's name had never "appeared in the volumes of Sparks."[62]

The *Life of Potter* is the story of a man fated, at death, to be buried in a potter's field. To the American Plutarch, it was rubbish. There is no humility in monumental biography. But there is humility in nature, in time, and in history. The same sun that shines on the Bunker Hill monument, Melville pointed out, shines on Israel's unmarked grave. Come winter, the same snow falls, dusting us all.

# 9

# MAN OF THE PEOPLE

Biographers of Andrew Jackson used to be cursed. On January 8, 1815, the general led American forces in a stunning defeat of an invading British Army, winning the Battle of New Orleans to end the War of 1812. Eyeing a future political career, he cast about for a biographer to chronicle his exploits. He settled on sixty-six-year-old David Ramsay, a South Carolina legislator and physician and gifted historian whose books included an 1807 *Life of Washington*. But before Ramsay had a chance to begin, he was shot in the back, three times, by a mad tailor, on the streets of Charleston. (Ramsay had earlier ventured a medical opinion that the tailor was dangerously insane and, on his deathbed, he insisted that his murderer could not be held accountable for his actions.)[1] Jackson next turned to his aide-de-campe, John Reid, a man half Ramsay's age, and much in Jackson's thrall. Reid set to work until, one day in January 1816, he took suddenly and strangely ill. He died eighteen hours later. Before his untimely demise, he had drafted only the first four chapters of the general's life; he hadn't gotten much further than the 1814 Battle of Enotachopo. (In which, to be sure, Jackson's merits were much extolled: only 20 of his own men lost, but 189 Indians dead on the battlefield, and many more to die afterward for, as Reid put it, "the greatest slaughter is in the pursuit.")[2]

His choices narrowing, Jackson tapped as his next and quite possibly doomed biographer, a twenty-six-year-old lawyer named John Eaton. Eaton had served under the general during the Creek War and was married to Jackson's ward.[3] Like Reid, he had never before written a book.[4] At The Hermitage, Jackson's thousand-acre cotton plantation outside Nashville, Eaton pored over Jackson's papers and wrote seven more chapters. The biography was published in 1817 as *The Life of Andrew Jackson*. The next year, Eaton was, for his service to Jackson, appointed to a vacant seat in the U.S. Senate. In 1823, Jackson was elected as the other senator from Tennessee and followed his biographer and friend to the nation's capital. The two men shared lodgings at a Washington boardinghouse. That same year, Jackson was nominated for the presidency. Eaton spearheaded Jackson's campaign.[5] John Quincy Adams refused to campaign at all. Following the tradition of the first five American presidents, Adams considered currying favor with voters beneath the dignity of the office, believing, too, that any man who craved the presidency ought not to have it. Adams called this his Macbeth policy: "If chance will have me king, why, chance may crown me, Without my stir."[6] Jackson's supporters leaned more toward Lady Macbeth's point of view. They had no choice but to stir; their candidate was, otherwise, unelectable.[7] How they stirred has shaped American politics ever since.[8] They told a story, the story of Andrew Jackson's life. In 1824, Eaton published a revised *Life of Jackson*, founding a genre, the campaign biography. At its heart lies a single, telling anecdote. In 1781, when Jackson was fourteen and fighting in the American Revolution, he was captured. A British officer, whose boots had gotten muddy, ordered the boy to clean his boots: Jackson refused, and the officer beat him, badly, with a sword. All his life, he bore the scars to show for it.[9] Andrew Jackson would not kneel before a tyrant.

Since 1824, no presidential election year has passed without a campaign biography, printed about the time a candidate is nominated, chiefly for the purpose of getting him elected. (Although, since Reagan's "New Beginning" in 1984, the campaign biography, as book, has been somewhat supplanted by the campaign film, screened at the nominating convention.)[10] The United States has had some very fine presidents, and some not so fine. But their campaign biographies are much of a muchness. The worst of them read like an Election Edition Mad Libs and even the best of them tell, with rare exception, the same Jacksonian story: scrappy maverick who splits rails and farms peanuts and shoots moose battles from the log cabin to the White House by dint of grit, smarts, stubbornness, and love of country.[11] From Eaton's Jackson, it's more or less a straight line, right through Harrison, Garfield, Eisenhower, Reagan, and Clinton, all the way to Kaylene Johnson's 2008 biography of Republican vice presidential nominee Sarah Palin: *Sarah: How a Hockey Mom Turned the Political Establishment Upside Down.* Jackson wouldn't polish those boots. Nixon learned how to be a good vice president by warming the bench during college football games.[12] Palin forged bipartisan political alliances in step-aerobics class.[13] Parties rise and fall. Wars begin and end. The world turns. But American campaign biographies have been following the same script for two centuries. East of piffle and west of hokum, the Boy from Hope always grows up to be the Man of the People.

As a presidential candidate, Andrew Jackson was, at the start, a hard sell. The nation's first five presidents, Washington, Adams, Jefferson, Madison, and Monroe, were diplomats, statesmen, philosophers, even. It was difficult to imagine how *any* man could fill the shoes of the men who fought the Revolution and drafted the Constitution. A generation had passed. John Quincy Adams, son of the second president, seemed the most suitable prospect; a former Harvard professor of rhetoric and U.S. senator, he spoke fourteen languages and had served as ambassador to the Netherlands, Portugal, Russia, and Britain. As secretary of state, he had drafted the Monroe Doctrine. But Andrew Jackson? He was provincial, and poorly educated. Of Jackson's bid for the presidency Jefferson declared, "He is one of the most unfit men, I know of for such a place."[14] Granted, the Hero of New Orleans was wildly popular with the American people, but then, so were gin and mountebanks. To Jefferson, Jackson, who had served less than a year in the Senate, was no more than a military man who, for all his extraordinary valor, had a reputation as a despot: brutal, tempestuous, and vengeful. The army needed men like Andrew Jackson. Whether the presidency needed him was another matter. Even the general himself is reported to have said, "I know what I am fit for. I can command a body of men in a rough way, but I am not fit to be President."[15]

The election of 1824 brought the first campaign buttons; the first public opinion polls (undertaken by and published in pro-Jackson newspapers); and the first campaign biography, written for John C. Calhoun.[16] But the biography that went farthest toward establishing the genre's enduring conventions was Eaton's *Life of Jackson*. When Eaton revised it in 1824, he turned what was a history, if a decidedly partial one, into political propaganda. Eaton cut out or waved away everything compromising (the duels Jackson had fought, the men he had executed), lingered longer over everything wondrous (mainly, battles), and converted into strengths what pundits had construed as Jackson's weaknesses.[17] Eaton's Jackson wasn't reckless; he was fearless. He had almost no political experience: he was, therefore, ideally suited to fight corruption.[18] He lacked a political pedigree; his father, a poor Scotch-Irish immigrant, died before he was born, but this only made Jackson more qualified for the Oval Office, since he was, to use a phrase coined during his presidency, a "self-made man."[19]

In 1824, with Eaton's biography behind him, Jackson won both the popular vote and a plurality, though not a majority, of the electoral vote. The election was thrown to the House, which chose Adams. Furious, Jackson returned to his Hermitage, vowing revenge. Eaton began still further revisions to his *Life of Jackson*, which he had printed in Cincinnati, Philadelphia, Baltimore, and even in Boston, where it was spuriously attributed to "a Citizen of Massachusetts."[20]

When Jackson trounced Adams in 1828, he rewarded his Boswell by naming him secretary of war, alarming Washington, possibly even more than the rest of Jackson's spoils-system appointments, because Eaton had, just before Jackson's inauguration, married a widow of dubious repute. The scandal of Eaton's marriage dominated Jackson's first two years in office. In a cabinet meeting in 1829, the president vouched for Mrs. Eaton's virtue: "She is as chaste as a virgin!" Only Jackson's secretary of state, Martin Van Buren, called upon the Eatons socially, a maneuver believed by many to have ensured his place as Jackson's successor. (As James Parton put it in his best-selling 1860 *Life of Jackson*: "The political history of the United States for the last thirty years dates from the moment when the soft hand of Mr. Van Buren touched Mrs. Eaton's knocker.")[21] What came to be called the "Petticoat War" led to much lampooning—one cartoon pictured the president, bent over a washtub, scrubbing a petticoat, complaining, "the more I rub this, the worst it looks"—but it got a whole lot less funny after it led to the dissolution, in 1831, of Jackson's entire cabinet.[22]

Jackson retired the national debt. He killed the Bank of the United States. He invented the pocket veto. When the

Supreme Court ruled against his plan to force the Cherokee to move to lands west of the Mississippi, Jackson went ahead, anyway.[23] By any measure, Andrew Jackson vastly expanded the powers of the president. What he could not do was to protect John Eaton, the man who had scrubbed clean his own reputation. In 1831, Eaton and his wife were banished from Washington. A curse, when it hits, hits hard.

In the 1850s, when James Parton began research for his own book about Jackson, he found, in the nation's libraries and bookstores "mountains of lies and trash" known as " 'Campaign literature,' a peculiar product of the United States." Measured against the puffery that came after it, Parton thought, Eaton's campaign biography was a model of restraint.[24] Still, Eaton's *Life*, along with Jackson's presidency, rewrote the presidential job description. When Henry Clay ran against Jackson in 1832, his biographer was left to apologize for Clay's experience:

> Much as we admire Henry Clay the Orator, Henry Clay the Statesman, Henry Clay the distinguished and commanding Speaker of the House of Representatives, Henry Clay the Minister Plenipotentiary, Henry Clay the Secretary of State, Henry Clay the grave and able Senator, Henry Clay the favorite of the people, yet do we love far more to dwell upon 'the orphan-boy' following the plough in the slashes of Hanover, and occasionally trudging his way, with a grist of corn, to a distant mill, to provide bread for a widowed mother and younger brothers and sisters.[25]

The Incumbent beat the Orphan in a landslide.

In 1834, Davy Crockett penned the first presidential campaign *auto*biography. Vying for the Democratic nomination, he then wrote an ornery biography of his rival, upbraiding him for having traded coonskin caps for fancier hats.[26] "Mr. Van

Buren's parents were humble, plain, and not much troubled with book knowledge, and so were mine," Crockett allowed. But Van Buren had since put on airs: "He couldn't bear his rise; I never minded mine."[27] In 1839, William Henry Harrison's biographer, in a book called *The People's Presidential Candidate*, tried both to nod to Tippecanoe's founding forebears (his father, a staggeringly wealthy Virginia slaveholder, had signed the Declaration of Independence), and to insist that he was nevertheless no more than an ordinary farmer who had "never been rich" and lived quietly among his crops and cows "upon his farm at North Bend, on the Ohio."[28] Harrison, who was sixty-seven, and fighting rumors of senility, had only ever distinguished himself in war. If he were elected, one of his advisers suggested, it would be "on account of the past, not the future. Let him then rely entirely on the past. Let him say not one single word about his principles, or his creed— let him say nothing—promise nothing." Harrison obliged, earning the nickname "General Mum." When a Democratic newspaper editor joked that "Old Granny" Harrison could be persuaded to turn down the nomination, and "sit the remainder of his days in his log cabin" if he were treated to "a barrel of hard cider," Whigs turned this on its head, dubbing Harrison—who lived in a mansion—the "Log-Cabin Candidate." Whigs built log cabins on wheels, hitched them to horses, and drove them across the country, handing out mugs of hard cider along the way. They built campaign headquarters out of logs. A Philadelphia distiller, E. C. Booz, sold whisky in bottles shaped like log cabins (thereby contributing "booze" to the American lexicon). One Albany newspaper tried to expose the chicanery behind calling an aristocrat a mountain man by printing a glossary:

Patriotism.—Guzzling sour cider.
Calumny.—The truth.
Argument.—Hurrah for Old Tip.

Personal Abuse.—Telling facts.
Log Cabin.—A palace.[29]

Harrison died of pneumonia a month after his inauguration (which is why his successor, John Tyler, came to be called
"His Accidency"), but the log cabin proved long-lived.[30] "I did
not happen to me to be born in a log cabin," Daniel Webster, a three-time presidential aspirant, sighed, adding, desperately, "but my elder brothers and sisters were." (As the literary
scholar James D. Hart once observed, "Webster, a politician
with older siblings, a mother who was not widowed, and a
birthplace not built of logs, obviously sensed that his career
could not extend beyond the Senate.")[31]

"Political biography," the *Democratic Review* reported,
mid-century, "has, for many years, consisted of the vilest fan-
faronade and farrago."[32] During the election of 1848, frontier,
log-cabin Jacksonianism had become so crucial to presidential
campaigning that critics of the Whig nominee, Zachary Taylor, charged that his only qualification for office was "sleeping
forty years in the woods and cultivating moss on the calves of
his legs."[33] (Where Jackson had run as the "Farmer from Tennessee," Taylor ran as the "Farmer from Kentucky.")[34] A biographer of Taylor's opponent, Lewis Cass, defended his work by
insisting that a candidate's life was "the property of the people,
who have a right to canvass and discuss in detail each item of
his history"[35] By now, one biography wasn't quite enough. The
Democrats issued two lives of Cass, one for the North, and one
for the South. Taylor's supporters offered no fewer than fourteen.[36] When Polk tried to run without a campaign biography,
Whig critics demanded to know, "Who is James K. Polk?"[37]

In 1852, Nathaniel Hawthorne's college roommate, Franklin Pierce, received the Democratic nomination. Hawthorne,
who had just finished *The Blithedale Romance*, offered to write
"the necessary biography."[38] He was an ardent admirer of
Jackson; he saw his friend as yet another young Hickory.[39]

He wrote the book in just over a month and was rewarded, when Pierce won the election, with the consul at Liverpool (although, as a northerner endorsing a pro-slavery candidate, Hawthorne lost a good number of friends). Hawthorne had much to offer: Pierce was obscure; Hawthorne was a celebrity.[40] He also lent a masterful canniness to the book's most telling anecdote. In 1846, Pierce had served under the man he was now running against, Winfield Scott, commander of the southern army in the Mexican War. (Scott's supporters promoted his ties to Jackson by publishing, in one volume, *The Lives of Winfield Scott and Andrew Jackson*.)[41] During battle outside Mexico City, Pierce's horse fell on him. Whigs, who called Pierce "the hero of many a bottle," said he was drunk. But Hawthorne turned what happened next into an endorsement of Pierce from the mouth of his opponent. Scott approached as Pierce attempted to remount:

> "Pierce, my dear fellow, . . . you are not fit to be in your saddle."
>
> "I am," replied Pierce, "in a case like this."
>
> "You cannot touch your foot to the stirrup," said Scott.
>
> "One of them I can," answered Pierce.
>
> The General looked again at Pierce's almost disabled figure, and seemed on the point of taking his irrevocable resolution.
>
> "You are rash, General Pierce," said he; "we shall lose you, and we cannot spare you."[42]

Franklin Pierce proved one of the most ineffective American presidents, ever. He served one term and died, in 1869, of cirrhosis.

"I wrote the life of Lincoln which elected him," William Dean Howells once boasted to Mark Twain.[43] Howells wrote his *Life of Abraham Lincoln*, in 1860, when he was twenty-three.

(He would go on to write more than two hundred books, including *The Rise of Silas Lapham*, and to serve as long-time editor of the *Atlantic*.) It is the most affecting campaign biography I have ever read, but that probably has as much to do with my love for Lincoln as with my admiration for Howells, who managed to write at once the best example of the genre and a cunning parody of it. "It is necessary that every American should have an indisputable grandfather," Howells began. About Lincoln's ancestry, he had not a clue. "There is a dim possibility that he is of the stock of the New England Lincolns, of Plymouth colony; but the noble science of heraldry is almost obsolete in this country, and none of Mr. Lincoln's family seems to have been aware of the preciousness of long pedigrees."[44] Howells had only weeks to write; he had never met Lincoln; and, as it happened, he didn't think his ancestors mattered; that was his point: we aren't electing the man for his ancestors; we're electing him for his ideas.

Howells proceeded to indulge in every one of the genre's conventions but then, somehow, to transcend them, too. Lincoln's childhood was characterized by nothing so much as "his struggle with the accidents of ignorance and poverty." He lived in "the rude cabin of the settler." He split timbers for rails. "Until he was twenty-three, the ax was seldom out of his hand, except in the intervals of labor, or when it was exchanged for the plow, the hoe, or the sickle."[45] But Howells knew that, to lead a country falling apart, Lincoln had to bring more than brawn. "'He has mauled rails!'" scoffed Democratic critics. "What backwoods farmer has not?"[46]

To this question, Howells had an answer. Lincoln wasn't Somebody's son. He wasn't a military hero. He was, by nature, a scholar. The scene you can't forget, in Howells, is young Lincoln reading *Commentaries on the Laws of England* in the woods: "He threw himself under a wide-spreading oak, and expansively made a reading desk of the hillside. Here he would pore over Blackstone day after day, shifting his position as the sun rose and sank, so as to keep in the shade, and utterly unconscious of everything but the principles of common law." Lincoln didn't battle his way out of poverty. He read his way out. His was a democracy of literacy.

After the Civil War, campaign biographies got goofier, borrowing from Howells's Lincoln not his love of law and learning, but his name, and his rough-hewn timbers. Grant and Garfield were born in log cabins; Garfield's biographers provided illustrations of the family home, and even measurements.[47] (Garfield's life was, literally, a Horatio Alger story, *From Canal Boy to President*.)[48] McKinley—*From Tent to White House*—lacked even for logs.[49] Coolidge was born behind clapboards, in a house attached to his father's general store, but his was nevertheless "another story of the Log Cabin to the White House."[50] "The story of Hoover," born on a farm in Iowa, orphaned at nine and a millionaire before he was forty, was "the story of America."[51] Al Smith, the Democratic nominee in 1928, was among the first graduates of the "University of Hard Knocks."[52] Franklin Delano Roosevelt, whose speech nominating Smith for the presidency was itself published as a campaign biography, left his own biographer in a quandary. His origins were hardly humble. This didn't stop one biographer from answering yes to the question posed by his book's title, "Is Roosevelt an Andrew Jackson?" It wasn't actually a lie to say that he was born in "the old family house on the ancestral farm." (FDR was careful never to call it an "estate.") And then there were the hardships of Groton: "The Boys slept in dormitories. The alcoves were small and bare. There was one tiny window. There was a bed, a chair, a bureau. That was all."[53]

Adlai Stevenson displayed remarkable candor when he admitted, in 1952: "I wasn't born in a log cabin. I didn't work my way through school nor did I rise from rags to riches, and there's no use trying to pretend I did."[54] He wasn't enough of an Everyman to compete against the "Man from Abilene," Dwight Eisenhower, whose biographer played Ike's hometown for all it was worth: "The lusty pioneer energies that built it had moved farther West, but they left behind a robust, independent settlement whose rugged population knew the value of hard work and took for granted the virtues of sturdy individualism."[55] (That's lusty, robust, rugged, hard, and sturdy, all in one sentence.) Ike's running mate, the son of a grocer, merited his own campaign biography: "Life in the home of Frank and Hannah Nixon was good, but it was never soft." (In a detail much like the footage of teenage Bill Clinton shaking Kennedy's hand at the White House, Nixon's biographer made a point of mentioning that, as a boy, Nixon slept beneath a portrait of Lincoln.)[56] When Jimmy Carter ran for president, in 1975, he wrote a campaign autobiography called *Why Not the Best?* He, too, had the Jacksonian goods, which were getting harder to come by. (Except, maybe, in Alaska.) "We lived in a wooden clapboard house alongside the dirt road which led from Savannah to Columbus, Georgia," Carter remembered. "There was no source of heat in the northeast corner room where I slept."[57] (Sarah Palin's childhood bedroom was "unheated," too. Aside from a wood stove.)[58]

Candidate John McCain didn't grow up on a farm, but he shared with John Eaton's Andrew Jackson a rebellious youth and a "hair-trigger temper." Jackson, "like too many young men, sacrificing future prospects to present gratification," spent money on trifles, and was forever "irritable and hasty."[59] McCain, whose high school nickname was Punk, was a regular James Dean. "Clad in blue jeans, motorcycle boots, and his overcoat, smoking a cigarette that dangled from his lips, McCain would sneak into Ninth Street in Washington, go to Waxy Maxy, and buy the latest record by Elvis Presley."[60] Like

Jackson, McCain was first catapulted to national prominence for his military valor and, in McCain's case, for the tragedy of his long and terrible imprisonment and torture in Vietnam. That happened. It matters. John McCain refused to polish those boots. That this meant McCain ought to be president was a message of Paul Alexander's *Man of the People: The Maverick Life and Career of John McCain*. *Man of the People*, a book first published in 2002. But, really, it was a lot older than that.

Americans first voted for a president whose campaign touted him as a rugged, stubborn, hot-tempered war hero, a man of the people, in 1824. There is no older or more hackneyed gambit in American politics, no maneuver less maverick. The Erie Canal is younger. We don't live in the Age of Jackson any more. But even people who did had their doubts about Old Hickory, and about the kind of campaigning his first biographer began, with its overblown claims. When Abraham Lincoln was elected president, in 1860, he named his own Boswell consul to Venice. Still, something troubled him. In the White House, he read Howells's *Life of Lincoln*, more than once. He checked it out of the Library of Congress, twice. It was in his office when he was assassinated. In the margins, he made corrections. Where Howells had written that Lincoln was, in the 1820s, "a stanch Adams man," Lincoln crossed out "Adams" and wrote, "anti-Jackson." And when Howells told of how, as a young congressman, Lincoln had traveled miles and miles, by foot, to the Illinois legislature, Lincoln scribbled in the margin: "No harm, if true; but, in fact, not true. L."[61]

# 10

# PICKWICK IN AMERICA

In the summer of 1841, Charles Dickens found himself with not quite enough to do. "I am in an exquisitely lazy state, bathing, walking, reading, lying in the sun, doing everything but working," he wrote his friend John Forster.[1] Dickens was twenty-nine and wrote, as a rule, on rampage. When he was sixteen, he taught himself shorthand and started working as a court reporter. At twenty, he was hired by a newspaper; two years later, he became a political correspondent for the *Morning Chronicle* and began writing sketches of London life under the name of Boz. The first number of *Pickwick Papers* appeared in March 1836, three days before Dickens married Catherine Hogarth, the daughter of the *Chronicle*'s editor.[2] By October of that year, he was making enough from *Pickwick* to leave the paper. He wrote from nine to two every day, "walking about my room on particular bits of all the flowers in the carpet."[3] Then he left the house and walked the streets for as long as he had written.[4] ("Nothing to see but streets, streets, streets. Nothing to breathe but streets, streets, streets.")[5] For most of his career, Dickens was also the editor of a weekly magazine.[6] Almost all his novels were published in either weekly or monthly installments, Dickens writing not more than a chapter or two ahead of his illustrator and not much further ahead of his readers.[7] He only ever missed a deadline once, after someone he loved died. He never used an amanuensis or a secretary.[8] For thirteen months in 1837 and 1838, he wrote *Oliver Twist* and *Nicholas Nickleby* at the same time, abandoning Fagin in Newgate to pursue Mr. Squeers only to leave Bill Sykes hanging while failing to rescue sorry little Smike.[9]

Everyone in Dickens is either a jailer or a prisoner, and some, like Dickens himself, are both: the author, his own turnkey. "Men have been chained to hideous prison walls and other strange anchors 'ere now," Dickens once wrote, "but few have known such suffering and bitterness at one time or other, as those who have been bound to Pens."[10] Whenever an extra in a Dickens novel needs to make an escape, he exits stage left, to an unseen America; characters with better billing merely gesture westward, like so many weathercocks.[11] Mr. Monks flees "to a distant part of the New World," where he meets his end in an American penitentiary. Amy Dorrit wishes her worthless brother Tip would decamp for Canada. Herbert Pocket fancies "buying a rifle and going to America, with a general purpose of compelling buffalo to make his fortune." Sam Weller's father proposes sneaking Mr. Pickwick out of Fleet Street prison ("Me and a cab'net-maker has dewised a plan for gettin' him out"), by concealing him in a piece of furniture ("A pianner, Samivel, a pianner!"), and sending him across the ocean, where all his troubles will be over, because he could "come back and write a book about the 'Merrikas as 'll pay his expenses."[12] It needed only the piano.

Readers were so keen to see Mr. Pickwick set sail that in 1837 Edward Lloyd published a knockoff called *Pickwick in America*. Here Mr. Pickwick meets his first Virginian:

> "America is a fine place, sir, is it not?" inquired Mr. Pickwick, looking with a searching glance into the countenance of the gentleman of the gigantic brimmer . . . .

"A fine place!—I calculate you're right there to an iota;" replied the singular little gentleman; "every swamp in America is
a perfect pride of paradise."

When Dickens sued Lloyd for plagiarism, Lloyd defended
himself by arguing, successfully, that *Pickwick in America* was
so bad that no one could seriously believe Dickens had written it.[13]

By September 1841, close on the heels of *The Old Curiosity
Shop*, Dickens was near to finishing *Barnaby Rudge*, a novel
of revolution that, like *A Tale of Two Cities*, begins in 1775. At
its climax, Joe Willet, who has just returned from fighting in
the American Revolution, breaks into a prison to rescue the
woman he loves, who happens to be the daughter of a lock-
smith.[14] Dickens had written seven books in six years. He had
only ever been out of England for a week or two, and only as
far as France.[15] He and his wife had, by now, four children. You
can hear the keys jangling, as if in Miss Murdstone's very jail
of a purse.[16] "Haunted by visions of America, night and day,"
Dickens wished to avail himself of Mr. Weller's stratagem. He
wrote his publisher, "It would be a good thing, wouldn't it, if
I ran over to America about the end of February, and came
back, after four or five months, with a One Volume book?"[17]

The hitch was his wife, who didn't want go without the
children (the oldest was four, the youngest only six months);
neither did she want her husband to go alone.[18] "Kate cries
dismally if I mention the subject," Dickens wrote Forster. "But,
God willing, I think it *must* be managed somehow!"[19] Dickens
sometimes signed letters from Mr. and Mrs. Dickens, "Bully
and Meek."[20] Forster had no doubt it would be managed.

There had never been a literary celebrity like Dickens.
"Since the voyages of Columbus in search of the New World,
and of Raleigh in quest of El Dorado, no visit to America has
excited so much interest and conjecture as that of the author

of *Oliver Twist*," Thomas Hood jeered in the *New Monthly Magazine* (Hood had a nagging suspicion that "Boz was all Buzz").[21] On January 4, 1842, Dickens and his wife boarded the steamer *Britannia*. Dickens called it the *Merrikin*.[22] The bed in his cabin was so thin, he informed the artist Daniel Maclise, he thought he could put it in an envelope and mail it with just one extra stamp. "The pillows are no thicker than crumpets."[23] Maclise had made a pencil drawing of the Dickens's four children, which they'd had framed. Catherine took it out and set it on the table.[24]

They set sail. "Free from that cramped prison called the earth, and out upon the waste of waters," both Dickens and his wife were seasick.[25] "I have only been on deck *once!*" Dickens wrote Forster, a fortnight into the voyage.[26] He was so sick, he wrote, that he suffered "no desire to get up, or get better, or take the air" and was possessed of "a kind of lazy joy—of fiendish delight, if anything so lethargic can be dignified with the title—in the fact of my wife being too ill to talk to me."[27] When Martin Chuzzlewit and Mark Tapley sail to the States on a packet-ship called the *Screw*, Tapley takes care of a poor woman and her three half-starved children while Chuzzlewit lies abed, moaning.

> "Why, you don't suppose there is a living creature in this ship who can possibly have half so much to undergo on board of her as *I* have, do you?" he asked, sitting upright in his berth and looking at Mark, with an expression of great earnestness not unmixed with wonder.
>
> Mark twisted his face into a tight knot, and with his head very much on one side pondered upon this question.[28]

Dickens always wrote this way, cleaving a man from his conscience by splitting one character into two and then locking them together in a prison, or a contract, or a marriage. Dickens novels are cunningly arranged to appear all a-clutter, like a Victorian parlor, turkey-work ottomans and mahogany card tables higgledy-piggledy with chintz armchairs and marble columns topped with busts of Roman statesmen, a curiosity shop of characters, but somewhere, caped by heavy, velvet drapes, there always hangs a pair of pendant portraits.[29] Twain had his Huck and his Jim. Dickens had his Chuzzlewits and his Tapleys, his England and America, locked in a cell, bound by a knot, fastened by a screw.

Dickens in America is a story of the limits of literary criticism in a democratizing print culture. In May 1841, Edgar Allan Poe reviewed *The Old Curiosity Shop* alongside another novel, *Night and Morning*, by the Englishman Edward Bulwer Lytton. Bulwer, Poe wrote, "has arrived at the capability of producing books which might be mistaken by ninety-nine readers out of a hundred for the genuine inspiration of genius," while Dickens, "by the promptings of the truest genius itself, has been brought to compose, and evidently without effort, works which have effected a long-sought consummation—which have rendered him the idol of the people, while defying and enchanting the critics." Readers might mistake Bulwer for a great novelist, Poe warned, but a true critic could see that Dickens really was one.[30]

While Dickens sailed across the Atlantic, Poe read *Barnaby Rudge*, which was published serially in the United States in a magazine called *The New-Yorker*.[31] Rudge has a pet raven named Grip (so did Dickens) who is forever crying, "Never say die!" Rudge is an idiot; Grip is "Grip the clever, Grip the wicked, Grip the knowing." Rudge's familiar is the Chuzzlewit to Rudge's Tapley. Rudge is arrested and sent to Newgate:

A smith was speedily in attendance, who riveted upon him a set of heavy irons. Stumbling on as well as he could, beneath the unusual burden of these fetters, he was conducted to a strong stone cell, where, fastening the door with locks, and bolts, and chains, they left him, well secured; having first, unseen by him, thrust in Grip, who, with his head drooping and his deep black plumes rough and rumpled, appeared to comprehend and to partake, his master's fallen fortunes.[32]

Poe was much taken with Grip. He wrote "The Raven" two years later; he knew "What this grim, ungainly, ghastly, gaunt, and ominous bird of yore / Meant in croaking 'Nevermore.'" Poe thought *Barnaby Rudge* was sloppy and poorly plotted, but he nevertheless took the occasion of reviewing it to assail his fellow American critics as "literary Titmice" who mistake popularity for quality: "The worth of a work is most accurately estimated, they assure us, by the number of those who peruse it." Dickens might be popular but a discriminating critic could see past that, to notice that he was also good; Dickens was, for Poe, the best illustration of the fallacy of "the dogma that no work of fiction can fully suit, at the same time, the critical and the popular taste."[33]

People have been complaining about criticism since criticism began.[34] Readers used to be, mainly, priests and courtiers. Then came the printing press, the Reformation, men of letters, the novel, and an explosion of books. Book reviewing only dates to the eighteenth century, when, for the first time, there were so many books being printed that magazines—magazines were new, too—started printing notices of them, just to keep track. In 1749, Ralph Griffiths, best known for having been arrested for publishing *The Memoirs of Fanny Hill*, launched *The Monthly Review*, in which he pledged to take notice of every single book printed. He soon began printing something more: critical essays. (Smollett called Griffiths' reviewers "obscure Hackney Writers, accidentally enlisted in the Service of an undistinguishing Bookseller," which is curious, because Smollett was one of them.)

Unwilling to ignore even a single title, *The Monthly* saddled its critics with piles of books; sinking beneath the latest stack of Gothic novels, Coleridge complained in 1796, "I am almost weary of the Terrible." The idea that a magazine ought to pick only certain titles as worthy of review was an innovation of the *Edinburgh Review*, which, in hindsight, may have overlooked rather too much, having failed, in its day, to give notice to even a single work by Austen, Byron, Hazlitt, Keats, Scott, and Shelley.[35]

In the United States, where there were, at first, far fewer books, and they were more expensive, a review was meant to serve as a substitute. Then, when there were more books, and they were cheaper, a review was meant to tell you whether or not a book was worth buying, except, if it was a book written by an American author, few American reviewers were willing to criticize it, which is why Poe considered American criticism spineless.[36] "Our criticism is in some danger of falling into the pit of a most detestable species of cant," he warned.[37]

When critics prove insufficiently critical, Poe argued, what is worthwhile and what is popular become indistinguishable, and the distance between the critic and the reader closes.[38] But that distance was, at the time, new, and, at the moment, it looks like it might turn out to have been an anomaly. In the nineteenth century's age of factories and suffrage, popular readership was growing fast: literacy rates were rising, the price of books was falling, and magazines, where fiction like Dickens's was first published, were cheaper still. (Henry James once reproached Dickens for participating in the "manufacture of fiction.") With so many and more varied readers, who, anymore, could judge what books were good, or even, what was worth reviewing? In 1802, *The Monthly Epitome*, a rival to the *Edinburgh Review*, proceeded on the notion that judging literary merit was too important to be left to critics; it published with the subtitle *Readers Their Own Reviewers*.[39]

Edward Bulwer Lytton was not without opinions about the relationship between critics and readers. In "The Spirit of Criticism," he expressed the view that the vast majority of English book reviewers "would scarcely be competent to teach English at a preparatory school." Still, he had no greater respect for readers, worrying that, as the literary marketplace was opening up, "all powerful opinion, that of the majority, will rule." When a sales rank becomes a vote count novelists become politicians, Bulwer warned in 1831, the year he was elected a member of Parliament, and then: you're either in, or you're out.[40]

But Dickens didn't unify the House of Critics and the House of Readers. For a very long time, critics—Poe excepted—dismissed him as a caricaturist: facetious, melodramatic, antic, clumsy, and, on political questions, dangerously out of his depth. There never lived a man as hideous as Quilp. Mr. Gradgrind is not to be credited; Nell is not to be borne. Mirth cannot answer tyranny. *Bleak House* is belabored. The novels before *Copperfield* are meringue and treacle; those that follow are burned pot roast. Mr. Dickens does not satisfy.

That Dickens was not well educated—he had read Henry Fielding, and not a lot else—fueled some of this early critical disdain, as if, although he saw much and wrote more, he did not know enough. Dickens, this argument goes, was simply not a *thinker*.[41] Henry James charged Dickens with neither loving humanity nor understanding it.[42] More often, and especially later, as modernists slaughtered Victorians by the herd, critics accused Dickens of loving not too little but too much. Aldous Huxley found him sickening, "He had an overflowing heart; but the trouble was that it overflowed with such curious and even rather repellant secretions."[43] Dickens's humor is a problem, too: there's either too much or too little of that, too, or, more often, it's the wrong kind and must, therefore, be counted against him.[44] Trollope conceded Dickens's "drollery," which makes it sound awful, only to condemn it as "very much below the humour of Thackeray." More, he worried that Dickens's popularity undermined the very project of criticism: so many people seemed to find Dickens funnier. "The primary object of a novelist is to please; and this man's novels have been found more pleasant than those of any other writer," Trollope admitted. "From all which, there arises to the critic a question whether, with such evidence against him as to the excellence of this writer, he should not subordinate his own opinion to the collected opinion of the world of readers."[45] Who decides?

In 1939, Edmund Wilson helped turn the critical tide. Wilson argued that Dickens was not only "the greatest dramatic writer that the English language had had since Shakespeare," but also an astute and even profound social critic—he had a singular vantage on the Pecksniffian moral dishonesty of Victorianism—even if he was fundamentally "not interested in politics." Months later, in an equally influential essay, George Orwell described Dickens as *chiefly* interested in politics; it was just that his politics weren't half as radical as some people wanted them to be: neither Karl Marx nor parliamentary reform save Oliver Twist; Mr. Brownwell saves Oliver Twist.[46] Lionel Trilling threw up his hands: "With a body of work as large and enduring as that of Dickens, taste and opinion will never be done."[47] That, of course, was a classy dodge. An answer to this critical dilemma lies in what happened to Dickens when he tried to tell the story of America.

On January 22, 1842, the *Britannia* reached Boston, a port that, in Dickens's honor, Americans took to calling Boz-town. Ribbons fluttered from lampposts. Hackneys lined up at the dock, fighting for the chance to drive Dickens to his hotel. Bundled in a coarse-hair brown peacoat, his feet stuffed into cork-sole boots, Dickens looked a fright; Catherine wanted him to change his clothes before getting off the ship. "Never mind that, dear," Dickens said. "We are on the other side now."[48]

Dickens bounded through the snow-covered streets of Boston, something like a lunatic. When he reached the Tremont Hotel, he yelled, "Here we are!" Wherever he went, it seemed, he screamed or shouted or collapsed in laughter. James Fields, later editor of the *Atlantic Monthly* called him the "Emperor of Cheerfulness."[49] Dickens was, then and always, amused, often convulsively so, by things that other people didn't even seem to notice. (Of his accommodations at the Tremont, he wrote Forster, "I slept in this room for two nights, quite satisfied with the belief that it was a shower bath.")[50] He sat for a portrait by Francis Alexander which the painter's apprentice found remarkable for capturing "that inexpressible look of kindly mirth" that seemed to forever play on Dickens's face, a "singular *lighting up of the face* which Dickens had, beyond any one I ever saw."[51] Mr. Dickens appeared to glow.

Henry Wadsworth Longfellow and Charles Sumner, who were both teaching at Harvard at the time, visited Dickens and took him for a ten-mile walk. He has "a slight dash of the Dick Swiveller about him," Longfellow wrote.[52] Richard Henry Dana, Jr., thought so too: "He is of the middle height, (under if anything) with a large expressive eye, regular nose, matted, curling, wet-looking black hair, a dissipated looking mouth with a vulgar draw to it, a muddy olive complexion, *stubby* fingers & a hand by no means patrician, a hearty, offhand manner, far from well bred, & a rapid, dashing way of talking. He looks 'wide awake,' 'up to anything,' full of cleverness, with quick feelings & great ardour. You admire him, & there is a fascination about him which keeps your eyes on him, yet you cannot get over the impression that he is a low bred man." Dana came to this assessment of Dickens's intellectual powers: "His forces are all light infantry & light cavalry, & always in marching order. There are not many heavy pieces, . . . the scientific corps is deficient, & I fear there is no chaplain in the garrison."[53]

At a dinner held in his honor in Boston, Dickens explained that he had come to America to make the acquaintance of his democratic readers. He had received letters "from the dwellers in log-houses among the morasses, and swamps, and densest forests, and deepest solitudes of the Far West."[54] He wanted to meet the people who wrote those letters; he wanted to watch them swoon. Dickens's longing for his readers was every bit as aching and desperate as their longing for him. He once wrote his wife about what it felt like to watch the actor William Macready listen to one of his stories: "If you had seen Macready last night, undisguisedly sobbing and crying on the sofa as I read, you would have felt, as I did, what a thing it is to have power."[55] On the page, Dickens was a very tyrant.

Dickens considered himself something of an honorary American, and Americans thought of him that way, too. Writing in a New York newspaper in 1842, a very young Walt Whitman hailed Dickens as a "democratic writer."[56] The *United States Magazine* lauded his "democratic genius."[57] "He was more truly democratic than any American who had yet written fiction," William Howells later remarked, and fair enough.[58] In Dickens, the poor rise, the rich fall, and everyone wants freedom. But, as Chesterton observed, what Dickens did was to make democracy funny.[59] And it turns out that this is what Americans did not find altogether amusing.

From Boston, Dickens visited prisons and factories and penitentiaries (Emerson found him tiresome on the subject of asylums) and by the beginning of February, just a month after he arrived, wrote Forster, "The American poor, the American factories, the institutions of all kinds—I have a book, already."[60] Then he went to New York, where everything began to go wrong. In the United States, Dickens's books sold wildly, but all the income he had received from their sale amounted to no more than fifty pounds.[61] But when Dickens argued on behalf of copyright reform—"I,—the greatest loser by the existing Law, alive"—New York newspapers damned him as coarse and mercenary, a poet of poverty who loved nothing better than money. On February 22, Dickens complained, "I have never in my life been so shocked and disgusted, or made so sick and sore at heart, as I have been by the treatment I have received here."[62]

He traveled on, southward, his dismay growing, his spirits sinking. He visited a prison outside of Philadelphia. "Over the head and face of every prisoner who comes into this melancholy house, a black hood is drawn; and in this dark shroud, an emblem of the curtain dropped between him and the living world, he is led to the cell from which he never again comes forth, until his whole term of imprisonment is expired." What must it be, to be so confined? At first, Dickens imagined, "the man is stunned." But "by degrees the insupportable solitude and barrenness of the place rouses him from this stupor, and when the trap in his grated door is open, he humbly begs and prays for work. 'Give me some work to do, or I shall go raving mad!'" He visited the cell of a man who had been held in solitary confinement for six years. "He wore a paper hat of his own making."[63] To have no communion with humanity is what Dickens dreaded most. It was the shadow of his own terror—no work for the doing, no readers for his writing, no audience for the performance—nothing but the walls, and a hat of paper.

"This is not the Republic I came to see," he wrote Macready, bitterly, from Baltimore. "This is not the Republic of my imagination."[64]

At the United States Hotel, he met with Poe (who had mailed him copies of his reviews of *The Old Curiosity Shop* and *Barnaby Rudge*) and promised he'd try to help him find an

English publisher.[65] Writers importuned him at every turn. In St. Louis, an old man came to Dickens's hotel every day, his pockets "running over with manuscript": he "had paraphrased the entire Book of Job, and wanted to read it to Mr. Dickens and get his opinion of it." ("God help him, poor fellow!" said Dickens.) Everywhere Dickens went, crowds crushed him, as much in the fame of fame as in the fame of accomplishment. When the train in which he was traveling reached Washington, a woman carried along by the force of the crowd cried to a man next to him,

> "What's the matter? What is it all about, say, John, what is it?"
>
> "Why," answered the man, looking over his shoulder, "they've got Boz here!"
>
> "Got Boz!" said she; "what's Boz? what do you mean?"
>
> "Why," said the man, "it's Dickens. They've got him in here!"
>
> "Well, what has he been doing?" said she.
>
> "He ain't been doing nothing," answered the man. "He writes books."
>
> "O," said the woman, indignantly, "is that all?"[66]

In Washington, Dickens conveyed to Congress a letter urging the passage of an International Copyright Law, addressed "To the American People" from "Twelve British Authors," signed first—and probably drafted—by Edward Bulwer Lytton.[67] He met the president and observed the workings of Congress, reporting to Macready that American politics were grotesque:

> Look at the exhausted Treasury; the paralyzed government; the unworthy representatives of a free people; the desperate contests between the North and the South; the iron curb and brazen muzzle fastened upon every man who speaks his mind, even in that Republican Hall, to which Republican men are

sent by a Republican people to speak Republican Truths—the stabbings, and shootings, and coarse and brutal threatenings exchanged between Senators under the very Senate's roof—the intrusion of the most pitiful, mean, malicious, creeping, crawling, sneaking party spirit into all transactions of life.[68]

He wrote Sumner, "We are now in the regions of slavery, spittoons, and senators."[69] His disgust at slavery left him physically ill; he made it as far south as Richmond and then turned west. The American people were not only savage, he wrote Forster from Sandusky, they were also humorless: "I should think there is not, on the face of the earth, a people so entirely destitute of humour, vivacity, or the capacity of enjoyment. It is most remarkable. I am quite serious when I say that I have not heard a hearty laugh these six weeks, except my own; nor have I seen a merry face on any shoulders but a black man's."[70]

America is where Dickens's love affair with his readers fell apart. Ask them to pay an author, and you get but one answer: "Dollars, banks, and cotton are *our* books, sir."[71] The emperor of cheerfulness turned sarcastic. "The man's read in America! The Americans like him! They are glad to see him when he comes here!" he wrote Forster from Niagara Falls. "The Americans read him; the free, enlightened, independent Americans; and what more *would* he have?" And then he added, "The national vanity swallows up all other countries on the face of the earth, and leaves but this above the ocean."[72] But, of course, it was Dickens's vanity that knew no shore.

He could hardly have been more eager to get home. "We sail from New York, per George Washington Packet *Ship* (none of your steamers) on Tuesday the Seventh of June. Hoo-ray—ay—ay—ay—ay—ay—ay!!!!!"[73] He brought on board the *George Washington* a spaniel named Timber Doodle; a wife, homesick; and his great expectations for America, dashed.[74]

The republic he had admired was a sham: its newspapers vicious, its politics brutal, its people humorless. He wrote Forster, "I am a Lover of Freedom disappointed."[75]


It didn't stop him writing. "Charles Dickens has just come home in a state of violent dislike of the Americans—& means to devour them," Mary Shelley wrote.[76] "Here I am in my own old room, with my books, and pen and ink and paper . . .—dog—and Raven," Dickens wrote Sumner in July. "The Raven, I am sorry to say, has become a Maniac."[77] So had Dickens. He was always something of a maniac when he was writing. He had told Sumner to expect an indictment of slavery, which is just what Sumner was hoping for.[78] In October, while Dickens was writing *American Notes for General Circulation*—the title is a swipe at Americans' preference for money over books—Longfellow, who had sailed to England, was staying in his house.[79] Longfellow read the manuscript in Dickens's study, writing to Sumner, "It is jovial and good-natured, and at times very severe. You will read it with delight and, for the most part, approbation."[80] When Longfellow left, to sail back to Boston, he carried Dickens's manuscript with him, to deliver it to his American publishers.[81] During the voyage, Longfellow, at Sumner's request, wrote his own polemic, *Poems on Slavery*.[82] ("Heaven speed your Slavery poems!" Dickens wrote him. "They will be manful, vigorous, and full of indignant Truth, I know. I am looking for them eagerly.")[83]

*American Notes* was widely considered the worst thing Dickens had ever written. The *Edinburgh Review* berated him for overstepping.[84] So young, so poorly educated—"we do not suppose that his conversation has lain much among Professors"—so plainly not a gentleman of breeding, "how can he have acquired the knowledge and the speculative powers necessary for estimating the character of a great people, placed in circumstances not only strange to him, but new in the history of mankind?"[85] Mr. Dickens "is a man of very 'liberal' opinions in politics," a reviewer in *Blackwood's* remarked, but "We greatly doubt whether he has read or thought sufficiently long and deeply on such matters, to enable him to offer confident opinions on them. In his own peculiar line, he is original, admirable, and unrivalled—and that line, too, is one which lies level with the taste of *the million* of persons of all shades of political opinions."[86]

In the United States, *American Notes* earned Dickens the enmity of just about every American who read it. "Truth is not his object for a single instant," Emerson wrote in his journal. "We can hear throughout every page the dialogue between the author and his publisher, 'Mr Dickens the book must be entertaining,—that is the essential point. Truth! damn truth.'" Poe called it "one of the most suicidal productions every deliberately published by an author, who had the least reputation to lose."[87] (Dickens had also failed to find Poe an English publisher; Poe's opinion of Dickens was falling fast.)[88] It was, however, a kinder book than Dickens meant it to be. He had wanted to include a first chapter called "Introductory and Necessary to Be Read," a truculent defense. He had seen much in the United States that he admired, but he would write as a critic ought, and chronicle the "blemishes of a nation." Forster convinced him to leave that out.[89]

Before Dickens went to America, his publishers had agreed to pay him an advance of £150 a month while he was traveling, in exchange for the account of his travels he was to write upon his return, after which they would pay him £200 a month for his next novel. But if either the travel book or novel sold poorly, Dickens would have to pay back the advance. Dickens was reduced to these infelicitous terms because he hadn't had a success since *The Old Curiosity Shop*. His readers missed

*Pickwick.* "Nor had the temporary withdrawal to America been favorable to an immediate resumption by his readers of their old and intimate relations," Forster hinted.[90] They missed Dickens the jolly.

Right after finishing *American Notes*, Dickens wrote *Martin Chuzzlewit*. ("I have nearly killed myself with laughing" he wrote, while writing the American chapters.) "What are the Great United States for, sir, if not for the regeneration of man?" General Choke asks, in the course of swindling Chuzzlewit into investing in the Eden Land Company. When Chuzzlewit and Tapley arrive in Eden, they find not the promised thriving republican city but festering swamps, rotting cabins, and dying settlers. "There's one good thing in this place, sir, . . . and that is, that it's a reg'lar little United States in itself." (Hannibal Chollop, who carries "a brace of revolving-pistols in his coat-pocket," allows that Eden is "moist, perhaps.") Chuzzlewit gets sick, and nearly dies.

> In the hideous solitude of that most hideous place, with Hope so far removed, Ambition quenched, and Death beside him rattling at the very door, reflection came, as in a plague-beleaguered town; and so he felt and knew the failing of his life, and saw distinctly what an ugly spot it was. Eden was a hard school to learn so hard a lesson in; but there were teachers in the swamp and thicket, and the pestilential air, who had a searching method of their own.

Dickens had found something out, in America. "So low had Eden brought him down. So high had Eden raised him up."[91]

Charles Dickens returned to the United States in 1867; he had wanted to go sooner, but he had been unwilling to be apart from Ellen Ternan, and he couldn't possibly bring her with him. In Dickens's honor, Bulwer hosted a farewell dinner. Dickens and Bulwer entered Freemasons Hall, arm in arm. Bulwer toasted first the queen, and then Dickens, "a different kind of royalty." When Dickens rose to speak, he attempted to explain why he was returning to a country he had famously found so disappointing. "Since I was there before, a vast entirely new generation has arisen in the United States."[92] Americans had changed, and Dickens had changed.

In the United States for six months, Dickens gave eighty readings and earned a quarter of a million dollars.[93] He was frantic and exhausted, all at once, and even before he began. Henry James found the readings charmless.[94] Mark Twain described them as "glittering frostwork."[95] The trip destroyed Dickens's health.[96] He died of a stroke two years later, at the age of fifty-eight.

In a three-volume biography that began appearing within a year of Dickens's death, Forster revealed something that, outside of Dickens's family, no one but he had ever known: that when Dickens was twelve, his father had gone to debtors' prison, and Dickens had been sent to work at a blacking factory.[97]

Reading Forster's biography, Carlyle had decided that at the very bottom of Dickens, a reader finds, "deeper than all, if one has the eye to see deep enough, dark, fateful, silent elements . . . the elements of death itself." But nothing, he thought, was darker than Dickens on America.[98]

*American Notes* and *Martin Chuzzlewit* constitute an unforgiving portrait of a troubled republic: ambitious, cruel, ungenerous, brutal, and divided. The problem wasn't that Dickens's America was inaccurate; it's that it came from a man known for his benevolence, his cheerfulness, and his democratic sympathies. Dickens's America is a dismal swamp, a failing bank, and a man, alone in a prison, wearing a paper hat. "However contemptible he found our pseudo-equality, William Dean Howells wrote, "he was more truly democratic than any American who had yet written fiction," and true enough.[99] Chesterton once observed that one of the things Dickens did best was to make democracy funny.[100] Also true. But, about democracy in America, Dickens's humor was black. "How could he ever go to America!" Mrs. Lupin cries, missing Mark Tapley. "Why didn't he go to some of those countries which are not quite barbarous; where the savages eat each other fairly, and given an equal chance to every one!"[101]

In 1870, when the American writer Bret Harte heard word of Dickens's death, he wrote a poem called "Dickens in Camp," about listening, as a boy, to a haggard old miner read *The Old Curiosity Shop* around a roaring campfire in the Sierras.

. . . as he read, from clustering pine and cedar

A silence seemed to fall.

But gone is "he who wrought that spell," Harte wrote: "Lost is that camp, and wasted all its fire."[102] And forgotten is that America that Dickens never found, that Eden, republic of dreams.

# 11

# THE HUMBUG

Edgar Allan Poe once wrote an essay called "The Philosophy of Composition," to explain why he wrote "The Raven" backwards. The poem tells the story of a man who, "once upon a midnight dreary," while mourning his dead love, Lenore, answers a tapping at his chamber door, to find "Darkness there and nothing more." He peers into the darkness, "dreaming dreams no mortal ever dared to dream before," and meets a silence broken only by his own whispered word, "Lenore?" He closes the door. The tapping starts again. He flings open his shutter and in, "with many a flirt and flutter," flies a raven, "grim, ungainly, ghastly, gaunt, and ominous bird of yore." The bird speaks just one word: *Nevermore.* That word is the poem's last, but it's where Poe began. He started, he said, "at the end, where all works of art should begin," and "first put pen to paper" at what became the third to last stanza:

> "Prophet," said I, "thing of evil! Prophet still if bird or devil!
> By that heaven that bends above us—by that God we both
>    adore,
> Tell this soul with sorrow laden, if within the distant Aidenn,
> It shall clasp a sainted maiden whom the angels name
>    Lenore—

Clasp a rare and radiant maiden whom the angels name
   Lenore."
      Quoth the Raven "Nevermore."[1]

"The Philosophy of Composition" is a lovely little essay, but, as Poe himself admitted, it's a bit of jiggery-pokery, too.[2] Poe didn't actually write "The Raven" backwards. The essay is as much an exercise as the poem itself, a contrivance, a flourish. Here is a beautiful poem; it does everything a poem should do, is everything a poem should be. And here is a clever essay about the writing of a beautiful poem. Top that. Nearly everything Poe wrote, including the spooky stories for which he's most remembered, has this virtuosic, showy, lilting, and slightly wilting quality, like a peony just past bloom. Poe didn't write "The Raven" to answer the exacting demands of a philosophic Art, or not entirely, anyway. He wrote it for the same reason he wrote tales like "The Gold-bug": to stave off starvation. For a long while, Poe lived on bread and molasses; weeks before "The Gold-bug" was published, he was begging strangers on the street for fifty cents to buy something to eat.[3] "'The Raven' has had a great 'run,'" Poe wrote a friend, "but I wrote it for the express purpose of running—just as I did the 'Gold-Bug,' you know. The bird beat the bug, though, all hollow."[4] The public that swallowed that bird and bug, Poe quite strenuously resented. You either love Poe or you don't but, either way, unless you happen to be, say, Coleridge, Poe doesn't love you.[5] A writer more condescending to more adoring readers is hard to think of. "The nose of a mob is its imagination," Poe wrote, "By this, at any time, it can be quietly led."[6]

Poe died, under very mysterious circumstances, in October 1849. Drunk and delirious, he seems to have been dragged around Baltimore to cast votes, precinct after precinct, in one of that city's infamously corrupt congressional elections, until he finally collapsed. From Ryan's tavern, a polling place in the

Fourth Ward, Poe was carried, like a corpse, to a hospital. He died three days later.[7] He was forty years old.

"My whole existence has been the merest Romance," Poe wrote, the year before his death, "in the sense of the most utter unworldliness."[8] This is Byronic bunk. Poe's life was tragic, but he was about as unworldly as a bale of cotton. Poe's world was Andrew Jackson's America, a world of banking collapse, financial panic, and grinding depression that had a particularly devastating effect on the publishing industry, where Poe sought his perch. Poe's biography really is a series of unfortunate events. But two of those events were global financial crises: the Panic of 1819 and the Panic of 1837, the pit and pendulum of the antebellum economy. Poe died at the end of a decade known as "the Hungry Forties," and he wasn't the only American to fall face down in the gutter during a seven-year-long depression brought on by a credit collapse.[9] He did not live out of time. He lived in hard times, dark times, up and down times. Indigence cast a shadow over everything Poe attempted. Poverty was his raven, tapping at the door, and it was Poe, not the bird, who uttered, helplessly, another rhyme for "Nevermore." "I send you an original tale," Poe once began a letter, and, at its end, added one line more: "P.S. I am poor."[10]

Edgar Poe was born in Boston, on January 19, 1809, to a talented actress named Eliza Poe and her hapless husband, David, who deserted her. When Edgar was two, his mother died of consumption. The Poe orphans had little more to depend upon than the charity of strangers. The children were separated and Edgar landed in the home of a wealthy Richmond merchant named John Allan and his sickly, childless wife, Fanny. Allan, who ran a firm called the House of Ellis and Allan, never adopted the boy, and never loved him, either. Poe, for his part, took Allan's name but never wanted it. (He signed letters, and published, as "Edgar A. Poe.") In 1815, Allan moved his family to London, to take advantage of the booming British market for Virginia tobacco.[11] Poe attended posh boarding schools.[12] Then, during the Panic of 1819, the first bust in the industrializing nineteenth century, banks failed, factories closed, and Allan's business imploded. The House of Ellis and Allan fell. Allan, plagued with two hundred thousand dollars of debt, sailed back to Virginia. Poe turned poet. The earliest verses in his hand that survive were written when he was fifteen. "Last night with many cares and toils oppress'd / Weary . . . I laid me on a couch to rest." Adolescent melancholy, and nothing more. But those lines are scribbled on a sheet of paper on which Allan had calculated, just above Poe's scrawl, the compound interest on a debt.[13]

In 1823, Poe fell in love with Jane Stannard, the unhinged mother of a school friend. A year later, Stannard died, insane. Poe spent much time at her graveside. "No more" became his favorite phrase. (Poe would later insist that mourning the death of a beautiful woman is, of all sorrows, the most *poetical*; he loved to play with names.)[14] In 1825, Allan inherited a fortune from an uncle. Allan rose; Poe kept falling. At sixteen, Poe went to the University of Virginia where he drank and gambled and, in a matter of months, racked up debts totaling more than two thousand dollars. Allan refused to honor them, even though Poe was at some risk of finding himself in debtor's prison. Poe ran off. There followed a series of huffy pronouncements and stormy departures; most ended in Poe begging Allan for money. "I am in the greatest necessity, not having tasted food since Yesterday morning," Poe wrote. "I have nowhere to sleep at night, but roam about the Streets." Allan was unmoved. Poe enlisted in the army and served for two years as Edgar A. Perry. In 1829, Fanny Allan died. Andrew Jackson was inaugurated. Poe, while awaiting a commission to West Point—having sent an application, and Allan's fifty dollars, to Jackson's secretary of war, John Eaton—submitted the manuscript for a book of poems to a publisher, who told him that he would publish it only if Poe would guarantee him against the loss. Allan refused to front the money. Poe moved to Baltimore, where he lived with his invalid grandmother; his aunt, Maria Clemm; his nine-year-old cousin, Virginia; and his brother, Henry, an alcoholic who was dying of consumption.

Jackson, meanwhile, refused to renew the charter of the Bank of the United States, run by Nicholas Biddle. Biddle insisted on the need for federal regulation of paper currency. Jackson and his supporters, known as "gold-bugs," wanted no paper money at all.[15] ("Gold-bug" was also slang for millionaire.) Between 1830 and 1837, while Biddle and Jackson battled, 347 state-chartered banks opened across the country. They printed their own money. In 1832, the year Jackson vetoed the extension of the national bank's charter, $59 million of paper bills were in circulation; four years later, that number had reached $140 million. All this paper was backed up by very little coin.[16] At the end of Jackson's two terms, American banks held $57 million in paper money and only $10.5 million in gold.[17]

Poe, who was broke, didn't need a bank. He could treasure up funds, he came to believe, in his own brain. He read as much as he could, charging books out of the Baltimore Library. "There *are* minds which not only retain all receipts, but keep them at compound interest for ever," he once wrote. "Knowledge breeds knowledge, as gold gold."[18] Poe may have thought his mind was a mint, but when his book of poems was finally published, it earned him nothing (exactly what all his collections of poetry earned). He sold one of Maria Clemm's slaves. "I have tried to get the money for you from Mr. A a dozen times," Poe wrote to one of his many creditors, "but he always shuffles me off." And then he added, lying, "Mr. A is not very often sober."[19]

"I have an inveterate habit of speaking the truth," Poe once wrote.[20] That, too, was a lie. (That Poe lied so compulsively about his own life has proved the undoing of many a biographer.)[21] In 1830, Poe finally made it to West Point, where he pulled pranks. "I cannot believe a word he writes," Allan wrote on the back of yet another letter from his wayward charge.[22] After Poe was court-martialed, Allan, who had since married a woman twenty years his junior, cut Poe off entirely. Poe went to New York but, unable to support himself by writing, he left the city within three months, returning to Baltimore, to live with Mrs. Clemm and little Virginia. He published his first story, "Metzengerstein." He won a prize of fifty dollars from the Baltimore *Weekly Visitor* for "MS in a Bottle." The editor, who met him, later wrote, "I found him a state of starvation."[23] In these straits, Poe wrote "Berenice," a story about a man who disinters his dead lover and yanks out all her teeth—"the white and glistening, and ghastly teeth of Berenice"—although this gets even grosser when, after he's done it, he realizes she was still alive. It has been plausibly claimed that Poe wrote this story to make a very bad and cruel and long-winded joke about "bad taste."[24] Also: he was hungry.


John Allan died in 1834, a rich man. He left his vast estate, three plantations and two hundred slaves, to his second wife and their two children. He left Edgar A. Poe not a penny. The next year, Poe was hired as the editor of a new monthly magazine, the *Southern Literary Messenger*, in Richmond. He was paid sixty dollars a month, a modest salary but for him, a fortune.[25] In 1836, Poe married Virginia Clemm. She was thirteen; he was twenty-seven; he said she was twenty-one.

He called her his "darling little wifey."[26] ("*I* was a child and *she* was a child, / In a kingdom by the sea; / But we loved with a love that was more than love— / I and my Annabel Lee.") Poe held the job at the *Messenger* for only fifteen months. He boasted that, under his editorship, the magazine's circulation grew from 700 to 5,500, but, as the Poe scholar Thomas Whalen has discovered, this, too, was a lie. The magazine had thirteen hundred subscribers when Poe started, and eighteen hundred when he left.[27]

Poe lied about the *Messenger*'s circulation because he was attempting to forge a career in the world of magazine publishing during very troubled economic times. And, plainly, he was a very troubled man. Quarreling with the publisher of the *Messenger*, Poe left the magazine and, in February 1837, moved to New York. The *New-Yorker*, a weekly magazine edited by Rufus Griswold, welcomed him, praising Poe's work at the *Messenger*.[28] Harper & Brothers was just about to publish Poe's novel, *The Narrative of Arthur Gordon Pym*.

Unfortunately, Poe arrived in New York just in time for Panic of 1837.[29] With all that paper money, speculators had gone wild; in the West, there had been a land grab and, in the East, a housing bubble; in New York, real estate values had risen 150 percent.[30] When the crash came, in the last weeks of Jackson's presidency, bankruptcies swept the nation. In New York, riots broke out as the swelling ranks of the city's poor broke into food shops. "Down with the panic makers," one newspaper warned, promising, "A bright sun will soon dispel the remaining darkness." But the skies didn't clear. In April, one New Yorker wrote in his diary, "Wall Street. The blackness of darkness still hangeth over it. Failure on failure." By the fall of 1837, nine out of ten eastern factories had closed. Five hundred desperate New Yorkers turned up to answer an ad for twenty day laborers, to be paid at the truly measly wage of four dollars a month.[31]

Then *Pym* failed. Poe's publisher had tried to pass the novel off as an authentic travel journal even as its author left a trail of clues to his oh-so clever hoax—"pym" being, for instance, an anagram for "imp." This didn't go over especially well. One reviewer called the book "an impudent attempt at humbugging the public."[32] Poe did not write another novel. He moved to Philadelphia and wrote more stories. During the seven-year depression that followed the Panic, as Whalen has shown, Poe wrote 90 percent fewer poems and twice as many tales. He insisted that this was an aesthetic choice. The tale, he insisted, affords "the best prose opportunity for display of the highest talent."[33] Any piece of truly worthy writing must be able to be read at a sitting in order to achieve a single dramatic effect, the *Nevermore*-ish end with which, Poe said, every work of Art must begin.[34] Maybe. But writing a book was exactly the kind of long-term investment Poe could not afford to make, especially with so little prospect of return. In the 1820s, books cost, on average, two dollars; during the depression, that price fell to fifty cents.[35]

Poe had already started writing gothic stories before the economy collapsed. But, as a man of no independent means whatsoever, he was especially vulnerable to market forces, and he knew it. (That's probably why he worked so hard at appearing so otherworldly, so Romantic.) Poe tried to deduce, from careful study, what sold best. "The history of all Magazines," he concluded, "shows plainly that those which have attained celebrity were indebted for it to articles *similar in nature—to Berenice*."[36] Gothic stories—supernatural tales set, often, in medieval ruins—had been popular for decades. They were also rather interesting to write on a rainy day, as Mary Shelley discovered, and great fun to parody, as Jane Austen found out (both *Frankenstein* and *Northanger Abbey* were published in 1818, when Poe was in England). The genre had since gone to seed; most of it, in Poe's lifetime, was fairly rotten. It did sell well, though. A philosophy of composition? No, what Poe developed was a philosophy of the literary marketplace. He had little choice. "The general market for literary wares," he reported, during one of the worst years of the depression, "is in a state of stagnation."[37]

The problem with Poe comes to this. He needed to turn his pen to profit—his mind was a mint!—but he also wanted to signal, as with *Pym*, that he was lowering himself. *Look! See! I'm brilliant! Even at writing dreck!* This kind of thing isn't usually terribly charming. Once in a while, someone attempted to point this out. Early on, a fellow writer explained to Poe why the brothers Harper had declined to publish Poe's *Tales of the Folio Club*:

> They object that there is a degree of obscurity in their application, which will prevent ordinary readers from comprehending their drift, and consequently from enjoying the fine satire they convey. It requires a degree of familiarity with various kinds of knowledge which they do not possess, to enable them to relish the joke; the dish is too refined for them to banquet on.[38]

Poe found this advice difficult to take. In "How to Write an Article for Blackwood Magazine," a story he wrote in 1838, he tried telling the joke more broadly. An aspiring writer of gothics visits *Blackwood*'s editor, seeking instruction. "Your writer of intensities must have very black ink, and a very big pen, with a very blunt nib," the editor advises, then offers some examples of recent successes:

> Let me see. There was "The Dead Alive," a capital thing!—the record of a gentleman's sensations when entombed before the breath was out of his body—full of tact, taste, terror, sentiment, metaphysics, and erudition. You would have sworn that the writer had been born and brought up in a coffin. Then we had the "Confessions of an Opium-eater"—fine, very fine!—glorious

imagination—deep philosophy—acute speculation—plenty of fire and fury, and a good spicing of the decidedly unintelligible. That was a nice bit of flummery, and went down the throats of the people delightfully. They would have it that Coleridge wrote the paper—but not so. It was composed by my pet baboon, Juniper.[39]

Still not so endearing.

Poe calibrated and recalibrated. Just how many ways can a writer insult his readers and get away with it? If you take Poe's best horror stories at face value, they are terrifying, wonderfully, flawlessly, terrifying; they are masterpieces. They're also dripping with contempt. "Half banter, half-satire," is how Poe once described them.[40] "The Tell-Tale Heart" reads more like three-quarters burlesque, especially when you think about the literary output of Juniper the baboon. A madman with superacuity murders an old man and entombs the corpse beneath the floor. When the police arrive, the madman begins to hear the beating of his victim's heart.

> I felt that I must scream or die!—and now—again—hark! louder! louder! louder! *louder!*—
>
> "Villains!" I shrieked, "dissemble no more! I admit the deed!—tear up the planks!—here, here!—it is the beating of his hideous heart!"

Most of Poe's stories have this campy, floozy *Boo!* business at the end.[41] Poe knew these were cheap tricks. No one plays them better than he does. It wasn't to everyone's taste. The first editor to read "The Tell-Tale Heart" rejected it, writing back, "If Mr. Poe would condescend to furnish more quiet articles, he would be a most desirable correspondent."[42]

What Poe most wanted was to never again answer to an editor. "As soon as Fate allows," he wrote in 1839, "I will have a Magazine of my own—and will endeavor to kick up a dust."[43]

Instead, Poe became, that same year, assistant editor of the Philadelphia-based *Burton's Gentleman's Magazine*. "That Magazines can live, and not only live but thrive, and not only thrive but afford to disburse money for original contributions," Poe wrote, "are facts which can only be solved, under the circumstances, by the really fanciful but still agreeable supposition, that there is somewhere still existing an ember not altogether quenched among the fires of good feeling for letters and literary men."[44] But, as the depression deepened, magazines struggled, too. At *Burton's*, Poe had to send letters to his writers informing them, "the intense pressure has obliged Mr. B. with nearly if not every, publisher of the country, to discontinue paying for contributions."[45] Drinking and fighting with Burton are the usual reasons given for Poe's departure, in 1841. (He was sacked.) But, really, he was in an impossible position.

Poe then asked Nicholas Biddle to give him a thousand dollars to launch his own magazine, which he proposed calling *The Penn*.[46] Biddle, broken by the Bank War, did not oblige. Poe returned to New York and took a job as book review editor of *Graham's Magazine*. He wrote much of the copy himself. George Graham paid his writers a scale that ranged from two to twelve dollars a page. He paid Poe only four dollars, explaining, "The character of Poe's mind was of such an order, as not to be very widely in demand."[47]

At *Graham's* and elsewhere, Poe wrote a prodigious amount of rather extraordinary literary criticism.[48] He was an exceptionally keen critic: untiring, unsparing, and, very often, unkind. A master of precision, he was particularly picky about diction. "The history of the borders is filled with legends," James Fenimore Cooper had written. "'*Abounds* with legends,' would be better," Poe suggested, "for it is clear that if the history were *filled* with legends it would be all legend and no history."[49] Cooper was a popular writer; this, to Poe, was a good sign that he was a bad one. That's why he gave Cooper so little rope. "The most 'popular,' the most 'successful' writers among us, (for a brief period, at least,) are, ninety-nine times out of a hundred, persons of mere address, perseverance, effrontery—in a word, busy-bodies, toadies, quacks."[50] (Poe aspired to be that one of out a hundred who was not.) Poe also found obnoxious and offensive the prevailing fashion for an American literature (which probably accounts for why Emerson called Poe nothing more than a "jingle man") and therefore waged a one-man campaign against the Young Americans' call for a national literature, charging them with adhering "to the gross paradox of liking a stupid book the better, because, sure enough, its stupidity is American."[51]

Poe also hated Transcendentalists and literary Bostonians because, "self-bepuffed," they praised one other's work.[52] He began his review of one much-hyped novel, "For the sake of everything puffed, puffing and puffable, let us take a peep at its contents!"[53] There was, in Andrew Jackson's America, a Literary Bubble, and Poe was determined to burst it. As Poe saw it, he was the nation's only real critic; everyone else was just a puffer.[54] If Rufus Griswold's correspondence is any measure, Poe was right. "I puff your books, you know," a testy Griswold once wrote a publisher, "without any regard to their quality."[55]

For all this, Poe was, unsurprisingly, much attacked, as in a column titled "POE-LEMICAL."[56] And still he fought. Literature was to Poe a religion, Graham once wrote, and Poe, "its high priest" who, "with a whip of scorpions scourged the money-changers from the temple."[57] Poe was looking, in other words, for a gold standard of literary value, against the nothingness of papery puffery.[58]

After Poe left Philadelphia, he changed the name of his proposed magazine to *The Stylus*; on its cover he wanted a picture of a hand holding a pen and, beneath it, a Latin epigram that translates as, "sometimes a pen of gold and sometimes a pen of iron."[59] *The Stylus* never got off the ground. Poe began to think of his life as a kind of forced labor in "the Magazine Prison-House."[60] But the market forces that confined Poe to that prison affected other writers, and readers, too. Something had happened in the world, in the midst of the Panic. When Poe wrote to Henry Wadsworth Longfellow and Washington Irving, soliciting contributions, he began his letter: "I need not call your attention to the signs of the times." Magazines were cheaper than books and richer than newspapers. What Poe sensed, and rightly, was the commercial and especially the stylistic ascendancy of magazine literature, despite the morbid financial times. The era of the magazine, with its clipped prose, relentless currency, and swift circulation, had arrived. No more "the verbose and ponderous." The "energetic, busy spirit of the age," Poe wrote, "tended wholly to the Magazine literature—to the curt, the terse, the well-timed, and the readily diffused."[61]

In these hard times, Poe was, nevertheless, desperate for something other than magazine writing to fall back onto. When Jackson's successor, Martin Van Buren, left office in 1841, to be replaced by William Henry Harrison and then, a month later, His Accidency, John Tyler, Poe schemed for a sinecure. In a letter dated, no coincidence, on the Fourth of July, he wrote, "I would be glad to get almost any appointment— even a $500 one—so that I have something independent of letters for a subsistence. To coin one's brain into silver, at the nod of a master, is to my thinking, the hardest task in the world."[62] Also, his mind had a tendency to mint counterfeits. He wrote to a friend in Washington, stating his qualifications. "I battled with right good will for Harrison, when opportunity offered," Poe lied. "For the rest, I am a literary man—and I see a disposition in government to cherish letters. Have I any chance?[63]

Poe had the idea that the Tyler administration needed a cryptographer. "Nothing intelligible can be written which, with time, I cannot decipher," he boasted. Just months earlier, he had published an essay on "secret writing," celebrating the ancient art of writing "in such manner as to elude general comprehension."[64] Poe liked ciphers because he liked to send messages that readers lacking his particular genius could not decode. When he published a cryptogram he had devised, he was astonished when even a single reader wrote with the solution. "From among at least 100,000 readers," Poe wrote the code-breaker, "you and I are the only persons who have succeeded."[65]

Poe had no real chance at a political appointment. But cryptography did lead him to an ingenious solution to his problem, the dilemma of a poet determined to both court— and *dupe*—the mob. In 1841 Poe published "The Murders in the Rue Morgue," the thrilling story of a crime solved by a code-cracking French detective named C. Auguste *Dupin*. (The murderer turns out to be an orang-outang.) With Dupin, Poe channeled his desire to write above his readers into a character much like himself, a man who had once been wealthy but who, "by a variety of untoward events, had been reduced to such poverty that the energy of his character succumbed beneath it." Dupin has a very Poe-ish intelligence; he is "fond of enigmas, of conundrums, hieroglyphics; exhibiting in his solutions of each a degree of acumen which appears to the ordinary apprehension praeternatural." And, like Poe, he gloats at the distance between his own powers of perception and everyone else's: Dupin boasts, "with a low chuckling laugh, that most men, in respect to himself, wore windows in their bosoms."

If Dupin sounds uncannily familiar, that's only because Sir Arthur Conan Doyle, like every other author of detective fiction, is, incalculably, in Poe's debt.[66] "The children of Poe" is what Stephen King once called his guild, and very reasonably. But horror stories, however much they borrow from Poe (especially his exquisite psychological sophistication), predate him, and have very many other sources. Not so the literary sleuth. All detective stories and police procedurals begin with the intellectually imperious C. Auguste Dupin: methodical, eccentric, calculating . . . and insulting. We, mere readers, are so many Watsons, Hastingses, and Goodwins. Poe is the only Holmes.

Poe wrote his most popular story, "The Gold-bug," just before the nation at last emerged from depression. In January 1842, his wife had begun to cough blood; she would eventually be consumed, as Poe's mother had been, by tuberculosis. The squalid conditions in which the Poes lived didn't help.[67] Poe begged Graham for an advance of two months salary.[68] In March, Poe met Charles Dickens, who was on his American tour.[69] By April, Poe had resigned his editorship at *Graham's*, claiming he found the magazine "namby-pamby," but he had also taken to drinking again.[70] (After Poe's death, Graham, who was fond of Poe, commended his bookkeeping: "He kept his accounts, small as they were, with the accuracy of a banker.")[71] When Rufus Griswold replaced Poe as editor of *Graham's*, a friend of Poe's printed a squib: "We would give more for Edgar A. Poe's toe nail, than we would for Rueful Grizzle's soul."[72] Shortly afterwards, Poe reviewed Griswold's *Poets and Poetry of America*, remarking that Griswold had included in his anthology poets Poe deemed beneath contempt. (Privately, Poe went further, calling Griswold's book "an outrageous humbug.")[73] The battle between Griswold and Poe would shape Poe's legacy for a century.

"My only hope of relief is the 'Bankrupt Act,'" Poe wrote in June.[74] He shopped around "The Mystery of Marie Roget," attempting to sell the story, a sequel to "Murders in the Rue Morgue," at a discount, telling one editor that Graham would have paid him $100; "Of course I could not afford to make you an absolute present of it—but if you are willing to take it, I will say $40."[75] A friend who visited him that fall was mortified to find that Poe and his wife and Mrs. Clemm had a hard time, and took a long while, to come up with anything to serve him to eat.[76] Then Poe, who, despite his claim that he had campaigned for Harrison, had very little commitment to any particular political party, offered to prostitute *The Stylus* to the Tyler administration. "It has been hinted to me that I will receive the most effectual patronage from Government, for a journal which will admit occasional papers in support of the Administration."[77]

Early in 1843, Poe went to Washington, to curry favor, but he drank too much and abused his hosts. He promised to join a temperance society.[78] A journalist who met Poe on the streets of the capital found him "seedy and woebegone." Poe, who had not eaten in two days, begged for a loan of fifty cents.[79] Just weeks later, Poe heard about a contest, sponsored by the *Dollar Newspaper*, for the best short story. The prize was a hundred dollars: "*Very Liberal Offers and No Humbug*" read one version of the contest announcement.[80] Poe had recently finished "The Gold-bug" and had sold it to Graham for fifty-two dollars.[81] Thinking to earn that extra forty-eight dollars, he returned Graham's money and submitted his story to the jury. He won first prize. The theme, another sign of the times, was clear enough: "The Banker's Daughter" took second prize; third went to a story called "Marrying for Money."[82]

"The Gold-bug" was printed in the *Dollar Newspaper* in June and July 1843. Its Dupin-like protagonist, William Legrand, "had once been wealthy; but a series of misfortunes had reduced him to want." Legrand lives on Sullivan's Island, off South Carolina, with a Newfoundland and "an old Negro, called Jupiter." Jupiter tells a spooky story: Legrand has discovered a strange beetle and, ever since, has been puzzling over "a syphon wid de figgurs on de slate—de queerest figgurs I ebber did see. Ise gittin' to be skeered." Poe's racism ran very deep. Jupiter is the gothic tale-teller inside "The Gold-bug," an echo of Juniper, the gothic-tale-writing baboon of "How to Write an Article for Blackwood Magazine." Dark and darker.

"The Gold-bug" is a tangle of puns, many of them, as the literary scholar Marc Shell has pointed out, having to do with currency. Legrand has found a bug the color of gold. "De bug is a goole bug," says Jupiter. It is, that is, a ghoul bug. It looks as if it's made of gold, but it's not. "Dey aint *no* tin in him, Massa," says Jupiter. There's nothing in him, no tin, and no gold, either. Legrand has also found a parchment, made of goat's skin, *kid's* skin. It contains a map to a treasure buried on the island by the pirate, Captain Kidd. This pun Legrand himself has to figure out, to find the buried treasure. (Kidd's map is, in this sense, a guide to Poe's tales themselves: is Poe kidding or not? Are the tales a joke, and worthless, or brilliant, and priceless?)[83] The parchment is covered with invisible ink, which, as Legrand eventually discovers, conceals a cryptogram. After decoding the cipher, Legrand takes Jupiter, the dog, and the befuddled narrator on a hunt for the buried treasure, which turns out to be a chest of jewels and silver and gold coins "of incalculable value," or, more precisely, $1.5 million.

Poe's intent in writing "The Gold-bug," one reviewer noted, "was evidently to write a popular tale: money, and the finding of money being chosen as the most popular thesis."[84] When a critic called the prize "A Decided Humbug" and suggested that no editor could possibly have paid Poe a hundred dollars for such "unmitigated trash," Poe sued for libel and won a retraction.[85] Still the story is, itself, a kind of hoax. It aspires to popularity by assaulting the very idea of a popular audience. Poe's tales, like paper money, promise value even as they flaunt their own worthlessness. Like the beetle of its title, "The Gold-bug," the story, is "no tin," too.

After "The Gold-bug," Poe's life went from bad to worse.[86] In late 1843, when Poe's friends heard that Poe's wife and mother-in-law were starving, they gave him fifteen dollars, only to come across him, an hour later, drunk on the street.[87] In 1844, Poe was down to his last four dollars.[88] The publication of "The Raven" the next year didn't rescue him from poverty but it did propel him, almost overnight, to literary celebrity. This he simply sabotaged. He became editor and then owner of *The Broadway Journal*, a New York weekly. But the tone of his criticism grew more rancorous, especially with the ill-advised publication in *Godey's Lady's Book* of a series of sketches called "The Literati of New York City: Some Honest Opinions at Random Respecting Their Authorial Merits, with Occasional Words of Personality." Invited to Boston to deliver a lecture on American poetry, he read, instead, a poem he wrote when he was a child (and later, in the *Broadway Journal*, confessed, without apology, that he had been drunk). He tried to keep the magazine afloat, writing to a friend, pleading, "So help me Heaven, I have sent and gone personally in all the nooks & corners of Broker-Land & such a thing as the money you speak of—is *not to be obtained*."[89] The *Broadway Journal* folded in 1846. Virginia Poe's prolonged illness left her husband in tatters. "I drank, God only knows how often or how much," Poe admitted.[90] He had a breakdown. His wife died in January 1847. Near the end of his own life, Poe may have descended again into lunacy. "I was never *really* insane, except on occasions where my heart was touched," he insisted, just months before his death, when he was, at best, disordered to the point of necromaniacal incoherence. "I have been taken to prison once since I came here for getting drunk; but *then*

I was not. It was about Virginia."[91] The cause of his death remains mysterious.

Poe was buried in Baltimore on October 9, 1849.[92] "Nothing further then he uttered—not a feather then he fluttered." Days after Poe's funeral, Rufus Griswold wrote a breathtakingly belligerent obituary; Poe's passing "will startle many but few will be grieved by it." Then Maria Clemm, in a singularly unfortunate act of either ignorance or avarice, gave Griswold power of attorney and sold him Poe's papers. (Poe's papers turned out to be worth something after all.) Griswold became Poe's literary executor. A year later, he wrote a biography of Poe in which he distorted the historical record, publishing slanders and forgeries, to make Poe seem a fiend.[93]

Between Poe's lies and Griswold's forgeries, it's no easy thing to take the measure of Edgar A. Poe. *Was the man an utter genius or a complete fraud?* is a question that has riddled Poe scholarship for a century and a half.[94] James Russell Lowell wrote, the year before Poe died: "There comes Poe, with his raven, like Barnaby Rudge, / Three fifths of him genius and two fifths sheer fudge."[95] The muddle goes back to Poe himself, who was forever calculating: half banter? half satire? Two dollars a page, or four? Less Byron, more gore?

> And the raven, never flitting, still is sitting, still is sitting
> On the pallid bust of Pallas just above my chamber door;
> And his eyes have all the seeming of a demon's that is
>     dreaming,
> And the lamp-light o'er him streaming throws his shadow on
>     the floor;
> And my soul from out that shadow that lies floating on the
>     floor
>         Shall be lifted—nevermore!

Three-fifths Romantic; two-fifths poor.

# 12

# PRESIDENT TOM'S CABIN

In 1852, when Harriet Beecher Stowe finished *Uncle Tom's Cabin*, she wrote to her congressman, Horace Mann (who happened to be Nathaniel Hawthorne's brother-in-law), to beg a favor. Might he know how to get a copy of her book to Charles Dickens? "Were the subject any other I should think this impertinent & Egotistical," Stowe wrote, making of demurral a poor cloak for ambition.[1] (Stowe's mealy-mouthed "affectation of humility" was the least of what Dickens would grow to despise about her; what really blew his stack was when she pried into the private lives of public men: "Wish Mrs. Stowe was in the pillory," he cursed, when Stowe reported, in the *Atlantic*, on Byron's romance with his half-sister, just the sort of exposé that led Dickens, who conducted a secret, adulterous affair for thirteen years, to burn his papers.)[2] But Stowe had reason to expect Dickens's sympathy with her antislavery screed. A decade earlier, the English novelist, upon completing an unhappy tour of the United States, judged the country "the heaviest blow ever dealt at liberty." And in *Martin Chuzzlewit* (1844), he smeared that "noble patriot," Thomas Jefferson, "who dreamed of Freedom in a slave's embrace."[3] Dickens was quoting from the Irish poet, Thomas Moore, who visited the United States in 1803, the year after rumors that the then-president had fathered children by one of his slaves became public, by way of the *Richmond Recorder*, in which a scurrilous Scots journalist named James Callender alleged that Jefferson "keeps, and for many years past has kept, as his concubine, one of his own slaves. Her name is SALLY." (Callender drowned himself in the James River in 1803, but even smarmy, unstable scandalmongers sometimes get a story straight.) Moore had written: "The weary statesman for repose hath fled / From halls of council to his negro's shed, / Where blest he woos some black Aspasia's grace, / And dreams of freedom in his slave's embrace."[4] Onto this, Dickens tacked a coda: "and waking sold her offspring and his own at public markets."

The sexually sated author of the Declaration of Independence pocketing a tidy sum by peddling his own progeny lends an Oliverian twist to what was already a seedy story. It is not, however, true. After Thomas Jefferson died, on July 4, 1826, his slaves were sold at auction, but not Sally Hemings's children, as the legal scholar Annette Gordon-Reed chronicled in *The Hemingses of Monticello: An American Family*, in 2008. Four of Sally Hemings's children were alive when Jefferson died; two had already left Monticello; Jefferson freed the other two in his Will.

Dickens may have been taking license; more likely, he genuinely believed Jefferson had sold his own children. There were plenty of places he could have gotten this impression. In 1838, the abolitionist newspaper, the *Liberator*, reported that Jefferson's children, twelve years after their father's death, still toiled in bondage. An eyewitness claimed to have seen one of them on the auction block at the most infamous slave market in America: "the DAUGHTER of THOMAS JEFFERSON SOLD in New Orleans, for ONE THOUSAND DOLLARS." This rumor, picked up by the London *Morning Chronicle*, isn't true, either. But Sally Hemings did have a daughter. Her name was Harriet. She left Monticello in 1822, when she was twenty-one. "Harriet. Sally's run," Jefferson wrote in his "Farm Book," where he kept track of his human property, a population that needing minding, since Jefferson was the second-largest slaveholder in Virginia. But Harriet didn't *run*. "She was nearly as white as anybody, and very beautiful," remembered one of Jefferson's overseers, who also said Jefferson gave him fifty dollars to give to the girl, and paid for her ride, by stage, to Philadelphia. A widely circulated rumor, reported by yet another literary English rambler, Frances Trollope (Anthony Trollope's mother), in her 1832 *Domestic Manners of the Americans* turns out to be right: "when, as it sometimes happened, his children by Quadroon slaves were white enough to escape suspicion of their origin, he did not pursue them if they attempted to escape."

Truth notwithstanding, the false report—that Jefferson's daughter was pawned off to the highest bidder—made a good story, or, at least, that's what William Wells Brown thought when he wrote *Clotel; Or, The President's Daughter*, the first African American novel, published in 1853, a year after *Uncle Tom's Cabin*. Brown knew a thing or two about what Stowe, in her Dickensian subtitle, called "Life among the Lowly." Stowe's novel opens in Kentucky; Brown was born there. He worked for a Mississippi River slave trader, dying the hair of gray-haired slaves black, that they might fetch a better price; he had seen his own sister carried away to be sold at auction; he had tried to escape with his mother in 1833 and succeeded, the next year, only by leaving her behind. In 1847, two years after the celebrated abolitionist and former slave Frederick Douglass published the story of his life, Wells told his own not entirely unvarnished tale, *The Narrative of William W. Brown, a Fugitive Slave, Written by Himself*. When Stowe's novel made publishing history (it sold ten thousand copies in its first week), Brown was living in London, rallying British sympathy for the American abolitionist movement. Mostly, he lectured. But drumming up support by writing a novel suddenly seemed a fine idea. And what better plot than the shocking story that had animated the pen of Dickens himself?

Brown's characters are different from Uncle Tom, Eliza, and Topsy, but they're no less didactic, and his novel, like Stowe's, follows their desperate fates, trial heaped upon tribulation, like so many ice floes crowding the Mississippi. Clotel, sold at auction, makes her escape by disguising herself as an Italian gentleman. Captured, she is imprisoned in a "negro pen" in Richmond. She flees but, crossing a bridge from Virginia to Washington—"within plain sight of the President's house"— she is once again trapped. With a last look toward heaven, she leaps into the Potomac: "Thus died Clotel, the daughter of Thomas Jefferson," writes Brown, at the close of a novel in which he had included a chapter titled "Truth Stranger Than Fiction."[5]

It took a very long time for historians to take this story seriously or even to begin to bother to sort out fact from fiction. Just why was the subject of Gordon-Reed's 1997 tour-de-force, *Thomas Jefferson and Sally Hemings: An American Controversy*, a book that was as much a painstaking investigation of the documentary record as a devastating brief on standards of evidence in historical research. For Gordon-Reed, the real scandal wasn't what happened between Jefferson and Hemings. The real scandal was how far historians, and especially the clan of Jefferson biographers, had been willing to go to ignore evidence right in front of them, documents like Jefferson's "Farm Book," even, but, especially, testimony about things said and done by the Hemingses themselves, as if what the Hemingses said and did didn't matter, as if their testimony couldn't possibly be true.[6] Taking a lawyer's view of the case, Gordon-Reed pieced together the evidence, weighed it, and delivered a summation: Jefferson fathered those children. And he freed them,

or let them go when they reached the age of twenty-one, because Sally Hemings had extracted from him, in 1789, at the
beginning of their thirty-eight-year affair, a promise that he
would do exactly that.

Gordon-Reed's *Thomas Jefferson and Sally Hemings* was
published the same year as Joseph Ellis's elegiac biography,
*American Sphinx: The Character of Thomas Jefferson* in which
Ellis had asserted—intuited, actually, since there is no hard
evidence for this whatsoever—that Jefferson who, as is well
documented, had been an ardent lover of women, and who
had gotten his wife pregnant seven times in ten years, had
never slept with the very beautiful Sally Hemings (who greatly
resembled his wife, her half-sister, a woman Jefferson adored),
because, the day his wife died (when Jefferson was thirty-six),
he had lost interest in sex, altogether and forever, to the point
of impotence.[7] The man was a statue. *American Sphinx* won the
National Book Award.

A few months later, Eugene Foster, a retired University
of Virginia professor of pathology, published in *Nature* the
results of DNA tests he had undertaken, working with scientists in Oxford, Leicester, and Leiden, on Hemings and
Jefferson blood. Foster tested the descendants of Field Jefferson, Thomas Jefferson's uncle, and of Eston Hemings, Sally
Hemings's youngest son. (The Y chromosome passes down
through males virtually intact, but Jefferson's only son by his
wife died in infancy, which is why Foster had to find his Jeffersonian Y elsewhere.) The link proved a relationship: Eston
Hemings's male descendants have the Jeffersonian Y. This
doesn't prove that all of Sally Hemings's children, or even
Eston, were fathered by Thomas Jefferson. It proves only that
Eston's father was *a* Jefferson. Alas, there just isn't another Jefferson handy, there at Monticello, and with a Y in his pocket,
during the months Hemings conceived. Ellis, in preface to the
paperback edition of his biography, graciously conceded the

argument. "Prior to the evidence," he wrote, "one might have reasonably concluded that Jefferson was living a paradox. Now it was difficult to avoid the conclusion that he was living a lie."[8] Sally Hemings's children were all but certainly Thomas Jefferson's.

Lost in the DNA-driven consensus, however, was Gordon-Reed's point. It ought never to have taken a lab test to bolster a claim deducible from the documentary record. At a conference at Monticello in 1999, Gordon-Reed revisited the case:

> It is true that we do not and will never have the details of what went on between Jefferson and Hemings and their children. This does not mean that we have nothing to go on. Perhaps the most persistent, and ultimately damaging, feature of the original debate over whether the relationship existed at all was the tight rein placed upon the historical imagination. One was simply not to let one's mind wander too freely over the matter. Brainstorming, drawing reasonable inferences from actions, attempting to piece together a plausible view of the matter were shunted into the category of illegitimate speculation, as grave an offense as outright lying.

Deductions can be wrong. But they're not illicit: they're how history, at its best, makes sense of a senseless world.

Gordon-Reed's single most revealing source was Madison Hemings's memoir, printed by an Ohio newspaperman named S. E. Wetmore in an obscure newspaper called the *Pike County Republican*, in March 1873. (Wetmore first heard about Hemings from a census taker in neighboring county who, in his 1870 census, noted next to his name: "This man is the son of Thomas Jefferson.") Five months after Wetmore published Hemings's story, James Parton—he of "Mrs. Eaton's knocker"—writing in the *Atlantic*, summarily dismissed it: "Mr. Hemings has been misinformed."

Parton believed that Hemings was either a fraud or a fool. He did not seek him out; he did not consider what he said; he did not even bother to refute him. He disregarded him. Gordon-Reed attributed this error to a number of stereotypes: Parton saw Hemings as an angry ex-slave, a "darky with delusions of grandeur," a feeble-minded, childlike pawn of a politically motivated white man. Parton probably did see Hemings this way. But it is also true that Madison Hemings's credibility had already been damaged, long before James Parton came along, by every nineteenth-century writer, black and white alike, who made use of the Jefferson-Hemings legend. Callendar poked a hole. Dickens left a dent. William Wells Brown dealt a blow. Abolitionists wanted, urgently, desperately, frantically, to end slavery. Their aim was to arouse sympathy. They told very many stories. Picturing white men preying on black women was their stock and trade. Stowe went further: she turned black men into feckless, sexless children. (That's one reason, but just one, why James Baldwin eviscerated *Uncle Tom's Cabin* in *Notes of a Native Son*; another was Stowe's failure to answer, or even to address, "the only important question" about slavery: "what was it that moved her people to such deeds"?)[9] Hawking hackneyed stories at the expense of black men's humanity came with a cost: who would believe Madison Hemings? (Nor did it help that Wetmore, in a shout-out to Stowe, titled the column in which he printed Hemings's memoir "Life among the Lowly.") Answering slavery with sentimentality carried a price, too: who could imagine Jefferson's daughter doing anything but dying?

This wasn't only James Callendar's fault, or Harriet Beecher Stowe's, or James Parton's. Journalists, novelists, historians: everyone had a hand. For decades, on both sides of the Mason-Dixon line, the gaveling off of Thomas Jefferson's children was a story either too awful to be true or too useful to be proven false. Sally Hemings lived in Richmond until 1836. Eston Hemings lived twenty years more. Madison Hemings only died in 1878. An enterprising investigator might have looked up any of them up, long before 1873, except . . . what if their stories weren't as poignant as what he wanted to print?

Instead of taking Parton's witnesses at their word, Gordon-Reed questioned them. Parton alluded to a letter he had in possession, written by yet another biographer, Henry Randall, in 1868. In an interview, Thomas Jefferson Randolph, Jefferson's grandson, told Randall that Sally Hemings "had children which resembled Mr. Jefferson so closely that it was plain that they had his blood in their veins," but this, Randolph insisted, was because they were the children of Peter Carr, Jefferson's nephew.[10] This was enough to satisfy Randall, and Parton, too. But Gordon-Reed asked, in her cross-examination of the evidence: If Randolph didn't have something still more scandalous to hide, why admit that he was related to the Hemingses? She also eliminated Carr, and also his brother, by pointing out something that Randall and Parton, had they bothered to look, could have discovered. To Monticello, Jefferson came and went (he was gone at least two-thirds of the time); the Carr brothers were nearly always near-to-hand.[11] "Why could not Peter Carr or Samuel Carr get Sally Hemings pregnant when Thomas Jefferson was not at Monticello," asked Gordon-Reed, "not once in fifteen years?"[12] (The DNA results subsequently vindicated her. Foster tested the Carr Y, too. It didn't match.)

Gordon-Reed rested her case, and set about writing history. She reasoned from analogy. She speculated. She asked her reader to trust her knowledge of human nature. Arguments from human nature can be persuasive, but, when the wind blows, they tend to totter. For one thing, "human nature" has a history. Enlightenment meditations on the subject, like David Hume's 1739–40 *Treatise of Human Nature*, influenced Jefferson's views on race. (Hume thought that blacks were "naturally inferior to the Whites," and even inhuman: "There scarcely ever was a civilized nation of that complexion, nor even any individual, eminent either in action or speculation.") For another, arguments from human nature are only as subtle and perceptive as the people who make them. Most of us are easily duped. "Error, Sir," Laurence Sterne wrote in *Tristram Shandy* (Jefferson's favorite novel), "creeps in thro' the minute holes and small crevices which human nature leaves unguarded." It was Ellis's confidence that he understood Jefferson's character, after all, which led him to his impotence theory.

Harriet Hemings had seven white great-grandparents; she was, in the idiom of the time, an "octoroon." She was also, because of a precedent-defying seventeenth-century Virginia statute, Thomas Jefferson's property. In English law, children inherit their status from their fathers. Relying on that law, a woman with an African mother and an English father successfully sued for her freedom in Virginia in 1655. Not long after, the House of Burgesses, eager to avoid another legal challenge, turned English law upside down.[13] In 1662, two years after the founding of the Company of Royal Adventurers to Africa— that is, just when the British were beginning to dominate the slave trade—Virginians answered doubts about "whether children got by an Englishman upon a Negro woman should be slave or ffree" by reaching back to an archaic Roman rule, *partus sequitur ventrem* (you are what your mother was).[14]

Generations passed. There was much begetting. About 1735, an Englishman named Captain Hemings had sex with a "Full blooded African Woman," a slave, whose name has not survived. She gave birth to a daughter. Hemings tried to buy the child, apparently to free her, but her owner refused to sell; he was curious to see how the girl would turn out. Hemings tried to steal her; he failed. In 1746, the girl, Elizabeth Hemings, came to be the property of an Englishman named John Wayles, when he married Frances Epps. (Eleven-year-old Hemings was part of the marriage settlement.) Wayles married three times; his children by his first wife included a daughter, Martha, born in 1750. After the death of his third wife, Wayles did not marry again. But he did start having sex with Elizabeth Hemings, by whom he had six children, including a daughter, Sally, born in 1773. In 1772, Martha Wayles married Thomas Jefferson. After John Wayles's death in 1773, Elizabeth Hemings and all of her children came to live at Monticello. In 1782, when Sally Hemings was nine, Martha Jefferson died. Mrs. Jefferson, on her deathbed, extracted from her altogether bereft and nearly unmoored husband a promise that he would never remarry. Four years later Jefferson drafted a bill passed by the Virginia legislature decreeing that "a marriage between a person of free condition and a slave, or between a white person and a negro, or between a white person and a mulatto, shall be null." In 1789, when sixteen-year-old Sally Hemings was living with forty-three-year-old Jefferson in Paris, she became pregnant (she later either miscarried or lost the child during or soon after childbirth).

Gordon-Reed argued that Hemings made a deal with Jefferson. (Madison Hemings called it a "treaty.") She knew she could stay in Paris, where she would be free; slavery was illegal in France. She decided to return to Virginia because, as most people would, she missed her family. And, crucially, Jefferson promised her that he would free all her children when they reached the age of twenty-one. Maybe Hemings loved Jefferson; maybe he loved her, too. (In 1974, Fawn Brodie wrote a history supposing this to be the case, and more than one romance novel assumes the same.) Gordon-Reed knew that this question is important, since Jefferson and Hemings are more than people, they're symbols, too. But symbols only get you so far. "The romance is not in saying that they may have loved one another," Gordon-Reed wrote. "The romance is in thinking that it made any difference if they did."[15] Nothing redeems slavery.

Jefferson, the architect of our freedom, could not reckon slavery's toll. "The whole commerce between master and slave is a perpetual exercise of the most boisterous passions, the most unremitting despotism on the one part, and degrading submission on the other," he wrote in 1782, the year his wife died. "The man must be a prodigy who can retain his manners and morals undepraved by such circumstances." Jefferson could not abide slavery. Neither could he imagine his life, or the Union, without it. And he knew its end would not come without bloodshed. "I tremble for my country when I reflect that God is just; that his justice cannot sleep forever."[16]

Moral impotence is a muffled agony. American sphinx? American Achilles.

Sally Hemings bore her last child in 1808. In 1815, the aging former president—who never admitted, publicly, anyway, that he was the father of Hemings's children—wrote a letter in which he wrestled with a matter—a "mathematical problem"—that had long vexed him. Just how many generations had to pass before a child with a full-blooded African ancestor could be called "white"?

> Let us express the pure blood of the white in the capital letters of the printed alphabet, and any given mixture of either, by way of abridgment in MS. Letters.

Let the first crossing be of $a$, a pure negro, with A, a pure white. The unit of blood of the issue being composed of the half of that of each parent, will be $a/2 + A/2$. Call it, for abbreviation, $h$ (half blood).

The letter goes on for a while. Suffice to say: $b$ is the second crossing, $q$ is a quadroon, $c$ is the third crossing.

Let the third crossing be of $q$ and C, their offspring will be $q/2 + C/2 = A/8 + B/4 + C/2$, call this $e$ (eighth), who having less than ¼ of $a$, or of pure negro blood, to wit 1/8 only, is no longer a mulatto, so that a third cross clears the blood.

To Thomas Jefferson, Harriet Hemings was $e$. What more she meant to him probably does depend as much on your view of human nature as on the documentary record. After Harriet Hemings took a stagecoach to Philadelphia in 1822, she traveled on to the nation's capital, where her older brother, Beverly, lived as a white man. "She thought it to her interest, on going to Washington, to assume the role of a white woman," said Madison Hemings, the only one of Sally Hemings's children to live his life as an African American. *She thought it to her interest.* He seems never to have forgiven her. "And by her dress and conduct as such I am not aware that her identity as Harriet Hemings of Monticello has ever been discovered." Finding her now would be difficult. "Harriet married a white man in good standing in Washington City, whose name I could give," Madison said, "but will not, for prudential reasons."

Truth isn't always stranger than nineteenth-century fiction but, usually, it's less melodramatic. Thomas Jefferson's daughter didn't leap to a watery grave. As late as the 1860s, years after *Clotel* was published, she was still alive—within plain sight of the White House after all—pursuing whatever liberty, and happiness, she could find.

# 13

# PRIDE OF THE PRAIRIE

In 1856, when he was forty-seven years old and long since a legend, Christopher Houston Carson, better known as Kit, told the story of his life. "I was born on the 24 December 1809 in Madison County, Kentucky," he began. Before he was two, his family moved to Missouri. At sixteen, he was apprenticed to a saddle maker but he ran away, joined a caravan heading for Santa Fe, and never looked back. Across the Rockies, up and down the Missouri, from Salt Lake to Sutter's Fort, he trapped beaver, hunted buffalo, traded furs, and mined for copper. He ate roots and elk and, in a pinch, roasted a foal cut from a mare's womb. He was a mountain man. Once a year he treated himself to coffee, two dollars a pint. He ran from grizzly bears and chased down horse-thieves. He killed very many Indians. He was shot twice, once in a gunfight with thirty Blackfeet, once in a showdown with a drunken Frenchman.[1] In 1843–44 and again in 1845, he guided the explorer John C. Frémont on his grueling overland expeditions to California and Oregon. During the Mexican War (1846–48), he covered sixteen thousand miles, by mule, delivering messages from the front to President James K. Polk in Washington, and back again.[2] Afterwards, he settled in Taos—for a while anyway—to raise a family and a flock of sheep with his wife,

Josepha Jamarilla; he had married her in 1843, when he was thirty-four and she was fourteen.[3]

In dictating his memoirs, Carson, who was illiterate, left out more than he told. He offered not a word about his two Indian wives—Singing Grass, an Arapaho woman who died in 1842, after the birth of their second daughter; and Making-Out-Road, a Cheyenne girl who turned out not to suit him. Still, his tale must have taken a while to tell. When he was finished, he gave the manuscript to a Taos businessman and ersatz literary agent named Jesse B. Turley. Turley wanted to find someone to write a biography of Carson, based on the memoirs. He thought about tackling it himself, but he soon thought better of it and instead offered the job to Washington Irving. Irving said no; he was busy writing his *Life of Washington*. Eventually, Turley signed an agreement with DeWitt Clinton Peters, a U.S. Army surgeon who knew Carson well. Carson had "dictated the facts," it remained only for Peters to write the book. Peters, Turley, and Carson would divide the profits. In 1858, a New York publisher brought out Peters's *Life and Adventures of Kit Carson . . . from Facts Narrated by Himself.* In its preface Peters boasted, "This book is a book of solid truth."[4]

As solid butter in Death Valley, that is. The manuscript of Carson's memoirs—rediscovered in Paris in 1905—is barely fifty pages; Peters' book is more than five hundred. Ah, but those four hundred and fifty pages of padding! Where Carson explained running away from his apprenticeship with a six-worded-shrug—"The business did not suit me"—Peters squared his shoulders and roared: "Saddlery is a honorable employment; but saddlery never made a greater mistake than when it strove to hitch to its traces the bold impulse, the wild yearning, the sinewy muscle of Kit Carson."[5]

Peters reputedly earned $20,000 from *The Life and Adventures of Kit Carson.* Out West, that kind of cash would have bought a lot of coffee. But neither Carson nor Turley ever saw a penny of it. Still, Carson hadn't done it just for the money. He wanted to set the record straight. He soon found out he had failed. When parts of the book were read to him, he is reported to have said he reckoned Peters had "laid it on a leetle too thick."[6]

Kit Carson, man of the mountains, man among men, made his literary debut in 1845 and 1846, in Frémont's wildly popular reports of his expeditions, in which the explorer painted his intrepid guide as a latter-day Leatherstocking, a Hawkeye who drew "from association with uncultivated nature, not the rudeness and sensualism of the savage, but genuine simplicity and truthfulness of disposition, and generosity, bravery, and single heartedness to a degree rarely found in society."[7] Almost overnight, Carson became both a national hero and a stock character in pulp fiction. In 1849, he turned up in a twenty-five-cent novel published in Boston, Charles Averill's *Kit Carson*, in which Carson is described as "a man of powerful proportions and Herculean stature" (Carson was actually five-foot-four).[8] In one scene, the coon-hatted Hercules, the Pride of the Prairie, rescues a young easterner from marauding Indians by shooting ten "howling savages" with ten shots of his trusty rifle. "Hold my powder horn for me, stranger," Carson shouts, "while I jest pick off a couple of these infarnal varmints, with *Old Sacramento!*"[9]

In his memoirs, the real Carson was at pains to explain that while he had tried to rescue more than a few captives, he wasn't always successful. In New Mexico late in 1849, he trailed Apaches who had attacked a wagon train and captured a settler named Ann White. After enduring two long weeks of captivity, White was killed just moments before Carson and his party reached her. Rummaging through the abandoned Apache camp where White had been prisoner, Carson found a copy of Averill's just-published *Kit Carson*; Ann White had carried it with her all the way from Missouri. "The book was the first of its kind I had ever seen, in which I was made a great hero, slaying Indians by the hundred," Carson recalled, ruefully. "I have often thought that as Mrs. White would read the same, and knowing that I lived near, she prayed for my appearance and that she would be saved." She had held out hope for a man who never existed. Later, when a friend offered him a gift of Averill's book, Carson told him: "Burn the damn thing."[10]

But this was not to be the last encounter between Kit Carson and his taller, prouder, and deadlier doppelganger. Beginning in 1860, after new technologies—the steam press and the stereotype plate—slashed publishers' printing costs, even more outrageous Carson caricatures began appearing in dime novels, ten-cent books so full of gore and war they were dubbed "blood-and-thunders." Between 1860 and 1900, Carson made an appearance in more than seventy stories.[11] In *The Fighting Trapper; Kit Carson to the Rescue* (written in 1874 by a New Jersey school superintendent named Edward Ellis using the pen-name "Captain James Fenimore Cooper Adams"), he kills Indians two at a time, a knife in each hand.[12] In this genre, that counts as restraint. Not long before he died, in 1868, Kit Carson was shown a dime novel cover featuring a picture of a dashing young Kit "slaying seven Indians with one hand, while he clasped a fainting maiden with the other." As the story goes, the old man stared at it for a while, fiddled with his spectacles a bit, and declared, "That there may have happened, but I ain't got no recollection of it."[13]

It was a bit of a surprise, then, that Hampton Sides's 2006 book about Carson was called *Blood and Thunder: An Epic of the American West*. What part of the dime novel tradition is worth echoing? Sides's book was an ambitious and sprawling account of the winning of the American West; it ranged over a century and across a continent. Carson, on horseback, is never far from center stage. But Sides's book was decidedly not a biography; Carson didn't even rate a place in the book's subtitle. After having decorated so many book covers, Carson is probably better left off: he had become controversial. By the end of the twentieth century, Carson had been reinvented as one of the West's most notorious villains, the "Columbus of the West," as he was sometimes called, and not by people who mean that as a compliment. The nineteenth-century dime novel's rifle-toting hero had become—and is arguably, and ironically, the chief source for—the late twentieth-century's genocidal madman. In 1990, vandals spray-painted swastikas and the word "Nazi" on Carson's tomb in Taos. In 1993, the Kit Carson Historic Museum held a debate titled "Kit Carson: Indian Fighter or Indian Killer?"[14]

But Carson made no appearance on Sides's cover for another reason. Sides admired Carson. He even shared a kind of lineage with him. During the American Revolution, Kit Carson's father served under Wade Hampton, a prodigiously wealthy South Carolina plantation owner. Kit Carson's brother, Hampton Carson, was named after him, as have been so many southern boys, including Wade Hampton Sides. Hampton Sides was no kin to Christopher Houston Carson, but he has that tie to Carson's father's commander, and he made his peace with it. "Yes, Christopher Carson was a lovable man," Sides wrote. "He was also a natural born killer."[15] With that, he dismissed decades of freighted and fruitless debate, having decided, instead, to use Carson as both his story's hero and its villain.

An editor-at-large for *Outside* magazine, Sides placed his story's action in a vivid landscape of mesas and deserts, pueblos and canyons. Las Vegas is "a hodgepodge of adobe houses, set among rustling cornfields irrigated by a muddy acequia that seeped from the Gallinas River."[16] On a march through what is now western Arizona and eastern California, American soldiers trudged "past mesquite and creosote, through octillo and paloverde, across dunes of rippled sand. They beheld the splendid weirdness of the century plant and the joshua tree and encountered saguaro cactus for the first time, the giant of the Sonoran desert, with its mighty fluted trunks and sagging humanlike arms."[17]

If, against this backdrop, Carson was Sides's main character, he led a large ensemble cast of larger-than-life American men: John C. Fremont, Thomas Hart Benton, Stephen Kearney. But Sides was especially keen to make Carson yield the stage to Indians: Apache, Kiowa, Hopi, Comanche, Ute, and, most of all, Navajo. Here, too, he lingered over the telling detail. Describing Navajo warriors he wrote: "They wielded clubs and carried shields made of buckskin layers taken from a deer's hip, where the hide is thickest. They had images of serpents painted on the soles of their moccasins to give them a snakelike sneakiness as they approached their quarry. Their steel-tipped arrowheads were daubed with rattlesnake blood and prickly pear pulp mixed with charcoal taken from a tree that had been struck by lightning."[18]

In *Blood and Thunder*, Sides chronicled American expansion into what is now the southwestern United States, beginning with the overland travels of men like Carson and Frémont and the skirmishes leading up to the Mexican War, a gruesome two-year conflict in which nearly 14,000 Americans and as many as 25,000 Mexicans were killed. At that war's end, with the Treaty of Guadalupe Hidalgo in 1848, the United States acquired 1.2 million square miles of territory—most of what is now California, New Mexico, Arizona, Nevada, Texas, and Utah, and parts of Colorado and Wyoming—increasing the size of the country by more than 66 percent.[19]

Sides carried his sweeping narrative through the 1850s, largely through the vehicle of Kit Carson's comings and goings. Much of this, however, was by way of set up for the sorry story Sides most wanted to tell: in 1864, Carson, now a U.S. Army colonel commanding nearly a thousand men, reduced the Navajo people to starvation by burning their crops and killing their livestock. The brutality of the campaign, intended to force the Navajo to agree to relocate, was without precedent. Carson estimated that his men destroyed nearly two million pounds of food. In the Navajo stronghold of the Canyon de Chelly, Carson's troops burned and chopped down three thousand peach trees. And then they burned the Navajos' baskets and smashed their pots, so that they couldn't carry or store what little food they had. "If there was ever a grandeur or majesty to warfare, surely none could be found here," Sides wrote.[20] In the end, eight thousand Navajos left their land, only to be led on a disastrous three-hundred-mile march known as the Long Walk.

Sides's ambition was to tell the whole of this epic story, from the opening of the Santa Fe Trail in 1824 to the Navajo Long Walk forty years later, not just from Carson's vantage, but also, and simultaneously, from the point of view of Navajo leaders like the long-lived Narbona and his son-in-law, Manuelito. Born in 1766, Narbona became a great warrior; beginning in the 1810s, he fought the Spanish and later the Mexicans, and led the Navajo to signal victories. He witnessed the first arrival to his land of people he called "the New Men," the Americans. On the eve of the New Men's war with Mexico, in 1846, he shrewdly advocated peace with the well-armed Americans. By then, Narbona was an old man but still, at six-foot-three, a giant, "with sharp chiseled features and a mane of long white hair"—U.S. Army officers compared his appearance to that of George Washington.[21] In 1849, Narbona was shot to death by American soldiers, and then scalped, during a botched treaty negotiation near Chaco Canyon. The Philadelphia artist and naturalist Richard Kern, who was there when Narbona died, later regretted that he had failed to secure the Navajo leader's skull for his friend Dr. Samuel Morton, the famous phrenologist. Wrote Kern, "I think he had the finest head I ever saw on an Indian."[22]

More than once, Sides stretched his evidence about Narbona and other Indian men too thin. When Narbona halts a move it is because "he realized he could not lead his people farther west without angering the gods"; when he meets the Americans he asks himself, "What fickle spirits drove these men?"[23] It's one thing, and an admirable thing, to want to offer readers real-life characters to serve as foils to Kit Carson; it's another thing to make up interior monologues.

Sides's *Blood and Thunder* was a well-written account of a vast swath of history with which few Americans are familiar. Sides was also writing in a big-market genre with ties to an even more popular form. The dime novel western and the blockbuster military history are two branches of the same family tree. Sides himself explained as much. There is quite a lot of bloodshed and a good deal of bluster and stormy weather in *Blood and Thunder*: the rolling thunder of horse hooves, the roaring thunder of artillery, the lightning flash of gunfire, and the belief, among the Navajo, that thunder is manly: "A female rain was a gentle, steady mist; a male rain was an angry black thunderstorm."[24] But the "blood and thunder" of Sides's title was a very pointed reference, an homage to the dime novel.[25]

Sides's book has other borrowings from the dime novel genre: it was full of the blood-and-thunder's rhythm and romance and especially its gushing relish of reliable violence: *journey, journey, back-story, skirmish . . . GUNFIGHT!! scouting, diplomacy, failed diplomacy, kiss the wife . . . BATTLE!!* As a critic writing in the *Atlantic Monthly* in 1879 said about the dime novel, you can expect about a hundred deaths every two chapters: "The whole vast action pivots, as it were, around the muzzle of an extended revolver."[26]

Dime novels first appeared just as the Civil War broke out. Their most avid early readers were soldiers in the Union and Confederate Armies. Blood-and-thunders were "sent to the army in the field by cords, like unsawed firewood," one contemporary reported.[27] A *Kit Carson* in every rucksack. After the war, dime novel westerns cultivated a vast, largely eastern, and altogether male audience: they were the first mass market fiction sold to men and boys. At a time when the average working-class wage was six dollars a week, even newsboys could afford them. And there were plenty to choose from. Writers like Edward Ellis, using dozens of pen names, cranked out at least four titles a year; one author claimed he could turn out a new story in twenty-four hours. At the Beadle and Adams publishing house on William Street in New York, dime novels were manufactured on a literary assembly line: writers working on the third floor sent their manuscripts to editors, one floor down, who sent them downstairs to the typesetters, who carried their plates to the basement for printing and shipping. In forty years, Beadle and Adams published over seven thousand novels. The company's chief distributor had a standing order for sixty thousand copies of every new title. Four hundred twenty million pages! As the 1879 *Atlantic* critic wryly observed, blood-and-thunders constituted "the greatest literary movement, in bulk, of the age."[28]

American intellectuals couldn't stand them—and they couldn't understand them. "Why these works are popular is a problem quite as much for the moralist and the student of national character as for the critic," wrote William Everett in Boston's *North American Review* in 1864. Everett chose a sample and reported, with dismay, "Ten of these novels have we faithfully read through, and more up-hill work in the main we never had; and this while Anthony Trollope and Dickens are living, and Thackeray is only just dead."[29]

In the 1870s, the plot of dime novel westerns changed, radically. As Bill Brown explained in *Reading the West: An Anthology of Dime Westerns*, sometime after the Navajo Long Walk, "white greed replaced Indian savagery as the most familiar source of villainy." Now it was the job of straight shooters like the fictional Carson to protect peace-loving Indians from bloodthirsty, or at least land-hungry, whites. But both before and after this plot reversal, Brown argues, all dime novel westerns did the same thing: they unified the North and the South in a fiction that "disengaged the story of the West from the story of the nation."[30] Readers, from soldiers to bankers to shop boys, could take pleasure in accounts of violence, lots of violence, utterly unconnected to their lives or their politics or their nation.

Sides's book, too, disengaged the story of the West from the story of the nation, though with infinitely more subtlety and sophistication. The Mexican War, for Sides, was finally more about James K. Polk, the man, than about manifest destiny, the ideology. Sides bothered to explain that Polk, as a teenager, was probably rendered impotent by an excruciatingly painful prostate surgery and that, as president, he was "a joyless, childless man fueled by an expansionist agenda."[31] He did not bother to explore how the American expansionist ideology known as manifest destiny appealed to both northerners and southerners alike; or how the dime novel western made that expansion appear inevitable and even glorious. Northerners, bound up in an evangelical religious revival, were attracted to its millennial vision. Southerners were eager to extend slavery into the western territories, to buttress their own political power, and open new markets to the domestic slave trade. More than a few Americans looked west in the earnest expectation that if Protestants reached the Pacific, Christ would return to Earth. And still more looked west to make room for their slaves. When the Civil War rent the North and South apart, the dime novel stitched them together again. When the devastating cruelty inflicted on people like the Navajo made news back east, dime novels just turned their plots upside down.

But these considerations, which bind conflicts between the North and South to the West, and into a coherent national story, have very little place in Sides's account. His story gallops; more ideas, harder questions, would rein it in to a slow trot. His West, under the Big Sky, is all skittering lizards, Indians on horseback, and mountain men eating pemmican. It is often a sad place, and much of what happens there is shameful, but it is very far away. And we see it, always, through the muzzle of a gun.

Dime novels haunted Kit Carson to the end. On the trail, he once met a man from Arkansas.

"I say, stranger, are you Kit Carson?" the man asked.

Carson said yes.

"Look 'ere," the Arkansan replied, casting his eye over Carson's diminutive frame. "You ain't the kind of Kit Carson I'm looking for."[32]

# 14

## LONGFELLOW'S RIDE

Henry Wadsworth Longfellow used to be both the best-known poet in the English-speaking world and the most beloved, adored by the learned and the lowly alike, read by everyone from Nathaniel Hawthorne and Abraham Lincoln to John Ruskin and Queen Victoria—and, just as avidly, by the queen's servants.[1] "Paul Revere's Ride" is Longfellow's best-known poem. It begins at a trot:

> Listen my children and you shall hear
> Of the midnight ride of Paul Revere.

It clips ("impatient to mount and ride, / Booted and spurred, with a heavy stride"); it clops ("impetuous, stamped the earth, / And turned and tightened his saddle girth"); then it gallops—

> A hurry of hoofs in a village street,
> A shape in the moonlight, a bulk in the dark,
> And beneath, from the pebbles, in passing, a spark
> Struck out by a steed flying fearless and fleet

—until, at last, it stops:

> So through the night rode Paul Revere;
> And so through the night went his cry of alarm

To every Middlesex village and farm,—
A cry of defiance, and not of fear,
A voice in the darkness, a knock at the door,
And a word that shall echo for evermore!

Generations of American schoolchildren have memorized
these lines and recited them in class, sweating it out, which is
why Longfellow is known as a schoolroom poet.[2] "Dear Mr.
Longfellow: I am a little girl nine years old. I have learned some
of your poems and love them very much," wrote Berta Shaffer, from Ohio, in 1880.[3] This is, no doubt, a kind of acclaim.
But for a poet's literary reputation, to be read by children—and
especially to be loved by children—is the sweet, sloppy kiss of
death. Beginning even before the rise of New Criticism, literary
scholars have paid almost no attention to Longfellow, dismissing "Paul Revere's Ride" as just another cloying Longfellow
poem, ho-hum, and dum-de-dum-de-dum-de-dum, a piece of
nineteenth-century romantic nationalism, drippy, contemptible, silly. "Rarely has so respected a writer been so discredited
by posterity," as the literary scholar Lawrence Buell once put it.[4]
"Feeble" is a word you often see, describing Longfellow's poetic
gifts.[5] Where was the ambiguity, the paradox, the difficulty, the
anxiety, the obscurity? What good was a poem that was *easy*?
Longfellow was soft. And, although in the last decades of the
twentieth century feminist critics subjected all things squishy
and sentimental to close inspection, arguing for the elevation
of writers like Susan Warner and Harriet Jacobs and Harriet
Beecher Stowe to canonical status, Longfellow didn't warrant
recovery, or even, really, a reading, presumably because he was a
man, and the canon had enough of those already. Meanwhile,
historians have pointed out, from the start, that Longfellow's
poem is, as history, rotten. (Longfellow wouldn't have cared.
"Nor let the Historian blame the Poet here, / If he perchance
misdate the day or year.")[6] Before Longfellow wrote his poem

about how Revere rode from Boston, warning Massachusetts minutemen that the redcoats were coming, Revere wasn't known for his ride (his obituary didn't even mention it); he never reached Concord; and he didn't ride alone. Longfellow, in other words, got almost every detail of what happened that night wrong. In 1896, *Century Magazine* published a parody—

> 'Tis all very well for the children to hear
> Of the midnight ride of Paul Revere;
> But why should my name be quite forgot,
> Who rode as boldly and well, God wot?
> Why should I ask? The reason is clear—
> My name was Dawes and his Revere

—which is read aloud, every year, on the nineteenth of April, on Cambridge Common, where brass horseshoes sunk into the pavement mark the path ridden by a man who had the bad luck to have a name that rhymes with everything grunting, earthy, and broken: jaws, caws, maws, paws, flaws. Poor Dawes.[7]

*Listen my children.* Longfellow, who, one supposes, could have done things differently if he'd been of a mind to, loved writing poems that everyone would read, poems everyone could read, poems in which people, unsophisticated people, even little people, might find pleasure and solace. (Emerson once wrote to Longfellow, "I have always one foremost satisfaction in reading your books—that I am safe.")[8] "Such songs have power to quiet," Longfellow wrote, in "The Day Is Done":

> Come, read to me some poem,
>     Some simple and heartfelt lay,
> That shall soothe this restless feeling,
>     And banish the thoughts of day.

Shooting down Longfellow's greeting-card verse—in which the anodyne yields to the lachrymose—has been, for modernist critics, nothing more demanding than target practice on a lazy afternoon, where the target is as big as Longfellow's much-visited and palatial Cambridge mansion. "Longfellow is to poetry what the barrel-organ is to music," Van Wyck Brooks wrote, in 1915. Lewis Mumford said Longfellow could be cut out of American literary history, and no one would miss him, or even notice.[9] T. E. Lawrence once joked that Ezra Pound was Longfellow's grandnephew, and he didn't mean that as a compliment.[10] Newton Arvin, who quite liked Longfellow, thought his trouble was his moralizing—"And come like the benediction / That follows after prayer"—although the problem, Arvin believed, wasn't that Longfellow was a moralist; it was that his morals were secondhand, and boring.[11] But Daniel Aaron once wisely pointed out that American literature isn't so swell that it can afford to junk the guy who wrote "Seaweed":

> Ever drifting, drifting, drifting
>     On the shiftless currents
> Of the reckless heart;
> Till at length in books recorded,
>     They, like hoarded
> Household words, no more depart.[12]

Longfellow was born by the sea, in Portland, Maine, in 1807. When he was sixteen, and away at Bowdoin, he wrote home to his mother that he was reading Thomas Gray, and that he admired the poet's obscurity. His mother wrote back that all she had read of Gray was his "Elegy Written in a Country Church-Yard"—"Approach and read (for thou canst read) the lay / Graved on the stone beneath yon aged thorn"—but that she admired it only so far. "Obscurity is favorable to the sublime, you think," she wrote her son, "but I am much better pleased with those pieces that touch the feelings and improve the heart than with those that excite the imagination only and raise perhaps an indistinct admiration. That is, an admiration of we know not exactly what."[13] Longfellow took that to heart.

After studying in Europe, Longfellow taught at Bowdoin. He wrote for Jared Sparks's *North American Review*; he published an indifferent work of prose. He became the Smith Professor of Modern Languages and Belles Lettres at Harvard in 1837; he was thirty years old. He published his first collection of poems, *Voices of the Night*, in 1839. He liked teaching but hated lecturing, and he didn't like being a professor enough to want to do it forever. Beginning in 1843, he made it a practice to buy the plates of his books, which gave him control of reprints; unlike most writers, and very much unlike his archnemesis, Edgar Allan Poe (who called him, unfairly, a plagiarist), Longfellow was a canny businessman. Most years, he earned more than two thousand dollars in royalties, a good enough living to allow him, in 1854, to quit teaching. For his final lecture, he lectured on the last canto of Dante's *Inferno*, a classy way to go out.[14]

A scholar of poetry and editor and translator of a landmark anthology, *The Poets and Poetry of Europe* (1845), Longfellow could speak eight languages and read more than a dozen. His own poems are thick with allusions, especially of the classical sort. But they were also so singularly accessible and so overwhelmingly popular that he has been blamed, preposterously, for the death of poetry, as if readers reared on Longfellow were ruined, forever, for anything tougher. He worked hard to make poetry look easy; his success was his failure.[15] "Liking Longfellow has become improper," Christoph Irmscher argued, in a discerning and persuasive reappraisal, mainly because Longfellow is "too likely to be admired by people who have no business commenting on literary works."[16] That includes kids.

Longfellow often wrote about his own much beloved children, doting on them in a fashion well within the conventions of his day but that now comes across, to many readers, as soppy and slightly sickening, as in "The Children's Hour," written when his children were fifteen, fourteen, nine, six, and four:

> I hear in the chamber above me
>> The patter of little feet,
> The sound of a door that is opened,
>> And voices soft and sweet.

Longfellow had a knack for writing about children; he was also motherly—"This having a babe is like dropping an anchor in to the dark, deep waters of Futurity," he wrote, when his first son was born—and his work has been described as "maternal," which of course, does no one's work any good, the maternal being generally and stupidly thought to be opposed, at least since the Enlightenment, to the intellectual.[17] Anyone who could possibly like Longfellow, the argument goes, is a twit.

That Longfellow has been neglected, and relegated to the domestic, the maternal, and the juvenile, means that he was never subjected to the scrutiny of New Historicists, either. If he had, they might have picked up on something strange about "Paul Revere's Ride," which is that one way of reading it is that it is a poem, not about liberty and Paul Revere, but about slavery and John Brown.

This story starts in 1837, the year Longfellow arrived at Harvard, where he met Charles Sumner, four years his junior, who was lecturing at the law school. They both joined a literary society called the Five of Clubs. Longfellow and Sumner became best friends and remained best friends—passionate friends—for the rest of their lives. Together, they dined and talked and confided and read one another's work; apart, they wrote endless letters, letters of news and gossip and longing. "Querido Carlos," Longfellow addressed Sumner. When Longfellow got married, Sumner, a bachelor, went with him on the honeymoon. Not long after the two men first met, Sumner left Cambridge to study in Europe, bearing letters of introduction written by Longfellow, and they began an intimate correspondence. The historian Frederick Blue, who has carefully documented their friendship, calls them an odd couple, which gets it just about right: Sumner was dogmatic and abrasive, even ferocious; Longfellow was gentle and retiring and contented, a famously *nice* man. Sumner pursued politics; politics made Longfellow cringe. They divided their talents. They once posed together for a portrait; it is called "The Politics and Poetry of New England."[18] Everyone knew which was which.

At the beginning of 1842, Longfellow entertained Dickens during his American tour; he took him to Boston's North End, to see Copps Hill and the Old North Church. Not long after, Longfellow sailed for Europe. ("I am desolate," Sumner wrote, at Longfellow's departure.)[19] In London, Longfellow again ran into Dickens, and listened to him fulminate over slavery and American hypocrisy. Meanwhile Sumner, back in the States, had become an active and ardent abolitionist. He wrote Longfellow from across the ocean, begging him to put his pen to the cause. "Write some stirring words that shall move the whole land," Sumner urged. "Send them home, and we will publish them." Longfellow obliged; on the return sea voyage, he wrote seven poems, in his cabin, during "stormy, sleepless nights." His *Poems on Slavery* was published later that year; they're not that stormy. Longfellow had no appetite for combat and no interest in attacking slaveholders (that was for Sumner to do); instead, he wrote, mournfully—modern readers would say mawkishly—about the plight of slaves. His poems on slavery were, in his view, "so mild that even a Slaveholder might read them without losing his appetite for breakfast."[20] Still, he was proud of them, writing to his father, "Some persons regret that I should have written them, but for my own part I am glad of what I have done." They earned him the gratitude of abolitionists but also much opprobrium, especially from Poe, who wrote a review dismissing *Poems on Slavery* as "intended for the especial use of those negrophilic old ladies of the north, who form so large a part of Mr. LONG-FELLOW's friends."[21]

Longfellow, therefore, backed off.[22] (He was unwilling, even, to do battle with Poe; that, too, he left to Sumner.) To write about slavery was to enter the world of politics—Sumner's world—a world Longfellow had no interest in entering. When the Liberty Party urged Longfellow to run for Congress, he declined. "Though a strong anti-Slavery man, I am not a member of any society, and fight under no single banner," Longfellow explained, adding, "Partizan warfare becomes too violent—too vindictive for my taste; and I should be found but a weak and unworthy champion in public debate."[23] Instead, he turned his poetic attention to history—a turn that would produce "Evangeline," "The Song of Hiawatha," "The Courtship of Miles Standish," and, of course, "Paul Revere's Ride." Longfellow is often considered to have held himself above politics but, really, he was afraid of it. He had little taste for political speech—even Sumner's—and less for the fray. Hearing Sumner speak at a Free Soil rally in Cambridge in 1848, Longfellow found the spectacle discordant: "it was like one of Beethoven's symphonies played in a saw-mill. He spoke admirably well; but the shouts and the hisses and the vulgar interruptions grated on my ears. I was glad to get away."[24]

Longfellow may not have taken up politics in his poetry, but he followed it closely and his diary is full of references to slavery and sectionalism and, in 1850, to the Fugitive Slave Act. ("If anyone wants to break a law, let him break the Fugitive-Slave Law," he wrote. "That is all it is for.")[25] His account books, too, are filled with references to slavery: month by month, year after year, in dozens and dozens of carefully recorded entries,

Longfellow noted sums of money given to black newspapers, black schools, black churches, and, especially, to fugitive slaves. In 1854, for instance, his accounts include these items:

Jan. 25—For Slaves 3.00
Feb. 16—Slaves in Canada 5.00
March 29—Negro Church Buffalo
June 23—Mr. Spence Negro School 3.00

"June 13—To free a slave 5.00," he wrote in his account book for 1856, and "Dec.—To ransom Slave 3.00," two years later. Longfellow used some of the money he made writing poems to buy men, women, and children their freedom.[26]

Longfellow's intimacy with Sumner also meant that politics—the politics, in particular, of radical Republicans—was never far from his mind, or his heart. Sumner was elected to the U.S. Senate in 1851, but, instead of celebrating his much contested election, he hid out in Longfellow's house. "The papers are all ringing with Sumner, Sumner!" Longfellow wrote in his diary. "Meanwhile the hero of the strife is sitting quietly here, more saddened than exalted." Sumner, braced for battle, left for Washington. In 1856, he wrote to Longfellow of his plan to deliver what would be his most famous speech, "The Crime against Kansas." It is frothy, terrifying, and foreboding. "Even now, while I speak," Sumner thundered, "portents lower in the horizon, threatening to darken the land, which already palpitates with the mutterings of civil war." Better him than me, Longfellow must have thought. Longfellow called Sumner on slavery "the greatest voice on the greatest subject that had been uttered since we became a nation," and told him, "You have torn the mask off the faces of traitors; and at last the spirit of the North is aroused."[27]

That speech also led, later that year, to South Carolina congressman Preston Books beating Sumner on the head with a cane, beating him bloody and senseless. Longfellow was consumed with worry. Sumner's younger brother George raced to Washington to care for him, but Sumner was very badly injured; it would take him more than three years to recover.[28] He went to Europe, seeking medical treatment. Longfellow sent him magazines. "A new Magazine called 'The Atlantic Monthly' has just been established," Longfellow reported to Sumner, in 1857, enclosing the first issue (which contained Longfellow's "Santa Filomena").[29] "I groan with you over the iniquity of the times," Longfellow wrote Sumner, the next year, in the wake of the Dred Scott decision. "It is deplorable; it is heart-breaking; and I long to say some vibrant word, that should have vitality in it, and force. Be sure if it comes to me I will not be slow in uttering it."[30]

In Sumner's absence, Longfellow spent a good deal of time with George Sumner, one brother taking the place of another. In 1859, Longfellow went to see George Sumner deliver a Fourth of July oration in Boston. Sumner attacked those in the North who would hesitate to take a stand, who would continue, even after Dred Scott, to seek compromise and concession. "I honor the conservative who stands the guardian of order, of existing rights, and of instituted liberty, and who gracefully yields at last to the progress of an advancing civilization," Sumner said.

> But there are some who, calling themselves conservatives, conserve nothing, and who yield, not to the advances of civilization, but to the encroachments of barbarism; whose whole conservatism is constant concession; who tell us they are "as much opposed to barbarism as any one," but they wouldn't meet it on the field of politics,—"as much opposed to crime as any one," but they wouldn't hear a warning voice raised against it from the pulpit;—their politics are too pure, their Sunday slumbers too precious, to be disturbed by any allusions to such exciting matters as the advances of crime. And so they go on, conceding

everything,—not to civilization, but to barbarism,—not to liberty, but to liberticide—backing down before every presumptuous aggression—down—and down still—until they fall among the lost ones whom Dante has described. From them there is nothing to expect.[31]

Longfellow wrote to Charles that George's speech was "solid, sober, literally paved with facts, which he pounded in so hard as considerably to hurt some of the Boston aldermen; particularly the Dred Scott fact jammed the lovers of fiction very badly."[32]

Charles Sumner returned from Europe that November, two weeks after John Brown's raid on Harper's Ferry. Brown was convicted and sentenced to be hanged. That execution led Melville to write "The Portent":

> The cut is on the crown
> (Lo, John Brown),
> And the stabs shall heal no more.

But the death of John Brown led Longfellow to write, too. The day Brown was to be hanged, Longfellow wrote in his diary: "The second of December, 1859. This will be a great day in our history; the date of a new Revolution,—quite as much needed as the old one. Even now as I write, they are leading old John Brown to execution in Virginia for attempting to rescue slaves! This is sowing the wind to reap the whirlwind, which will come soon."[33]

This is Longfellow, an almost maddeningly restrained and genteel man, at his most ardent. Was there a way he could do his part, in his timid way, so as not to back "down—and down still," like the conservatives George Sumner had lambasted? John Brown had started "a new Revolution." Longfellow, writing poems about history, got to thinking about the old one.

Before heading to Washington to resume his Senate duties (his seat had been kept vacant during his recuperation),
Charles Sumner visited Longfellow in Cambridge. On January 5, 1860, Longfellow went to a reading at "the Revere
House"—a hotel in Bowdoin Square—and had dinner with
Sumner: "He goes to Washington tomorrow with rather
sad forebodings, I think." And, as before, when Sumner left,
Longfellow consoled himself with the company of Sumner's
younger brother. On April 5, 1860, he had George Sumner over
for dinner. "He proposes an expedition to the 'North End,' or
old town of Boston," Longfellow wrote in his diary. They went
on this outing the next day: "We go to the Copp's Hill burial
ground and see the tomb of Cotton Mather, his father and his
son; then to the old North Church, which looks like a parish
church in London. We climb the tower to the chime of bells,
now the home of innumerable pigeons. From this tower were
hung the lanterns of a signal that the British troops had left
Boston for Concord."

Whether Longfellow had already begun writing his poem
about Paul Revere before that outing with George Sumner
is uncertain. But he had certainly begun writing it by April
19, when he noted in his diary, "I wrote a few lines in 'Paul
Revere's Ride;' this being the day of that achievement." During the months Longfellow was working on the poem, he,
like everyone else, waited, and agonized, over the fate of the
union. On May 30, he went to see Frederick Douglass deliver
an oration in Boston. "At the Anti-Slavery meeting," Longfellow wrote in his diary, "heard Remond and Douglas, colored
men, speak; also Wendell Phillips. All good speakers." Meanwhile, in Washington, Charles Sumner was writing a speech
of his own, "The Barbarism of Slavery." Longfellow's thoughts
were with him, on June 4, when he wrote in his diary, "Charles
Sumner speaks to-day in the Senate at Washington." In a

speech that lasted more than four hours, Sumner spoke of the battle between liberty and slavery as a battle between civilization and barbarism. Slavery, Sumner said, was "Barbarous in origin; barbarous in its law; barbarous in all its pretensions; barbarous in the instruments it employs; barbarous in consequences; barbarous in spirit; barbarous whenever it shows itself, Slavery must breed Barbarians." He concluded, "The sacred animosity between Freedom and Slavery can end only with the triumph of Freedom."[34]

Longfellow had anxiously anticipated the speech, fretting that Sumner wasn't up to it, that his strength would fail him. He watched for the transcript to be printed in Boston newspapers, and, when it appeared, he made clippings and sent them to Sumner, applauding him: "You have done your work fearlessly, faithfully, fully! It was disagreeable, but necessary, and must remain as the great protest of Civilization against Barbarism in this age. Its great simplicity gives it awful effect. In rhetoric you have surpassed it before; in forcible array and arrangement of arguments, never!"[35]

Meanwhile, all this time, he went on writing "Paul Revere's Ride," a narrative poem about the struggle for liberty as a flight, a ride, a warning sounded in the night—a poem that is now read as a catchy and technically accomplished but aesthetically dull and politically insipid national romance. He finished writing it on October 13, 1860. Two weeks later, he went to the polls and cast his vote for Lincoln. On November 6, word came that Lincoln had won. "It is the redemption of the country," Longfellow wrote in his diary. "Freedom is triumphant."[36]

"Paul Revere's Ride" was published in the *Atlantic* in January 1861 and was read at the time as a call to arms, rousing northerners to action, against what Charles Sumner called the Slaveocracy—"a warning voice" waking those who would concede to barbarism from what George Sumner called "their precious Sunday slumbers." But the poem can also be read as concerning, not just the coming war, but slavery itself: "Paul Revere's Ride" is, in one sense, a fugitive slave narrative.

During the weeks Longfellow was writing "Paul Revere's Ride," the plight of slaves was very much on his mind. He was attending lectures by Frederick Douglass. He was listening to George Sumner condemn the Supreme Court's decision in Dred Scott. He was fervently reading speeches given by Charles Sumner. He was casting his vote for Lincoln. He was sympathizing with John Brown. Fearful of politics, Longfellow was, nevertheless, wishing he could do his part, quietly, gently, poetically. "I long to say some vibrant word, that should have vitality in it, and force," he had written to Sumner. And there is more: much in "Paul Revere's Ride" echoes lines from Longfellow's *Poems on Slavery*—especially "The Slave's Dream," "The Slave Singing at Midnight," "The Witnesses," and "The Warning"—poems full of fugitive slaves, riding through the night, haunted by the dead, hurrying through the darkness, calling out, bearing witness, singing what Longfellow calls (in "The Slave in the Dismal Swamp") "songs of liberty."

Longfellow's historical sources for his account of Revere's ride appear to have been limited, and, of course, the poem wasn't meant to be accurate. Longfellow loved lore. He began "Hiawatha": "Should you ask me, whence these stories? / Whence these legends and traditions, / . . . I should answer, I should tell you, /From the forests and the prairies." He had, though, seen at least one old document: a letter written by Paul Revere, in 1798, to Jeremy Belknap, founder of the Massachusetts Historical Society, describing the night of April 18, 1775. Longfellow almost certainly read this letter because it was published, in October 1832, in *New England Magazine*, in the same issue in which a very early poem of Longfellow's appeared.

Revere described starting out, in Boston: "I . . . went to the north part of the town, where I had kept a boat; two friends rode me across the Charles River, a little to the eastward where the *Somerset* man-of-war lay. It was then young flood, the ship was winding, and the moon was rising. They landed me in the Charlestown side." Longfellow, starting out his poem, stays close to Revere's account:

> with muffled oar
> Silently rowed to the Charlestown shore,
> Just as the moon rose over the bay,
> Where swinging wide at her moorings lay
> The Somerset, British man-of-war;

But then Longfellow leaves Revere's description behind. His ship takes on a different cast:

> A phantom ship, with each mast and spar
> Across the moon like a prison bar,
> And a huge black hulk, that was magnified
> By its own reflection in the tide.

Why? To Longfellow's abolitionist readers, the name *Somerset* would have readily called to mind the landmark 1772 Somerset case, which outlawed slavery in Britain. And here the "phantom ship" conjures something more. It is as dark and haunting as a slave ship—a dominant conceit in abolitionist writing— "each mast and spar . . . like a prison bar."[37] Longfellow had written about just such shackled ships in "The Witnesses," where across the "Ocean's wide domains . . . Float ships, with all their crews, / No more to sink nor rise":

> There the black Slave-ship swims,
>     Freighted with human forms,

Whose fettered, fleshless limbs
Are not the sport of storms.

Revere, in his letter to Belknap, next described leaving Charlestown. "I set off upon a very good Horse; it was then about 11 o'Clock, and very pleasant. After I had passed Charlestown Neck, and got nearly opposite where Mark was hung in chains." Mark, "hung in chains," refers to the rotting remains of a slave from Charlestown who was executed in 1750, after he and a slave woman named Phyllis were convicted of poisoning their master, a Charlestown merchant, with arsenic. Phyllis was burned at the stake, in Cambridge, not far from Longfellow's house, in a place called Gallows Hill; Mark was executed in Charlestown and his body was left, hung in chains, as a warning to Boston's slaves of the danger of rebellion. By the time Revere made his ride, in 1775, Mark's bones had been hanging at Charlestown Neck for a quarter-century, bearing witness.

Maybe it was Revere's remark about that landmark, Mark's bones, that sparked in Longfellow this thought, but, just here, the poem takes a turn. In Boston, the man who mounts the belfry of the Old North Church to light the lanterns looks out at Copp's Hill, the burying ground Longfellow had gone to with George Sumner, and where the Mathers lay entombed, but which was also, by the 1850s, far better known as the place where Boston's blacks were buried:

Beneath, in the churchyard, lay the dead,
In their night encampment on the hill,
Wrapped in silence so deep and still
That he could hear, like a sentinel's tread,
The watchful night-wind, as it went
Creeping along from tent to tent,
And seeming to whisper, "All is well!"

In "The Witnesses," Longfellow's dead whisper something else, from the depths:

These are the bones of Slaves;
  They gleam from the abyss;
They cry, from yawning waves,
  "We are the Witnesses!"

By now, Longfellow has departed quite radically from Revere's account (which, in any event, was written long after the fact). "In Medford, I awaked the Captain of the Minute men," Revere wrote Belknap, "and after that, I alarmed almost every House, till I got to Lexington." Revere stopped in Lexington for half an hour and had a bite to eat while he talked with John Hancock, Samuel Adams, and William Dawes. On the way to Concord, he stopped, again, to talk with Dr. Samuel Prescott, and was then captured by the British. But in Longfellow's poem, Revere races, onward,

through the gloom and the light,
The fate of a nation was riding that night;
And the spark struck out by that steed, in his flight,
Kindled the land into flame with its heat.

That flight, too, has a counterpart not only in abolitionist literature—where, in the wake of the Fugitive Slave Act, the fate of the nation was often said to ride on a slave's flight—but also in Longfellow's *Poems on Slavery*. In "The Slave's Dream," another horseman rides wildly through the night:

at furious speed he rode
  Along the Niger's bank;
His bridle-reins were golden chains,
  And, with a martial clank,
At each leap he could feel his scabbard of steel
  Smiting his stallion's flank.

This man, though, is a slave, dreaming of riding all the way home, to Africa. And while Revere, Longfellow's Son of Liberty, rides through New England farms and towns, to the sounds of the barnyard—

> He heard the crowing of the cock,
> And the barking of the farmer's dog,
> And felt the damp of the river fog,
> That rises after the sun goes down

—his son of slavery rides to the howls of African beasts:

> At night he heard the lion roar,
>     And the hyena scream,
> And the river-horse, as he crushed the reeds
>     Beside some hidden stream;
> And it passed, like a glorious roll of drums,
>     Through the triumph of his dream.

But that triumph is no triumph at all.[38] The slave never wakes from his dream. "The Slave's Dream" ends with death: "For Death had illumined the Land of Sleep, / And his lifeless body lay / A worn-out fetter, that the soul / Had broken and thrown away!" But "Paul Revere's Ride" ends with the rider, having wakened from its slumber every New England village and farm, riding on, into history ("You know the rest. In the books you have read"):

> For, borne on the night-wind of the Past,
> Through all our history, to the last,
> In the hour of peril men will hear
> The midnight message of Paul Revere,
> And the hurrying hoof-beat of his steed.

That, anyway, is what Longfellow wrote. But, in a letter written on November 23, 1860, Longfellow's brilliant editor, J. T. Fields, offered a decided improvement.

Dear Longfellow.

Dont you think it better to end Paul Revere's Ride on this line,

> In the hour of darkness and peril and need,
> The People will waken and listen to hear
> The hurrying hoof-beat of his steed,
> And the midnight message of Paul Revere.

It seems to me the last line as it stands above is stronger than the end as it now remains in the proof.

What do you say?[39]

Longfellow said yes.

"Paul Revere's Ride" is a poem about waking the dead. The dead are northerners, roused to war. But the dead are also the enslaved, entombed in slavery—another common conceit: Frederick Douglass once wrote about his escape as "a resurrection from the dark and pestiferous tomb of slavery." Who shall wake? Neglecting Longfellow, taking the Sumner out of Longfellow, juvenilizing Longfellow, has had its costs. Decades of schoolroom recitation not only have occluded the poem's meaning but have also made it exceptionally serviceable as a piece of political propaganda, not least because political propaganda and juvenilia have rather a lot in common. Everyone invokes Revere. Everyone reveres Revere. In 1967, at the Southern Christian Leadership Conference in Atlanta, Martin Luther King, Jr., said, "We still need some Paul Revere of conscience to alert every hamlet and every village of America that revolution is still at hand."[40] In 1975, during the Bicentennial, Gerald Ford came to Boston and gave a speech at the Old North Church, calling for renewed pride in America: he quoted Longfellow.[41] Edward Kennedy who, like all

the Kennedy children, was required by his mother to memo-
rize "Paul Revere's Ride," once recited it, in its entirety, during a meeting of the Senate Appropriations Committee, after
which the committee's chairman, Robert Byrd, recited it back
to him.[42] What was the point of that? The poem, as juvenilia,
has no point.

In 2009, on the anniversary of Paul Revere's ride, George
Pataki turned up in Boston. Pataki, a former Republican governor of New York, was thinking about running for president. In the North End, he positioned himself in front of an
equestrian statue of Paul Revere. He was there to launch an
organization called "Revere America." "We're standing near
where Paul Revere, on this day, 235 years ago began a ride,"
Pataki said. "He was looking to tell patriotic Americans, 'Our
freedom was in danger.' We're here today to tell the people of
America that once again our freedom is in danger." The danger
was health care legislation passed during the Obama years; the
aim of Revere America was to gather signatures on a petition
"to repeal and replace Obamacare."

"I say nothing of politics, for what is the use of talking,"
Longfellow wearily wrote Sumner, in January 1861, just after
"Paul Revere's Ride" was published and South Carolina se-
ceded from the union. "The events of the last month only
strengthen my convictions, and you know well enough what
they are."[43] We, too, know well enough what they are. Longfellow signed his next letter to Sumner, "Yours ever without
compromise or concession." Two weeks later, Longfellow
wrote in his diary, "The dissolution of the Union goes slowly
on. Behind it all I hear the low murmur of the slaves, like the
chorus in a Greek tragedy."[44] Listen, and you shall hear.

# 15

# ROCK, PAPER, SCISSORS

On the morning of November 2, 1859—Election Day—George Kyle left his house with a bundle of ballots tucked under his arm. Kyle was a Democrat. As he neared the polls in Baltimore's heavily Republican Fifteenth Ward, he encountered in the gathering crowd a ruffian who tried to snatch from him that sheaf of ballots. Kyle dodged and wheeled. He heard a cry: his brother, just behind him, had been whacked in the head. Next, someone clobbered Kyle. Kyle drew a knife. He didn't have a chance to use it. "I felt a pistol put to my head," he said. It fired, "tearing the skin from the side of my face." He fell. He must have dropped his knife. Maybe he lost hold of his ballots, too. When he rose, he drew his own pistol, hidden in his pocket. He spied his brother lying in the street. Someone else fired a shot, hitting Kyle in the arm. A man carrying a musket rushed at him. Another threw a brick, knocking him off his feet. George Kyle picked himself up and ran. He never did cast his vote. Neither did his brother, who died of his wounds. (Although, to be sure, so paltry a thing as death didn't stop everyone; more than a few dead and buried Baltimoreans voted in that election, if not early and often, at least oftener than any corpse ought.) Not surprisingly, the Democratic candidate for Congress, William Harrison, lost to the Republican, Henry Winter Davis. Three months later, when the House of Representatives convened hearings into the election, whose result Harrison contested, Davis's victory was upheld on the grounds that any "man of ordinary courage" could have made his way to the polls.[1]

"Are you not a man in the full vigor of manhood and strength?" a member of the House Committee on Elections asked another Harrison supporter who, like Kyle, went to the polls but turned back without voting (and who happened to stand six-foot-five and weigh more than two hundred pounds).[2] The hearings established a precedent. "To vacate an election," an election law textbook subsequently advised, "it must clearly appear that there was such a display of force as ought to have intimidated men of ordinary firmness."[3]

What was at stake, in the House Committee on Elections, was whether men like George Kyle, men who planned to vote for Harrison but failed, were too easily daunted. What wasn't at stake—because it was neither illegal nor unusual but, instead, necessary—was that Kyle carried with him to the polls a bundle of ballots. Kyle wasn't a poll worker. He was a voter. (A notably well-armed one. But still.) He didn't expect to get a ballot at the polls, from a precinct official. Nowhere in the United States in 1859 did election officials provide ballots. Kyle, like everyone else, brought his own. The ballots he carried, preprinted "party tickets," endorsed the slate of Democratic candidates, headed by Harrison. Voters didn't need to fill those ballots out. They just had to be able to get them—either from a partisan, at the polls, or at home, by cutting them out of the newspaper—and to cross the throngs to reach a solitary platform placed against the outside wall of a building (voters weren't allowed inside), climb that platform, and pass a bundle of ballots, one per office, through a single, high window and into the hands of an election judge. This, all things considered, was no mean feat, and not only in Baltimore. Between 1828 and 1861, eighty-nine Americans were killed at the polls on Election Day.[4]

The reform that ended this unsettling state of affairs was imported from Australia and not achieved in the United States until the 1890s. The American adoption of the "Australian ballot"—with its radical provision that governments should provide ballots—was hard fought.[5] It changed everything. It lies, if well hidden, behind every argument made about how we ought to vote now, from the promotion of paperless voting to the more recent backlash, favoring a paper trail. And it is also, like every other American election reform, a patch upon a patch.

The United States was founded as an experiment, a staggeringly brilliant experiment, in eighteenth-century republicanism, in which it was understood that only the wealthiest and best-educated men would vote—the only people who could be counted on to vote with the public good, and not private interest, in mind—and that they would do so publicly. What went on in Baltimore's Fifteenth Ward on November 2, 1859, was something altogether different. And how Americans vote in the twenty-first century looks, from an eighteenth-century point of view, even stranger. Just about every citizen over the age of eighteen and not in prison will be eligible to vote.[6] We won't be clobbered, stabbed, and shot. We will not have to bring our own ballots. But we will want to vote very, very quickly. We will insist that how we vote should be secret. The Founders didn't plan for this. No one planned for it. There is no plan. It's patches all the way down.

Americans used to vote with their voices—*viva voce*—or with their hands or, literally, with their feet. Yea or nay. Speak up. Raise your hand. All in favor of Jones, stand on this side of Town Hall; if you support Smith, line up over there. Every

town, county, and colony, and later, every state, determined
its own method of voting (although nearly everyone agreed
that Election Day ought to involve plenty of stumping and
a prodigious amount of drinking). In the colonies, as in the
mother country, casting a vote only very rarely required paper
and pen.[7] The word "ballot" comes from the Italian *ballota*, or
ball, and in the 1600s, a ballot usually was a ball, or at least
something ball-ish, like a pea or a pebble, or, not uncommonly,
a bullet. Colonial Pennsylvanians voted by tossing beans into
a hat.[8] Everyone knew how everyone else voted.[9] Paper voting, when it started, wasn't meant to conceal anyone's vote; it
was just easier than counting beans. Our forebears considered
casting a "secret ballot" cowardly, underhanded, and despi-
cable; as one South Carolinian put it, voting secretly would
"destroy that noble generous openness that is characteristick
of an Englishman."[10]

The first recorded colonial use of paper voting comes from
Salem, Massachusetts: in 1629, church members elected their
pastor by writing his name down on slivers of parchment. In
1634, John Winthrop, the first governor of Massachusetts,
was elected "by paper"; thirteen years later, a Bay Colony
law dictated voting "by wrighting the names of the persons
Elected."[11] Outside of Massachusetts, which had an unusually
high literacy rate, this would have been entirely impractical.
Only very slowly did voting by paper grow common enough
that the word "ballot" came to mean not a ball but a piece of
paper. Well after American Independence, most elections remained the stuff of corn and beans and hands and feet.[12]

The Constitution, drafted in 1787, left the conduct of elections up to the states: "The times, places and manner of holding
elections for Senators and Representatives, shall be prescribed
in each state by the legislature thereof; but the Congress may
at any time by law make or alter such regulations." Further
than this limited federal oversight the framers would not go.

And even this needed Madison's insistence, during the Constitutional Convention, that "it was impossible to foresee all the abuses" that states might make of unimpeded power over the conduct of elections.[13]

The Constitution makes no provision for how Americans should vote not only because the men who wrote it wanted to leave such matters (mostly) to the states, but also because, as only Madison glimpsed, they could not possibly have foreseen how unwieldy elections would very soon become. With the exception of Benjamin Franklin, who anticipated Malthus, the nation's founders could scarcely have imagined that the population of the United States, less than four million in 1790, would increase tenfold by 1870. Nor did they prophesy the party system. Above all, they could not have fathomed universal suffrage, which entirely defied eighteenth-century political philosophy. The framers expected only a tiny minority to vote, and these men didn't elect George Washington; they voted only for delegates to the Electoral College, an institution established to further restrain the popular will. (The original proposal, at the Constitutional Convention, was for the president to be elected by Congress, called, in the debates, the "national legislature." A motion "to strike out 'National Legislature' & insert 'citizens of U.S.'" was defeated, twelve states to one. That the people, even given limited suffrage, would elect the president directly was almost inconceivable. The election of the president by Congress, however, violated the separation of powers. The Electoral College, proposed after the defeat of the motion for direct election, was an ill-begotten compromise.)[14]

The states, left to their own, adopted electoral methods best described as higgledy-piggledy. The constitutions of five the original states mentioned voting by ballot.[15] "An opinion hath long prevailed among diverse good people of this state," wrote the framers of New York's 1777 constitution, "that voting at elections by ballot would tend more to preserve the liberty and freedom of the people than voting *viva voce*"; they proposed a "fair experiment" with the paper ballot.[16] In 1799, Maryland became the first state to require paper voting in all statewide elections. The Twelfth Amendment, ratified in 1804, mandated that members of the Electoral College "vote by ballot." By no means, however, did paper voting become universal. The citizens of Kentucky voted *viva voce* until 1891.

Early paper voting was, to say the least, a hassle. You had to bring your own ballot, a scrap of paper. Then you had to (a) remember and (b) know how to spell the names and titles of every candidate and office. If "John H. Jones" was standing for election, and you wrote, "John Jones," your vote would be thrown out. (If you doubt how difficult this is, try it. I disenfranchise myself with "comptroller.") Shrewd partisans began bringing prewritten ballots to the polls, and handing them out . . . with a coin or two. Dolling out cash—the money was called "soap"—wasn't illegal; it was getting out the vote.

Meanwhile, the eighteenth century's brilliant experiment in republicanism gave way to the unruly exuberance of nineteenth-century democracy. Of the twenty-four states in the union by 1825, seventeen held annual elections for state legislators. There was, in other words, a great deal of voting. And more and more voters. New states entering the union adopted constitutions without any property qualifications for voting, putting pressure on older states to eliminate those restrictions. The electorate doubled, and then tripled. And still it kept growing. As suffrage expanded—by the time Andrew Jackson was elected president in 1828, nearly all white men could vote—scrap-voting had become more or less a travesty, not least because the newest members of the electorate, poor men and immigrants, were the least likely to know how to write.[17]

In stepped political parties, whose rise to power was made possible by the rise of the paper ballot. Party leaders began to *print* ballots, usually in newspapers—early American news-papers were brazenly partisan—either on long strips, listing an entire slate, or on pages meant to be cut to pieces, one for each candidate, like the bundle of ballots George Kyle tucked under his arm on Election Day in 1859. These ballots came to be called "party tickets," because they looked like train tickets (and which is why, when we talk about someone who votes a single-party slate, we say that he "votes the party ticket"). The printing on ballots of party symbols (like the Free Soil-ers' man-pushing-a-plow) meant that voters not only didn't need to know how to write; they didn't need to know how to read, either.[18]

At first, party tickets looked to be illegal. In 1829, a Bos-ton man named David Henshaw tried to cast as his ballot a sheet of paper on which were printed the names of fifty-five candidates, his party's entire slate. Election officials refused to accept his ballot. Henshaw sued, arguing that he had been disenfranchised. When the case was heard before the state's Supreme Court, the decision turned on whether casting a printed ballot violated a clause in the state's 1789 constitution, requiring a written one. The Massachusetts constitution, only three decades old, had already been outpaced by the times. "It probably did not occur to the framers of the constitution," the Court observed, in a landmark ruling in Henshaw's favor, "that many of the town might become so populous as to make it convenient to use printed votes."[19]

The ticket system made voting easier, but only at the cost of limiting voters' choices. It also consolidated the power of the major parties while, curiously, promoting insurgency, too: party malcontents could print their own ballots, promoting their own slate of candidates; "knife" a candidate by stacking up a pile of tickets and then slicing out someone's name from the whole stack at once; or distribute "pasters," strips of paper with the name of a candidate not on the party ticket, to be pasted over his opponent's name. (Polls were stocked with vats of paste.)[20]

Party tickets led to massive fraud, corruption, and intimidation. A candidate had to pay party leaders a hefty sum to ensure that his name would appear on the ticket and to cover the costs of printing tickets and buying votes. (One estimate put the price of a congressional seat in New York City at over $200,000.)[21] It became more and more important to make sure all that soap was paying off. Ballots grew bigger, and more colorful, so brightly colored that there was no way a voter could hide his vote.

But wanting to hide that vote now began to seem, to reformers in both England and America, eminently reasonable. In 1831, the Scottish Benthamite, James Mill, argued for a secret ballot to curb the influence of landlords upon their tenants and factory owners upon their workers, in the wake of the expansion of the suffrage in Britain.[22] The next year, the state of Maine became the first to require that all ballots be printed in the same color, to protect voters, like George Kyle, trying to cast minority ballots in a polling place besieged by rowdy members of the majority, including paid "shoulder strikers," thugs "accomplished in the arts of scuffling and ballot-stuffing."[23] It didn't do much good. In 1851, a Massachusetts legislature dominated by Free Soilers and Democrats mandated the use of uniform envelopes, to be supplied by the secretary of state. That didn't do much good, either. "To say that the citizen shall vote with a sealed bag, or not at all," critics argued, "is an act of despotism." What honest man was ashamed of his vote? The secret ballot, insisted the Virginian John Randolph in 1847, "would make any nation a nation of scoundrels, if it did not find them so." In 1853, when the Massachusetts legislature changed hands, the new majority made envelopes optional, having accepted the argument of Rufus Choate that it was its duty to give every citizen the right "to vote as his fathers, did, with an open ballot."[24]

By the time the House Committee on Elections investigated the contested 1859 Baltimore congressional election, bullying and fisticuffs at the polls were to be expected, and endured. (Women were disenfranchised until the passage of the Nineteenth Amendment in 1920, although, as nineteenth-century suffragettes were wont to argue, maybe, if women had been allowed to vote earlier, there would have been rather more decorum at the polls.) "Were the voters of the 11th ward men of ordinary courage?" a committee member asked a frustrated voter who had only this answer: "Men of ordinary courage, extraordinary courage, and some with no courage at all."[25]

Meanwhile, on the other side of the world, someone came up with a startling idea. What if the government were to provide not just envelopes, but ballots, too?

The exact origins of the idea are somewhat murky. The first Australian ballot law, written by a jurist named Henry Samuel Chapman, was passed in Victoria in March 1856 (a similar law, authored by Francis S. Dutton, was passed in New South Wales the following month, and whether Chapman or Dutton is more justifiably dubbed "Father of the Ballot" remains, in some quarters, a matter strenuously debated). Victoria's Electoral Act of 1856 detailed, quite minutely, the conduct of elections, ordering that no campaigning could take place within a certain distance of the polls and requiring that election officials print ballots and erect a booth or hire rooms, to be divided into compartments where voters could mark those ballots secretly.[26]

This, of course, is exactly how we vote in the United States today. Not that there hasn't been tinkering: New South Wales gets the undisputed acclaim for introducing, in 1877, the placement of an empty square next to a candidate's name, requiring voters to indicate their selections by marking an X in the box.

(Chapman's law required crossing out the names of everyone you *didn't* want to vote for.)[27] Then there's a deuced clever scam called the Tasmanian Dodge (for which, yes, Tasmania gets full credit): get your hands on a blank ballot, fill it out, and then pay someone to cast it while smuggling out another blank. A good Tasmanian dodger could vote as many times as he liked, without ever casting a ballot. (The dodge was eventually defeated by numbering ballots.)[28]

When the Australian ballot was propounded in Britain, James Mills's son, John Stuart Mill, emerged as its most articulate opponent. The younger Mill first took up the subject in 1859, just a few months before George Kyle's brother died in Baltimore. Voting, Mill insisted, is not a right but a trust: if it were a right, who could blame a voter for selling it? Every man's vote must be public for the same reason that votes on the floor of the legislature are public. If a congressman or a member of Parliament could hide his vote, would we not expect him to vote badly, in his own interest and not in ours? A secret vote is, by definition, a selfish vote. Only when a man votes "under the eye and criticism of the public" does he put public interest above his own.[29]

Mill's argument, while widely debated, met with a perplexing reply: even if voting is a public trust (which not all of Mill's opponents granted), voters need to exercise it privately to exercise it well because the electorate, unlike the legislature, consists of men of unequal rank. The powerless will always be prevailed upon by the powerful; only secrecy can protect them from undue influence. Parliament adopted the Australian ballot in 1872.[30]


The most zealous American champion of the Australian ballot, Henry George, sailed to Australia in 1852, when he was thirteen, as a foremast boy. He washed up in San Francisco in 1858; three years later he married an Australian. He first advocated the Australian ballot in December 1871, just months after the *New York Times* began publishing its investigation into the gross corruption of elections in New York City under the party boss, William Marcy Tweed. (In 1868, a presidential election year, Tweed's amply rewarded "repeaters" cast more than 50,000 illegal votes.)[31] Without the Australian ballot, George wrote, "we might almost think soberly of the propriety of putting up our offices at auction."[32]

George had a point. In San Francisco, party bosses handed out "quarter eagles," coins worth $2.50; in Connecticut, where 16 percent of the electorate could be bought, votes cost between two and twenty bucks. In Indiana, tens of thousands of men sold their suffrages for no more than a sandwich, a swill, and a fiver.[33] If people were so poor and desperate they'd sell their votes for lunch, well, maybe letting everyone vote just couldn't work. Maybe the Founders were right. But George, while granting, in an 1883 essay, that elections had become a national scandal, resisted the conclusion "that democracy is therefore condemned or that universal suffrage must be abandoned."[34] The next year, a New York lawyer named William Ivins published in *Harper's* a scathing indictment of machine politics: "Our elections are not elections in any true sense of the word," Ivins declared. "When we vote we simply register our choice as between two or three men who have already been elected by a machinery unknown to the law."[35]

In 1886, Henry George ran for mayor of New York. He lost. But the party he created, the United Labor Party, became the first national party to demand the Australian ballot.[36] Two years later, the Kentucky state legislature attempted the reform in Louisville. After the voting that year, an observer wrote to the *Nation*: "The election last Tuesday was the first municipal election I have ever known which was not bought outright."[37]

In 1888, Massachusetts became the first state to legislate the Australian ballot. (Its law served as the model for all that followed.) That success put pressure on David Hill, the Democratic governor of New York, who had vetoed an Australian ballot bill three times, arguing that its restriction on campaigning at the polls violated freedom of speech.[38] Hill's veto was only broken in 1890 after fourteen men carried to the floor of the New York legislature a petition weighing half a ton.[39] But Massachusetts and New York proved the only states to deliberate at length over the Australian ballot. Elsewhere, state legislatures swiftly yielded to their example, and to the argument made in national magazines and especially by the *Nation*.[40] In the presidential election of 1896, nine out of ten American voters cast secret, government-printed ballots.[41] William McKinley won, with 271 electoral votes. William Jennings Bryan lost, with 176. The death toll? Zero.


On Election Day, I usually walk around the corner to vote in the basement gymnasium of a neighborhood elementary school, beneath a canopy of basketball hoops. At a table just inside the gym, a precinct volunteer hands me a piece of white paper about the size and weight of a file folder. I enter a booth built of aluminum poles, tug shut behind me a red-white-and-blue curtain, and, with a black marker tied by a string to a tabletop, I mark my ballot, awed, as always, by the gravity of the moment, democracy's sacrament, consecrated with pen and paper.

Except for the basketball hoops, much about how I usually vote was laid out in An Act to Provide for Printing and Distributing Ballots, passed in Massachusetts in 1888.[42] Does it work? With the American adoption of the Australian ballot, many kinds of corruption, violence, and intimidation simply ended, which is why reports of peaceful elections in

Massachusetts and New York proved so persuasive across the country. George Kyle, for one, would have been relieved not to have to walk to the polls with that bundle of ballots tucked under his arm, and, between the clouting, the gunfire, and the ruffians wielding muskets and bricks, my ordinary courage would surely not have taken me even half as close to the polls as his did. Still, the Australian ballot didn't accomplish what Henry George hoped it would: it can scarcely be said to have removed money from elections. Money found other ways in. And it did not, in every case, guarantee free elections. In the South, the Australian ballot, by opening the door to literacy tests, proved crucial to the disenfranchisement of black men, who had been granted suffrage in 1870 by the Fifteenth Amendment. As a Democratic campaign song sung in Arkansas in 1893 put it:

> The Australian ballot works like a charm
> It makes them think and scratch
> And when a Negro gets a ballot
> He has certainly met his match.[43]

Arguably, the Australian ballot also shifted the American conversation about voting from a fundamental debate about democracy to the instrumental and profit-driven advocacy of technology; it launched a kind of voting machine arms race. Machines for casting and counting votes date to the 1880s; the first punch card machine patent was granted in 1888; the next year marked the debut of the Acme Counting Ballot Box; the mechanical curtain-and-lever machine dates from 1899. (Voting machines, like printed ballots, were initially challenged on the grounds that they were unconstitutional.)[44] With the important exception of the Voting Rights Act of 1965, outlawing literacy tests, the twentieth century's election reforms have mostly had to do with managing machines, machines that can break, machines that can be made to fail.[45]

That all Americans can all vote is a consequence of nineteenth-century politics. How our votes are counted is, generally, a product of twentieth- and twenty-first-century technology. Both are patched on to eighteenth-century political philosophy. About the only time the patch is noticeable is when people think about the Electoral College, which is so glaringly a throwback to an earlier and outdated set of assumptions about the relationship between the people and their rulers that it's hard not to notice it. A patch, even a patch upon a patch, isn't necessarily bad. Times change. If the Founders had written more about elections, we might still be voting with corn and beans. But it's probably worth remembering that we vote in defiance of eighteenth-century republicanism, and not in its spirit, and that voting in our kitchens, on the family computer, would remove from the act of casting a ballot its very last vestiges of civic occasion and public office. The United States adopted the Australian ballot to solve problems created by the sudden and dramatic expansion of the electorate in a time of vast economic inequality and very low literacy. For all the good that it did, that reform swept away the notion, however utopian, of voting as a public trust; the staging, at the polls, of heated political debates; and the marking of Election Day as a boisterous public holiday celebrating our vital political culture. The voting booth was a brilliant invention. What happens to the American electorate inside that tiny, curtained space is a bit like what happens when Clark Kent enters a telephone booth, takes off his glasses, and puts on his tights: we, mere citizens, become We the People. We choose our rulers, and, even more elementally, we grant them the right to rule us. With the stroke of a pen, we offer our consent to be governed; we constitute the nation. But, sometimes, it's a little cramped in there.

# 16

# OBJECTION

The day the strikers' wives pelted the scabs with rotten eggs and a strikebreaker and Irish ex-cop named Edward Casey cracked Jimmie Morris's skull, the governor of Wisconsin called in the National Guard. They came from Milwaukee. By morning, four companies of infantry, a battery of artillery, and a squadron of cavalry armed with rifles and Gatling guns had taken up position outside the gates of the Paine Lumber Company, in Sawdust City, also known as Oshkosh. The city and the company had been founded in 1853, when a New Yorker with the unlikely name of Paine, no champion of the rights of man, he, came out from Canisteo; now the place was run by his son, George. Even Oshkosh's mayor was on George Paine's payroll. By the time of the strike, in 1898, the two thousand German, Irish, Polish, and Danish immigrants who worked at Paine Lumber, the largest of Oshkosh's two dozen sawmills, were turning out four hundred thousand doors a year, making Oshkosh, population twenty-eight thousand, the door capital of the world. Morris, sixteen, had been supporting his mother and six younger brothers and sisters ever since his father was maimed in the mill. He earned forty-five cents a day. The factory doors, Paine doors, were locked once the workers got in, at 6:45 a.m., and kept locked, except for a lunch break, until the guards came and turned the key, twelve hours after that day dawned. "Why gentlemen," Clarence Darrow said to the jury, when the leaders of the strike were brought to trial, "the only difference I can see between the state prison and George M. Paine's factory is that Paine's men are not allowed to sleep on the premises."[1]

The trouble had started that May, after workers sent Paine a letter demanding better wages, a weekly pay day, the end of woman and child labor, and recognition of their union. Thomas Kidd, thirty-eight, general secretary of the Amalgamated Woodworkers International, came from the union's headquarters in Chicago, to organize. Paine had been replacing men with women and children; by that spring, children made up a quarter of his workforce; not a few, like Jimmie Morris, had taken jobs once held by their fathers.[2] Paine threw the letter in the wastebasket; he said he found it "unbusinesslike." Sixteen hundred workers went on strike. "Oshkosh is in the hands of a mob," the mayor said. The sheriff deputized dozens of men as strikebreakers. After the Civil War, National Guard units had been formed, in northern states, to deal with labor unrest; they were funded, in part, by donations from businessmen.[3] But in Oshkosh, the guardsmen turned out to be sympathetic with the strikers; after less than a week, the mayor sent them back to Milwaukee. The mills were closed. But the day after thirteen hundred citizens of Oshkosh attended Morris's funeral, District Attorney Walter Quartermass launched an investigation into the strike, and that's what broke it. The mills reopened on August 3. Casey was indicted for murder. (He was later acquitted.)[4] Kidd was charged with leading a conspiracy to destroy George Paine's business. The state of Wisconsin had come up with an argument by which Kidd could be convicted as a criminal: there is no right to strike.[5]

The trial was "watched all over the country as a test case," the *Milwaukee Sentinel* reported.[6] Quartermass brought in a special prosecutor, F. W. Houghton, who happens to have been among the men who had volunteered their services to the sheriff. That summer, he had made a series of speeches to the Law and Order League.[7] When Paine turned up in court, he sat, not with the crowd, but in front, next to Houghton, who shook his hand, with warmth. Across the aisle, up from Chicago to defend Thomas Kidd, sat Clarence Darrow, whose best trick was to turn a defense into a prosecution. He would pursue Paine to the ends of the earth; he said he wanted to be wherever Paine was, until the day they both died and then, by God, he wanted to be where Paine was not.[8]

Darrow is not only American history's best-known trial lawyer but also its most famous skeptic. In *Clarence Darrow: American Iconoclast* (2011), Andrew E. Kersten observed that Darrow "was dedicated to smashing the structures and systems of social control that impinged on the liberties and freedoms of average people and that caged their aspirations" and regrets, as have many before, that Darrow was not a "systematic thinker."[9] You want to count on Darrow, but you can't. He sounds better than he was. He betrayed people all the time. He was terrible to women. His political philosophy was amateur, and jury-rigged. John A. Farrell, in *Clarence Darrow: Attorney for the Damned* (2011), went further into the archives and deeper into Darrow's crags, to offer this: "He did not believe in free will, nor good and evil, nor choice. There were no moral absolutes, no truth, and no justice. There was only mercy."[10] You can count on that.

Darrow played a role in some two thousand trials.[11] In more than a third of those cases, he was paid nothing.[12] The only case he ever volunteered for is also the one that secured his lasting fame (and gained Spencer Tracy an Oscar nomination, for portraying him in *Inherit the Wind*): defending John Scopes, charged by the state of Tennessee with the crime of teaching evolution. In the nation's schools and colleges,

Darrow said, "the sharp-shooters of bigotry" were picking off teachers who cared about ideas.[13] "I knew that education was in danger from the source that has always hampered it—religious fanaticism."[14]

More usually, Darrow was sought out. "By no effort of mine," he wrote, looking back on his life, "the distressed and harassed and pursued came to my office door."[15] He defended 102 men who were facing the death penalty, and not one was executed, which is good, because Darrow thought he might not survive it, if one of them had been.[16] "It would almost, if not quite, kill me if it should ever happen," he knew.[17] "I had a strongly emotional nature which has caused me boundless joy and infinite pain. I had a vivid imagination. Not only could I put myself in the other person's place, but I could not avoid doing so. My sympathies always went out to the weak, the suffering, and the poor. Realizing their sorrows I tried to relieve them in order that I might be relieved."[18] Sometimes, there is honesty in modesty even as false as that.

Darrow wasn't a philosopher; he wasn't even an iconoclast. He was an agonist. He would argue one way; he would argue another; he just didn't want to see bigotry thrive or watch a man die. He liked to say creeds were dope.[19] "No one can find life tolerable without dope. The Catholics are right, the Christian Scientists are right, the Methodists are right, the drunkards are right."[20] He thought his own dope was pessimism.[21] It wasn't. His dope was compassion. He despaired for humanity mainly because he didn't meet many of his kind of addict. The problem is, you can't teach sympathy; like imagination, you either have it or you don't.[22]

Clarence Sewall Darrow was born in Farmdale, Ohio, in 1857. "I have been told that I come from a very old family," is how he began his autobiography. "A considerable number of people say that it runs back to Adam and Eve." He lifted that from Dickens's *Martin Chuzzlewit*.[23] Everything he read, he used.

Darrow's father, Amirus, was a woodworker and an undertaker. He made furniture and he made coffins, which is one reason Darrow was, all his life, so helplessly obsessed with death. Amirus was also, as Darrow put it, "the village infidel." Darrow's parents read Jefferson, Voltaire, and Rousseau. They were abolitionists; their house was a stop on the Underground Railroad. Clarence got his middle name from William Seward, a radical Republican who went on to become Lincoln's secretary of state.

Some Darrow biographers skip over Darrow's childhood, arguing that earlier biographers have made too much of it, by which they mean, chiefly, Irving Stone.[24] In a swashbuckling biography from 1941, Stone stressed the influence of Darrow's boyhood on his character: "many a midnight the boy had been awakened to ride to the next village on top of a load of hay that concealed an escaping Negro slave." Many a later lawyer read Stone on Darrow and was stirred. Stone, like most popular biographers, was a fabulist. He had John Brown patting little five-year-old Clarence on the head; Brown was hanged in 1859, when Clarence was only two.[25]

But Darrow himself made much of his early years, and when a fellow does that, a biographer has to hearken. "Since my childhood I have never once changed my mind," Darrow wrote in *Farmington*, a barely fictionalized autobiographical novel.[26] Darrow always attributed his cast of mind to his father, who taught him "that doubt was the beginning of wisdom."[27] Amirus also told his son the story of how, when he was eight years old, his father had made him watch a hanging, and how he had never forgotten how it felt to know that, just by watching, and not speaking up, you had helped kill a man.[28]

Darrow was tall and sure-footed, a fine first baseman. ("I once thought that when the time should come that I could

no longer play ball there would be nothing left in life.")[29]
He knew the smell of sawdust. He was forever whittling; he
was cursed with a whittler's itch; in the city, he learned to
scratch it by doing crossword puzzles. How did he come to
be a lawyer? "We lived across the street from a tin-shop, and
the tinner was the justice of the peace." He liked to go over
there and watch the trials. "I enjoyed the way the pettifoggers
abused each other."[30] After a stretch studying at Allegheny
College, Darrow taught school for three years, studying law
books at night. He then went, for just a year, to the University
of Michigan.

"The law is a bum profession, as generally practiced," he
thought. "It is utterly devoid of idealism and almost poverty
stricken as to any real ideas."[31] Darrow was, always and at
heart, a teacher.[32] He used the law to teach one idea, and then
another, but the idea he was really hoping to impart in the
classroom he made of his courtroom was doubt.

He passed the bar, got married, and joined a practice in
Andover, Ohio, not ten miles from where he was born. He
might have been a small-town pettifogger till the end of his
days except that, in 1887, he read Henry George's *Progress and
Poverty*. At the time, the richest 1 percent of Americans owned
51 percent of the nation's wealth (today that number is 35 percent) and the poorest 44 percent owned less than 2 percent.[33]
He also read John Altgeld's *Our Penal Machinery and Its Victims*" and decided to move to Chicago, partly to meet Altgeld
who was, at the time, a superior court judge. He helped Altgeld campaign, successfully, for governor and took a job as a
lawyer for the Chicago & Northwestern Railway. He earned a
reputation as a public speaker. He met George, on the lecture
circuit, but his passion for George's single-tax solution waned:
"The error I found in the philosophy of Henry George was its
cocksureness, its simplicity, and the small value that it placed
on the selfish motives of men."[34]

In 1894, Darrow quit working for the railroad to defend the president of the American Railway Union, Eugene Debs— "the bravest man I ever knew"—who was charged in connection with his role in the Pullman strike.[35] Between 1881 and 1894, there had been, on average, one major railroad strike a week.[36] In the Gilded Age, labor was, generally and literally, crushed. In a single year, of some seven hundred thousand men working on the railroads, more than twenty thousand were injured on the job and nearly two thousand killed. After the Panic of 1893, the Pullman Company cut wages an average of 28 percent; the next year, workers in Chicago went on strike. President Grover Cleveland ordered U.S. marshals to Illinois; Governor Altgeld objected. When the marshals came, riots broke out and the U.S. Attorney General issued a blanket injunction, ordering the strikers back to work. For ignoring the injunction, Debs was convicted of contempt of court and sentenced to six months.[37]

Although Darrow's defense of Debs was unsuccessful, it brought him enough attention that, two years later, he ran for Congress. Altgeld was up for reelection, and he and Darrow campaigned on behalf of Nebraska congressman William Jennings Bryan, who won the Democratic presidential nomination after giving a convention speech in which he placed upon his head an imaginary crown of thorns, a martyr to country and party. The *New York Times* called Bryan an "irresponsible, unregulated, ignorant, prejudiced, pathetically honest and enthusiastic crank."[38] In Illinois, the whole Democratic ticket lost. Darrow blamed Bryan, who lost the presidency. Altgeld, no longer governor, joined Darrow's law practice. And Darrow, a convert to free love, divorced his wife. To make the divorce stick, he needed to get out of town for a while. He made a deal with the Amalgamated Woodworkers: he would defend Kidd for 250 dollars, so long as the union agreed to publish Darrow's closing argument.[39] He had a pretty fair idea what he wanted to say about what men like George M. Paine were doing to the people who worked in the mills. He took a train north, skirting the western shore of Lake Michigan, to Milwaukee, and then boarded a railway car heading along a spur, northwest, to a town not much older than he, on the shores of Lake Winnebago.

*Wisconsin v. Kidd* was called to order in Oshkosh Municipal Court, in City Hall, on Friday, October 14, 1898. George Zentner, a picket captain, and Michael Troiber, a picketer, were also charged in the conspiracy. Both had worked for Paine; both were immigrants, as were four out of five people living in Oshkosh, which was, at the time, the second largest city in Wisconsin.[40] Oshkosh's paper of record, the *Daily Northwestern*, declared the case "second only to the trial of Eugene V. Debs" in national importance.[41] Darrow went further. This trial, he said, was part of "the great battle for human liberty, a battle which was commenced when the tyranny and oppression of man first caused him to impose upon his fellows and which will not end so long as the children of one father shall be compelled to toil to support the children of another in luxury and ease."[42] In American history, there have been few more skilled orators.

"Most jury trials are contests between the rich and poor," Darrow once wrote, in an essay called "How to Pick a Jury." Jury selection took four days.[43] The trick, he advised, is to find, for each seat on the jury, a man so likely to identify with your client that, "really, he is trying himself." And so: "If a Presbyterian enters the jury box and carefully rolls up his umbrella, and calmly and critically sits down, let him go. He is cold as the grave."[44]

In Oshkosh, the Honorable Arthur Goss was having none of it; he ruled against Darrow's effort to expand his number of peremptory challenges.[45] Next, Darrow objected to Houghton, on the ground that he was a prejudiced party. Then Houghton objected to Darrow, as counsel, on the ground that he wasn't from Wisconsin. Both objections were overruled.

Opening arguments took two days. The state had to prove that Kidd had instigated the strike; the defense that he had not. (Darrow would change the stakes.) The prosecution called strikers who testified that Kidd had been at their meetings. Quartermass read a speech Kidd had made after Jimmie Morris's funeral. Houghton called Paine to the stand. Paine said his plant was worth a million dollars, and that the strike had cost him $25,000.[46]

On cross-examination, Darrow got Paine to admit that he had tried to get a judge to file an injunction against Kidd, but that no judge would file it.[47] He implied that Paine had also attempted to bribe Kidd. He began building an argument that the only reason this case had gone to trial was because Paine wanted it to.[48] He was also trying to establish that the point of a strike wasn't to damage anyone's business; it was to relieve suffering. He asked Paine if he employed girls at the mill. Paine said yes.

"What do those girls do?" Darrow asked.

"Ah," said Paine. "Those girls take little bits of sticks and saw them up on little saws."[49]

These saws, that cut doors and deprived men of their limbs, were *playthings*? Here, one supposes, Darrow scratched his head, something he did to suggest that someone had just spoken nonsense. (Observed one reporter: "The scratch behind the ear, however, apparently has no purpose whatsoever.")[50]

When, on Tuesday, October 25, the state rested, Darrow moved that all charges be dismissed: this wasn't a criminal case; this was an act of malice. The motion was denied.[51]

Darrow began his defense by calling Kidd, who testified that Paine employed children and that the wages he paid grown men averaged between eighty-five and ninety cents a day, "a lower rate than paid in any city in the United States." The state objected; this was hearsay. Darrow asked Kidd about the speech he had made. Kidd said, "At no time nor place have I advised violence in carrying out the strike."[52] Darrow called the district attorney to the stand (a favorite ploy). Hadn't workers complained to you before that Paine was breaking the law, in hiring children under the age of fifteen? Quartermass admitted as much.[53] When the matter of just how much these children were paid came up, Houghton volunteered, "I wish I could have been able to get as much when I was a child of their age."[54] I do believe the attorney for the defense scratched his head.

"The case all through has been closely fought," the *Northwestern* reported, and the battles between Houghton and Darrow "very spicy." But Darrow's main line of defense had been thwarted. He intended to prove the existence of a conspiracy led by Paine, but Hoss ruled all the evidence in that regard inadmissible. Houghton had called sixty-two witnesses; Darrow called only twenty-five.[55]

Then came closing statements. "An actor may fumble his lines," Darrow once wrote, "but a lawyer needs to be letter-perfect."[56] He spoke, as he always did, without notes.


Clarence Darrow wore baggy pants and a string tie. His shoulders were so wide he needed special shirts. He moved like a bull. He slicked his hair down, which didn't stop it from being unruly. He looked a far sight more like an underslept pettifogger than a big city lawyer. He liked to play dumb, "as if he were no lawyer at all, but a cracker-barrel philosopher groping for a bit of human truth," as Ben Hecht put it. He would "crack his suspenders like the explosion of a .45," a Chicago newspaperman once said. "I used to think he'd break a rib."[57]

This is a trial for conspiracy, Darrow told the jury and, true, here was "a conspiracy, dark and damnable": "Somebody is guilty of one of the foulest conspiracies that ever disgraced a free nation." But Thomas I. Kidd had nothing to do with it. No. "Back of all this prosecution is the effort on the part of George M. Paine to wipe out these labor organizations out of existence, and you know it." Crack the suspenders. "That's all there is to it."[58]

Darrow took his time. He began with Paine. Paine had persuaded Quartermass to file charges; he had used his influence to have Houghton appointed special counsel. The trial was his doing. He had bent the great state of Wisconsin to his will. And "after he gets through with it," Darrow told the jury, "I hope he will pass it back to you." Paine could go to hell. The men, women, and children who worked in his mill: they were already there. Take a man like Troiber. He had come to Oshkosh, "as thousands of others have come from all nations of this earth, to lend his brawn and muscle and life to the building up of this great land—and he worked for ninety cents a day until he grew old and stunted and haggard and worn, and thought he had a right to demand something more; and then George M. Paine conspired to lock him up in jail, and he hired these lawyers as bloodhounds to bay him inside the doors."[59]

Past that, Darrow told the jury, he did not give a fig about the facts in this case. Did Troiber hit a man who tried to cross the picket line? "I do not know," Darrow said. "I do not care." Were the children who worked at Paine's fifteen, or younger? "I do not care. It is a disgrace to the civilization in which we live that they were there at all." Had the woodworkers dared to form a union? Yes, but "I do not care." Did Kidd urge them to strike? No, but Darrow didn't care. Fourteen weeks that strike lasted, peaceably, with not enough excitement "to make up one decent Fourth of July celebration." There had been that riot, yes, and that poor boy, Jimmie Morris, had got his skull cracked. Who was to blame for that? "I do not know," Darrow said. "I do not care." Here's what he did know: Kidd was a goddamned saint. "If I had been here to conduct this strike instead of Kidd," he told the jury, "the men would not have been so gentlemanly and orderly, let me tell you that."[60]

As to the most damning evidence: Did Kidd make the speech that was read in court, and made to sound so sinister? Yes, and the son of a carpenter once made a speech just like that to some fishermen in Judea.[61] Come to think of it, that speech was just like a letter in a Dickens story: "Dear Madam—I will be home at 7. Chops and tomato sauce." After Mr. Pickwick wrote that note to his landlady, she brought him to court for breach of promise. And a lawyer "who practiced law in London then," Darrow told the jury, "but who has moved to Oshkosh since, brought out that letter and he read it to the jury and he said, 'Gentlemen of the jury, 'Chops and tomato sauce.' Gentlemen of the jury, what is the meaning of those words, 'chops and tomato sauce'? Gentlemen of the jury, are a widow's affections to be trifled away by chops and tomato sauce?" Kidd uttered the words, "fellow citizens," and Houghton called him a socialist. Chops, gentlemen, and tomato sauce.

No, Darrow didn't care about the facts, nor, for that matter, did he care about the case. He cared, only, about one question: "whether when a body of men desiring to benefit their condition, and the condition of their fellow men, shall strike, whether those men can be sent to jail."[62]

And then Darrow said to the jury: "I know that you will render a verdict in this case which will be a milestone in the history of the world, and an inspiration and hope to the dumb, despairing millions whose fate is in your hands."[63] He had spoken for eight hours.

Darrow's success as a lawyer lay, in part, with his talent as an historian. Every case he ever argued was the most important case in the history of the world. Or, at least, he was able to make it seem that way. The Kidd trial, if not, perhaps, a milestone in the history of the world, was a landmark in the Gilded Age debate about prosperity and equality. There were two ways of looking at what Darrow called "the great questions that are animating the world today."[64] Either wealthy businessmen like Paine and Pullman were ushering in prosperity for all, or else the interests of the Paines and the Pullmans of the world were at odds with everyone else's interests. In Oshkosh, Darrow won that argument.[65] The jury was out for fifty minutes. All three defendants were acquitted.

Darrow went on to serve as labor's leading lawyer. In 1903, he represented the United Mine Workers in Pennsylvania, in arbitration. "Five hundred dollars a year is a big price for taking your life and your limbs in your hand and going down into the earth to dig up coal to make somebody else rich."[66] While Darrow spoke, the chair of the arbitration commission had to beg the audience to stop applauding. The miners got their raise, and back pay to boot. Six years later, in the first trial covered by wire services, he defended Big Bill Haywood, secretary of the Western Federation of Miners, accused, on entirely trumped up charges, of playing a role in the murder the former governor of Idaho. "Don't think for a moment that if you kill Haywood you kill the labor movement of the world or the hopes and aspirations of the poor," Darrow told the jury. "Haywood can die, if die he must, but there are others who will live if he dies, and they will come to take his place and carry the banner which he lets fall." Haywood was acquitted.

In 1910, Darrow agreed to defend the McNamara brothers, to be hanged if convicted of bombing the *Los Angeles Times* building. The *Times* was antilabor. Twenty-one people died in the bombing. At the time Darrow took the case, he was twenty-five thousand dollars in debt, supporting a wife, an ex-wife, and at least one mistress. When he realized that his clients were guilty, he changed their plea, but not before the district attorney discovered that an investigator hired by Darrow had tried to bribe two jurors. Darrow was indicted and tried, twice. In the first trial, he was found not guilty; the second resulted in a hung jury. Darrow always maintained his innocence or, more shiftily, his blamelessness: "My conscience refuses to reproach me."[67]

After that, Darrow left the labor movement. He went on to do his best work speaking and writing against fundamentalism, eugenics, the death penalty, and Jim Crow. "America seems to have an epidemic of intolerance," he wrote.[68]

"Gentlemen, the world is dark," Darrow told that jury in Oshkosh, "but it is not hopeless."[69] After all, no attorney for the damned ever lacks for work.

# 17

# CHAN, THE MAN

"Enter Charlie Chan" is the title Earl Derr Biggers gave to chapter 7 of *The House Without a Key*, published serially in the *Saturday Evening Post* in 1925, and set in Hawaii, where Biggers, a Harvard Lampooner who was born in Ohio and who, before he started writing novels, mainly wrote humor for a magazine called the *Boston Traveler*, had once gone for his health. Honolulu: ukulele music, ginger blossoms, coconut palms, grass mats, a luau. Miss Minerva Winterslip, a Boston spinster far from home, discovers, on a cot on her veranda, a dead body in white pajamas. A lizard skitters over the corpse, leaving a trail of tiny, crimson footprints. The spinster, shaken and trembling, telephones the dead man's brother, Amos, who promptly summons the authorities. A police captain and a coroner arrive, followed by a third man, of appearance, most curious: "He was very fat indeed, yet he walked with the light dainty steps of a woman. His cheeks were as chubby as a baby's, his skin ivory tinted, his black hair close-cropped, his amber eyes slanting."

"Amos!" cried Miss Minerva. "That man—why he—"

"Charlie Chan," Amos explained. "I'm glad they brought him. He's the best detective on the force."

"But—he's Chinese!"

Miss Minerva, overcome, collapses. Chan, despite being as chubby as a baby and as dainty as a woman and being, really, anything *but* a man, walks away with the chapter, the novel, and Biggers's career. But first, he inspects the scene on Miss Minerva's veranda. "No knife are present in neighborhood of crime," he reports, in inexplicably bludgeoned English spoken in a "high, sing-song voice." The captain assigns him the case. "The slant eyes blinked with pleasure. 'Most interesting,' murmured Chan." Miss Minerva balks. Chan steps forward and gives the lady from Boston a stare. "Humbly asking pardon to mention it," he smiles, bowing. "I detect in your eyes slight flame of hostility. Quench it, if you will be so kind."[1]

A star was born. The honorable Chinese detective from Honolulu would appear in five more Biggers novels, and long before the seventh chapter. Biggers, who knew very little about Hawaii and less about China, found this mystifying. Once, when a reporter wrote to ask him how he came up with the character, Biggers wrote back, in Chan's voice:

> Boss looks me over, and puts me in a novel, *The House Without a Key*. "You are a minor character, always," he explains. "No major feelings, please. The background is your province—keep as far back as is humanly possible." Story starts to begin serial career, and public gets stirred up. They demand fuller view of my humble self. "What is the approximate date of beginning of next Charlie Chan story?" they inquire of the boss. And is my face red?
>
> Boss glares at me, plenty gloomy. "Good Lord!" he cries, "am I saddled with you for the remainder of my existence?"
>
> "You could be saddled with horse," I bristle.[2]

Chan's Hollywood career was launched in 1926, with a film adaptation of *The House Without a Key*, starring the Japanese actor George Kuwa, after which Chan went on to appear in forty-six more movies; he was most memorably played, in the

1930s, by a Swede named Warner Oland. He also appeared in countless comic strips and, in the 1970s, in sixteen episodes of Hanna-Barbera's *The Amazing Chan and the Chan Clan*, which aired on CBS television on Saturday mornings and featured a dog named Chu Chu, Jodie Foster's voice as one of Chan's ten children, and the cri de coeur, "Wham, bam, we're in a jam!"[3]

Charlie Chan is also one of the most hated characters in American popular culture. In the 1980s and 1990s, distinguished American writers, including Frank Chin and Gish Jen, argued for laying Chan to rest, a yellow Uncle Tom, best buried. In trenchant essays, Chin condemned the Warner Oland movies as "parables of racial order" and Jen called Chan "the original Asian whiz kid."[4] In 1993, the literary scholar Elaine Kim bid Chan good riddance—"Gone for good his yellowface asexual bulk, his fortune-cookie English"—in an anthology of contemporary Asian American fiction titled *Charlie Chan Is Dead*, which is not to be confused with the beautiful and fantastically clever 1982 Wayne Wang film, *Chan Is Missing*, and in which Chan is alive and well and all over the place, it's just that no one can find him anymore.[5]

"Role of dead man require very little acting," as Charlie Chan liked to say.[6] (Don't ask me what that means. Aphorisms, like tiger in zoo, all roar, no claw.) In *Charlie Chan: The Untold Story of the Honorable Detective and His Rendezvous with American History* (2010), Yunte Huang, who was born in China, went to graduate school in the United States, and taught at Harvard before he went on to teach American literature at the University of California, Santa Barbara, confessed, abashedly, to being a Chan fan: "Sometimes late at night, I turn on the TV and a Chinaman falls out. He is hilarious."[7] Most interesting.

Earl Derr Biggers did not invent Charlie Chan. "How can I write of Chinese?" he asked Chan, in that fictional conversation with his fictional detective. "I could not distinguish

Chinese man from Wall Street broker." (Chan had an answer for that. Chan had an answer for everything. "Chinese
would be the one who sold you the honest securities.")[8] A
great delight of Huang's quirky, smart, and entertaining
book is his sleuthing out the real story behind Charlie Chan.
Chan was an actual guy, a detective with the Honolulu Police
Department; Biggers read about him in the newspaper. His
real name was Chang Apana. He was born, around 1871, in
Waipio, a village outside Honolulu. His mother, Chung Shee,
was also born in Hawaii. People from China had settled in
what were then called the Sandwich Islands, beginning in
the 1780s. Sugarcane had been cultivated in China for centuries, and the first person to grow it for sugar processing
in the Sandwich Islands was a man named Wong Tze-chun,
who arrived from China in 1802. Chang Jong Tong, Chang
Apana's father, probably traveled from China to Hawaii in
the 1860s. In the second half of the nineteenth century, forty-
six thousand Chinese laborers made that journey. In 1866,
when the sugarcane trade was booming, Mark Twain went to
Hawaii to report for the *Sacramento Union*. "The Government
sends to China for coolies and then farms them out at $5 a
month each for five years," Twain wrote.[9] When Chang Jong
Tong's five years were up, he took his wife, and their three
children, and headed home, to the tiny village of Oo Sack,
south of Canton.

Yunte Huang himself grew up—"in the waning days
of Mao's China"—in a village in southeastern China not
much different from Oo Sack. Huang wrote of a boyhood
spent working, and playing with insects—ants, fireflies,
grasshoppers—for toys, and imagined that Apana might have
done the same. Imagining Apana's life is what Huang is often
reduced to, though, because Apana never learned to read or
to write, either Chinese or English (although, later in life, he
taught himself to read Hawaiian), which partly accounts for
his scant appearances in the historical record.

In Oo Sack, a part of the world devastated by famine and the Opium Wars, the boy and his family were starving. In 1881, when Apana was about ten years old, his parents sent him to Oahu, with an uncle; he never returned to China. Somehow—here, too, the trail vanishes—he became a cowboy, a *paniolo*, because, ten years later, he was a stableman for a wealthy family, the Wilders, at their horse ranch in Honolulu. When Samuel Wilder, a steamship magnate, was married in Hawaii, in 1866, to Elizabeth Judd, the daughter of a missionary (and said to be the first white girl born in Hawaii), both Mark Twain and King Kamehameha attended the wedding. In 1897, the Wilders's youngest daughter, Helen, hired Chang Apana as the first officer for a local chapter of the Humane Society. It was his job to stop people from beating their horses. He was very good at this. He was, for one thing, different from most of the people who lived in Honolulu's Chinatown, which was where he mostly patrolled, making arrests and issuing fines, in a city with some twenty-five thousand Chinese. He was nicknamed "Kanaka Pung" because he looked more Hawaiian than Chinese. "I was the only one without my queue in the '80s and 90's," he later recalled. He was neither chubby like a baby nor dainty like a woman. He was five feet tall and wiry and had a nasty scar on his brow. He wore a cowboy hat and carried a bullwhip.

In 1898, the United States went to war with Spain, a war waged, mainly, in the Pacific; Hawaii became a territory of the United States; and Chang Apana was recruited by the Honolulu Police Department, which was growing, because of the first two of those developments. In a force of more than two hundred men—the officers mainly Hawaiians, and the chiefs mostly white, or *haole*—he was the only Chinese.[10] He excelled and was promoted to detective. In the 1910s, he was part of a crime-busting squad. His escapades were the stuff of legend. He was said to be as agile as a cat. Thrown from a second-floor window by a gang of dope fiends, he landed on his feet. He leapt from one rooftop to the next, like a human fly. When he reached for his whip, thugs scattered and miscreants wept. He once arrested forty gamblers in their lair, singlehanded. He was a master of disguises. Once, patrolling a pier at dawn, disguised as a poor merchant—wearing a straw hat and stained clothes and carrying, tied to a bamboo shoulder pole, baskets of coconuts—he raised the alarm on a shipment of contraband, even while he was being run over by a horse and buggy, and having his legs broken. He once solved a robbery by noticing a strange thread of silk on a bedroom floor. He discovered a murderer by observing that one of the suspects, a Filipino man, had changed his muddy shoes, asking him, "Why you wear new shoes this morning?"[11]

At times, Huang got a little carried away by the legend, caught up in the perfumed, tropical romance of it all. "Apana once climbed up walls like a pre-Spiderman sleuth and slipped into an opium dive," he wrote.[12] But, more often, Huang's history is bracing and expansive, moving from Apana's exploits to chronicle the squalor of Honolulu's Chinatown and the miseries endured by each wave of immigrant workers—Chinese, Japanese, Korean, and Filipino—in a world of brutal and unbending racial hierarchy. (Before Hawaii outlawed the death penalty in 1957, twenty out of the twenty-four civilians executed on the islands were Filipino, two were Korean, two Japanese, one Puerto Rican, and one Hawaiian; as Huang observes, "not a single white man was among them.") One of Apana's jobs was to capture lepers, for forced transport to a leper colony on the island of Molokai, to die. Hawaiians called leprosy *mai pake*, "Chinese sickness," because it came to the islands in the 1830s and appeared to have arrived with the Chinese. Apana got that scar above his right eye while trying to capture a Japanese man who had contracted leprosy and who, armed with a sickle, refused to be sent to Molokai, on a journey over what came to be called the Bridge of Sighs.[13]

Earl Derr Biggers started out as a police reporter for the *Cleveland Plain Dealer*. He published a lot of doggerel, many short stories, and two plays. He produced his first novel in 1913. He sailed to Hawaii seven years later.[14] He always said, though, that he only came across Chang Apana, in 1924, back in the States, while paging through a Hawaiian newspaper in the Reading Room of the New York Public Library: "In an obscure corner of an inside page, I found an item to the effect that a certain hapless Chinese, being too fond of opium, had been arrested by Sergeants Chang Apana and Lee Fook, of the Honolulu Police. So Sergeant Charlie Chan entered the story of *The House Without a Key*."[15]

The year Biggers decided to write about Chan, Congress passed the most restrictive anti-immigration act in U.S. history, the Immigration Act of 1924, which, among other things, excluded from American citizenship foreign-born "Asiatics" (a new racial category, invented by eugenicists in the 1910s and codified in 1923).[16] The trick of Huang's book, which he didn't quite pull off, was to explain why so many Americans became so enamored of Charlie Chan, at just this moment. Why, hating and fearing the Chinese, did they love the Chinese detective? Was he—so unmanned, so obsequious, so humbly offering his services—reassuring? Or was there more to it, or something different? On this question, Huang dodged. He began by rejecting cause and effect, insisting that the Immigration Act neither led Biggers to write about Chan nor created an audience for him: "Crude historical determinism," Huang insisted, "is mostly a self-fulfilling prophecy, an insult to the magic of the literary imagination." Then he wrote about America in the

1920s, and especially about the golden age of detective fiction, to point out, quite rightly, that Chan has rather a lot in common with a certain chubby, dainty, and foreign detective named Hercule Poirot, a Belgian in England who is forever being mistaken for a Frenchman, who is also very clever, can't keep the order of verbs and adjectives straight, speaks in aphorisms, and was created by Agatha Christie in 1920. But then Huang waved Poirot away. All detectives have ticks, and quirks of speech, and little affectations. Chan is, somehow, in some ineluctable way, more foreign—the original inscrutable. Huang was left to conclude, vaguely, that "the fictional Chan was part of the Zeitgeist of America in the 1920s."[17] Well, yes. But what else?

He was, Huang argued, a "Chinaman," a word that, beginning in the nineteenth century, worked, in the United States as a slur, in a way that, say, "Frenchman" or even "Irishman" never did. One of the best parts of Huang's book was his account of the invention of the Chinaman, an account that ranges from Chang and Eng, the "Siamese twins," who, born in Siam, were of Chinese ancestry, and were displayed in the United States beginning in 1829; to gold-rushing, railroad-building California, from the 1850s on onward, where white Californians wrote songs like this—

My name is Sin Sin, come from China
In a bigee large shipee, commee long here;

to the Chinese Exclusion Act of 1882; to the laundrymen in Earl Derr Biggers's childhood Ohio.[18]

"What is a Chinaman?" Huang asked. And one of his answers was, "I am." Huang was a sophomore at Peking University in 1989, when the student protests broke out in Tiananmen Square. He camped out on the square and would have been there, on June 4, when the tanks rolled in, and killed hundreds of demonstrators, except that his family had telegrammed, three days before, that his mother was "gravely ill," and he had journeyed home, to the countryside. His family was lying. His mother was just fine. But China, for Huang, was never the same. Two years later, he left for the United States and landed in Tuscaloosa, running a Chinese restaurant called Si Fang. He gave a great deal of thought to what it meant to be seen, in America, as a Chinaman, a purveyor of chop suey. He left Alabama and worked his way through graduate school in Buffalo as a deliveryman for a Chinese fast food joint. Then, at an estate sale in upstate New York, he came across some Charlie Chan books and fell in love with the honorable detective from Honolulu. "I have met thousands of Chans," Huang wrote, and "I find him to be the strangest and most impressive Chan ever." He wrote other books, scholarly studies of "transpacific imagination" and "transpacific displacement." But finding Chan became his passion. He drove across Ohio, looking for the place, in Akron, where, according to the census, a man named Charlie Chan ran a laundry, in 1900. He read in endless archives. He flew to Honolulu and went to Chang Apana's house at 3737 Waialae Avenue.[19] What is a Chinaman? Huang was fascinated by this question and spent ten years gumshoeing all over America, trying to answer it, missing China, missing Chan, wishing for a world where soldiers don't kill students, and where a racist parody isn't so much racist, as parody.

Chang Apana met Earl Derr Biggers in 1928. By then, people in Honolulu had taken to calling Apana Charlie Chan. In 1926, Biggers published another Chan mystery, *The Chinese Parrot* and, with the royalties, bought a house in Pasadena, where he hired a Chinese servant named Gung Wong. The next year, Biggers published *Behind That Curtain*, and *The Chinese Parrot* was made into a silent film, starring the Japanese actor Kamiyama Sojin. (No print of either Sojin's *Chinese*

*Parrot* or the 1926 film of *The House Without a Key*, starring George Kuwa, survives.)[20] Biggers sailed from California to Hawaii in the summer of 1928 and met with Apana on July 5, at the Royal Hawaiian Hotel. Apana's nephew, Chang Joe, served as an interpreter. Biggers later recalled Apana as "a man who can laugh even as he reaches for the whip." There is no record of what Apana thought of Biggers. The two men posed for a photograph, taken by the Hawaii Tourist Bureau. The photograph, in which neither man is smiling, was printed in the newspaper with the caption, "AUTHOR MEETS 'LIVE' CHINESE DETECTIVE."[21]

In 1929, Biggers published *The Black Camel* and, soon after, *Charlie Chan Carries On*, which sold 35,400 copies in its first four months alone. In 1930, Biggers earned more than seventeen thousand dollars in royalties. ("You know how much Apana get?" Apana's nephew, Walter Chang once asked an interviewer. "Not even nickel!") That year, Fox cast Warner Oland as Chan, in an adaptation of *Charlie Chan Carries On* (of which no print survives). Oland, born in Sweden in 1879, had, beginning in 1918, specialized in playing Oriental villains, including Dr. Fu Manchu. (Oland's mother was Russian, and he had Slavic features.) Biggers, on learning that Oland would be playing Chan, wrote to his publisher, "hope to heaven he understands what sort of character Charlie is—not a sinister Fu Manchu." But when he saw the film, Biggers was pleased: "after all these weary years, they have got Charlie right on the screen."

In the 1930s, the Chan movies kept Fox afloat. Oland studied Chinese, traveled to China, and learned Chinese calligraphy. He was paid forty thousand dollars per film.[22] Fox made sixteen Chan films between 1931 and 1939, when Oland died in the middle of shooting the seventeenth. Biggers once tried to get Apana a part in a Chan film, for which he would have been paid five hundred dollars. Apana turned it down. But

Apana loved the movies. Walter Chang remembered going to meet his uncle at the police station, at two o'clock in the afternoon, to go to a matinee, to watch movies, any movies, and especially Charlie Chan movies. "He like the movies. Oh, the movies." Keye Luke, a dashing Canton-born American artist and actor who played Lee Chan, Charlie's Number One Son, in seven Oland-Chan films, loved them, too. Luke, who died in 1991, was exasperated with the argument that Oland, as Chan, "demeans the race": "Demeans! My God!" Luke said in an interview. "We thought we were making the best damn murder mysteries in Hollywood."[23]

In May 1931, Fox shot *The Black Camel* on location, in Honolulu—the only Oland-Chan movie filmed in Hawaii. The movie is about the making of movies, and the art of deception. ("Hollywood is famous furnisher of mysteries," says Chan.) The murder victim is an actress, in Hawaii to shoot a film on location. Bela Lugosi, who had just finished being Dracula, plays a very creepy psychic named Tarneverro. Chan tries to pass himself off as a Chinese merchant; Tarneverro sees through him.

Chang Apana, now in his seventies, was invited to come watch the filming. He and Oland met, on Kailua Beach, and posed for a photograph together. Apana looks amused. Oland is grinning. Oland inscribed the back of photograph, "To my dear friend, Charlie Chang, 'The bravest of all,' with best of luck, from the new 'Charlie Chan,' Warner Oland."

Apana missed hardly a day of shooting. In one scene, someone tells Charlie Chan that he ought to have a lie detector. "Lie detector?" Chan asks. "Ah, I see! You mean wife. I got one." Apana laughed and laughed. It was a rehearsal, though, and no one captured on tape the sound Yunte Huang most wanted to hear.[24]

# 18

# THE UPROOTED

In May 1939, Ralph Ellison, who was twenty-five at the time, asked an old man hanging out in Eddie's Bar on St. Nicholas Avenue near 147th Street, "Do you like living in New York City?" The man said:

> Ahm in New York, but New York ain't in me. You understand? Ahm in New York, but New York ain't in me. What do I mean? Listen. I'm from Jacksonville Florida. Been in New York twenty-five years. I'm a New Yorker! Yuh understand? Naw, naw, yuh don't get me. What do they do; take Lenox Avenue. Take Seventh Avenue; take Sugar Hill! Pimps. Numbers. Cheating those poor people out a whut they got. Shooting, cutting, backbiting, all them things. Yuh see? Yuh see what Ah mean? *I'm* in New York, but *New York ain't in me!*[1]

Ellison took all that down, on a nice neat form. He was asking because it was his job to ask: he was muddling through the Depression on a crummy paycheck from the Works Progress Administration, which people liked to call the Whistle, Piss, and Argue department but which was something to do, anyway, and better than the dole. At its peak, the WPA's Federal Writers' Project employed more than seven thousand writers—from newspaper reporters to playwrights, anybody who used to make some kind of living by writing, and couldn't any more—including Saul Bellow, Zora Neale Hurston, John Cheever, and Richard Wright. (At the time, one in four people in publishing were out of work.) You had to take a pauper's oath, to get hired, and the whole thing was axed, four years after it got started, by congressmen who were convinced it was a communist front. But, before that, Ellison and all those thousands of other writers chronicled American life by interviewing ordinary people. They also reinvented the interview and changed American journalism forever. It was mired in bureaucracy and inefficiency, but it was also the best public literary works project, before or since. Its folklore director, Benjamin Botkin, had a mad, beautiful vision. He wanted to turn "the streets, the stockyards, and the hiring halls into literature."[2] From more than ten thousand interviews, the Writers' Project produced some eight hundred books, including *A Treasury of American Folklore*, and in 1939, a volume called *These Are Our Lives*.[3] That's not counting the novels, though, which is what became of a lot of those interviews. In *The Invisible Man*, which won the National Book Award when it was published in 1952, an old woman, up from the South, saves Ellison's narrator, a newer arrival, after he collapses on Lenox Avenue, telling him, "You have to take care of yourself, son. Don't let this Harlem git you. I'm in New York, but New York ain't in me, understand what I mean?"[4]

That man in Eddie's bar, who left Jacksonville, Florida, at the beginning of World War I, was part of what historians call the Great Migration, which can be confusing, because historians also talk about the Great Migration of Puritans who left England between 1630 and 1641. There's great, and then there's great. The seventeenth-century migration to New England—twenty thousand people—was great because the Puritans thought it was great, and said so, every time they got within ten paces of a pulpit. I am founding a city on a hill, a beacon unto the world! I am leading an errand into the wilderness! The twentieth-century migration from the cotton belt was great, in numbers, but whether it was great, for the people who made it, was something to wonder about. Was this really the Promised Land? Was this, Seventh Avenue, home? "Should I have come here?" Richard Wright, who was born in Mississippi and moved to Chicago in 1927, asked, in *Black Boy*. Between 1915 and 1918, five hundred thousand blacks left the South; 1.3 million between 1920 and 1930. They drove; they hitched rides; they saved till they could buy a ticket on a train. They went to cities, especially Chicago, Detroit, New York, Philadelphia, and Los Angeles. They fled Jim Crow, laws put on the books after Reconstruction. Georgia was the first state to demand separate seating for whites and blacks in streetcars, in 1891; five years later came *Plessy v. Ferguson*. By 1905, every southern state had a streetcar law, and more: in courthouses, separate Bibles; in bars, separate stools; in post offices, separate windows; in libraries, separate branches. In Birmingham, it was a crime for blacks and whites to play checkers together in a public park.[5] By 1970, after civil rights killed Jim Crow and the Great Migration stopped, six million people had left their homes. It was bigger than the Gold Rush. It was bigger than the Dust Bowl Okies. Before the Great Migration, 90 percent of all blacks in the United States lived in the South; after it, 47 percent lived someplace else. At the beginning of the twenty-first century, more African Americans lived in the city of Chicago than in the state of Mississippi. Isabel Wilkerson, who earned a Pulitzer while working as the *New York Times*'s Chicago bureau chief and went on to teach journalism and serve as the director of the Narrative Nonfiction program at Boston University, called the exodus "the most underreported story of the twentieth century."[6]

To report that story, Wilkerson became something of a one-woman WPA project.[7] Wilkerson's research, which took her more than ten years, is not unlike another chunk of work done by the Federal Writers' Project: documenting the history of slavery, before its memory faded altogether. In the 1930s, about one hundred thousand people who had once been owned by other people were still alive.[8] Writers' Project writers fanned out to find them and collected two thousand life stories.[9] Before that, all historians could use, to write about slavery, were a handful of slave narratives, published in the decades before the Civil War, by people who escaped; accounts written, here and there, by travelers to the South; and tottering piles of letters and diaries written by slaveholders. Oral histories are, as evidence, not without problems. Much depends on the sensitivity, acuity, and fidelity of the interviewer. But without those WPA interviews—firsthand accounts, by people who lived for part of their lives as slaves—the history of slavery would be a lopsided travesty.

Wilkerson, realizing that the generation of Americans who lived under Jim Crow wouldn't be around much longer, set out to talk to them. Her own parents migrated to Chicago, her mother from Georgia, her father from Virginia; she'd heard their stories from childhood. She wanted to hear more. She interviewed twelve hundred people, from all over the country. She found them at pensioners clubs, senior centers, and funerals. ("I hung around playgrounds; I hung around the street, the bars," Ellison told Ann Banks, when she interviewed him, for *First Person America*, an excellent and invaluable study and anthology. "I went into hundreds of apartment buildings and just knocked on doors. I would tell some stories to get people going and then I'd sit back and try to get it down as accurately as I could. Sometimes you would find people sitting around on Eighth Avenue just dying to talk.")[10] Wilkerson spoke for a long time with three dozen people and then chose three, and interviewed them for hundreds of hours.[11] Her book is the story of those three lives, told, really, as an act of love. She took her title from Wright:

> I was taking a part of the South
> To transplant in alien soil,
> To see if it could grow differently,
> If it could drink of new and cool rains,
> Bend in strange winds,
> Respond to the warmth of other suns
> And, perhaps, to bloom.

And her deeply affecting, finely crafted, and, frankly, heroic book can be read an elegant homage to Wright's *12 Million Black Voices: A Folk History of the Negro in the United States* (Wright's text accompanied photographs taken by the Farm Security Administration). Wright expressed, in vernacular, an argument of the Chicago School of sociologists, who, beginning in the 1920s, had been studying the Great Migration, calculating averages, finding the mean, compiling reports (presaging Moynihan's), about black life in the urban North.[12] "Perhaps never in history has a more utterly unprepared folk wanted to go to the city," Wright wrote.[13] In the Chicago School argument, the folk, in the city, crash into modernity; uprooting means loss, especially loss of community, an argument that has been long debated and which Wilkerson didn't so much take on as steer clear of. Her folk don't crash; they struggle; they study; they strive and even thrive. More to the point, she didn't call them folk, and, for all that her work shares with Wright's, her project had less in common with the documentary populism of the 1930s, which, like Chicago School sociology, was always about the collective, where truth was to be found in the aggregate (if you could just talk to enough people, take enough photographs, conduct enough surveys, you could, finally, record what it meant to be human), than with the new narrative journalism of the 1960s, which was always about the individual, where truth was to be found in allegory (if you could just find the right person to talk to, and it had to be an ordinary person, you could write, from that one, the story of everyone). Wilkerson's work, in other words, was more novelistic than documentary, more *Invisible Man* than *12 Million Black Voices*, and less Studs Terkel (another Writers' Project writer) than J. Anthony Lukas (who, like Wilkerson, spent much of his career at the *New York Times*).[14]

Wilkerson took on one of the most important demographic upheavals of the last century—a phenomenon whose dimensions and significance have eluded many a scholar—and told it, as a novelist would, through the lives of three people no one has ever heard of, as a certain kind of journalist might. Narrative nonfiction is risky; it has to be grabby, telling, and true. To bear analytical weight, it has to be almost frighteningly shrewd. In Wilkerson's book, *The Warmth of Other Suns*, three lives, three people, three stories, are asked to stand for six million. Can three people explain six million? Do they have to? Your answers probably depend, mostly, on your intellectual proclivities. You're reading this book, about stories; chances are, you lean toward thinking stories, good stories, explain. But, if you're an empiricist, the only real way to decide is to see it tried. And so, of six million lives, of three stories, here's one.

Mae Ida Brandon was born in a wood house in Chickasaw County, Mississippi, in 1913. She was ornery, and a tomboy, and told people to call her Ida Mae—it sounded less old-fashioned—as soon as she could tell anybody what to do. She walked a mile to a one-room schoolhouse that went to the eighth grade, which was the highest you could go to, and where she was once whipped with a switch for spelling Philadelphia wrong, a place she had never heard of. She hated picking cotton, and was bad at it, but she liked killing snakes. Once, when she was six or seven, sometime, anyway, before her father died, she rode a horse to the blacksmith's to get a piece of plow sharpened, and the blacksmith's two sons, white boys, dangled her over a well, to watch her squirm. When she was thirteen, two brothers, the Carter boys, said something to some white lady, as best she could remember, and were lynched the next day. "If it is necessary, every negro in the state will be lynched," James. K. Vardaman had said in 1903, the year he was first elected governor of Mississippi; the year Ida Mae was born was the year that he joined the U.S. Senate. In those years, by one reckoning, someone in the South was hanged or burned alive every four days. The rest of the Carters up and moved to a place called Milwaukee, which Ida Mae hadn't heard of either.[15]

George Gladney came to court Ida Mae Brandon in 1928, when she was fifteen and he was twenty-two, and, though her mother, Miss Theenie, thought he was too dark and too old ("He's old enough for your daddy"), he was serious. "He wasn't no smiling man," Ida Mae said. In 1929 she married him. They moved to a cabin near the Natchez Trace, sharecroppers for a man named Edd Pearson. They worked all day and all year and at the end of it they broke even, which was considered lucky, because most sharecroppers ended up with nothing but debt to show for it, at least by the boss's accounting. A woman was expected to pick one hundred pounds of cotton a day. ("It was like picking a hundred pounds of feathers," Wilkerson writes, "a hundred pounds of lint dust." That description takes on more meaning after, late in the book, Wilkerson travels to Chickasaw with Ida Mae, and they pick cotton together.) She learned to make blackberry cobbler and tomato pie. She kept chickens and wore a dress made out of a flour sack. She had her first baby, a girl, in 1930; it felt like thunder. "I could see the pain comin' down on top of the house and keep comin.'" Another girl came, soon enough but was taken, even sooner, by the flux, come on when she was set under a tree with her sister. They named their boy James Walter, after a white boy in town Ida Mae took care of, thinking it might bring him luck.[16]

One night in 1937, someone came knocking on the door, Mr. Edd and four more white men, with guns. They were looking for George's cousin, Joe Lee. They were sure he had stolen some turkeys. They found him, sneaking out the back. They tied him with hog wire and dragged him to the woods and beat him with chains and then drove him to town and left him in jail. The turkeys, which had wandered off, wandered back in the morning. George got Joe Lee out of jail and used grease to peel his clothes off him because they were stuck on, with blood. He went home and told Ida Mae, "This the last crop we making."[17] They sold everything they owned, piece by piece, on the sly, and told anyone who asked, "We just running out of room." They got a ride in a truck from Miss Theenie's house to the depot carrying quilts and the children and a Bible and a shoebox full of fried chicken and boarded the Mobile and Ohio Railroad. They stopped in Chicago. "What did it look like at that time, Chicago?" Wilkerson asked. "It looked like Heaven to me then."[18]

They got off the train in Milwaukee, where Ida Mae's sister had gone. Miss Theenie had guessed, but Ida Mae had told no one that she was pregnant, and now she wanted to go home to have the baby. She gave birth to a girl, in 1938, in Miss Theenie's house, and named her Eleanor, after the First Lady. That year, Theodore Bilbo, a U.S. senator from Mississippi, helped filibuster against a bill making lynching a crime. "If you succeed in the passage of this bill," Bilbo said, "you will open the floodgates of Hell." When Ida Mae went back north, she didn't go to Milwaukee; she went to Chicago, where George had found work as an iceman. In 1940, she went to a firehouse in the South Side of Chicago and voted, for the first time in her life. Roosevelt defeated Wilkie. George got a job at the Campbell's soup factory. Ida Mae got a job at the Walther Memorial, working as a hospital aide. Most of all, she liked to watch the babies being born. "They always come out hollering."[19]

In 1966, when Ida Mae Gladney was fifty-three, Martin Luther King, Jr., came to Chicago. "Chicago has not turned out to be the New Jerusalem," he told the crowd. ("They had him way up on something high," Ida Mae said. "I never did get to see him good.") The next year, Ida Mae and her whole family—Velma, James, and Eleanor had all married and had their own children by now—bought a house together, a three-family in South Shore, for $30,000. Next thing, every white family on the block moved out. "Lord, they move quick," Ida Mae said.[20]

Isabel Wilkerson met Ida Mae Gladney in 1996, when Ida Mae was eighty-three years old. She was still living in that house her family bought in 1967, in the second-floor apartment. She sat, and looked outside her bay window, at the street. Watching her, Wilkerson writes, as if from her notebook: "*A man is selling drugs out of a trash can. She can see, plain as day, where he puts them and how he gets them out of the trash can for the white customers in their SUVs with suburban license plates. Another hides his stash in his mouth. And when the customers come up, he pulls a piece of inventory from his tongue.*" They call Ida Mae "Grandma." They warn her when not to come out, "Because we don't know what time we gon' start shootin.'"[21]

Not long after Wilkerson met Ida Mae, she went with her to a neighborhood watch meeting, in Beat 421, at the

South Shore Presbyterian Church. Beat 421 is in State Senate District 13, which, in 1997, had a new senator. When Barack Obama came to Beat 421 to explain what state senators do, Ida Mae listened politely.

The story of Ida Mae Gladney's life, as told by Wilkerson, makes an argument or, really, a bunch of arguments (it is also, of course, a history, in brief, of the twentieth century). In the Great Migration, more men went than women. Women went because their husbands decided to go; they didn't usually have much choice. People who left the South were generally better educated than people who didn't. Up to a point, their move follows the familiar patterns of other immigrants although, as Wilkerson wrote, everyone she talked to balked at being called an immigrant. (Wilkerson called the exodus "an unrecognized immigration.") The Great Migration was not about the boll weevil, which is what economists often concluded. Cotton was getting harder to grow; the soil was exhausted; the boll weevil had come; everyone was broke; sharecroppers left their crops because their crops were failing. But of twelve hundred people she interviewed, Wilkerson pointed out, not a single one of them, when asked why they left the South, mentioned the boll weevil. Instead, they talked about Jim Crow, and about lynching, and about violence and humiliation and brutality and misery—Ida Mae being held by the ankles by two white boys, over a well where, if she were dropped, no one would ever find her. "We cannot fight back," Wright wrote, "we have no arms; we cannot vote; and the law is white."[22] There was no escaping it, except . . . Ellison interviewed a man in Harlem named Leo Gurley who told him a tall tale about a man named Sweet, in Florence, South Carolina. "He was one sucker who didn't give a damn bout the crackers," Gurley said. "It was this way: Sweet could make hisself invisible."[23]

Leaving the South took extraordinary fortitude. What the North and West held, the dreams and the disappointments, no one could have foreseen. Wilkerson, somewhat too sketchily, considered postwar urban history—white flight, the closing of factories, the disappearance of industrial jobs.[24] By the beginning of the twenty-first century, there was no more Jim Crow, she observed, but "hypersegregation": in the 2000 census, Detroit's population was 80 percent black; Dearborn's was 1 percent. Most often, she outlined debates about what historians had called the "second ghetto," only to reject them. "Perhaps it is not a question of whether the migrants brought good or ill to the cities they fled to or were pushed or pulled to their destinations," she wrote, "but a question of how they summoned the courage to leave in the first place or how they found the will to press beyond the forces against them and the faith in a country that had rejected them for so long"[25] The questions of social scientists—What is the structure of poverty?—and of policy makers—How can this be fixed?—were not Wilkerson's questions. "We watch strange moods fill our children, and our hearts swell with pain," Wright wrote. "The streets, with their noise and flaring lights, the taverns, the automobiles, and the poolrooms claim them, and no voice of ours can call them back."[26] The people on Ida Mae's street, Wilkerson writes, echoing Wright, "are the lost grandchildren of the Migration."[27] We worry; we grieve; we know not what to do. This is narrative nonfiction, lyrical and tragic and . . . fatalist. The story exposes; the story moves; the story tells; the story ends. What Wilkerson urged, finally, wasn't argument at all; it was compassion: hush, and listen.

That old man in Eddie's bar told Ralph Ellison, in 1939, "Son, if Ah had-a got New York in me Ahd a-been dead a long time ago." When Ida Mae Gladney visited Mississippi with Isabel Wilkerson, someone asked, "Ida Mae, you gone be

# 19

# RAP SHEET

Steven Hayes and Joshua Komisarjevsky, who met in 2006 in a Hartford drug treatment center and shared a room in a halfway house in between stints in prison, were both seasoned burglars, though Hayes, a forty-four year-old crack addict, was quite a bit older than Komisarjevsky, the twenty-six-year-old great-grandson of a Russian princess. In the spring of 2007, both men were paroled. Hayes, whose arrest record stretched back to 1980, had served about three years of a five-year sentence for third-degree burglary, and Komisarjevsky had finished half of a nine-year sentence for the same crime, in the second degree. Hayes moved in with his mother, in Winsted, in Litchfield County; Komisarjevsky went back to his hometown, Cheshire, a suburb about twenty miles north of New Haven. They kept in touch. On July 23, 2007, authorities said, Hayes and Komisarjevsky broke into the Cheshire home of William Petit, Jr., an endocrinologist, and tortured the family through the night, raping Petit's wife, Jennifer Hawke-Petit, and at least one of the couple's two daughters. In the morning, Hayes and Komisarjevsky are said to have forced Hawke-Petit, a school nurse who suffered from multiple sclerosis, into the family car and taken her to a local bank, where she withdrew $15,000, after which an alarmed teller alerted the police.

The two men allegedly then brought Hawke-Petit back to the house, killed her, set the house on fire, and fled, though not far: they crashed the Petits's SUV into a police barricade, just past the end of the driveway.[1]

Inside the house, a four-bedroom colonial, police found three bodies. Hawke-Petit, age forty-eight, had been strangled. Seventeen-year-old Hayley Petit, who, that September, was to start college at Dartmouth, died of smoke inhalation. Her eleven-year-old sister, Michaela, was found tied to a bed, her body badly burned after having been doused with gasoline. Only William Petit, who had been bound with rope, beaten in the head with a baseball bat, and left for dead in the cellar, survived.

Hayes and Komisarjevsky were tried on multiple counts of kidnapping, sexual assault, arson, and murder.[2] The state sought the death penalty.

Every murder raises terrible questions, questions no trial, no law, no punishment can answer. What forces make it possible for one human being to take the life of another? Murders can be solved and even explained—at least, that's the operating assumption of criminal investigation and the narrative logic behind every whodunit—but it can be difficult, and viscerally painful, to think about any specific murder with any clarity, or for very long. Maybe the brisk trade in lurid violence as spectacle has something to do with it; one either watches or averts one's eyes; dispassionate reflection rarely enters into it.[3] Scholars from theologians and psychologists to evolutionary biologists have offered theories about murder—theories of evil, theories of disease, theories of disposition—but the analytical burden placed on any general discussion of murder, freighted, as it is, with the weight of atrocity, is nearly unbearable.[4] Nothing suffices, or can.

Between the convulsive emotional response to a single murder and an elusive general theory of murder lies another kind of contemplation: the study of the murderousness of nations. The United States also has the highest homicide rate of any affluent democracy; in 2008, it was nearly four times higher than the rate in France or Germany, and six times higher than in the United Kingdom.[5] Why? Historians haven't often asked this question. Even historians who like to try to solve cold cases usually stop there, ceding to sociologists and other social scientists the study of what makes murder rates rise and fall or what might account for why one country is more murderous than another. Only in the 1970s did historians begin studying homicide in any systematic way. In the United States, that effort was led by Eric Monkkonen, who died in 2005.[6] Monkkonen's research was taken up by Randolph Roth, who offered, in *American Homicide* (2009), a massive investigation of murder, in the aggregate, and over time. Roth's argument was profoundly unsettling. There is and always has been, he claimed, an American way of murdering. It is, he believed, the price of our politics.

In the archives, murders are easier to count than other crimes. Rapes go unreported, thefts can be hidden, adultery isn't always actionable, but murder will nearly always out. Murders enter the historical record through coroners' inquests, court transcripts, parish ledgers, and even tombstones.[7] "Fell by the hands of William Beadle / an infatuated Man who closed the / horrid sacrifice of his Wife / & Children with his own destruction," reads the headstone of Lydia Beadle of Wethersfield, Connecticut, who was murdered, along with her five children, in 1782. The number of uncounted murders, known as the "dark figure," is thought to be quite small. Given enough archival research, historians can conceivably count, with fair accuracy, the frequency with which people of earlier eras have killed one another, with this caveat: the farther back you go in time—and the documentary trail doesn't go back much farther than 1300—the more fragmentary the record and the bigger the dark figure.[8] Pieter Spierenburg, a professor of historical criminology at Erasmus University in Rotterdam, sifted through the evidence in *A History of Murder: Personal Violence in Europe from the Middle Ages to the Present* (2009). Homicide rates, conventionally represented as the number of murder victims per 100,000 people in the population per year, have been falling across Europe for centuries. Spierenburg attributes this long decline to what the German sociologist Norbert Elias called the "civilizing process" (shorthand for a whole class of behaviors requiring physical restraint and self-control, right down to using a fork instead of eating with your hands or stabbing at your food with a knife), and to the growing power of the centralizing state to disarm civilians, control violence, enforce law and order, and, broadly, hold a monopoly on the use of force.[9] (Anthropologists sometimes talk about a related process, the replacement of a culture of honor with a culture of dignity.) In feuding medieval Europe, the murder rate hovered around 35. Duels replaced feuds. Duels are more mannered; they also have a lower body count. By 1500, the murder rate had fallen to about 20. Courts replaced duels. By 1700, the murder rate had dropped to 5. In 2000, that rate was generally well below 2, where it has held steady for the past century.[10]

In the United States, the picture could hardly be more different. The American homicide rate has been higher than Europe's from the start and higher at every stage since. It has also fluctuated, sometimes wildly. During the colonial period, the homicide rate fell, but in the nineteenth century, while Europe's kept sinking, the U.S. rate went up and up. In the twentieth century, the rate in the United States dropped to about 5 in the years following World War II but then rose, reaching about 11 in 1990. It has since fallen once again, to just above 5, a rate that is, nevertheless, two and a half times higher, on average, than that of any other affluent democracy.[11]

What accounts for the remarkable difference? Guns leap to mind: in 2008, firearms were involved in two-thirds of all murders in the United States.[12] Roth insisted that the prevalence of guns in America, and our lax gun laws as compared to most of Europe, can't account for the whole of the spread. And so: have Americans not undergone the same "civilizing process"? Apparently not, say some Europeans. Unmoored from Europe, colonial Americans seem to have gone murderously adrift. Spierenburg speculated that democracy came too soon to the United States. By the time European states became democracies, the populace had already accepted the authority of the state. But the American Revolution happened before Americans had gotten used to the idea of a state monopoly on force. Americans therefore preserved for themselves not only the right to bear arms—instead of yielding that right to a strong central government—but also medieval manners: impulsiveness, crudeness, and a fidelity to a culture of honor. We're backwards, in other words, because we became free before we learned how to control ourselves.[13]

Perhaps unsurprisingly, not everyone buys this argument. The civilizing process has had its critics, although it remains more fashionable than, say, modernization theory. Even stipulating Elias, though, mapping a schematic theory of self onto the murder rate seems, methodologically, bizarre. Monkkonen took a different but equally conjectural approach. When he died, he had been working on an article called "Homicide: Explaining America's Exceptionalism," in which he offered, by way of hypothesis, four factors to account for the centuries-long differences between American and European homicide rates: mobility, federalism, slavery, and tolerance. Mobility breaks social ties; federalism is a weak form of government;

slavery rationalized a culture of violence among white southerners (where the murder rate has always been disproportionately high, as it has, and remains, in all the so-called law-and-
order states); and American judges and juries have historically
proven less willing than their European counterparts to con-
vict murderers, tolerating, among other crimes, racial murders
and killings by jealous spouses.[14]

Roth, a professor of history at Ohio State, aimed to bring
into this debate hard facts and rigorous methods.[15] He headed
a collaborative project, begun by Monkkonen, called the Historical Violence Database, containing records of murders in
several of the original thirteen colonies; nineteenth-century
records from five states, seven cities, and thirty-four counties;
and a wealth of twentieth-century statistics, chiefly from the
Uniform Crime Reports kept by the FBI beginning in 1930.[16]
As a discussion of the available data, *American Homicide* was
unrivaled. As an explanation, though, it was pretty dubious.
Roth's work involved three steps: first, he used his database
to count murders and then, using surviving censuses to count
people, he calculated the homicide rate and, finally, he attempted to explain what factors correlate with that rate, across
four centuries.[17] It's that last step that was wobbliest.

Most criminologists trace the homicide rate back only a
few decades. The fluctuation in the homicide rate since the
1940s has at least something to do with demography. The
overwhelming majority of murderers and murder victims
are young adult men. When Baby Boomers reached that age
bracket, the homicide rate soared. Once they aged out of their
most lethal years, the rate fell.[18] Roth argued that the demographic explanation of the postwar crime boom and bust,
while important, falls short, but where other social scientists
have investigated economic conditions like joblessness or government policies like gun control to fill the explanatory gap,
Roth was swayed by an argument made by a criminologist

named Gary LaFree in a 1998 book called *Losing Legitimacy: Street Crime and the Decline of Social Institutions in America.* LaFree observed that the homicide rate correlates, inversely and nearly perfectly, with public faith in government and trust in elected officials.[19] So, for instance, the Vietnam era, marked by declining confidence in elected officials, correlates with a rising homicide rate. He measured that faith and trust by relying on national opinion surveys taken beginning in 1958, which asked questions like, "How much of the time do you trust the government to do what is right?"[20]

Roth attempted to graft LaFree's argument onto all of American history. He determined that four factors correlate with the homicide rate: faith that government is stable and capable of enforcing just laws; trust in the integrity of legitimately elected officials; solidarity among social groups based on race, religion, or political affiliation; and confidence that the social hierarchy allows for respect to be earned without recourse to violence. When and where people hold these sentiments, the homicide rate is low; when and where they don't, it's high.[21]

Whatever you think of the value of public opinion polls, LaFree at least had them. Roth didn't. How do you measure the belief that government is stable in 1695 or 1786 or 1814 or 1902? You can't. You can only look at what was happening in those years and tell a story about what you think people believed about their government, and, if you know what the homicide rate was, it's hard not to simply fit a story to your data. The homicide rate in New England fell from a high, in 1637, of 120 to under 1, in 1800, chiefly by dropping, rather dramatically, after every war except the Revolution.[22] Roth argued that the rate fell, overall, as judicial institutions were established, and people developed faith in them, and it fell, precipitously, after every war because wars against hostile neighbors brought the colonists together. But it would seem equally plausible to argue something else: the homicide rate in colonial New England tracks the European decline quite nicely, overall, and it drops, in a stepwise fashion, after each and every war, because the population of young men declines during every war, which means there are fewer potential murderers and murder victims around. Both interpretations make sense; neither has been demonstrated.

The implications of Roth's argument were, as he realized, distressing. If a high American murder rate is a function of not placing our entire trust in government, are we simply doomed to endure a high murder rate? Else the argument reads like an indictment of dissent. Roth took his case all the way to the White House: "The statistics make it clear that in the twentieth century, homicide rates have fallen during the terms of presidents who have inspired the poor or have governed from the center with a popular mandate, and they have risen during the terms of presidents who presided over political and economic crises, abused their power, or engaged in unpopular wars." The homicide rate appears to correlate with presidential approval ratings.[23] If Roth was right, electing a bad president is dangerous and inciting people to hate any president, good or bad, is deadly. But what's measuring what? Which is the cart, and which the horse? The homicide rate might also correlate with housing starts, and what then? And the presidential approval rate might be understood as a proxy for all sorts of measures of a well- or poorly adjusted society. Or maybe there's another horse, somewhere, some third factor, that determines both the presidential approval rate and the homicide rate. Or maybe that dark figure is a lot bigger than anyone thought. It's hard to say, partly because, in using quantitative methods to make an argument about the human condition, Roth had wandered into a no-man's-land between the social sciences and the humanities. After a while, arguments made in that no-man's-land tend to devolve into meaninglessness:

good government is good, bad government is bad, and everything's better when everything's better. Correlating murder with a lack of faith and hope may contain its horror, but only because, in a bar graph, atrocity yields to banality.

Every September, the FBI issues a report on crime, a compilation of statistics for the previous year. It does not offer an interpretation of this vast quantity of data. "We leave that up to the academics and the criminologists and the sociologists," said an FBI spokesman, upon the release of the 2009 report.[24] For all the number crunching, one thing's clear: there is no such thing as an average murder. And, even if there were, what happened at the Petits's house in Cheshire, Connecticut, on July 23, 2007, wouldn't be it, and not just because of that crime's particular depravity. Much about the case is out of the ordinary. The victims were white and wealthy; murder victims are disproportionately black and poor.[25] Exceptional, high-profile crimes often lead to legislative action driven by citizen initiative. California's controversial three-strikes law, a ballot measure, was first proposed by a Fresno photographer whose daughter was murdered.[26] In 2008, in response to the Petit murders, the Connecticut legislature doubled and tripled mandatory penalties for second- and third-time offenders.[27] "Big cases make bad laws" is a criminological axiom, and one with which Mark A. R. Kleiman agreed in *When Brute Force Fails: How to Have Less Crime and Less Punishment* (2009). Kleiman blamed big cases and bad laws for another distinctive feature of American life: 2.3 million people were, at the time, in jail in the United States. That worked out to nearly one out of every one hundred adults, the highest rate anywhere in the world, and four times the world average.[28] Prison crowding was likely one reason why Steven Hayes and Joshua Komisarjevsky were paroled. While the crime rate was 15 percent lower in 2009 than it was twenty-five years before, the incarceration rate was four times higher. At what point, Kleiman wondered, will incarceration be a greater social ill than crime? He proposed, for lesser offenders, punishments that are swift and certain, but not necessarily severe; a night in jail, instead of a warning, for missing a meeting with a parole officer, for instance, and ten nights the next time.[29] Whether or not Kleiman's recommendations were practical, Connecticut, reeling from the Petit murders, was heading in exactly the opposite direction.

The FBI may leave the analysis of crime to academics, but, over the last few decades, the government has, increasingly, left the punishment of criminals up to citizens. William Petit and his sister-in-law Johanna Chapman-Petit served as the honorary cochairs of Three Strikes Now, a grassroots organization lobbying the state legislature to adopt California-style mandatory sentencing of life without possibility of parole for third-time offenders.[30] The Cheshire case dominated the state's death penalty debate, too, a debate that had long centered on race. In a state whose population is 86 percent white, five of the ten men on death row at the time were black.[31] (Both Hayes and Komisarjevsky were white.) Earlier in 2009, the Connecticut legislature voted to abolish the death penalty. William Petit publicly denounced the bill and Jodi Rell, the state's Republican governor, refused to sign it.[32]

Capital punishment has been on the books in Connecticut since 1635. Three strikes has been tried before, too. In colonial America, very many crimes, including murder, were punishable by death, and, for lesser crimes, Connecticut, like many colonies, mandated the death penalty for third-time offenders.[33] That began to change on September 7, 1768, when a burglar named Isaac Frasier was hanged in Fairfield, Connecticut. "He early discovered a thievish Disposition," said the town's minister in a sermon at the gallows titled *Excessive Wickedness, the Way to an Untimely Death*. Convicted of burglary in New Haven, Frasier was whipped and branded and had his ears cropped. Caught again in Fairfield in 1766, he received the same punishment "and was solemnly warned that death would be his punishment on a third Conviction." When Frasier robbed another house, he was sentenced to death. "The Government of Connecticut have always been remarkably tender of putting persons to Death," one observer noted. But when Frasier applied to the legislature for clemency, he was denied. Said the pastor at the gallows, "Justice requires that you should suffer."[34]

An outcry followed. Two weeks after Frasier's death, a Hartford newspaper published an essay called "An Answer to a very important Question, viz. Whether any community has a right to punish any species of theft with death?" The writer's answer—an emphatic no—borrowed extensively from Cesare Beccaria's 1764 treatise, *Of Crimes and Punishments*.[35] Beccaria, an Italian nobleman, argued against capital punishment, which was, at the time, widespread in Europe, too, on two grounds: first, in a republic, men do not forfeit their lives to the government; and, second, capital punishment does not deter crime. Beccaria argued (and Kleiman merely revisited that argument) that punishments, to be effective, must be swift and certain, but not necessarily severe. Punishments, Beccaria insisted, should be proportionate to crimes, whose dangerousness could be measured, in "degrees," by their injury to society. For the crime of first-degree murder, Beccaria considered life in prison both more just, and a more effective deterrent, than execution.

The first American edition of Beccaria's treatise was published 1777, and it reached a wide audience in Connecticut beginning in 1786, when it was serialized in a New Haven newspaper.[36] "If we glance at the pages of history," Beccaria wrote, "we will find that laws, which surely are, or ought to be, compacts of free men, have been, for the most part, a mere tool for the passions of some." This argument held particular appeal for a people who had just finished waging a war against the passions of King George; adopting Beccaria's recommendations came to seem, in a fundamental sense, American, as if the United States had a special role to play, as a republic, in the abolition of capital punishment. In 1784, the Yale senior class debated whether the death penalty was "too severe & rigorous in the United States for the present Stage of Society."[37]

In the 1790s, five states abolished the death penalty for all crimes other than murder. By the 1820s, all northern states reserved capital punishment only for first-degree murder. When incarceration replaced all corporal and most capital punishment, Americans built prisons, and sentenced criminals to jail time. In 1846, Michigan became the first state to abolish the death penalty, altogether. Twice, in the middle of the nineteenth century, the governor of Connecticut asked the state's legislature to do the same, to no avail.[38]

Over the course of the twentieth century, capital punishment was abolished in much of the world, and in all of Europe, but not in the United States.[39] Germany, Austria, and Italy stopped executing criminals after World War II; Denmark, Belgium, New Zealand, and the Netherlands in the 1950s; and Britain, Australia, and Canada in the 1960s. In many parts of the United States, the death penalty, was, if not outlawed, abandoned. By the time of the Chesire case, save for a serial murderer named Michael Ross who was killed by lethal injection in 2005 after he waived his right to appeal because he wanted to die, no one had been executed in Connecticut, or, for that matter, anywhere else in New England, since 1960.[40]

Not so elsewhere. More than a thousand people were executed in the United States in the last quarter of the twentieth century. In 2010, Hayes and Komisarjevsky were found guilty and sentenced to death, to be killed by lethal injection. China,

Iran, and Saudi Arabia execute more criminals, but, among affluent democracies, the death penalty, like the U.S. homicide and incarceration rates, marks an American exception, or, looked at another way, an anachronism. Long ago, Beccaria pointed out the meaningfulness of the correspondence, over time, between crime and punishment, between one kind of violence, and another. If the history of murder contained a lesson, Beccaria believed, it was this: "The countries and times most notorious for severity of punishment have always been those in which the bloodiest and most inhumane of deeds were committed."

Murder has a history, but it isn't always edifying, and sometimes the history of crime and punishment has a chilling sameness. The prospect of death didn't deter Barnett Davenport, a Connecticut murderer who was hanged in 1780, at the age of nineteen. "No man becomes a devil in a minute," Davenport said, just before mounting the gallows. His life of crime began when, at age twelve, he stole some watermelons from a neighbor's garden. More than once, he was caught. But by the time he was eighteen, he had advanced from pilfering eggs and potatoes to stealing horses. He fought in the Revolution and then deserted. He went to live in the house of a man named Caleb Mallery, near Litchfield. On February 3, 1780, "a night big with uncommon horror" (and a year with an elevated homicide rate), Davenport killed Mallery, Mallery's wife, and their seven-year-old granddaughter, by beating their heads in with a pestle. Next, he pried open the family's money chest and took from it a pile of bills and a handful of coins. Then he set the house on fire, leaving inside, to die, two more children, aged six and four. He was quickly captured, and swiftly hanged. In his confession, he recalled that Caleb Mallery had cried out, in between blows, "Tell me what you do it for?"[41] History does not record the murderer's reply.

# 20

# TO WIT

A good idea, before writing your presidential inaugural address, is to read everyone else's. Or, you could skip the rest, and just read Lincoln's. Presidential eloquence doesn't get much better than the argument of Lincoln's first inaugural, "Plainly, the central idea of secession is the essence of anarchy"; the poetry of his second, "Fondly do we hope, fervently do we pray, that this mighty scourge of war may speedily pass away," and its parting grace: "With malice toward none, with charity for all, with firmness in the right as God gives us to see the right, let us strive on to finish the work we are in."[1]

Reading Lincoln left James Garfield nearly speechless. After Garfield was elected, he, like most of the United States' more bookish chief executives, or at least their speechwriters, undertook to read the inaugural addresses of every president that preceded him. "Those of the past except Lincoln's, are dreary reading," Garfield confided to his diary. "I have half a mind to make none."[2] Lincoln's are surpassingly fine; most of the rest are utterly unlovely. "Lincoln never used a two- or three-syllable-word where a one-syllable word would do," Ted Sorensen told John F. Kennedy, after finishing his own reading. He applied that rule to the writing of Kennedy's speech, not just the "Ask not," but also the "Call to": "Now the trumpet

summons us again—not as a call to bear arms, though arms
we need; not as a call to battle, though embattled we are—but
a call to bear the burden of a long twilight struggle."³ Lincoln
could hardly have said it better.

Economy isn't everything. "Only the short ones are remembered," Richard Nixon concluded, after reading all the
inaugurals, an opinion that led him to say things briefly but
didn't save him from saying them badly: "The American
Dream does not come to those who fall asleep."⁴ Even when
they make more sense than that, American presidential inaugurals are not, on the whole, gripping. "The platitude quo-
tient tends to be high, the rhetoric stately and self-serving,
the ritual obsessive, and the surprises few," Arthur Schlesinger,
Jr., observed in 1965, and that's still true.⁵ A bad inaugural
doesn't always augur a bad presidency. It still sinks your spirit,
though. In 1857, James Buchanan berated abolitionists for
making such a fuss about slavery: "Most happy will it be for
the country when the public mind shall be diverted from this
question to others of more pressing and practical importance."
Ulysses S. Grant kvetched: "I have been the subject of abuse
and slander scarcely ever equaled in political history." Theodore Roosevelt all but thumped his chest. Eisenhower opted
for a numbered list. George H. W. Bush compared freedom
to a kite. For meaninglessness, my money's on Carter: "It is
that unique self-definition which has given us an exceptional
appeal, but it also imposes on us a special obligation to take
on those moral duties which, when assumed, seem invariably
to be in our own best interests." But, for monotony, it's difficult to out-drone Warren G. Harding ("It is so bad that a
sort of grandeur creeps into it," H. L. Mencken admitted): "I
speak for administrative efficiency, for lightened tax burdens,
for sound commercial practices, for adequate credit facilities,
for sympathetic concern for all agricultural problems, for the
omission of unnecessary interference of . . . ."⁶ I ellipse, lest I

nod off. The American Dream does not come to those who fall asleep.

In 1880, when Garfield was elected, there were fewer inaugurals to plow through but they were harder to come by. Barack Obama was able to Google. Sorensen, who mimeographed, had to walk over to the Library of Congress.[7] Garfield's staff had to hunt down each and every inaugural, one by one, and copy them out by hand. They weren't compiled and printed as a set until 1893.[8] They were, however, written to be read as much as heard. Arguably, they still are. Before 1921, when Woodrow Wilson used an amplifier, even the crowd couldn't make out what he was saying, and before Calvin Coolidge's was broadcast over the radio in 1925, the inaugurals were, basically, *only* read. That has changed. Since Truman's 1949 speech, inaugurals have been televised and, since Clinton's 1993, streamed on the Internet.[9] "Our founders saw themselves in the light of posterity," Clinton said. "We can do no less." Inaugurals are written for the future but look, mostly, to the past ("We are the heirs of the ages," Theodore Roosevelt said), which might help explain why so many prove so unsatisfying in the present.[10] Obama's inaugural, the fifty-seventh in American history, was the first to be YouTubed, live. On the day itself, most people watch and listen. Speaking to posterity no longer means writing for readers. Still, the first thirty-four of our country's inaugural addresses will forever survive only as written words. Since 1893, a complete set of texts has been reissued every decade or so. Bedside reading they're not.

"Made the first actual study for inaugural by commencing to read those of my predecessors," Garfield wrote in his diary, on December 20, 1880, when he still had plenty of time. (New presidents used to be sworn in on March 4. In 1933, the Twentieth Amendment changed the date to January 20 to shorten the awkward interregnum between election and inauguration.) He started with Washington's first (the oldest) and second (at 135 words, the shortest). The next day, he read Adams's overworked and forgettable one and only. "His next to last sentence contains more than 700 words. Strong but too cumbrous." (Also, indefinite: nineteen of those seven hundred words are "if.") That afternoon, Garfield listened as a friend read Jefferson's first aloud, probably more forcefully than had Jefferson, who was, famously, a mumbler. "Stronger than Washington's, more ornate than Adams'," was the verdict of the president-elect about Jefferson's 1801 inaugural, widely considered nearly as transcendent as Lincoln's two, for its clarion call for bipartisanship, "Every difference of opinion is not a difference of principle. We have called by different names brethren of the same principle. We are all Republicans, we are all Federalists," though it's the next, if admittedly more ornate, sentence that steals my breath: "If there be any among us who would wish to dissolve this Union or to change its republican form, let them stand undisturbed as monuments of the safety with which error of opinion may be tolerated where reason is left free to combat it."[11]

On December 22, Garfield trudged through a few more lesser addresses: "Curious tone of self-depreciation runs through them all—which I cannot quite believe was genuine. Madison's speeches were not quite up to my expectations. Monroe's first was rather above." And then, what with Christmas, trips to the dentist, and choosing a Cabinet, Garfield's interest in reading inaugurals flagged. Instead, he devoured a novel, hot-off-the-presses, Disraeli's three-volume, autobiographical *Endymion*, finishing it on New Year's Eve, two weeks after he started it, concluding in his diary, twenty minutes before midnight: "It shows adroitness, great reserve on dangerous questions, with enough frankness on other questions to make a show of boldness." Even that much he could not say for the inaugurals stretching from John Quincy Adams (the first inaugurée to wear pants instead of knee-breeches) to James Buchanan (a man Kennedy once aptly described as "cringing in the White House, afraid to move," while the nation teetered on the brink of civil war). By mid-January, Garfield's staff had stitched all the inaugurals into a book for him to read. But, bound or unbound, Garfield found them a slog. Did he really have to write one? He wasn't so sure: "I am quite seriously discussing the propriety of omitting it."

He could have done. The Constitution says nothing about an inaugural address. It calls only for a president to be sworn in, as per Article 2, Section 1: "Before he enter on the Execution of his Office, he shall take the following Oath or Affirmation:—'I do solemnly swear (or affirm) that I will faithfully execute the Office of the President of the United States, and will to the best of my Ability, preserve, protect and defend the Constitution of the United States.'" George Washington took that oath in New York City on April 30, 1789 (late—weeks after March 4—but only because the election hadn't been concluded until mid-April). Just hours before the ceremony, a special congressional committee decided that it might be fitting for Washington to rest his hand on a Bible, but, since no one in Federal Hall had a copy, there followed a mad dash to find one. At mid-day, Washington took his oath standing on a balcony above a crowd assembled on Wall Street. Then he kissed the Bible and uttered four more words: "So help me God." Ever since, most have done the same, but some have dispensed with the kiss, a few have skipped those four words, and, in 1853, Franklin Pierce even refused the Bible.[12]

After Washington was sworn in, he entered Federal Hall and made a speech before Congress. He didn't have to. He thought it would be a good idea. Like most things Washington did, this set a precedent. Washington's first inaugural was addressed to "Fellow Citizens of the Senate and the House of

Representatives."[13] He made no pretense of speaking to the American people; he was speaking to Congress. In 1801, Jefferson, the first president inaugurated in Washington, D.C., the nation's new capital, was also the first to address his remarks to the American people—"Friends and Fellow Citizens"—but, the day he delivered it, he, too, was really only speaking to Congress, assembled in the half-built U.S. Capitol. Monroe, in 1817, was the first to deliver his inaugural in the open air (before a crowd of eight thousand, who couldn't hear a thing), although this came about only because the Capitol was undergoing renovations and tetchy House members refused to let Senators carry their chairs into a temporary House chamber.[14] Only since 1829, with Andrew Jackson's rowdy and jubilant inauguration, have presidents spoken to the citizenry in any way more than symbolically; as many as twenty thousand Americans showed up to strain, in vain, to hear him. Appealing directly to the American people proved to be the death of William Henry Harrison who, in 1841, was the oldest president to take office. Determined to prove his hardiness, Harrison delivered his address hatless and without so much an overcoat on a bitterly cold and wet day. "In obedience to a custom coeval with our government and what I believe to be your expectations I proceed to present to you a summary of the principles which will govern me in the discharge of the duties which I shall be called upon to perform," Harrison began, in the windy introductory paragraph of a speech that, so far from being a summary, took more than two hours to deliver, and, at more than eight thousand words, still reigns as the longest. Harrison caught a cold that day; it worsened into pneumonia; he died a month later.

"I must soon begin the inaugural address," Garfield scolded himself, in his diary on January 25, 1881. He had finished his dreary reading. There was no real avoiding the writing. "I suppose I must conform to the custom, but I think the address should be short." Three days later he reported, "I made some progress in my inaugural, but do not satisfy myself. The fact is I ought to have done it sooner before I became so jaded."

Washington was far from jaded, but he struggled, too. With the help of David Humphreys, he wrote the better part of a first draft, seventy-three pages of policy recommendations. Eager to assure Americans that he had not the least intention of founding a dynasty, he reminded Congress that he couldn't: "the Divine providence hath not seen fit that my blood should be transmitted or my name perpetuated by the endearing though sometimes seducing, channel of personal offspring." James Madison judiciously deleted that.[15] Jefferson wrote his own. Jackson made a stab at a draft, but his friends, calling it "disgraceful," rewrote it entirely. After reading a draft of William Henry Harrison's inaugural, cluttered with references to ancient republics, Daniel Webster pared it down, and declared when he was done, "I have killed seventeen Roman pro-consuls as dead as smelts."[16]

Lincoln gave a draft of his first inaugural to his incoming secretary of state, William Seward, who wisely proposed a new ending, offering an olive branch to seceding southern states:

> I close. We are not we must not be aliens or enemies our fellow countrymen and brethren. Although passion has strained our bonds of affection too hardly they must not. I am sure they will not be broken. The mystic chords which proceeding from so many battle fields and so many patriot graves pass through all the hearts and all the hearths in this broad continent of ours will yet again harmonize in their ancient music when breathed upon by the guardian angel of the nation.

But it was Lincoln's revision that made this soar:

> I am loathe to close. We are not enemies, but friends. We must not be enemies. Though passion may have strained, it must not break our bonds of affection. The mystic chords of memory,

stretching from every battlefield and patriot grave to every living heart and hearthstone, all over this broad land, will yet swell
the chorus of the Union, when again touched, as surely they
will be, by the better angels of our nature.[17]

Revision usually helps. Raymond Moley drafted Franklin
Roosevelt's first inaugural, but Louis Howe added, "The only
thing we have to fear is fear itself." Sorenson wrote much of
Kennedy's, but it was John Kenneth Galbraith who proposed
an early version of "Let us never negotiate out of fear, but let
us never fear to negotiate."[18] Carter, who had a vexed relationship with speechwriters, wrote his own unmemorable inaugural, although James Fallows managed to convince him to
open by thanking Gerald Ford.[19] Former speechwriter Robert
Schlesinger once pointed out that Ronald Reagan gave, over
the course of his career, iterations of what was essentially the
same talk, known as The Speech.[20] His inaugural was yet another version. Clinton solicited advice from dozens of people,
including Sorensen, and then tinkered. About her husband,
Hillary Clinton once said, "He's never met a sentence he
couldn't fool with."[21]


James Garfield wrote his inaugural alone. "I must shut myself
up to the study of man's estimation of himself as contrasted
with my own estimate of him," he wrote, with much misgiv-
ing, on January 19. "Made some progress on the inaugural," he
reported a few weeks later, "but still feel unusual repugnance to
writing." At last he settled on an outline: "1st a brief introduction, 2nd a summary of recent topics that ought to be treated
as settled, 3rd a summary of those that ought to occupy the
public attention, 4[th] a direct appeal to the people to stand by
me in an independent and vigorous execution of the laws." In
*Presidents Creating the Presidency: Deeds Done in Words*, Karlyn Kohrs Campbell and Kathlesen Hall Jamieson argued that

the inaugural serves four purposes: reconstituting the people; rehearsing shared values; setting forth policies; and demonstrating the president's willingness to abide by the terms of his office.[22] That list happens to be a near match to Garfield's outline. But it misses what's changed about inaugurals over the years, and what was new-ish about Garfield's. The nation's first century of inaugural addresses, even when they were addressed to the people, served to mark an incoming president's covenant with the Constitution, not with the citizenry. As the political scientist Jeffrey Tulis pointed out in his landmark 1987 study, *The Rhetorical Presidency*, every nineteenth-century inaugural except Zachary Taylor's mentions the Constitution. John Quincy Adams called the Constitution our "precious inheritance." To Van Buren it was "a sacred instrument." James K. Polk called it "the chart by which I shall be directed." A few nineteenth-century inaugurals, including William Henry Harrison's, consist of careful constitutional analysis. Only half of the inaugurals delivered in the twentieth century even contain the word "Constitution," and none does much more than name it.[23]

"Since the presidencies of Theodore Roosevelt and Woodrow Wilson," Tulis argued, "popular or mass rhetoric has become a principal tool of presidential governance." Americans came to not only accept that our presidents will speak to us, directly, and ask for our support, plebiscitarily; they began to expect it, even though the Founders surely did not. Tulis and other scholars who wrote on this subject during the Reagan years generally found the rise of the rhetorical presidency worrying. By appealing to the people, charismatic chief executives were bypassing Congress, and ignoring the warnings of—and the provisions made by—the Founders, who considered popular leaders demagogues: politicians who appealed to passion, and not to reason. The rhetorical presidency, Tulis warned, was leading to "a greater mutability of policy, an erosion of the processes of deliberation, and a decay of political discourse."[24]

Scholars then quibbled with Tulis's theory. In *The Anti-Intellectual Presidency: The Decline of Presidential Rhetoric from George Washington to George W. Bush*, political scientist Elvin T. Lim argued that the problem isn't that presidents appeal to the people; it's that they pander to us. Speech is fine; blather is not. By an "anti-intellectual president"—a nod to Richard Hofstadter's 1963 *Anti-Intellectualism in American Life*—Lim meant, with a handful of exceptions, everyone from McKinley forward, presidents who, in place of evidence and argument, offered platitudes, partisan jibes, emotional appeals, and lady-in-Pasadena human-interest stories.[25] Sloganeering in speechwriting became such a commonplace that, in 2009, the National Constitution Center hosted a contest for the best six-word inaugural. ("New deal. New day. New world.") Public-spirited, yes; nuanced, not so much.

Lim dated the institutionalization of the anti-intellectual presidency to 1969, when Nixon established the Writing and Research Department, the first White House speechwriting office. There had been speechwriters before, but they were usually also policy advisers. With Nixon's administration was born a class of professional whose sole job it was to write the president's speeches and who have been rewarded, in the main, for the amount of applause their prose could generate. FDR's speeches were interrupted for applause, on average, twice (and no one applauded when he said fear is all we have to fear). Bill Clinton's last state of the union address was interrupted 120 times. (The dispiriting transcript reads, "I ask you to pass a real patients' bill of rights. [Applause.] I ask you to pass common sense gun safety legislation. [Applause.] I ask you to pass campaign finance reform. [Applause.]") For every minute of George W. Bush's states of the union, there were twenty-nine seconds of applause.[26]

Lim interviewed forty-two current and former White House speechwriters. But much of his analysis rested on running inaugurals and other presidential messages through something called the Flesch Readability Test, a formula involving the average number of words in a sentence and the average number of syllables per word. Flesch scores, when indexed to grade levels, rate the *New York Times* at college level; *Newsweek* at high school; and comic books at fifth grade. Between 1789 and 2005, the Flesch scores of inaugural addresses descended from a college reading level to an eighth-grade one. Lim took this to mean that inaugural addresses are getting stupider.[27] That's not clear. How we write, and how we read, have changed. This chapter of this book, with the exception of the sentence after this one, gets an eleventh-grade rating. However, were circumstances such that a disquisition on presidential eloquence were to proffer, to a more loquacious narrator—one whose style and syntax were characterized by rhetorical flourishes that, to modern ears, might, indeed, give every appearance of being at once extraordinary and antiquated, and yet more particularly, obnoxious—were, that is, this composition to present to such a pen-man a propitious opportunity for maundering, not to say, for circumlocution, that tireless soul would be compensated, if a dubious reward it would prove, by a Flesch score more collegial, nay, indeed: this extracted digression rates "doctoral." In Flesch terms, in other words, just about any body of prose you could take from 1789 would be less "readable" than something written in 2005; it can still be malarkey. "Readability" turns out to be not such a useful measure, across time. Still, Lim was onto something. Late twentieth-century speechwriters, most of whom trained as journalists, did favor small words and short sentences, as do many people whose English teachers made them read Strunk and White's 1959 *Elements of Style* ("Omit needless words") and Orwell's 1946 "Politics and the English Language" ("Never use a long word where a short one will do"). Lim got this, but only sort of. Harding's inaugural comes in at ninth-grade reading level; George H. W. Bush's at sixth-grade. Harding's is flowerier, but it isn't smarter or subtler. ("It is flap and doodle," Mencken wrote. "It is balder and dash.") Bush's and Harding's inaugurals are equally empty-headed; both suffer from what Orwell called "slovenliness."[28] The problem doesn't lie in the length of sentences or the number of syllables. It lies in the absence of precision, the paucity of ideas, and the evasion of every species of argument.

Three days before his inauguration, Garfield scrapped his entire first draft and started again. (Actually, he didn't quite scrap it; he filed it; you can read his several drafts at the Library of Congress.) He finished his speech at 2:30 in the morning, just hours before he became president (thereby beating Clinton, who put down his pen at 4:30 a.m.).

Every inaugural address is a history lesson. (The time has come, Barack Obama said, in his inaugural, "to choose our better history.")[29] Garfield began, as almost everyone does, with a celebration of the American experiment. "We cannot overestimate the fervent love of liberty, the intelligent courage, and the sum of common sense with which our fathers made the great experiment of self-government." Like most presidents, Garfield's remarks on the American experiment echoed Washington's. "The preservation of the sacred fire of liberty and the destiny of the republican model of government," Washington said, are, finally, "staked on the experiment entrusted to the hands of the American people." John Adams deemed this "an experiment better adapted to the genius, character, situation, and relations of this nation" than of any other. Jefferson called the United States "the world's best hope." Jackson agreed: "The eyes of all nations are on our Republic." On the future of this American experiment, Polk said, are staked "the hopes and happiness of the whole human family."[30]

That experiment was, for nearly a century, a trial of liberty in an age of slavery. Monroe, wondering at "how near our government has approached to perfection," asked, as if slavery didn't exist, "On whom has oppression fallen in any quarter of our Union? Who has been deprived of any right of person or property?" Van Buren acknowledged slavery as source of "discord and disaster" to "our great experiment"; he therefore lauded our forefathers' "forbearance" of the peculiar institution. William Henry Harrison urged the same: "The attempt of those of one state to control the domestic institutions of another can only result in feelings of distrust and jealousy, the certain harbingers of disunion, violence, and civil war, and the ultimate destruction of our free institutions." Pierce went further: "I believe that involuntary servitude, as it exists in different states of this confederacy, is recognized by the Constitution." Lincoln was the first to state the question starkly: "One section of our country believes slavery is right and ought to be extended, while the other believes it is wrong and ought not to be extended. This is the only substantial dispute." In his second inaugural, he asked the Union to forgive the Confederacy: "It may seem strange that any men should dare to ask a just God's assistance in wringing their bread from the sweat of other men's faces, but let us judge not, that we be not judged."[31]

Garfield, who wrestled, alone in his study, with man's estimation of man, proved the first post–Civil War president to achieve anything like Lincoln's frankness. "The elevation of the Negro race from slavery to the full rights of citizenship is the most important political change we have known since the adoption of our Constitution in 1787," Garfield declared. And then he issued a warning: "Those who resisted the change should remember that under our institutions there is no middle ground for the Negro race between slavery and equal citizenship." About the southern suppression of the black vote, he insisted, "To violate the freedom and sanctities of the suffrage is more than an evil. It is a crime which, if persisted in, will destroy the government itself." William McKinley, in the first inaugural of the twentieth century, announced, "We are reunited. Sectionalism has disappeared." It had not. In 1909, William Taft had still to insist, "The Negroes are now Americans."[32]

With McKinley, American presidents began speaking about taking the American experiment abroad. "We are provincials no longer," Woodrow Wilson said, in 1917. Through depression and war, Franklin Roosevelt assured Americans that the experiment would not fail: "If I know aught of the spirit and purpose of our nation, we will not listen to comfort, opportunism, and timidity. We will carry on." By the era of Truman and Eisenhower, the republic wasn't an experiment; it was an act a faith, the bulwark against communism.[33]

Religious faith, though, has had only a small place in the great majority of inaugurals, except in the celebration of religious liberty (as when, for instance, William Henry Harrison gave thanks for "that good Being who has blessed us by the gifts of civil and religious freedom"). That changed in 1980, when Ronald Reagan announced, "It would be fitting and good, I think, if on each Inauguration Day in future years it should be declared a day of prayer." Eight years later, George Bush, in his inaugural, obliged: "My first act as President is a prayer. I ask you to bow your heads: Heavenly Father, we bow our heads and thank You for Your love." And every president since Reagan has followed his precedent in tacking on, at the end of the inaugural, some form of "God Bless America."[34]

Reagan's vision for what the country needed— "government is not the solution to our problem, government is the problem"—differed, of course, from Clinton's—"There is nothing wrong with America that cannot be cured by what is right with America." But they shared a fondness for sloganeering. "The divide of race has been America's constant curse," Clinton said, in his second inaugural. Obama's March 2008 speech on race tried to lift that curse. "America can change. That is the true genius of this nation," he said. "This union may never be perfect, but generation after generation has shown that it can always be perfected."[35]

James Garfield read the story of America, and then he did his imperfect best. The inaugural he delivered, on March 4, 1881, didn't match Lincoln's eloquence. Still, it is very fine:

> My countrymen, we do not now differ in our judgment concerning the controversies of past generations, and fifty years hence our children will not be divided in their opinions concerning our controversies. They will surely bless their fathers and their fathers' God that the Union was preserved, that slavery was overthrown, and that both races were made equal before the law. We may hasten or we may retard, but we cannot prevent, the final reconciliation.[36]

Enough said.

# NOTES

## Introduction

1. Mabel B. Casner and Ralph Henry Gabriel, *The Rise of American Democracy* (New York: Harcourt, Brace, 1938), v–vi, 667–71, and a loose-leaf page of advertising copy pasted into the copy owned by Widener Library, Harvard University. Casner and Gabriel later published a revision titled *The Story of American Democracy* (New York: Harcourt, Brace, 1942). *The Story of America* was the title of yet another textbook, written by Mary D. Chase and published in 1935.

2. Abigail Adams to John Adams, March 31, 1776, in *Familiar Letters of John Adams and His Wife Abigail Adams*, ed. Frank Shuffelton (New York: Penguin, 2004), 148.

3. John Adams to Abigail Adams, April 14, 1776, in ibid., 154.

4. For Jefferson's many drafts, and an account of how the document was written, see Pauline Maier, *American Scripture: Making the Declaration of Independence* (New York: Knopf, 1997).

5. John Adams to Jonathan Sewall, February 1760, in *The Works of John Adams*, ed. Charles Francis Adams (Boston: Little, Brown, 1856), 1:56; Alexander Hamilton, *Records of the Federal Convention of 1787*, ed. Max Farrand (New Haven: Yale University Press, 1937), 1:299.

6. Philip S. Foner, *The Democratic-Republican Societies, 1790–1800* (Westport, CT: Greenwood Press, 1976), 25.

7. Edward J. Larson, *A Magnificent Catastrophe: The Tumultuous Election of 1800* (New York: Free Press, 2007), 185; Robert J. Dinkin, *Campaigning in America: A History of Election Practices* (New York: Greenwood Press, 1989), 23.

8. *Aurora*, October 14, 1800.

9. *The Gazette of the United States*, October 15, 1800.

10. See Dorothy Ross, "Historical Consciousness in Nineteenth-Century America," *American Historical Review* 89 (October 1984): 909–28.

11. Alexis de Tocqueville, *Democracy in America*, trans. Arthur Goldhammer (New York: Library of America, 2004), introduction.

12. Charles Dickens to W. C. Macready, March 22, 1842, in *Letters of Charles Dickens*, ed. Madeline House et al. (Oxford: Clarendon Press, 1965–2002), 3:156.

13. Thomas Carlyle to John Forster, July 3, 1843, in *The Collected Letters of Thomas and Jane Welsh Carlyle*, ed. Clyde de L. Ryals and Kenneth J. Fielding (Durham, NC: Duke University Press), 16: 224–25.

14. Charles Dickens to W. C. Macready, April 1, 1842, in *Letters of Charles Dickens*, 3:175–76.

15. Frederick Douglass, "The Meaning of July Fourth for the Negro," in *Frederick Douglass: Selected Speeches and Writings*, ed. Philip S. Foner, abridged and adapted by Yuval Taylor (Chicago: Lawrence Hill Books, 1999), 196–97.

16. Henry George, "To the Voters of San Francisco, May 3, 1878," in Henry George, *Collected Journalistic Writings*, ed. Kenneth C. Wenzer (Armonk, NY: M. E. Sharpe, 2003), 1:142; George, *Progress and Poverty: An Inquiry into the Cause of Industrial Depressions, and of Increase of Want with Increase of Wealth* (San Francisco: W. M. Hinton, 1879). On George and his influence, see especially Edward J. Rose, *Henry George* (New York: Twayne, 1968).

17. Frederick Jackson Turner, "Contributions of the West to American Democracy," *Atlantic Monthly* (1903); and Turner, *The Significance of the Frontier in American History*, ed. Harold P. Simonson (New York: Ungar, 1963).

18. Charles and Mary Ritter Beard, *The Rise of American Civilization* (New York: Macmillan, 1927), 2 vols.

19. Arthur M. Schlesinger, Jr., *The Age of Jackson* (Boston: Little, Brown, 1945), 312–13, 372–73.

20. Hofstadter disliked being classed with consensus historians and also regretted the title of his book. See his preface to the 1967 edition, reproduced in Richard Hofstadter, *The American Political Tradition and the Men Who Made It*, with a foreword by Christopher Lasch (New York: Vintage, 1989), xxv–xxxiv. And see also Hofstadter, *The Progressive Historians: Turner, Beard, Parrington* (New York: Knopf, 1968).

21. Hofstadter, *The American Political Tradition*, xxxix.

22. Michael Holzman, "The Ideological Origins of American Studies at Yale," *American Studies* 40 (1999): 78, 87.

23. Bernard Bailyn, *The Origins of American Politics* (New York: Knopf, 1968).

24. Bernard Bailyn, "The Challenge of Modern Historiography," *American Historical Review* 87 (1982): 1–24; Eric Foner, "History in Crisis," *Commonweal*, December 18, 1981, 723–26; Herbert G. Gutman, "The Missing Synthesis: Whatever Happened to History?" *Nation*, November 21, 1981, 521, 553–54; and Thomas Bender, "Wholes and Parts: The Need for Synthesis in American History," *Journal of American History* 73 (1986): 120–36.

25. Arthur M. Schlesinger, Jr., *The Disuniting of America* (New York: Norton, 1992), especially the epilogue.

26. For sharply divergent accounts of the controversy over the national history standards, see Lynne Cheney, *Telling the Truth: Why Our Culture and Our Country Have Stopped Making Sense and What We Can Do About It* (New York: Simon and Schuster, 1995); and Gary Nash, *History on Trial: Culture Wars and the Teaching of the Past* (New York: Knopf, 1997).

27. Eric Foner, *The Story of American Freedom* (New York: Norton, 1998).

28. Sean Wilentz, *The Rise of American Democracy: From Jefferson to Lincoln* (New York: Norton, 2005), 197, xx.

29. Charles Dickens, *American Notes for General Circulation* (London, 1842), chap. 8.

30. Hofstadter, *American Political Tradition*, xl.

## 1. Here He Lyes

1. Some of Smith's published writings are collected in John Smith, *Writings: With Other Narratives of Roanoke, Jamestown, and the First English Settlement of America* (New York: Library of America, 2007). And see especially Philip L. Barbour's magnificently annotated and definitive three-volume *Complete Works of Captain John Smith* (Chapel Hill: University of North Carolina Press, 1986).

2. Alden T. Vaughan, "John Smith Satirized," *William and Mary Quarterly* 45 (1988): 730–31; Philip Barbour, *The Three Worlds of Captain John Smith* (Boston: Houghton Mifflin, 1963), 393.

3. Smith, *Writings*, 203, 690.

4. Barbour, *Complete Works*, 1:lviii.

5. Smith, *Writings*, 691.

6. Karen Kupperman, *Jamestown Project* (Cambridge: Harvard University Press, 2007), 15, 58, 64–68.

7. Smith, *Writings*, 44, 42.

8. Barbour, *Complete Works*, 1:207.

9. Edmund Morgan, *American Slavery, American Freedom: The Ordeal of Colonial Virginia* (New York: Norton, 1975), 56, 72, 78.

10. Barbour, *Complete Works*, 1:276

11. Smith, *Writings*, 1100–1101; Barbour, *Complete Works*, 1:xlv, 232–33.

12. William M. Kelso, *Jamestown: The Buried Truth* (Charlottesville: University of Virginia, 2007).

13. Smith, *Writings*, 41.

14. Ibid., 125.

15. Kupperman, *Jamestown Project*, 11.

16. Kelso, *Jamestown*, 2, 170, 214.

17. Kupperman, *Jamestown Project*, 1, 9.

18. John Hope Sweet, ed., *Envisioning an English Empire: Jamestown and the Making of the North Atlantic World* (Philadelphia: University of Pennsylvania Press, 2005), with a preface by Karen Kupperman, xv.

19. Barbour, *Complete Works*, 2:128–29.

20. Ibid., 3:271.

21. Barbour, *Three Worlds*, 276.

22. Smith, *Writings*, 123.

23. Kupperman, *Jamestown Project*, 69.

24. [Henry Adams,] "A Discourse of Virginia," *North American Review* 104 (1867).

25. Henry B. Rule, "Henry Adams' Attack on Two Heroes of the Old South," *American Quarterly* 14 (1962): 177, 179; Adams, "Discourse"; Jarvis M. Morse, "John Smith and His Critics: A Chapter in Colonial Historiography," *Journal of Southern History* 1 (May 1935): 125.

26. Morse, "John Smith and His Critics," 125, 128, 132.

27. Morison as quoted in Vaughan, "John Smith Satirized," 712.

28. Laura Polanyi Striker and Bradford Smith, "The Rehabilitation of Captain John Smith," *Journal of Southern History* 28 (1962): 474–81.

29. James West Davidson and Mark Hammond Lytle, *After the Fact: The Art of Historical Detection* (New York: Knopf, 1982), 4–6.

30. Smith, *Writings*, 673.

31. Ibid., 125.

32. Adams, "Discourse of Virginia."

## 2. A Pilgrim Passed I

1. Samuel Eliot Morison, *Sailor Historian: The Best of Samuel Morison*, ed. Emily Morison Beck (Boston: Houghton Mifflin, 1977), 402–6, quote on 402.

2. David McCord, "Some Reflections on Style," in ibid., xxxiii.

3. Samuel Eliot Morison, *Those Misunderstood Puritans* (North Brookfield, MA: Sun Hill Press, 1992), 11.

4. Morison, *Sailor Historian*, 383.

5. Ibid.

6. William Bradford, *Of Plymouth Plantation, 1620–1647*, ed. Samuel Eliot Morison (New York: Knopf, 1952), 61, 58, 44, 441.

7. Morison, in ibid., xi, xxiv.

8. Morison, introduction, in ibid.

9. Bradford, ibid., 3.

10. Morison, in ibid., xxvi; Bernard Bailyn, interview with the author, March 14, 2006.

11. Morison, in *Of Plymouth Plantation*, xxvii.

12. Ibid., xxv.

13. Nathaniel Philbrick, *Mayflower: A Story of Courage, Community, and War* (New York: Viking, 2006), 7.

14. Ibid., 36, 33.

15. "An Interview with Nathaniel Philbrick," by Viking Press, http://www.bookbrowse.com/author_interviews/full/index.cfm?author_number=415.

16. Bernard Bailyn, *Morison: An Appreciation* (Boston: Massachusetts Historical Society, 1977), 11.

17. Edmund S. Morgan, "An Address to the Colonial Society of Massachusetts, on the Occasion of Its Centennial," *New England Quarterly* 66 (September 1993): 361.

18. Gregory M. Pfitzer, *Samuel Eliot Morison's Historical World: In Quest of a New Parkman* (Boston: Northeastern University Press, 1991), 199.

19. Morison, in *Of Plymouth Plantation*, vii.

20. Ibid., x.

21. Increase Mather, *An Earnest Exhortation to the Inhabitants of New-England* (Boston: John Foster, 1676), 3.

22. Jill Lepore, *The Name of War: King Philip's War and the Origins of American Identity* (New York: Knopf, 1998), 121.

23. Ibid., 72.

24. Ibid., 89.

25. Ibid., 173, xvi.

26. Philbrick, *Mayflower*, xvii.

27. Thomas Church, *Entertaining Passages relating to Philip's War* . . . *with some account of the Divine Providence towards Benj. Church, Esqr.* (Boston: B. Green, 1716), ii.

28. Lepore, *The Name of War*, 17.

29. Philbrick, *Mayflower*, 357.

30. Morison, in *Of Plymouth Plantation*, xxx.

31. Pfitzer, *Morison's Historical World*, 113.

32. Bailyn, *Morison*, 10.

33. Morison, *Sailor Historian*, 385.

34. Pfitzer, *Morison's Historical World*, 114.

35. Philbrick, *Mayflower*, 357–58.

36. Church, *Entertaining Passages*, 54.

37. Samuel Eliot Morison, *By Land and by Sea: Essays and Addresses* (New York: Knopf, 1953), 234.

38. Perry Miller, "Errand into the Wilderness," in *Errand into the Wilderness* (1956; repr., Cambridge: Belknap Press of Harvard University Press, 1984), 15. Citations refer to 1984 reprint.

39. Samuel Eliot Morison, *Vistas of History* (New York: Knopf, 1964), 105.

40. Morison, in *Of Plymouth Plantation*, vii.

41. Samuel Eliot Morison, *Massachusettensis de Contoribus; or, The Builders of the Bay Colony* (Boston: Houghton Mifflin, 1930), vi.

42. Pfitzer, *Morison's Historical World*, 234–35.

43. Bailyn, *Morison*.

## 3. The Way to Wealth

1. Benjamin Franklin, *Papers of Benjamin Franklin*, ed. Leonard W. Larabee et al. (New Haven: Yale University Press, 1959–2008), 7: 234, 174, 219. Poor Richard's proverbs can be found in the *Papers*. Portions of this chapter appeared, in a different form, in *The Whites of Their Eyes* (Princeton: Princeton University Press, 2010).

2. Benjamin Franklin, *Autobiography*, ed. J. A. Leo Lemay and P. M. Zall (New York: Norton, 1986), 10.

3. Franklin, *Papers*, 7:328–29.

4. Carl Van Doren, *Benjamin Franklin* (New York: Viking Press, 1938), 268.

5. Franklin, *Papers*, 14:345.

6. Ibid., 1:331.

7. Franklin, *Autobiography*, 66–71.

8. Ibid., 248.

9. Franklin, *Papers*, 5:432.

10. Ibid., 1:17, 19.

11. Ibid., 1:311.

12. Robert Newcomb, "The Sources of Benjamin Franklin's Sayings of Poor Richard," Ph.D. dissertation, University of Maryland, 1957, 65, 54, 77, 32.

13. J. A. Leo Lemay, *The Life of Benjamin Franklin* (Philadelphia: University of Pennsylvania Press, 2006–9), 2:172

14. Franklin, *Papers*, 2:300–301.

15. Lemay, *Life of Franklin,* 2:188

16. Franklin, *Papers*, 2:127.

17. Ibid., 2:136.

18. Lemay, *Life of Franklin,* 2: 526

19. Franklin, *Papers*, 3:30–31.

20. Franklin, *Autobiography*, 11–12; Franklin, *Papers*, 4:107.

21. Franklin, *Papers*, 1:328–31.

22. Ibid., 6:123.

23. Ibid., 7:320.

24. Ibid., 7:340–41.

25. Ibid., 7:350.

26. Van Doren, *Benjamin Franklin*, 276–77.

27. Franklin, *Autobiography*, 272–73.

28. Van Doren, *Benjamin Franklin*, viii–ix.

29. Ibid., 272.

30. Franklin, *Papers*, 12:4–5.

31. *The Examination of Doctor Benjamin Franklin* (London, 1766).

32. Franklin, *Autobiography*, 79.

33. Franklin, *Papers*, 1:130.

## 4. The Age of Paine

1. Thomas Paine, *The Complete Writings of Thomas Paine*, ed. Philip Foner (New York: Citadel Press, 1945), 1:3, 17. Portions of this chapter appeared, in a different form, in *The Whites of Their Eyes*.

2. John Adams, *Papers of John Adams*, ed. Robert J. Taylor et al. (Cambridge: Harvard University Press, 1977–2010), 4:37, 41, 53, 29.

3. Craig Nelson, *Thomas Paine: Enlightenment, Revolution, and the Birth of Modern Nations* (New York: Viking, 2006), 49.

4. *Writings of Thomas Paine*, 1:19.

5. John Adams, *Diary and Autobiography of John Adams*, ed. L. H. Butterfield (Cambridge: Harvard University Press, 1961), 3:330–41.

6. Paul Collins, *The Trouble with Tom: The Strange Afterlife and Times of Thomas Paine* (New York: Bloomsbury, 2005), 22.

7. *Writings of Thomas Paine*, 1:49–50; Nelson, *Thomas Paine*, 108.

8. Nelson, *Thomas Paine*, 203.

9. Ibid., 9.

10. Mercy Otis Warren, *History of the Rise, Progress, and Termination of the American Revolution* (Boston, 1805), 1:378–80.

11. Eric Foner, *Tom Paine and Revolutionary America* (New York: Oxford University Press, 1976), 264.

12. Collins, *The Trouble with Tom*, 29.

13. Perry Miller, "Thomas Paine, Rationalist," *Nation*, February 23, 1946, p. 232; Sean Wilentz, "The Air Around Tom Paine," *New Republic*, April 24, 1995, p. 38; Bernard Bailyn, *Faces of Revolution: Personalities and Themes in the Struggle for American Independence* (New York: Knopf, 1990), np.

14. John Keane, *Tom Paine: A Political Life* (Boston: Little, Brown, 1995), xiii.

15. *Writings of Thomas Paine*, 1:286, 344, 404–5, etc.

16. Nelson, *Thomas Paine*, 202, 220, 228.

17. Ibid., 229–30.

18. Ibid., 241.

19. Ibid., 248, 274–75, 281.

20. Ibid., 285.

21. Foner, *Tom Paine and Revolutionary America*, xii.

22. *Writings of Thomas Paine*, 1:464, 599.

23. "Plea for a Patriot," *Galaxy* 21 (May 1876): 593.

24. Wilentz, "The Air Around Tom Paine," 38.

25. Harvey J. Kaye, *Thomas Paine and the Promise of America* (New York: Hill and Wang, 2005), 171.

26. Collins, *The Trouble with Tom*, 53, 57, 62, 64.

27. Nelson, *Thomas Paine*, 270, 308, 306; *Spirit of the Pilgrims*, June 1931, 341.

28. Colllins, *The Trouble with Tom*, 15.

29. Foner, *Tom Paine and Revolutionary America*, 257.

30. Warren, *History*, 1:379.

31. *Writings of Thomas Paine*, 1:601, 465.

32. Nelson, *Thomas Paine*, 9.

## 5. We the Parchment

1. James Madison, *The Debates in the Federal Convention of 1787, Which Framed the Constitution of the United States of America*, ed. Gaillard Hunt and James Brown Scott (New York: Oxford University Press, 1920), 577–79.

2. *The Constitution of the United States Together with an Account of Its Travels since September 17, 1787*, comp. David C. Mearns and Verner W. Clapp (Washington, DC: Library of Congress, 1942–58), 1–17. Much of this is condensed at "Signers of the Constitution: Text and History of the Constitution," National Park Service, last modified July 29, 2004, http://www.nps.gov/history/history/online%5Fbooks/constitution/history.htm. On more recent preservation efforts, see Catherine Nicholson and Mary Lynn Ritzenthaler, "Exposed to Air after Fifty Years!" *Common-place* 2, no. 4 (July 2002). For an account of the visitor experience to the National Archives, see Beth A. Twiss-Garrity, "Relics, Reverence, and Relevance," *Common-place* 2, no. 4 (July 2002).

3. "Before the American Revolution, no people had ever explicitly voted on their own written constitution." Akhil Reed Amar, *America's Constitution: A Biography* (New York: Random House, 2005), 8.

4. James Madison, *Federalist* No. 40: "The Powers of the Convention to Form a Mixed Government Examined and Sustained," *New York Packet*, January 18, 1788.

5. You can see this at "Parchment Constitution," The Patriot Post Shop, http://patriotshop.us/product_info.php?cPath=85&products_id=646.

6. Thomas Paine, *The Rights of Man, For the Use and Benefit of All Mankind* (London: Daniel Isaac Eaton, 1795).

7. The oldest one I've seen is from 1788, but it's not pocketable: *The Constitution of the United States* (Hartford: Hudson and Goodwin[?], 1788). The earliest pocket edition might be *The Declaration of Independence, and Constitution of the United States of America, To which is Prefixed the*

*Constitution of the State of New-York* (New York: John Bull, 1796), which is thirty-seven pages and 18 cm, a duodecimo. A few more are *The Declaration of Independence and the Constitution of the United States, with the several amendments . . . Together with President Washington's Farewell address* (Norwich, CT: Sterry & Porter, 1806), 60 pp.; *Declaration of Independence, and Constitution of the United States of America* (New York: J. Low, 1812); *Declaration of Independence and Constitution of the United States of America, with Its Amendments* (Boston, J. P. Jewett, 1856). Quite a lovely one is *The Declaration of Independence and Constitution of the United States of America* (New York: R. Spalding, 1864). The earliest polyglot one I've seen is *The Declaration of Independence, and the Constitution of the United States: In German, French, and English* (New York: Laidlaw Bros., 1888); it includes commentary.

8. "Andrew Johnson's Constitution," *Cincinnati Daily Gazette*, April 1, 1875.

9. Center for the Constitution at James Madison's Montpelier, *2010 Executive Summary: The State of the Constitution: What Americans Know*, http://center.montpelier.org/files/Executive%20Summary09.16.2010.pdf.

10. "The Constitution: Learn It or Lose It" reads the bumper sticker. http://www.libertystickers.com

11. Jamal Greene reports the findings of a study conducted at Harvard Law School: "between 1957 and 1986 only three federal court decisions referenced founding-era dictionaries. . . . In each of the four semi-decanal periods from 1987 to 2006—representing Justice Scalia's tenure on the Supreme Court—the number of founding-era dictionary references has been, respectively, 6, 11, 5, and 24."Greene, "Selling Originalism," *Georgetown Law Journal* 97 (March 2009): 689–90.

12. On Franklin's alphabet, see Jill Lepore, *A Is for American: Letters and Other Characters in the Newly United States* (New York: Knopf, 2000), chap. 1.

13. Herbert J. Storing, ed., with the assistance of Murray Dry, *The Complete Anti-Federalist*, vol. 1, *What the Anti-Federalists Were For* (Chicago: University of Chicago Press, 1981), 54.

14. William Manning, *The Key of Libberty* (Billerica, MA: Manning Association, 1922), with an introduction by Samuel Eliot Morison, 39–40. Manning wrote this essay in 1798, but it wasn't published until 1922. A modernized edition, and an excellent biography of Manning, can be found in William Manning, *The Key of Liberty: The Life and Democratic Writings*

*of William Manning, "'A Laborer,'" 1747–1814*, ed. Michael Merrill and Sean Wilentz (Cambridge: Harvard University Press, 1993).

15. H. Arnold Bennett, *The Constitution in School and College* (New York: G. P. Putnam's Sons, 1935), 103–6.

16. Nullification, Michael Kammen put it, was about "each side claiming to be more constitutional than the other." Michael Kammen, *A Machine That Would Go of Itself: The Constitution in American Culture* (2006; repr., New Brunswick, NJ: Transaction Publishers, 2009), 52–53. Citations refer to the 2009 edition. William Manning would have called this kind of thing fiddling. In 1833, Daniel Webster argued, on the floor of the Senate, against the nullifiers' use of the phrase "constitutional compact" to refer the Constitution, on grammatical grounds as much as political ones: "in our American political grammar, *constitution* is a noun substantive; it imports a distinct and clear idea of itself; and it is not to lose its importance and dignity, it is not to be turned into a poor, ambiguous, senseless, unmeaning adjective, for the purpose of accommodating any new set of political notions." Webster in ibid., 53–54.

17. Joseph Story, *The Constitutional Class Book: Being a Brief Exposition of the Constitution of the United States* (Boston: Hilliard, Gray, 1834), 334–45. In another book, Story tried to make his remarks on the Constitution "intelligible to every class of readers, by embodying them in plain and unambitious language." Joseph Story, *A Familiar Exposition of the Constitution of the United States, Containing a Brief Commentary on Every Clause* (Boston: Marsh, Capen, Lyon, and Webb, 1840), 6. By the 1830s, those new political notions included universal white male suffrage. "The people" now included more and more men with little or no education. With the expansion of suffrage came the growth of common schools.

18. "*Every good citizen*, capable of reading and understanding its meaning," Hickey wrote, "is bound by duty to his country, if in his power, to possess a copy of the Constitution." "The Constitution in its words is plain and intelligible," George Dallas wrote, "and is meant for the homebred, unsophisticated understandings of our fellow-citizens." William Hickey, *The Constitution of the United States of America, with an Alphabetical Analysis*, 2nd ed. (Philadelphia: T. K. & P. G. Collins, 1846, 1847), xviii, xxi, vi. Hickey is difficult to read. Here Hickey explains why he has written his book: "The length of time required in the ordinary course of business, for obtaining a practical knowledge of the operations of government, by persons entering into public life, and their embarrassments for the want of a

convenient mode of reference to the various sources of information, have suggested the utility of preparing, as a part of this work, and as germainne [*sic*] to its design, a means of collecting and rendering available to the public interest the experience and information acquired in this respect, in the progress of time, by attention to the business of legislation in the public service."

19. Wright, quoted in Kammen, *Machine,* 83.

20. Webster, quoted in ibid., 84.

21. William E. Cain, ed., *William Lloyd Garrison and the Fight Against Slavery: Selections from* The Liberator (Boston: Bedford Books of St. Martin's Press, 1995), 35–36.

22. Brown, writes American University law professor Robert Tsai, was a practitioner of "fringe constitutionalism." At Brown's trial, the prosecution introduced the constitution as evidence of Brown's treachery; the defense wanted to use it as evidence of his insanity, but this Brown would not allow. Instead, the defense argued that Brown had erected only "a mere imaginary Government." Robert L. Tsai, "John Brown's Constitution," *Boston College Law Review* 51 (January 2010): 151–207.

23. William Grimes, *Life of William Grimes, the Runaway Slave* (New York: n.p., 1825), 68. See also Ann Fabian, *The Unvarnished Truth: Personal Narratives in Nineteenth-Century America* (Berkeley: University of California Press, 2000), 86–88. Lysander Spooner, a radical abolitionist, argued that resistance to slavery was "a strictly constitutional right." Spooner quoted in Tsai, "John Brown's Constitution," 169.

24. Rush to Adams, June 1789, quoted in Eric Thomas Slauter, *The State as a Work of Art: The Cultural Origins of the Constitution* (Chicago: University of Chicago Press, 2009), 244.

25. "Divergent Views of Public Men," *Life,* September 17, 1956, 119–20.

26. James Ayres, "Busing Foes Take their Protest to Replay of Boston Massacre," *Boston Globe*, March 6, 1975.

27. Madison, who drafted the Bill of Rights, proposed "nor shall any national religion be established," and the Senate suggested prohibiting "establishing articles of faith or a mode of worship." Jack N. Rakove, ed., *The Annotated U.S. Constitution and Declaration of Independence* (Cambridge: Belknap Press of Harvard University Press, 2009), 222.

28. Sanford Levinson, *Constitutional Faith* (Princeton: Princeton University Press, 1988), 33.

29. People usually argue that the fact that the constitution is written means that it is unifying, but Levinson explored "the potential of a written

constitution to serve as the source of fragmentation and *dis*integration" (ibid., 17). Slauter discusses the history of the body politic in *The State as a Work of Art*.

30. "Our real constitution," one civics book author insisted in 1886, "is found in the interpretations which the courts have given to the written documents and the actual institutions which have been established under them." Jesse Macy, *Our Government: How It Grew, What It Does, and How It Does It* (1886; repr., Boston: Ginn and Company, 1887), 174. Citations refer to the 1887 reprint. There is, of course, a large literature on this question, but a very helpful discussion is Laurence H. Tribe, *The Invisible Constitution* (New York: Oxford University Press, 2008). By an invisible constitution Tribe means to distinguish his approach from those who write of an unwritten constitution, the latter generally referring to the body of constitutional law. He means, instead, what is, literally, not written into the Constitution but is still a part of it.

31. Wilson quoted in Kammen, *Machine*, 19. Oliver Wendell Holmes spoke of constitutional provisions as "organic living institutions." In 1955, Earl Warren wrote, "our legal system has been an organic growth, and not the overnight creation of any individual genius."

32. Ibid., *Machine,* 231. National Association for Constitutional Government, *Socialism in American Colleges* (Washington, DC, 1920). On the Sons of the American Revolution, Thomas Reed Powell once wrote, "we have Sons and Daughters of the Revolution who seek to guard us against further revolution, or even evolution. Causes may be celebrated even though they are lost causes. There are Sons and Daughters of the Confederacy. But there are no Sons and Daughters of the Confederation, unless perhaps because of some of their ideals we should so classify the late but unlamented American Liberty League." Thomas Reed Powell, "From Philadelphia to Philadelphia," *American Political Science Review* 32 (February 1938): 2. (This was Powell's presidential address to the American Political Science Association, December 27, 1937.)

33. On Beck, see Morton Keller, *In Defense of Yesterday: James M. Beck and the Politics of Conservatism, 1861–1936* (New York: Coward-McCann, 1958). On the distribution of Beck's lectures and books, see p. 159. Beck became a member of the Sons of the American Revolution in 1897 (54). For his growing conviction, in 1906, that trust-busting is un-American, see p. 80. Beck had started out as a Democrat, but his views changed: "Legalism, concern for the Constitution, reverence for the American past, would become hallmarks of his political thinking" (82). On Constitution

Day, 1919, Beck delivered an address titled "A Rising Sun or a Setting Sun?" Beck suggested that Benjamin Franklin would enjoy shaking Henry Ford's hand, etc. Beck concluded, though, that the sun was setting, since progressives had eroded constitutional principles. James M. Beck, *The Constitution of the United States: Yesterday, Today—and Tomorrow?* (New York: George H. Doran, 1924), chap. 22 (for Ford, see p. 258); Keller, *In Defense of Yesterday*, 128–29. By 1920, Keller writes, Beck's "name was put forward for Congress, the Senate, even the Presidency" (147). For the presidential address before the American Bar Association in 1921, he spoke on "The Spirit of Lawlessness" and railed against, among other things, jazz and modern art: "futurists, cubists, vorticists and other aesthetic Bolsheviki." Nothing could remedy the world except the founding fathers. He lashed out at "garbage historians" who would debunk Washington, including, in this category, Samuel Eliot Morison, who had said Washington was dull but honest (153, 156–57). Beck was a Republican congressman from 1927 to 1934. Keller argues that Beck "found that the nature and needs of corporate capitalism could not be reconciled with his ideals of limited constitutional government and free competition" (13).

34. "This is due, not to any conscious hostility to the spirit or letter, but to the indifference and apathy with which the masses regard the increasing assaults upon its basic principles." Beck, *Constitution of the United States*, 273.

35. Bennett, *The Constitution in School and College*, 103–6.

36. This is reported in Maxwell H. Bloomfield, *Peaceful Revolution: Constitutional Change and American Culture from Progressivism to the New Deal* (Cambridge: Harvard University Press, 2000), 76

37. A good example of a late nineteenth-century catechism for school-children is Alfred Bayliess, *Easy Lessons on the Constitution of the United States* (Chicago: W. W. Knowles, 1891). Bennett notes the rise of the guides containing clause-by-clause analysis, supplanting catechisms, but their chief defect, he argues, is "their relatively non-critical character. They are not designed sufficiently to provoke constructive criticism of our national political institutions" (*The Constitution in School and College*, 93–94). Conservative authors of civics textbooks counseled avoidance of criticism. DeKoven wrote in 1923: "revere the Constitution as the best form of government ever devised by the mind of man. Let him not try to diminish the power of any one of the three columns of government, particularly let him not attempt to question the restraining power of the Supreme Court" (ibid., 84–85). *Community Civics* (1922) damned the electoral

college as "worse than useless"; *A Texas Civics* (1927) called the method of amendment undemocratic (Bennett, *The Constitution in School and College*, 82–83).

38. Bennett, *The Constitution in School and College*, 101.

39. "I don't believe in one generation deciding what the others shall do," wrote one philosophy professor in 1931. "Our forefathers didn't know anything about a country of 120,000,000 people, with automobiles, trains, and radios." Kammen, *Machine*, 227. In 1935, Charles A. Beard published a second edition of his *Economic Interpretation*, with a new introduction, in which he attempted both to disentangle his historical research from the politics of his day and to defend himself against charges that his economic determinism was Marxist. Beard, *An Economic Interpretation of the Constitution of the United States* (New York: Macmillan, 1935), xii–xiii.

40. Arnold quoted in Kammen, *Machine*, 276).

41. For a photograph, see Associated Press, "Tea Party Group on Offensive over Blog Satirizing NAACP," *Cleveland.com*, July 19, 2010, http://www.cleveland.com/nation/index.ssf/2010/07/tea_party_group_on_defensive_o.html.

42. Hearst Corporation, *The American Public's Knowledge of the U.S. Constitution: A National Survey of Public Awareness and Personal Opinion* (New York: Hearst Corporation, 1987), 13.

43. Ibid., 12.

44. The ANES measures the knowledge not of the populace but of the electorate and, assuming that voters are better informed than nonvoters, ANES data overestimate political knowledge. Knowledge of particular policy issues seems to be no better. In 1964, fewer than four in ten Americans knew that the Soviet Union was not a NATO member. Surveys conducted in the 1980s found that only 22 percent of American voters knew that the United States had a no-first-strike nuclear policy. During the 2000 election, only 15 percent of those polled could identify even a single candidate running for Congress. The most influential study is Michael X. Delli Carpini and Scott Keeter, *What Americans Know about Politics and Why It Matters* (New Haven: Yale University Press, 1986). For a more recent treatment, see Ilya Somin, "Political Ignorance and the Countermajoritarian Difficulty: A New Perspective on the Central Obsession of Constitutional Theory," *Iowa Law Review* 89 (April 2004): 1312. Somin argues that the know-nothing percentage is closer to 34 percent because random guessing (when several survey questions offer only two possible answers) overestimates knowledge.

45. Beth Twiss-Garrity reports some early constitutional knowledge polling: "A 1943 National Opinion Research Center study showed that only 23 percent of respondents could correctly name some of the rights protected by the Bill of Rights. In 1947, the Gallup Poll noted that 41 percent had no knowledge of the contents of the Bill of Rights. On the bicentennial of the Constitution in 1987, a study by the College of Education at the University of Houston reported that 46 percent of those queried did not know that the Constitution created a system of government. In the most recent NCC poll, conducted by Minda Borun in November 2001, two-thirds of respondents could not identify the Constitution as the outline for U.S. government, while less than one-fourth could correctly pick three items in the Constitution from a list of six choices. People seemed to recognize their ignorance. In another NCC study, only 12 percent of respondents claimed to know 'a great deal' about the Constitution, with others avoiding taking the survey out of self-professed shame" (Twiss-Garrity, "Relics, Reverence, and Relevance"), but 71 percent of answers coded as incorrect were either partly or nearly correct.

46. Hearst Corporation, *The American Public's Knowledge*, 7–8. For a critique made along these lines, see Susan R. Burgess, Daniel J. Reagan, and Donald L. Davison, "Reclaiming a Democratic Constitutional Politics: Survey Construction and Public Knowledge," *Review of Politics* 54 (Summer 1992): 399–415.

47. Kammen, *Machine*, 24.

48. "Exalting originalism," the Columbia legal scholar Jamal Greene has observed, "was part of a deliberate effort by the Reagan Justice Department to rally Americans against a Federal Judiciary it perceived as frustrating its conservative political agenda." Greene, "Selling Originalism," 659–60.

49. Thurgood Marshall, speech presented at the annual seminar of the San Francisco Patent and Trademark Law Association, Maui, HI, May 6, 1987.

50. "The Mount Vernon Statement: Constitutional Conservatism: A Statement for the 21st Century," February 17, 2010, http://www.themountvernonstatement.com/.

51. Ben Frumin, "Mount Vernon to Right Wingers: You're Not Welcome Here," *Talking Points Memo Live Wire* (blog), February 17, 2010, http://tpmlivewire.talkingpointsmemo.com/2010/02/mount-vernon-to-right-wingers-youre-not-welcome-here.php. And see the photograph

illustrating Tracy D. Samuelson, "Mount Vernon Statement: A Fake Hitler Outdid Conservatives Online," *Christian Science Monitor*, February 18, 2010. http://www.csmonitor.com/Business/new-economy/2010/0218/Mount-Vernon-Statement-A-fake-Hitler-outdid-conservatives-online.

52. Scalia wrote in 1989, "The purpose of constitutional guarantees is precisely to prevent the law from reflecting certain *changes* in original values that the society adopting the Constitution thinks fundamentally undesirable." Scalia from "Originalism: The Lesser Evil," *University of Cincinnati Law Review* 57 (1989), quoted in Greene, "Selling Originalism," 658.

53. "The good news about the Court is that it is interpreting the constitutional principles affirmed by the American people at times when their political attention and energy was most focused on such matters; the bad news is that the Americans who made these considered constitutional judgments are dead." Bruce Ackerman, *We the People*, vol. 1, *Foundations* (Cambridge: Belknap Press of Harvard University Press, 1991), 263.

54. Greene, "Selling Originalism," 659.

55. Mark Levin, *Men in Black: How the Supreme Court Is Destroying America* (Washington, DC: Regnery Publishing, 2005), 9.

56. Reva B. Siegel, "Dead or Alive: Originalism as Popular Constitutionalism in *Heller*," *Harvard Law Review* 122 (November 2008): 224, 228. And see Jill Lepore, "Battleground America," *New Yorker*, April 23, 2012.

57. During the Reagan years, Cass Sunstein and Akhil Amar offered a historicist constitutional interpretation, based on civic republicanism, which was, at the time, flourishing in the work of the historians like J.G.A. Pocock, Bernard Bailyn, and Gordon Wood. Larry D. Kramer, *The People Themselves: Popular Constitutionalism and Judicial Review* (New York: Oxford University Press, 2004).

58. Ibid., 248; Michael N. Berman, "Originalism Is Bunk," *New York University Law Review* 84 (April 2009). Daniel Levin has argued, "The birth of the modern American heritage movement could easily be described as a series of acts of expiation by modern industrialists. Oil tycoon John D. Rockefeller rebuilt Colonial Williamsburg, and auto magnate Henry Ford created a condensed version of American history in Greenfield Village, Michigan, while Wall Street financed the reconstruction of Monticello." Daniel Levin, "Federalists in the Attic: Original Intent, the Heritage Movement, and Democratic Theory," *Law and Social Inquiry* 29 (Winter 2004): 108.

59. "First, it is easier to understand than other theories. Second, it caters to populist suspicion of legal elites. Third, it appeals to a sense of cultural nationalism." Greene, "Selling Originalism," 708.

60. "By returning to an origin myth of the Constitution featuring the document's ratification by the 'people,'" Levin argues, "originalists attempt to reconstruct American constitutionalism in a populist mode that casts liberal jurisprudence as essentially undemocratic." Levin, "Federalists in the Attic," 116, 107

61. Michael K. Holler, *The Constitution Made Easy* (Woodland Park, CO: Friends of Freedom, 2008), 30–31, 68–69, 38–39. See also http://www.theconstitutionmadeeasy.com/.

62. Michael Arnheim, *U.S. Constitution for Dummies* (Hoboken, NJ: Wiley, 2009), 112, 60–63, 238, 276.

63. Thomas Reed Powell, "Constitutional Metaphors," Review of James M. Beck's *The Constitution of the United States*, by James M. Beck, *New Republic*, February 11, 1925.

## 6. I.O.U.

1. The original reading diary is in box 2, in a folder titled, "Reading Diary in Newark Prison, January 1, 1797–August 5, 1798." The cover is missing. The book is about ten by eight inches. The binding is broken. It might have been bound in calf. Some 277 numbered pages of the blank book have been filled; the rest are blank; maybe a fifth of the volume is blank. It has been transcribed, although the transcription has left out long excerpts from books and includes only Pintard's writing. John Pintard's "Reading Diary in Newark Prison," transcript, in John Pintard Papers, New York Historical Society, box 2A. On the first page, Pintard quotes Boswell, from *Journal of a Tour to the Hebrides*: "Every man should keep minutes of whatever he reads. Every circumstance of his studies should be recorded; what books he has consulted; how much of them he has read; at what times; how often the same authors; and what opinions he formed of them, at different periods of his life. Such an account would much illustrate the history of his mind." The fullest account of Pintard is David Sterling, "New York Patriarch: A Life of John Pintard, 1759–1844," Ph.D. dissertation, New York University, 1958. But see also Walter Muir Whitehall, "John Pintard's 'Antiquarian Society,'" *New York Historical Society Quarterly* 45 (October 1961): 346–63. On the Newark Town Jail, see Sterling,

"New York Patriarch," 201–2; and for a further description, see the account in the New Jersey Historical Society finding aid for the sheriff's journal at "Manuscript Group 929, Newark Town Jail, Newark, NJ," http://www.jerseyhistory.org/findingaid.php?aid=0929. The number of lengths of the hall is from Bruce H. Mann, *Republic of Debtors: Bankruptcy in the Age of American Independence* (Cambridge: Harvard University Press, 2002), 117, 301n15.

2. Larry E. Sullivan, "Books, Power, and the Development of Libraries in the New Republic: The Prison and Other Journals of John Pintard of New York," *Journal of Library History* 21 (Spring 1986): 415. On the gridded table, see Margaret Heilbrun, "Nyork, Ncentury, N-YHS," *New-York Journal of American History* 65 (2003): 28. Quixote is from Pintard, "Reading Diary," 71. "Read a pamphlet lent me by Mr Murray, entitled National debt national prosperity, wherein the writer exhibits considerable ingenuity to prove the advantages of funded debt of G. Britain as having diffused money through the nation" (33). I believe this to be Robert Peel, *The National Debt Productive of National Prosperity* (Warrington, 1787). Pintard read the two-volume London 1785 edition of Johnson's *Dictionary*. I consulted the 1783 editing for the first and last words. The first entry is actually for the letter "A," but the first word is "abacus." Samuel Johnson, *A Dictionary of the English Language*, 7th ed. (London: W. Strahan et al., 1783). Pintard had tried, twice before, when not in prison, to read the dictionary. Pintard wrote in his diary on New Year's Day, 1798: "I am also reading or rather studying Dr Johnsons Dictionary of the English language which I began the 9th of Octo & read loiteringly having proceeded only as far as the word *Cheek* the 31st Decem. I shall endeavour to prosecute my reading with more vigor. I attempted this task the first winter I passed in Newark in 1793, but proceeded only as far as the word *absence*, which proved inauspicious, as I stopped there. I again took up the design June 1 of the last year, but read only as far as the word abide on the 3d June. My intention is not to lay it aside untill I have gone through this somewhat laborious undertaking, unless inevitably prevented. As I go along I take a memo of the various authors cited, and mark the interesting selections with which Dr J. has illustrated the meaning & acceptations of the words in the English language. No person can form the most distant idea of the powers & capacity of Johnsons mind, that has not attentively examined his Dictionary. His talent at defintion is truly astonishing" (Pintard, "Reading Diary," 48). And see the entry from April, 20, 1798, when he finishes: "Concluded reading Dr Johnsons great work his Dictionary of

the English Language, 6th Edition 2 Vols quarto, London, 1785. I began this task the 9th of October last before which time I had made two imperfect attempts in the winter of 1793 & in June 1797, but did not proceed far. The 1st Vol. contains 1028 pages, the 2d 2114, exclusive of the preface History of the English Language & Grammar. I read the words & definitions with critical attention, & marked all the most striking examples with which he illustrates the force & application of the words. I found by repeated observation that it required on an average nine minutes per page throughout. At the commencement my reading was slow, & attempted to mark in Ashs' Dictionary the words not used by Johnson. This retarded me & I gave it over. My reading increased progressively from 4 to 6, 10, 14, 16, 18, 20 pages per diem. On the 6th of April I read 50 pages which I found very fatiguing. I was engaged 157 days in this undertaking, from which I experience considerable improvement in the knowledge of the English Language, & which I shall regard as a signal instance of preserving application. I have made a list of authorities cited by Johnson which I propose copying in a blank leaf of the Dictionary & I kept a regular Journal of the progress of each days reading" (78).

3. "The lives of the poets afford great critical knowledge, and the style of Johnson merits close study. I am more indebted to him than any other writer, for the many valuable lessons imbibed from his moral pen. He first taught me to respect virtue and religion, and the frequent perusal of his various works, especially the Rambler & Rasselas, will prove an incentive to the practice of religious & social duties" (Pintard, "Reading Diary," 13). Pintard says much this same thing in a diary from 1793: "I feel myself more indebted to the writings of Johnson, and his minute biographer, Mr. Boswell, for many resolutions I have formed, to pursue a moral and religious course of conduct. . . . I purpose to read everything that has fallen from the pen of Johnson" (quoted in Sullivan, "Books, Power," 415). And again in 1833: "I feel more indebted to this eminent moralist than to any other English author" (ibid.).

4. Samuel Johnson, *Idler*, no. 22, September 16, 1758.

5. *The Ill Policy and Inhumanity of Imprisoning Insolvent Debtors* (Newport, RI: James Franklin, 1754), 6.

6. On the efficacy of the threat, see Joanna Innes, "The King's Bench Prison in the Later Eighteenth Century: Law, Authority and Order in a London Debtors' Prison," in *An Ungovernable People: The English and Their Law in the Seventeenth and Eighteenth Centuries*, ed. John Brewer and John Styles (London: Hutchinson, 1980), 254. She points out that a 1791 study

by the House of Commons found that of 12,000 bailable writs, only 1,200 led to imprisonment (that is, everyone else paid).

7. The best study remains George Philip Bauer, "The Movement against Imprisonment for Debt in the United States," Ph.D. dissertation, Harvard University, 1935. But a handy summary of the state abolition dates can be found in Charles Warren, *Bankruptcy in United States History* (Cambridge: Harvard University Press, 1935), 52.

8. On Pintard's bankruptcy proceedings, see Mann, *Republic of Debtors*, 234–39.

9. This story about Roman law is repeated everywhere, but a fairly reasonable authority for it is Richard Ford, "Imprisonment for Debt," *Michigan Law Review* 25 (November 1926): 24–25. Ford says that dismemberment, "though permitted by the letter of the law, was unknown in practice; the selling of the debtor into slavery was, however, very common."

10. Mann, *Republic of Debtors*, 286n8. See also Margot C. Finn, *The Character of Credit: Personal Debt in English Culture, 1740–1914* (New York: Cambridge University Press, 2003), 110. Joanna Innes, "The King's Bench Prison in the Later Eighteenth Century: Law, Authority, and Order in a London Debtors' Prison," in *An Ungovernable People: The English and Their Law in the Seventeenth and Eighteenth Centuries*, ed. John Brewer and John Styles (London: Hutchinson, 1980), 253, has a good account of the Middle Ages, too.

11. The proverb is quoted in Innes, "King's Bench Prison," 255.

12. Bauer, "Imprisonment for Debt," 37. On the frequency of debtor servitude: "In virtually all the colonies north of the Potomac an important variation of custom is to be noted—a tempered reversion to the idea of antiquity—namely the substitution of servitude for imprisonment as a way of satisfying judgments. This arrangement, while perhaps not more advantageous to the debtor, was at least on the surface more rational. The obvious absurdity of locking up a man who cannot meet his obligations, and so rendering him even less able to do so, would seem to have been avoided. But the true explanation of the phenomenon probably lies not so much in the superior reasoning of the colonial mind as in the economic conditions of the new country" (ibid., 30). See also Christine Daniels, "'Without Any Limitacon of Time': Debt Servitude in Colonial America," *Labor History* 36 (1995): 232–50.

13. Bauer, "Imprisonment for Debt," 75–76.

14. Defoe, himself twice arrested for debt, wrote, allegorically, about his coy mistress, Lady Credit, whose hand was hard to win: "If you court

her, you lose her." Paula R. Backscheider, "Defoe's Lady Credit," *Huntington Library Quarterly* 44 (1981): 89–100.

15. Bauer, "Imprisonment for Debt," 23–24, 31–32.

16. Ibid., 26.

17. Cotton Mather, *Fair Dealing between Debtor and Creditor: A very brief Essay upon the Caution to be used, about coming in to* DEBT (Boston, 1716), 3, 8.

18. Bauer, "Imprisonment for Debt," 55–57.

19. This was Oglethorpe's plan; it didn't quite work out that way. Some mention of this is made by Ford, "Imprisonment for Debt," 28.

20. Bauer, "Imprisonment for Debt," 60–61.

21. The best discussion of Fielding's debt is in Finn, *The Character of Credit.*

22. E.g., ibid.; also Barbara Weiss, *The Hell of the English: Bankruptcy and the Victorian Novel* (Lewisburg, PA: Bucknell University Press, 1986); Patrick Brantlinger, *Fictions of State: Culture and Credit in Britain, 1694–1994* (Ithaca: Cornell University Press, 1996); and Mary Poovey, *Genres of the Credit Economy: Mediating Value in Eighteenth- and Nineteenth-Century Britain* (Chicago: University of Chicago Press, 2008).

23. James Neild, *An Account of the Rise, Progress, and Present State of the Society for the Discharge and Relief of Persons Imprisoned for Small Debts throughout England and Wales* (London: J. Nichols and Son, 1808). See also G. Le G. Norgate, "Neild, James [1744–1814]," rev. Stephen M. Lee, in *Oxford Dictionary of National Biography*, ed. Lawrence Goldman, May 2009, http://www.oxforddnb.com/view/article/19859; and Bauer, "Imprisonment for Debt," 81.

24. John Howard, *The State of the Prisons in England and Wales* (London, 1777); the quotation is from section 1: "General View of Distress" (Warrington, 1780). See also Bauer, "Imprisonment for Debt," 83.

25. "After 1766, when local Sons of Liberty held their annual celebration, they regularly sent the remains of their banquet to City Hall for the refreshment of the famished prisoners lodged there" (Bauer, "Imprisonment for Debt," 77).

26. T. H. Breen, *Tobacco Culture: The Mentality of the Great Tidewater Planters on the Eve of Revolution* (Princeton: Princeton University Press, 1985).

27. When the states began drafting their constitutions, some attempted to abolish the imprisonment of debtors. Pennsylvania's liberal constitution decreed "That the person of a debtor, where there is not a

strong presumption of fraud, shall not be continued in prison, after delivering up, bona fide, all his estate real and persona, for the use of his creditors, in such manner as shall be hereafter regulated by law." By 1798, North Carolina, Vermont, Kentucky, Georgia, and Tennessee would all adopt this policy. Bauer, "Imprisonment for Debt," 92.

28. Ibid., 90–91.

29. "Members of the association 'for the relief of distressed Debtors confined in the Gaol' . . . address a memorial to the legislature, in which they say that from Jan. 2, 1787 to Dec 3, 1788, there have been 1,162 commitment to the goal for debt, 716 of which have been for amounts less than 20 shillings. These debtors are 'deprived of the comfort of their families, prevented from the opportunity of obtaining the means of subsistence by their own industry, subjected to the danger arising from putrid and contagious disorders . . . , and liable to become useless if not pernicious members of society from . . . acquiring habits of intemperance . . . .' The memorialists contend that society is greatly injured by confining debtors who owe small sums, because their labour is worth so much more than their debts; and they ask for a remedy through legislation" (December 12, 1788, I. N. Phelps Stokes, *Iconography of Manhattan Island, 1498–1909* [New York: R. H. Dodd, 1915–28], 5:1233). See also *A Sketch of the Origin and Progress of the Humane Society of the City of New-York* (New York: Van Winkle and Wiley, 1814), 5.

30. The detail about the shoes comes from Elizabeth Mankin Kornhauser, *Ralph Earl: The Face of the Young Republic* (New Haven: Yale University Press, 1991), 35. She cites Mary L. Booth, *History of the City of New York: From Its Earliest Settlement to the Present Time* (New York: Clark & Meeker, 1859).

31. An engraving of the New Gaol is reproduced in Raymond A. Mohl, "The Humane Society and Urban Reform in Early New York, 1787–1831," *New-York Historical Society Quarterly* 54 (1970): 31.

32. Kornhauser, *Ralph Earl*, 32–39.

33. On City Hall's debtors' prison, see Jill Lepore, *New York Burning: Liberty, Slavery, and Conspiracy in Eighteenth-Century Manhattan* (New York: Knopf, 2005), chap. 3. On the New Gaol, see Mohl, "Humane Society"; Mann, *Republic of Debtors*, 86–87; and various entries on this building in Stokes, *Iconography of Manhattan*.

34. The best social history of English debtors' prison is Innes, "King's Bench Prison."

35. As Innes points out, married women could not own property and so could neither contract nor default on debts (ibid., 263).

36. The New Gaol's debtors' constitution, though, lasted only about four years; after that, the prison descended, again, into chaos. James Ciment, "In Light of Failure: Bankruptcy, Insolvency and Financial Failure in New York City, 1790–1860," Ph.D. dissertation, City University of New York, 1992, 141–48, quote on 144. People who couldn't pay their fines were sentenced—by a jury of men imprisoned for debt—to solitary confinement.

37. Pintard fled to New Jersey then wrote to his creditors and said he'd be willing to go to jail, "could I foresee any possible advantage." David L Sterling, "William Duer, John Pintard, and the Panic of 1792," in *Business Enterprise in Early New York,* ed. Joseph R. Frese and Jacob Judd (Tarrytown, NY: Sleepy Hollow Press, 1979), 121.

38. Sterling, "New York Patriarch," 46–51.

39. James Grant Wilson, *John Pintard, Founder of the New York Historical Society* (New York: Printed for the Society, 1902), 17. On Pintard's relative prosperity, see Raymond A. Mohl, "Humanitarianism in the Preindustrial City: The New York Society for the Prevention of Pauperism, 1817–1823," *Journal of American History* 57 (December 1970): 580.

40. Robert Sobel, *Panic on Wall Street: A History of America's Financial Disasters* (New York: Macmillan, 1968; repr., Washington, DC: Beard Books, 1999), 17, 19. Citations refer to Beard Books edition.

41. Ciment, "In Light of Failure," 42. On Pintard's role in the American Museum, see Heilbrun, "NYork," 26. On Pintard and *New York Magazine,* and various other biographical details, including the partnership with Bleecker and the borrowing from widows and orphans, see Sterling, "Duer, Pintard, and the Panic of 1792." Another useful account is Sobel, *Panic on Wall Street,* chap. 1: "William Duer and the Panic of 1792." Sobel briefly discusses the founding of the exchange at the Tontine (10) and also talks about Pierre de Peyster challenging Duer to a duel in prison (27). Duer resigned his post as assistant secretary of the treasury in early 1790 (19).

42. Sterling, "Duer, Pintard, and the Panic of 1792," 106, 117.

43. Ibid., 117.

44. George W. Johnston, "John Pintard," typescript biographical essay dated January 16, 1900. Pintard Papers, box 3, in a folder titled "Notes on John Pintard and Governor Clinton."

45. Finn, *Character of Credit,* 53.

46. Jonathan J. Bean, "Duer, William," in *American National Biography Online (ANB)* (February 2000), http://www.anb.org.ezp-prod1.hul .harvard.edu/articles/10/10-00470.html; and also Robert F. Jones, *The*

*King of the Alley: William Duer: Politician, Entrepreneur, and Speculator,*
*1768*–1799 (Philadelphia: American Philosophical Society, 1992). "Keeping house" is detailed in Finn, *Character of Credit*, and also in Innes, "King's
Bench," 255–56.

47.  Sobel, *Panic on Wall Street*, 28.

48.  Ibid., 29.

49.  Pintard, "Reading Diary," July 23, 1797, 32. "August 6th Occupied
last week with papering & painting my chamber, which together with a
lassitude occasioned by the heat of the weather, have interrupted my regular studies."

50.  Ibid., March 31, 1798, 69.

51.  On finishing the dictionary, see ibid., April 20, 1798.

52.  On the jailbreak, see Mann, *Republic of Debtors*, 96–97.

53.  Pintard, "Reading Diary," entries for March 8, 1798 (63), and April
27 or 29, 1798 (80–81). Dodd's "Thoughts on Prison" was published in 1777.
This excerpt is copied from Pintard's diary.

54.  Ibid., July 4, 1798, 112–14.

55.  Pintard made a particular study of Blackstone, but the law books he
read included, for instance, the *Law of Bailment*.

56.  Sterling, "New York Patriarch," 212–13.

57.  In a landmark study published in 1935, Charles Warren made a
persuasive argument that still holds: "Whatever may have been the antici-
pation of the framers, the fact is that the Bankruptcy Power has developed
steadily, from being a regulation of traders for purely commercial purposes,
into a National policy of relief, for creditors and debtors of all classes and
for the restoration of business life, with debts adjusted or discharged."
Warren, *Bankruptcy*, 8. On this same point, see Bauer, "Imprisonment for
Debt," 101–2.

58.  Warren, *Bankruptcy*, 7–8.

59.  This Pintard diary entry from September 10, 1800, is quoted in
Johnston, "John Pintard," 3.

60.  See *A Sketch of the Humane Society*, 7. They began spooning out
soup not just to debtors but to beggars, too. The next year, the organization changed its name to the Humane Society of New York, with a goal
of reducing street begging. To get that cup of soup, beggars had to present
printed tickets, supplied to the prosperous of the city by the Humane Society. (Give a beggar a quarter and he'll buy a pint of beer, the idea was, but
give him a ticket, and all he can get is a quart of soup.) *Am. Med. and Phil.*
*Register* (April 1814), 4:632–37. Also see notes of mine from I. N. Phelps

Stokes, viz.: Nov. 6, 1802 (Stokes, *Iconography of Manhattan*, 5:1396): "The Society for the Relief of Distressed Prisoners announced 'that the alterations they have lately adopted in providing for the prisoners . . . , and the establishment of a Soup House for the benefit of the Poor, promise to be extensively useful.' Soup is supplied at four pence a quart, 'each quart to contain a portion of beef not less than 4 ounces, and a due proportion of vegetables.' Printed tickets are given to persons soliciting alms, each entitling the bearer to a quart of soup. John Rodgers is president. *Com. Adv.* N 6, 1802." The soup house is also described in Mohl, "Humane Society," 40–41.

61. Quoted in Ciment, "In the Light of Failure," 200.

62. Quoted in Warren, *Bankruptcy*, 20.

63. Heilburn, "NYork," 22.

64. Mohl, "Humane Society," 31. See also Clinton's entry in the *ANB*.

65. Sterling, "New York Patriarch," 246–51. A good brief summary of Pintard's rehabilitation as a public servant is in Mohl, "Humanitarianism," 580. See also David L. Sterling, "John Pintard (1759–1844): The First City Inspector of New York," *New-York Historical Society Quarterly* 43 (1959): 453–62.

66. He had lost his library to his creditors but in 1800 went into the book trade; "in 1807 he offered to sell his books on American history to The New-York Historical Society at cost, as a nucleus for its future library. In 1809 the collection was purchased" (Whitehill, "John Pintard's 'Antiquarian Society,'" 358). For Pintard as beloved founder of the NYHS, see, e.g., R.W.G. Vail, "Mr. Pintard Takes a Walk," in *Knickerbocker Birthday: A Sesqui-Centennial History of the New-York Historical Society* (New York: New-York Historical Society, 1954), 3–27. See also Heilburn, "NYork," especially 25–26. He also donated a substantial number of books to the New-York Historical Society Library, for which he served as a trustee (Sullivan, "Books, Power," 413). Pintard writes at some length about his work taking care of the library in a letter to his daughter in 1816 (*Letters from John Pintard to His Daughter* [New York: New-York Historical Society, 1940–41], 1:18). More on his care of the library is from January 27, 1818 (*Letters*, 1:107).

67. John Pintard, *To the Public: The Address of the New-York Historical Society* (New York, 1809), broadside.

68. This excerpt from Pintard's diary is quoted in Heilburn, "NYork," 28.

69. Mohl, "Humane Society," 41.

70. Bauer, "Imprisonment for Debt," 136.

71. Ciment, "In the Light of Failure," 142.

72. Pintard Papers, box 11, folder 3. John Pintard to unknown, December 11, 1809.

73. Ciment, "In the Light of Failure," 139, 130, 163.

74. Fay's ad: "To the Editor," *Columbian*, April 5, 1811, 3.

75. "The man who steals a $12 watch is jailed for three years," one opponent argued, but the swindler who "borrows $12,000, with no intention of re-paying . . . is taken to court . . . and is set free to go on his way to do it again." *Columbian*, November 2, 1810, and quoted in Ciment, "In the Light of Failure," 40.

76. Pintard, *Letters*, 1:26; August 13, 1816. "This is indeed the Era of Great Good," he wrote; November 12, 1825, 2:199; February 13, 1826, 2:228.

77. Whitehall, "John Pintard's 'Antiquarian Society,'" 357.

78. Pintard, in 1816, lists them all in a letter to his daughter. Sullivan ("Books, Power," 409) counts eleven; this probably comes from the list Pintard supplies in a letter dated December 31, 1816, at which point he is secretary of the Mutual Insurance Company, director of Steam Boat, Clerk of the Corporation of the Sailors Snug Harbor, recording secretary of the board of managers of the American Bible Society, secretary of the academy of arts, recording secretary of the historical society, curator of the literary and philosophical society, trustee of the city library, treasurer of the episcopal theological library, director of the savings bank and vestryman of st esprit (*Letters* 1:47).

79. Mohl, "Humane Society," 42; he says the society reported that the debtors' prison was vacant in 1824.

80. Pintard, *Letters*, 1:151; October 28, 1818. For the history of the society, see Mohl, "Humanitarianism." The society also published pamphlets for the poor, including reprints of *Poor Richard's Almanack* (ibid., 590).

81. Sullivan, "Books, Power," 416.

82. Cited in Ciment, "In the Light of Failure," 75–76; this is from Pintard's letters to his daughter, 1:193.

83. "The first Savings Bank in the United States was established in this city by the sagacity of John Pintard. It was known as the New York Bank for Savings. Pintard was President, with Peter Augustus Jay and Philip Hone as first and second vice-presidents. . . . Mr. Pintard was President of the Institution until his resignation in 1841, being then four-score and two years of age, and stricken with blindness" (Wilson, *John Pintard*, 31–32). Mohl discusses Pintard's role in the founding of the savings bank in

"Humanitarianism," 587–88. For more on Pintard's views on the bank, see the letter of December 4, 1816: "You will see by the Herald the plan of a *Savings Bank* for laying up the earnings of domestics & the labouring community of wh[ich] I am a Director, an office I reluctantly assumed but could not well avoid taking a share of trouble in organizing an Institution" (*Letters*, 1:38–39).

84. Pintard, *Letters*, 2:356. Pintard said that he only joined the SPP to start the bank. "My main object in joining it was to promote the incorporation of a savings Bank in this City" (*Letters*, 1:159; December 14, 1818).

85. It is important to note, though, that the bank was, really, a success, if a modest one. See Mohl, "Humanitarianism," 588, on deposits in the first years.

86. Pintard, *Letters*, 1:180; April 9, 1819.

87. Warren, *Bankruptcy*, 3, 9.

88. Ciment argues that "bankruptcy and insolvency statues were often written and passed (and repealed) in response to public outrage after periods when speculation and easy and excessive credit had sent the economy into a panic as in 1800, 1811, and 1841. Debtor law, then, was implicitly designed to curb or curtail commercial behavior that was considered unethical in and of itself or was believed detrimental to the economy generally" (Ciment, "In the Light of Failure,"172).

89. Bauer, "Imprisonment for Debt," 136–46; Ciment, "In the Light of Failure," 215, 187–89.

90. The best account of the 1841 law is Edward J. Balleisen, *Navigating Failure: Bankruptcy and Commercial Society in Antebellum America* (Chapel Hill: University of North Carolina Press, 2001).

91. *An Alphabetical List of Applicants for the Benefit of the Bankrupt Act . . . Within the Southern District of New-York . . . Giving Not Only the Names of the Applicants, but Their Residence, and Occupation . . . for Their More Certain Identity* (New York: Henry Anstice, 1843).

92. "As New York expanded, so did the legal 'limits.' By the end of the imprisonment era in 1831, the 'limits had come to include all of Manhattan below 14th Street" (Ciment, "In the Light of Failure," 126). Another description of the liberties or limits can be found in Mohl, "Humane Society," 36. In London, the limits were sometimes called "the Rules" (Innes, "King's Bench," 256).

93. Ciment, "In the Light of Failure," 140.

94. Bauer, "Imprisonment for Debt," 250.

95. Ciment, "In the Light of Failure," 123. On how this affected the mission of the Humane Society, see Mohl, "Humane Society," 51.

96. This study, from 1834, is cited in Ford, "Imprisonment for Debt," 30.

97. Bauer, "Imprisonment for Debt," 261–68.

98. "On the evening of February 29, 1832, the handful of individuals still incarcerated for debt in New York City spent their last night in jail" (Ciment, "In the Light of Failure," 167).

99. Ibid., 123–24n3, which points to Stokes, *Iconography of Manhattan*, 5:1643, 1669, 1693, 1694. This same year, Pintard writes, "It is worse than a shame, it is gross, for an American who has any pretension to education to be ignorant of his own country" (Pintard, *Letters*, 3:297–98; November 14, 1831).

100. Sterling, "Duer, Pintard, and the Panic of 1792," 123; Sobel, *Panic*, 31.

101. Pintard, *Letters*, 1:156; November 28, 1818.

102. On Pintard and the canal, see Sterling, "New York Patriarch," 309–10.

103. "He took an active part in inducing the legislature to have the city laid out under its present plan of streets and avenues. . . . Probably the greatest single influence upon New York's commercial position was cutting the Erie Canal. The War of 1812 checked and almost destroyed interest in the matter. John Pintard got up a great meeting, induced Clinton to take charge of the Canal, helped to complete it, and when the completion was celebrated, it was Pintard who was secretary of the meeting, who arranged the programme, who wrote the resolutions, carried the bottle containing Lake Erie water and emptied it into the Atlantic, and gave as much credit as possible to all the other men without taking any to himself" (Johnston, "John Pintard," 6).

104. John Pintard to Eliza Noel Pintard Davidson, July 5, 1816, in *Letters*, 1:17.

## 7. A Nue Merrykin Dikshunary

1. *Connecticut Journal*, June 4, 1800. On the strong objections to "lengthy," see "The Trial and Condemnation of Lengthy," *Monthly Magazine* (September 1800): 172. On the raisins and peppermints in Webster's desk, see Emily Ellsworth Fowler Ford, comp., *Notes on the Life of Noah Webster* (New York: privately printed, 1912), 2:377. (Ford's two-volume

study is both a biography and a collection of Webster's letters, memoires, and diary entries.) All Websterian definitions in this chapter come from either Noah Webster, *A Compendious Dictionary of the English Language* (New Haven, 1806), or Webster, *An American Dictionary of the English Language* (New Haven, 1828). An important biography is Harry S. Warfel, *Noah Webster: Schoolmaster to America* (New York: Macmillan, 1936); more recent is Joshua Kendall, *The Forgotten Founding Father: Noah Webster's Obsession and the Creation of an American Culture* (New York: Putnam, 2011).

2. Philadelphia *Aurora*, June 9, 1800.

3. Samuel Johnson Jr., *A Selected, Pronouncing and Accented Dictionary* (Suffield, CT: Edward Gray, 1800); Caleb Alexander, *A Columbian Dictionary of the English Language* (Boston, 1800); "Article XIV," *American Review and Literary Journal* 1 (1801): 210. A review of Alexander's *Columbian Dictionary* appears in *The Port Folio* 1 (1801): 247.

4. *Gazette of the United States*, June 10 and June 12, 1800.

5. Warfel, *Noah Webster*, 267; Philadelphia *Aurora*, August 4, 1800.

6. Noah Webster to Benjamin Rush, December 15, 1801, in *Letters*, ed. Harry S. Warfel (New York: Library Publishers, 1953), 228.

7. David Micklethwait, *Noah Webster and the American Dictionary* (Jefferson, NC: McFarland, 2000), 172.

8. Noah Webster, diary entry, June 6, 1786, in *Notes on the Life of Noah Webster* 1:157. For Webster's early career and the history of Webster's spelling book, see Lepore, *A Is for American*, chap. 1.

9. Benjamin Franklin, *A Scheme for a New Alphabet and Reformed Mode of Spelling* (1768), in *Papers of Benjamin Franklin*, http://www.franklinpapers.org; Noah Webster, *Collection of Essays and Fugitive Writings* (Boston: Thomas and Andrews, 1795), xi.

10. Jonathan Boucher, *Proposals for Printing, by Subscription, in Two Volumes, Quarto* (London, 1802).

11. Noah Webster to Thomas Dawes, August 5, 1809, in *Letters, 328*.

12. *Gazette of the United States*, June 10, 1800.

13. *Port Folio*, November 21, 1801.

14. "New French Political Nomenclature," *Monthly Magazine*, March 1800, 165; Thomas Jefferson to John Adams, August 15, 1820, in *The Writings of Thomas Jefferson* (New York: Derby and Jackson, 1852), 175.

15. Warfel, *Noah Webster*, 234.

16. Noah Webster to Oliver Wolcott, June 23, 1800, in *Notes on the Life of Noah Webster*, 1:478.

17. Noah Webster to Thomas Jefferson, [October] 1801, in *Letters*, 240–45.

18. Thomas Jefferson to James Madison, August 12, 1801, in *The Writings of Thomas Jefferson*, ed. Paul Leicester Ford (New York: Putnams, 1892–99), 8:81.

19. Noah Webster to the editor of the *Palladium*, February 17, 1835, in *Notes on the Life of Noah Webster*, 517.

20. Warfel, *Noah Webster*, 426.

21. Ibid., 424–25.

22. "Webster's Orthography," *United States Democratic Review* (July 1856): 541–50.

23. Thomas Dawes to Noah Webster, August 4, 1806, in *Notes on the Life of Noah Webster*, 2:9.

24. John Quincy Adams to Noah Webster, November 5, 1806, in ibid., 2:9–12.

25. Samuel Latham Mitchell to Noah Webster, June 19, 1807, in ibid., 2:20–22.

26. [James Savage], "Webster's Grammar, Dictionary &c &c," *Monthly Anthology*, 8 (March 1810).

27. Noah Webster to Thomas Dawes, August 5, 1809, in *Letters*, 328-331.

28. Noah Webster, *The Autobiographies of Noah Webster*, ed. Richard M. Rollins (Columbia: University of South Carolina Press, 1989), 177.

29. Noah Webster to the Friends of Literature, February 25, 1807, in *Letters*, 271–74.

30. Oliver Wolcott to Noah Webster, September 19, 1807, in *Notes on the Life of Noah Webster*, 2:26–27.

31. James Kent to Noah Webster, March 20, 1810, in ibid., 2:75–76.

32. Thomas Jefferson to John Adams, August 15, 1820, in *The Writings of Thomas Jefferson*, ed. Albert Ellery Bergh (Washington, DC: Thomas Jefferson Memorial Association, 1907), 15:272–73.

33. Noah Webster to Josiah Quincy, February 12, 1811, in *Notes on the Life of Noah Webster*, 2:101–2.

34. Ibid., 115–16. By the time he finished his dictionary, he had also completed another manuscript, nearly half as long, a contorted treatise on etymology called *A Synopsis of Words in Twenty Languages*. Despite Webster's attempts to find a publisher, the *Synopsis* has never been published and remains, largely unread, among Webster's papers at the New York Public Library.

35. Noah Webster to Rebecca Greenleaf Webster, July 10, 1824, and July 21, 1824, in *Notes on the Life of Noah Webster*, 2:205–7, 210–16.

36. Webster, autobiographical fragment in ibid., 2:293.

37. Noah Webster to James Madison, March 17, 1826, in ibid., 2:294–95.

38. James Kingsley, [Review of *An American Dictionary of the English Language*], *North American Review* 28 (1829): 433–81.

39. Noah Webster, *The Holy Bible . . . in the Common Version, with Amendments of the Language* (New Haven, 1833), vii–viii. See also Noah Webster, *Mistakes and Corrections. 1. Improprieties and errors in the common version of the Scriptures; with specimens of amended language in Webster's edition of the Bible* (New Haven, 1837); Noah Webster to Messrs. Morse, February 24, 1834, in *Letters*, 433. Webster's Bible is only ever given the briefest of treatments by his biographers. The sole scholarly treatment of Webster's Bible is Harry R. Warfel, "The Centenary of Noah Webster's Bible," *New England Quarterly* 7 (1934): 578–82. Also see W. H. Morse, "Noah Webster's Bible," *Herald of Gospel Liberty*, September 3, 1925.

## 8. His Highness

1. The most comprehensive account of Sparks's life and work is Herbert Baxter Adams, *The Life and Writings of Jared Sparks*, 2 vols. (Boston: Houghton, Mifflin, 1893), but see also the Papers of Jared Sparks, Houghton Library, Harvard University, Finding Guide; and George E. Ellis, *Memoir of Jared Sparks, LL.D.* (Cambridge, MA: John Wilson and Son, 1869). Marshall got a cut of the *Writings of Washington* because he and B. Washington had planned to bring out their own edition; Sparks bought them out. Sparks wrote, "my ambition was to make a perfect edition of his writings, one that should stand as a perpetual monument, worthy of his fame and of his country" (Adams, *Life of Sparks*, 1:407). On Sparks's arrival at Mount Vernon, see his diary entry for March 14, 1827 (ibid., 2:11).

2. On the *North American Review*, see Van Wyck Brooks, *The Flowering of New England, 1815–1865* (New York: Dutton, 1936), chap. 6.

3. "Mr. Jared Sparks's Liberties with George Washington," *Literary World* 8 (March 1, 1851): 165.

4. "You are in Paradise you say," Ann Storrow to Jared Sparks, May 20, 1827, in "Letters of Ann Gillam Storrow to Jared Sparks," ed. Frances Bradshaw Blanshard, *Smith College Studies in History* 6 (1921): 227. The reference to forty thousand letters is from Brooks, *Flowering*, 122.

5. "Having been here two weeks very diligently employed in taking a general survey of the papers," he reported to Judge Washington on March 30, "I am happy to inform you that my expectations in regard to their extent and value are fully realized." Washington must have written to Sparks, warning him about something, because, on April 17, Sparks reassured him, "I am fully aware of the delicacy you mention, and trust my judgment will guard me against any indiscretion which shall afford reasonable grounds of complaint." Adams, *Life of Sparks*, 2:11, 15, 27, 39.

6. Ron Chernow, *Washington: A Life* (New York: Penguin, 2010), xix.

7. Adams, *Life of Sparks*, 2:17, 19, 22, 43–44; Jared Sparks, *The Writings of George Washington*, 12 vols. (Boston: American Stationers' Company, John B. Russell, 1834–37). Sparks invested his small fortune in the American Stationers' Company, which went bankrupt in the Panic of 1837, bankrupting Sparks. See also Jared Sparks, *An Account of the Manuscript Papers of George Washington, which were Left by Him at Mount Vernon; with a Plan for their Publication* (Boston: n.p., 1827).

8. Edward G. Lengel, ed., *The Papers of George Washington: Digital Edition* (Charlottesville: University of Virginia Press, 2008), http://rotunda.upress.virginia.edu.ezp-prod1.hul.harvard.edu/founders/default.xqy?keys=GEWN-print&mode=TOC.

9. *The Diaries of George Washington*, ed. Donald Jackson and Dorothy Twohig, 6 vols. (Charlottesville: University of Virginia Press, 1976), 3:287. Although, in a separate account, he noted the weather: "Foggy again in the forenoon, but clear afterwds. & Warm" (3:289).

10. John Adams, *Diary and Autobiography of John Adams*, ed. L. H. Butterfield (Cambridge: Belknap Press of Harvard University Press, 1961), 2:156–57.

11. Adams quoted in François Furstenberg, *In the Name of the Father: Washington's Legacy, Slavery, and the Making of a Nation* (New York: Penguin, 2006), 64.

12. Ruffin quoted in ibid., 25.

13. William E. Woodward, *George Washington: The Image and the Man* (New York: Boni and Liveright, 1926), 82; J.D.A., "Washington's Enduring Fame," *New York Times*, October 24, 1926. "Bunk" itself dates only to c. 1900. Ford said history was bunk in 1916. Harold Ross founded a magazine that hates bunk in 1925. On debunking GW in the 1920s, see Karal Marling, *George Washington Slept Here* (Cambridge: Harvard University Press, 1988), chap. 8. In 1924, J. P. Morgan apparently bought up a collection of Washington's "smutty" letters in order to destroy them (ibid., 250).

14. Susan Lardner, "Exit Poll," *New Yorker*, March 19, 1984. Marling also identifies 1984, and Reagan's campaign, as the beginning of this Georgian revival (*George Washington Slept Here*, 385).

15. These include biographies by Richard Norton Smith, Richard Brookhiser, Joseph Ellis, James MacGregor Burns, and John Ferling.

16. Woodrow Wilson, *George Washington* (New York: Harper & Brothers, 1896), 100.

17. Chernow, *Washington*, 5–6, 10, 26–27, 30, 11.

18. Henry Wiencek, *An Imperfect God: George Washington, His Slaves, and the Creation of America* (New York: Farrar, Straus and Giroux, 2003), 112–13.

19. On Washington's apotheosis, see Paul K. Longmore, *The Invention of George Washington* (Berkeley: University of California Press, 1988); and Furstenberg, *In the Name of the Father*.

20. Robert Vincent Remini and Terry Golway, eds., *Fellow Citizens: The Penguin Book of U.S. Presidential Inaugural Addresses* (New York: Penguin, 2008), 1.

21. Owen Wister, *The Seven Ages of Washington: A Biography* (New York: Macmillan, 1907), 1.

22. "The Farewell Address: Transcript of the Final Manuscript," Papers of George Washington, http://gwpapers.virginia.edu/documents/farewell/transcript.html.

23. As Sparks observed, "the larger portion of his life was passed on a conspicuous public theatre." Sparks, *The Writings of George Washington*, 1:xiii.

24. Chernow, *Washington*, xix–xx. For a very useful discussion of Washington's reserve and the biographer's dilemma, see Pauline Maier, "Good Show: George Washington Plays George Washington," review of *The Papers of George Washington*, ed. W. W. Abbot, *The Diaries of George Washington*, ed. Donald Jackson and Dorothy Twohig, *The Journal of the Proceedings of the President, 1793–1797*, ed. Dorothy Twohig, *The First of Men: A Life of George Washington*, by John E. Ferling, and *The Invention of George Washington*, by Paul K. Longmore, *Reviews in American History* 17 (June 1989): 187–98. See also Edmund S. Morgan, *The Genius of George Washington* (New York: Norton, 1980).

25. Mason L. Weems, *The Life of Washington*, ed. Marcus Cunliffe (Cambridge: Belknap Press of Harvard University Press, 1962), 2–3; Paul Leicester Ford, *The True George Washington* (Philadelphia: Lippincott, 1896), 5.

26. "Setting Washington on stilts" is Mahon. But it's quoted in Ellis, *Memoir of Sparks*, 57.

27. "Biography . . . is a young art," as Virginia Woolf once wrote. Woolf, "The Art of Biography," in *The Death of the Moth and Other Essays* (1942; repr., New York: Harcourt, Brace, Jovanovich, 1974), 187. Citations refer to the 1974 reprint edition.

28. Earlier, Weems sold *Onania*, a treatise against masturbation; *The Lover's Almanac*; and, in 1799, a book dedicated to Washington called *The Philanthropist; Or, A Good Twenty-five Cents Worth of Political Love Powder*. The first editions of Weems's "Life and Memorable Actions of George Washington" were anonymous and short, but the book grew with each edition and, soon enough, Weems put his name on the title page, calling himself the former "Rector of Mount-Vernon Parish." Cunliffe, introduction, in Weems, *Life of Washington*, xvii.

29. Bushrod Washington had actually talked with Weems about making him his uncle's official biographer, but that fell through. The Weems–B. Washington negotiation is discussed in Furstenberg, *In the Name of the Father*, 139. Weems on Marshall: 141.

30. Furstenberg describes it as "destined to be one of the great failures of early American publishing" (ibid., 141).

31. On Jefferson's opinion of Marshall's *Life of Washington*, see an aside by Sparks in Adams, *Life of Sparks*, 2:37. Jefferson said Marshall had written the book principally "with a view to electioneering purposes" (Jefferson quoted in Furstenberg, *In the Name of the Father*, 140). On Marshall's supposed plagiarism, see William A. Foran, "John Marshall as a Historian," *American Historical Review* 43 (October 1937): 51–64. Foran identified instances of copying on 268 of 488 pages of the original edition; Marshall's twelve-page account of the Battle of Camden, for instance, was taken verbatim from William Gordon's history of the revolution. Most instances were slighter, but ubiquitous; e.g., where Jeremy Belknap had written, "The next morning as Vaughan was returning with thirteen men only, he crept up the hill which overlooked the battery, and observed that the chimneys of the barracks were without smoke, and the staff without a flag. With a bottle of brandy . . . he hired . . . a Cape Cod Indian, to crawl in an embrasure and open the gate"; Marshall wrote, without any acknowledgement, "the next morning as Vaughan was returning with thirteen men only, he crept up the hill which overlooked the battery, and observed that the chimneys of the barracks were without smoke, and the staff without a flag, hired a Cape Cod Indian with a bottle of rum, to crawl in

an embrasure and open the gate" (ibid., 54). Foran discusses Marshall's use of quotation marks on 60, to argue that their usage was well established at the time, and that Marshall understood that convention but ignored it. For Marshall's defense, see his remarks, quoted on 63.

32. Weems, *Life of Washington*, 12, 9.

33. Jared Sparks, *The Life of John Ledyard* (Cambridge, MA: Hilliard and Brown, 1828), vi.

34. Adams, *Life of Sparks*, 1:389. Not long after, he made his first application to Bushrod Washington to see the whole collection and was turned down. "Meditating on the importance of having a new History of America," Sparks wrote in his diary in 1823. "I would go to the fountain and read every thing on the subject." Ellis, *Memoir of Sparks*, 43.

35. Adams, *Life of Sparks*, 2:520–21. "I have brought home rich treasures,—two large trunks full of his papers, which belonged to Franklin, which have slumbered in a garret 40 years," Sparks wrote, after one trip. Jared Sparks to Hilliard Gray, April 25, 1837, box 140, folder 60, Henry Wadsworth Longfellow Dana Papers, Henry Wadsworth Longfellow House, Cambridge, MA.

36. Daniel Webster, "The Bunker Hill Monument, An Address delivered . . . on the Seventeenth of June, 1825," in *Daniel Webster's First Bunker Hill Oration*, ed. Fred Newton Scott (New York: Longmans, Green, 1895), 25.

37. Adams, *Life of Sparks*, 2:36–37, 39. Curiously, this assessment—that Weems's biography was truer than Marshall's—was exactly the reverse of what most critics and later scholars have assumed, although Sparks was in no position to point this out, and never did.

38. B. Washington had good cause for concern, in allowing the papers to be removed. He had lent some of them to John Marshall, and in 1827, he hadn't yet got them back. Worse, they had "been very extensively mutilated by rats, and otherwise injured by damps" (ibid., 2:213)

39. Longellow rented rooms there, too; he and Sparks were quite close. Longfellow's in-laws later bought it for him. Now it's the Henry Wadsworth Longfellow House, owned by the National Park Service. Sparks moved to a house on Kirkland Street and lived there for the rest of his life.

40. Ibid., 2:40.

41. John Adams is quoted in Longmore, *The Invention of Washington*, 213. This is more generously assented to by Madison, in Madison to Jared Sparks, January 25, 1828: "You will be aware, also, that some of his letters, especially when written in haste, show specks of inaccuracy which, though

not derogating at all from the greatness of his character, might disappoint readers abroad accustomed to regard him as a model even in the performances of his pen" (Adams, *Life of Sparks*, 2:218). When Sparks met Madison, he reported that Madison explained, "Washington was not fluent nor ready in conversation, and was inclined to be taciturn in general society. In the company of two or three intimate friends, however, he was talkative, and when a little excited was sometimes fluent and even eloquent" (ibid., 1:558).

42. "Will you review Mr. Somerville's book on France?" Sparks asked Bancroft in 1824, adding, "The work is not put together with much tact, but it contains a great deal of knowledge, and some good thoughts." Jared Sparks to George Bancroft, March 25, 1824, "Correspondence of George Bancroft and Jared Sparks, 1823–1832," ed. John Spencer Bassett, *Smith College Studies in History* 2 (1917): 75–76. When Bancroft poked fun at this direction and asked for clarification ("in reply have only to say, that I will make the article you speak of with pleasure and in the spirit of Xn. Philanthropy," Bancroft to Sparks, March 26, 1824, 76), Sparks wrote back, "I should suppose that from 10 to 15 pages would do, but you may write as much as you please. Make a few of the best extracts. You will find a very ambitious and unformed style occasionally; and the general getting up of the book indicates an unpractised hand; but there is much historical knowledge and some good thoughts, and I should like to have the author dealt gently with, although not extravagantly praised. I think you can let some parts of the book speak well for themselves; You can make a sort of analysis of things, and throw in such reflections as occur" (Sparks to Bancroft, March 31, 1824, 77). Sparks always planned to write a grand American history himself, but, in the end, he left it to Bancroft.

43. Bancroft to Sparks, July 10, 1824, 80. Or again, "If you will go directly upon it, do so, but make no *omissions*, nor alterations, except grammar and good sense require it. I have written with great care, will be personally responsible for every word of the article, and also for the selections" (Bancroft to Sparks, July 12, 1824, 80).

44. "I cannot as a man of honor, take part in this or permit it, without forfeiting my claim to self-respect," Bancroft wrote (Bancroft to Sparks, December 13, 1826, 124). Sparks replied, en route, in January 1827, that he wondered at Bancroft's "strange notions of an editor's task" (Sparks to Bancroft, January 2, 1827, 126).

45. Sparks's defense against this last pair of charges is especially interesting. See Jared Sparks, *Letter to Lord Mahon* (Boston: Little, Brown, 1852), 18–19.

46. These changes are recounted in many places, but see John Spencer Bassett, *The Middle Group of American Historians* (New York: Macmillan, 1917), chap. 2.

47. Bancroft reviewed it in the *North American Review*: "He has published such an edition of Washington's works as is never likely to be excelled" ("The Documentary History of the American Revolution," *North American Review* [April 1838]).

48. Hildreth, quoted in Brooks, *Flowering*, 327. Brooks's account of the controversy is on 125–26. Other accounts include J. Franklin Jameson, *The History of Historical Writing in America* (Boston: Houghton, Mifflin, 1891), 110–11; Scott E. Casper, *Constructing American Lives: Biography and Culture in Nineteenth-Century America* (Chapel Hill: University of North Carolina Press, 1999), chap. 3.

49. "Hawthorne's Life of Pierce.—Perspective," *Democratic Review* 31 (September 1852): 276–77.

50. "Mr. Sparks's Liberties," 165.

51. Weems, *Life of Washington*, 7.

52. John Marshall, *The Life of George Washington*, 2nd ed., 2 vols. (Philadelphia: C. P. Wayne, 1804–7; Philadelphia: James Crissy, 1832), 1:iii, 1–2. Citations refer to the Crissy edition.

53. "Of the first nineteen years of George Washington's life, little is known." David Ramsay, *The Life of George Washington* (New York: Hopkins & Seymour, 1807), 3.

54. Sparks, *Writings of Washington*, 1:4; Adams, *Life of Sparks*, 2:28–29. Which is, I believe, why the Daughters of the American Revolution revered her as a model housewife. Marling, *George Washington Slept Here*, 92. Wilson found calling her "a wise and provident mother" sufficient (*George Washington*, 47). Henry Wiencek and Joseph Ellis mention her name and leave it at that. Wiencek, *Imperfect God*, 31, 32; and Joseph J. Ellis, *His Excellency: George Washington* (New York: Knopf, 2004; repr., New York: Vintage Books, 2005), 8, 9. Citations refer to the Vintage edition.

55. Chernow, *Washington*, 15, 17–18.

56. *The Papers of George Washington*, ed. W. W. Abbott et al. (Charlottesville: University of Virginia Press, 1983), 1:1.

57. George Washington, [Proposed Address to Congress? April? 1789,] in *The Writings of George Washington*, ed. John C. Fitzpatrick (Washington, DC: U.S. Government Printing Office, 1931–44), 30:296–97n81.

58. On Sparks's relationship to Franklin's correspondence, and to that of Franklin's sister Jane Mecom, see Jill Lepore, *Book of Ages: The Life and*

*Opinions of Benjamin Franklin's Sister* (New York: Knopf, forthcoming), part 5.

59. Melville made a note in his London diary in December 1849, indicating that he was giving thought to writing about Potter. See Newton Arvin, *Herman Melville* (New York: William Sloane Associates, 1950; repr., New York: Grove Press, 2002), 244. Citations refer to Grove Press edition.

60. Jared Sparks, Review of *Sketches of the Life and Character of Patrick Henry*, by William Wirt, *North American Review* 6 (March 1818): 294. The *North American Review* only listed *Moby Dick* among books received. *North American Review* 74 (January 1852): 258.

61. Melville to Hawthorne and the reviews of *Moby Dick* are quoted in Robert S. Levine, introduction to *Israel Potter* (New York: Penguin, 2008), xi. A few months after a critic writing for the *Literary World* condemned "Mr. Jared Sparks's Liberties with George Washington," *Moby Dick* was reviewed (Evert A. Duyckinck, "Melville's *Moby Dick*," *Literary World*, November 22, 1851). Sometime soon after Duyckinck's review appeared, Melville canceled his subscription to *Literary World*, as per the "Historical Note" by Leon Howard and Hershel Parker in Herman Melville, *Pierre, or, The Ambiguities*, ed. Harrison Hayford, Hershel Parker, and G. Thomas Tanselle (Evanston, IL: Northwestern University Press, 1971), 376.

62. Herman Melville, *Israel Potter: His Fifty Years of Exile* (New York: G. P. Putnam, 1855), 25, 3, 5. The critical response to *Israel Potter* is easily followed in the reviews excerpted in Jay Leyda, *The Melville Log: A Documentary Life of Herman Melville, 1819–1891* (New York: Harcourt Brace, 1951; repr., New York: Gordian Press, 1969), 2:499–510.

## 9. Man of the People

1. Robert L. Brunhouse, ed., "David Ramsay, 1749–1815 Selections from His Writings," *Transactions of the American Philosophical Society* 55 (1965): 1–250; his death is related on 27. On Ramsay agreeing to write Jackson's biography, see Frank L. Owsley, Jr., "Editor's Introduction," in John Reid and John Henry Eaton, *The Life of Andrew Jackson* (Tuscaloosa: University of Alabama Press, 1974; 2007), v.

2. Owsley, in *Life of Jackson*, v–vii. Reid's account of the Battle of Enitachopco is on 137. A week after Jackson heard the news of his second biographer's untimely demise, he wrote to Reid's brother, "The book must be finished."

3. Jackson, a lawyer, served as the guardian for several children, and he and his wife, Rachel, who had no children of their own, had also adopted one of Rachel's nephews and raised as their own an Indian boy found, on a battlefield, in the arms of his dead mother.

4. Eaton reported that he agreed to take on the work only in the hope that sales of the biography would provide an inheritance for Reid's very young children. See Eaton's preface in *Life of Jackson*.

5. Eaton was the general's "bosom friend and almost adopted son." Margaret Bayard Smith, 1828, as quoted in Catherine Allgor, *Parlor Politics: In Which the Ladies of Washington Help Build a City and a Government* (Charlottesville: University of Virginia Press, 2000), 200.

6. Dinkin, *Campaigning in America*, 41.

7. On Jackson's sheer implausibility as a presidential aspiration, see ibid., 53.

8. On this general point, see, e.g., M. J. Heale, *The Presidential Quest: Candidates and Images in American Political Culture, 1787–1852* (London: Longman, 1982), 157: "The popular political culture of the United States today in no small measure had its origins in the electioneering of the Jacksonian era."

9. Eaton, *Life of Jackson*, 12.

10. William Burlie Brown, *The People's Choice: The Presidential Image in the Campaign Biography* (Baton Rouge: Louisiana State University Press, 1960), xiiii; Joanne Morreale, *A New Beginning: A Textual Frame Analysis of the Political Campaign Film* (Albany: SUNY Press, 1991).

11. This is an allusion to William M. Thayer, *From Log-Cabin to the White House. Life of James A. Garfield* (Boston, 1885). On the genre of campaign biography, see Brown, *People's Choice*; Miles, *Image Makers*; and Heale, *Presidential Quest*, chap. 8;

12. James Keough, *This Is Nixon* (New York: G. P. Putnam's Sons, 1956), 27.

13. Kaylene Johnson, *Sarah: How a Hockey Mom Turned the Political Establishment Upside Down* (Kenmore, WA: Epicenter Press, 2008), 41. "Wasilla mayor John Stein and police chief Irl Stambaugh participated in the same step-aerobics classes that Sarah attended. . . . The band of friends and fitness buffs representing all political persuasions rallied around her."

14. Jefferson quoted in Heale, *Presidential Quest*, 55: "He is one of the most unfit men, I know of for such a place. He has very little respect for Laws or Constitutions,—& is in fact merely an able military chief. His passions are terrible."

15. Dinkin, *Campaigning in America*, 47.

16. On the first campaign button, see Heale, *Presidential Quest*, 50. "Campaign biography was the most distinctive literary product of Jacksonian political culture. During the presidential election of 1824, the character and qualifications of the candidates became central issues in the absence of partisan difference." Scott E. Casper, "The Two Lives of Franklin Pierce: Hawthorne, Political Culture, and the Literary Market," *American Literary History* 5 (Summer 1993): 205–6. On the public opinion poll, see Dinkin, *Campaigning in America*, 42.

17. Owsley, in *Life of Jackson*, x. Beginning in 1824, Eaton also dropped Reid's name from the title page.

18. For more specifics of Eaton's depiction of Jackson's character, see especially ibid., 393–96; on his incorruptibility as retirement from political life, see 396; on rising above partisanship because a political outsider, see 396–98.

19. See "self-made man" in the *OED*. On Jackson's father's death, see Eaton, *Life of Jackson*, 9–10; and on how this made him learn the lessons of opposition to tyranny, see 10.

20. On the question of this edition, see Owsley's remarks in ibid., xviii.

21. James Parton, *Life of Jackson* (Boston: Houghton, Mifflin, 1860), 3:287.

22. Allgor, *Parlor Politics*, 227.

23. Lepore, *Name of War*, 209.

24. Parton, *Life of Jackson*, 1:vi–vii. For the record, Parton considered Jackson "unfit for the office."

25. Quoted in Hart, "Born in Log Cabins."

26. On Crockett's autobiography as a campaign narrative, see his entry in the *ANB*.

27. Davy Crockett, *The Life of Martin Van Buren* (Philadelphia: Nafis and Cornish, 1835, 1837), 26–27.

28. [Richard Hildreth], *The People's Presidential Candidate; Or the Life of William Henry Harrison, of Ohio* (Boston: Weeks, Jordan, 1839), 14–16, 194. See also Miles, *Image Makers*, 17.

29. Robert Gray Gunderson, *The Log Cabin Campaign* (Lexington: University of Kentucky Press, 1957), 73–79; 129–33.

30. Dinkin, *Campaigning in America*, 52.

31. Quoted in Hart, "Born in Log Cabins."

32. "Hawthorne's Life of Pierce," 276–77. By 1845, the campaign biography was already the subject of at least one burlesque. Robert Hopkins,

"Simon Suggs: A Burlesque Campaign Biography," *American Quarterly* 15 (1963): 459–63.

33. Dinkin, *Campaigning in America*, 55.

34. Heale, *Presidential Quest*, 165.

35. *Life of General Lewis Cass* (Philadelphia: G. B. Zieber, 1848), 11–12.

36. Heale, *Presidential Quest*, 159, and 248n3.

37. Dinkin, *Campaigning in America*, 53.

38. Hawthorne to Pierce, June 9, 1852, in Nathaniel Hawthorne, *The Letters*, ed. Thomas Woodson et al. (Columbus: Ohio State University Press, 1984–88). For fuller discussion, see also Richard J. Williamson, *The Impact of Franklin Pierce on Nathaniel Hawthorne: Friendship, Politics, and the Literary Imagination* (Lewiston, ME: Edwin Mellen Press, 2006).

39. For Hawthorne on Jackson, see Nathaniel Hawthorne, *Life of Franklin Pierce* (Boston: Ticknor, Reed and Fields, 1852), 23.

40. Casper, "Two Lives of Franklin Pierce," 203–5.

41. Joel Tyler Headley, *The Lives of Winfield Scott and Andrew Jackson* (New York: Scribner, 1852); see also Miles, *Image Makers*, 52.

42. Hawthorne, *Life of Franklin Pierce*, 100–101. "Hero of many a bottle" comes from Pierce's entry in the *ANB*.

43. Howells to Twain as per the preface of William Dean Howells, *Life of Abraham Lincoln* (summer 1860; repr. Springfield, IL: Abraham Lincoln Association, 1938), v.

44. Ibid., 17–18.

45. Ibid., 20–29.

46. Dinkin, *Campaigning in America*, 80.

47. Russell H. Conwell, *The Life, Speeches, and Public Services of Gen. James A. Garfield* (Indianapolis: Horon, 1880), 44, 47.

48. Horatio Alger, *From Canal Boy to President: The Boyhood and Manhood of James A. Garfield* (Boston: DeWolfe, Fiske, 1881).

49. Edward S. Ellis, *From Tent to White House Or, How a Poor Boy Became President* (New York: Street and Smith, 1898, 1899).

50. Richard Hofstadter, *Anti-Intellectualism in American Life* (New York: Knopf, 1963), 193–99.

51. Quoted in Hart, "Born in Log Cabins."

52. Quoted in ibid.

53. Casimir W. Ruskowski, *Is Roosevelt an Andrew Jackson?* (Boston: Bruce Humphries, 1939). Groton is mentioned in Brown, *People's Choice*, 56, 54. And see the anti-FDR biography, John T. Flynn, *Country Squire in the White House* (New York: Doubleday, Doran, 1940).

54. Quoted in Brown, *People's Choice*, 56.

55. Kevin McCann, *Man from Abilene* (New York: Doubleday, 1952), 14–15. In short, "Eisenhower is a symbol of his time and place as few other great men in history have ever been" (17).

56. Keough, *This Is Nixon*, 20–21.

57. Jimmy Carter, *Why Not the Best?* (Nashville: Broadman Press, 1975), 13, 32.

58. Johnson, *Sarah*, 18.

59. Eaton, *Life of Jackson*, 14.

60. Paul Alexander, *Man of the People: The Maverick Life and Career of John McCain* (Hoboken, NJ: Wiley, 2008), 15–19.

61. Howells, *Life of Abraham Lincoln*. The reprint edition includes facsimiles of all of Lincoln's notations.


## 10. Pickwick in America

1. Charles Dickens to John Forster, September 13, 1841, in *Letters of Charles Dickens*, 2:380–81. He was keen to take up a new writing project but fearful of it, since he had just been reading about how Scott had a breakdown from writing too much too fast, and he was worried that, if he kept writing at this clip, he would fall apart, too. Dickens's reading of Lockhart's *Life of Scott* while finishing writing *Barnaby Rudge* is discussed in Ada B. Nisbet, "The Mystery of *Martin Chuzzlewit*," in *Essays Critical and Historical Dedicated to Lily B. Campbell* (Berkeley: University of California Press, 1950), 202–3.

2. On *Pickwick's* extraordinary reception—people just could not stop laughing—see George H. Ford, *Dickens and His Readers: Aspects of Novel Criticism since 1836* (1955; repr., New York: Gordian Press, 1974), chap. 1. *Pickwick* appeared just as Victoria was crowned. Ford makes the interesting argument that Dickens at once looked "back to Regency high-spirits and forward to Victorian good spirits": "In his hands, the novel of high spirits became the novel of good spirits" (12–13). Ford also draws a curious, if unconvincing, comparison between Dickens and Thurber (16–17).

3. John Butt and Kathleen Tillotson, *Dickens at Work* (London: Methuen, 1957), 19–20. See also Mamie Dickens, *My Father as I Recall Him* (London: Roxburghe Press, 1896), chap. 3.

4. Peter Ackroyd, *Introduction to Dickens* (London: Sinclair-Stevenson, 1991), 7.

5. Dickens, *Little Dorrit*, chap. 3.

6. Dickens edited *Bentley's Miscellany* from 1837 to 1839; *Master Humphrey's Clock* from 1840 to 1841; *Daily News* in 1846; *Household Words* from 1850 to 1859; and *All the Year Round* from 1859 to 1870. On Dickens's painstaking habits as an editor, see Gerald Giles Grubb, "Dickens' Editorial Methods," *Studies in Philology* 40 (1943): 79–100; and "The Editorial Policies of Charles Dickens," *PMLA* 58 (1943): 1110–24. Dickens not only lived in what Edgar Allan Poe once called the "the Magazine Prison-House" ("Some Secrets of the Magazine Prison-House," *Broadway Journal*, February 15, 1845), he built it. On Dickens's role in making the magazine a popular genre, see, for instance, Gerald Giles Grubb, "Dickens' Influence as an Editor," *Studies in Philology* 42 (1945): 811–23.

7. Trilling tells this marvelous story: "perhaps no other man could have endured, as Dickens did, going out to buy a quire of paper for the next number of *Copperfield*, and, at the stationer's overhearing a lady asking for the new installment of *Copperfield*—no, not the one the shop-keeper offered her, she had read that; she wanted the *new* one: the one that, as Dickens realized, was yet to be begun on the paper he was just buying." Lionel Trilling, "The Dickens of Our Day [1952]," in *A Gathering of Fugitives* (Boston: Beacon Press, 1956), 47.

8. On Catherine Dickens taking dictation for correspondence, see Lillian Nayder, *The Other Dickens: A Life of Catherine Hogarth* (Ithaca: Cornell University Press, 2011), 67, 111. He also employed George Putnam to answer his correspondence in the United States. And he dictated *A Child's History of England* to Georgiana Hogarth (M. Dickens, *My Father as I Recall Him*, chap. 3). But, as far as I can tell, he never dictated his fiction.

9. *Nickleby, Chuzzlewit, Dombey, Copperfield, Bleak House, Little Dorrit*, and *Our Mutual Friend* were all published in nineteen monthly installments; *Edwin Drood* was to be published in eleven. Of the other six novels, five were published in weekly installments. (Each installment, or number, generally included three or four chapters.) "Dickens never wrote more than four or five numbers before the first was published" (Butt and Tillotson, *Dickens at Work*, 14). See also Grubb, "Dickens' Pattern of Weekly Serialization," *ELH* 9 (1942): 141–56.

10. Dickens quoted in Robert L. Patten, *Charles Dickens and His Publishers* (Oxford: Clarendon Press, 1978), 10. Patten writes, "Writing for money was not only a necessity for Dickens; it was also a principle" (10). Dickens didn't really achieve financial security until the end of 1840s.

11. In "The New World in Dickens's Writings: Part Two," *The Trollopian* 1 (1947): 11–12, Robert B. Heilman counts fugitives to America in five novels and fortune-hunters are all over the place.

12. Dickens, *Pickwick Papers*, chap. 45.

13. Bos, *Pickwick in America* (London: E. Lloyd, 1837?). There are eleven separate pamphlets in Houghton's collection, containing many American adventures. This passage is from part 1, chapter 3, page 18. Once Mr. Pickwick and Sam Weller reach America, most of what happens to them involves black people and slavery. There are, for instance, accounts of "nigger balls" etc., with many illustrations of the book's chief American characters, e.g., Maximillian Jupiter and Fat Boy. Houghton's records describe the series as: "A Dickens parody, doubtfully ascribed to Thomas Peckett Prest. Also ascribed to George W. M. Reynolds." See also Joseph J. Beard, "Everything Old Is New Again: Dickens to Digital," *Loyola of Los Angeles Law Review* 19 (2004–05), which compares *Dickens v. Lloyd* with the case of *The Wind Done Gone* and its relationship to *Gone With the Wind*.

14. Dickens, *Barnaby Rudge*, chaps. 71 and 72. In its preface, he explained that he had written a novel set in the 1780s to offer the only lesson that "all History teaches us": "That what we falsely call a religious cry is easily raised by men who have no religion, and who in their daily practice set at naught the commonest principles of right and wrong, that it is begotten of intolerance and persecution; that it is senseless, besotted, inveterate, and unmerciful."

15. Ackroyd, *Dickens*, 370.

16. Miss Murdstone's jail of a purse is in *Copperfield*, chap. 4.

17. Dickens to John Forster, September 13, 1842, in *Letters of Dickens*, 2:380–81; Dickens to William Hall, September 14, 1842, in ibid., 2:383.

18. Dickens to William Hall, September 14, 1842, in ibid., 2:383. "I can't persuade Mrs. Dickens to go, and leave the children at home; or to let me go alone."

19. Dickens to John Forster, September 13, 1842, in ibid., 2:380–81.

20. Dickens to David Colden, July 31, 1842, in ibid., 3:291.

21. [Thomas Hood], "Boz in America," *New Monthly Magazine*, 1842. "Boz was all Buzz," Hood to Dickens, quoted in Philip Collins, *Dickens: The Critical Heritage* (London: Routledge & K. Paul, 1971), 95.

22. Dickens to Daniel Maclise, January 3, 1842, in *Letters of Dickens*, 3:9. "Merrikin" is a reference to Dickens, *Pickwick Papers*, chap. 31.

23. Dickens to Daniel Maclise, January 3, 1842, in *Letters of Dickens*, 3:8.

24. G. W. Putnam, "Four Months with Charles Dickens," *Atlantic Monthly*, October 1870. And further to the display of the portrait, see Nayder, *The Other Dickens*, 113. On the portrait itself, see Daniel Maclise to Catherine Dickens, September 27, 1841: "Embrace Charley and May and Katy, and hang me if I believe you have named the younger yet—bus kiss the little unknown, too—we must include him in our projected group if it is only three dots and a line" (quoted in ibid., 111–12). The portrait is reproduced in ibid., 114. The raven is in it. Mrs. Dickens took the portrait out wherever she went. There's a very good chance Poe saw it when he met with Dickens in the United States Hotel.

25. "Free from that cramped prison called the earth": Dickens, *Martin Chuzzlewit*, chap. 15.

26. Dickens to Forster, January 17, 1842, in *Letters of Dickens*, 3:11.

27. Dickens, *American Notes*, 1: chap. 2.

28. Dickens, *Martin Chuzzlewit*, chap. 15.

29. Dickens, *The Old Curiosity Shop*, chap. 1.

30. Edgar Allan Poe, "The Old Curiosity Shop," *Graham's Magazine*, May 1841, and George H. Ford and Lauriat Lane, Jr., eds., *The Dickens Critics* (Ithaca: Cornell University Press, 1961), 20. Poe had earlier reviewed *Pickwick Papers*, calling Dickens a "far more pungent, more witty, and better disciplined writer of sly sketches, than nine-tenths of the Magazine writers of Great Britain." Poe in *Southern Literary Messenger* 11 (1836): 458. On Dickens and Poe, see especially Gerald G. Grubb, "The Personal and Literary Relationships of Dickens and Poe," *Nineteenth-Century Fiction* (5, nos. 1–3, June, September, and December 1950), 1–22, 101–20, 209–22.

31. The novel hadn't gone over well in England, either, one reviewer, auguring much that was to come, remarking that Dickens was "little at home on the ground of history and philosophical politics." In Collins, *Dickens: The Critical Heritage*, 91.

32. Dickens, *Barnaby Rudge*, chap. 58.

33. Edgar Allan Poe, Review of *Barnaby Rudge*, in *Graham's Magazine*, February 1842.

34. A recent discussion, with an emphasis on the structural problems that follow from the prepositioning of books, is Gail Pool, *Faint Praise: The Plight of Book Reviewing in America* (Columbia: University of Missouri Press, 2007).

35. Derek Roper, *Reviewing before the* Edinburgh, *1788–1802* (Newark: University of Delaware Press, 1978), 19–20, 29, 38, 46, 44.

36. "We rhapsodize rather than discriminate," he complained. Edgar Allan Poe on Rufus Dawes in *Graham's Magazine*, October 1842, and in *Essays and Reviews*, ed. G. R. Thompson (New York: Library of America, 1984), 491–92. This isn't just Poe's impression; it appears to have been the case, as per Nina Baym, *Novels, Readers, and Reviewers: Responses to Fiction in Antebellum America* (Ithaca: Cornell University Press, 1984), 19–21. Another place Poe wrote about this, anticipating Dickens's visit, which was much on his mind: "The analysis of a book is a matter of time and of mental exertion." Poe, "Exordium to Critical Notices," *Graham's Magazine*, January 1842, and in *Essays and Reviews*, 1028.

37. Poe, "Exordium to Critical Notices."

38. Which is a problem because "The most 'popular,' the most 'successful' writers among us," Poe wrote, "are, ninety-nine times out of a hundred, persons of mere address, perseverance, effrontery—in a word, busy-bodies, toadies, and quacks." "The Literati of New York City," *Godey's Lady's Book*, various issues in 1846, and in *Essays and Reviews*, 1118. He believed there were rules: "While the critic is *permitted* to play, at times, the part of the mere commentator—while he is *allowed*, by the way of merely *interesting* his readers, to put in the fairest light the merits of his author—his *legitimate* task is still, in pointing out and analyzing defects." Poe, "About Critics and Criticism," *Graham's Magazine*, January 1850, and in *Essays and Reviews*, 1040.

39. Pool reports that 150,000 books were published in 2007; about 2,000 of those books were reviewed in the *New York Times Book Review*, 5,000 in *Kirkus*, and 7,500 in *PW* (*Faint Praise*, 16, 24).

40. Leslie Mitchell, *Bulwer Lytton: The Rise and Fall of a Victorian Man of Letters* (London: Hambledon and London, 2003), xv, 111–12.

41. For example, G. H. Lewes wrote in 1872, "Thought is strangely absent from his works." Also see the discussion of Lewes's and Eliot's critiques in Sarah Winter, *The Pleasures of Memory: Learning to Read with Charles Dickens* (New York: Fordham University Press, 2011), 274–85.

42. Henry James, "The Limitations of Dickens," *Nation* (1865), and in *The Dickens Critics*, 48–54. The mature James on Dickens: "we somehow liked Dickens the more for having forfeited half the claim to appreciation. That process belongs to the fact that criticism, roundabout him, is somehow futile and tasteless" (117). James, at twenty-four, also went to see

Dickens read in New York. See *The Notebooks of Henry James* (New York: Oxford University Press, 1947), 319.

43. Aldous Huxley, "The Vulgarity of Little Nell" (1930), in *The Dickens Critics*, 153.

44. Not least because, as Rosemarie Bodenheimer put it, "Few of the reviewers who created the image of Dickens as the genius of English humor were inclined to consider the kind of intelligence on which humor depends." Bodenheimer, *Knowing Dickens* (Ithaca: Cornell University Press, 2007), 4.

45. Anthony Trollope, *Autobiography* (1882), in *The Dickens Critics*, 74–76. Trollope wrote about Dickens in several different places, all of them as pained and bewildered as this discussion. A nice summary of his hostility to the writer who influenced him more than any other is to be found in Ford, *Dickens and His Readers*, 106–8.

46. Edmund Wilson, "Dickens: The Two Scrooges" (1939), in *The Wound and the Bow: Seven Studies in Literature* (Boston: Houghton Mifflin, 1941), 4, 5, 22. Orwell on Dickens is in *Inside the Whale, and Other Essays* (London: Gollancz, 1940).

47. Lionel Trilling, introduction to *Little Dorrit* (1953), in *The Dickens Critics*, 279. But see also Trilling, "The Dickens of Our Day [1952]," in *A Gathering of Fugitives* (Boston: Beacon, 1956), 41–48. "The Dickens of Our Day" is a review of the now much-maligned Edgar Johnson biography, which Trilling celebrates. In his assessment of his own relationship to Dickens, Trilling writes wistfully both of once loving Dickens, and of once despising him: "I had been, as people used to say, brought up on Dickens, or at least I had been brought up on the myth of being brought up on Dickens, and there seemed to me no possibility that so familial a figure could have any true virtue for an intelligent and advanced person, such as I believed Erskin and Fadiman to be, such as I hoped to be myself" (42). Also this, on learning to accept Dickens as something other than a caricaturist: "We who have seen Hitler, Goering, and Goebbels put on the stage of history, and Pecksniffery institutionalized in the Kremlin, are in no position to suppose that Dickens ever exaggerated in the least the extravagance of madness, absurdity, and malevolence in the world—or, conversely, when we consider the resistance to these qualities, the amount of goodness" (44). Trilling, like Wilson, is at pains to distance himself from the doddering Dickens fanciers, because loving Dickens, and being curious about his life, even endlessly curious, which Trilling confesses himself to be, "does not mean that we are on our way to joining

the company of the genial madmen who belong to Dickens Fellowships and make Dickens Tours and, on a higher stage of development, write learned notes for *The Dickensian.* The mere desire for a true knowledge of Dickens's life requires detail, every possible detail—it is a life that cannot be understood in its essence unless it is seen in all its plethora of existence" (45).

48. Boz-town and looking a fright: *Dickens on America & the Americans,* ed. Michael Slater (Austin: University of Texas Press, 1978), 9. Hackneys and ribbons: Richard Henry Dana to Mrs. Arnold, February 14, 1842, in *Letters of Dickens,* 3:34. Dickens's outfit: N. C. Peyrouton, "Re: A Memoir of Morand," *Dickens Studies* 3 (1968): 27.

49. The best account of his arrival is James T. Fields, *Yesterdays with Authors* (Boston: Houghton Mifflin, 1871), 127–29.

50. Dickens to Forster, January 29, 1842, in *Letters of Dickens,* 3:36.

51. Putnam, "Four Months with Charles Dickens."

52. Dickens to Forster, January 30, 1842, in *Letters of Dickens,* 3:39. Longfellow on Dickens is from a letter to his father, in Henry Wadsworth Longfellow, *The Letters of Henry Wadsworth Longfellow,* ed. Andrew Hilen (Cambridge: Harvard University Press, 1972), 2:381. Longfellow's brother Samuel found Dickens's "rowdyism" vulgar: "He has none of that refinement and scholarly look which we are apt to attach to our idea of a literary man; in other words he is just what we ought to expect when we recollect his history instead of his books." In Edward Wagenknecht, "Dickens in Longfellow's Letters and Journals," *The Dickensian* 52 (1955): 7–21; quotation on 8.

53. R. H. Dana is quoted in *Letters of Dickens,* 3:39.

54. Dickens, speech in Boston on February 1, 1842.

55. Dickens to Catherine Dickens, December 2, 1844, in *Letters of Dickens,* 4:234–35. The letter is stained with tears.

56. Walt Whitman, "Boz and Democracy," *Brother Jonathan,* February 26, 1842. That Dickens understood his work as establishing a democratic literature is the argument of Sarah Winter in *Pleasures of Memory.* Winter is more interested, however, in the use to which Dickens's fiction was later put: "In the emerging twentieth-century literature curriculum, Dickens's authorial persona became associated with the cultural nationalism of an English literature curriculum in Britain, and an Anglo-American literary curriculum in the United States, along with a generic humanitarian ethic associated with a nascent concept of global citizenship suitable to the expansion and maintenance of colonies and empire" (11).

57. "The Reception of Mr. Dickens," *United States Magazine and Democratic Review,* April 1842, 315–20, and in Collins, *Dickens: The Critical Heritage,* 117.

58. William Dean Howells, *My Literary Passions* (New York: Harper, 1895), 99–100.

59. "No one but an Englishman could have filled his books at once with a furious caricature and with a positively furious kindness. In more central countries, full of cruel memories of political change, caricature is always inhumane. No one but an Englishman could have described the democracy as consisting of free men, but yet of funny men. In other countries, where a democratic issue has been more bitterly fought, it is felt that unless you describe a man as dignified you are describing him as a slave. This is the only final greatness of a man; that he does for all the world what all the world cannot do for itself. Dickens, I believe, did it." G. K. Chesterton, *Charles Dickens: A Critical Study* (New York: Dodd, Mead, 1911), 299.

60. Dickens to Forster, February 4?, 1842, in *Letters of Dickens,* 3:50. This was the kind of thing that really floored Thackeray, who, after his own visit to the United States, wondered, "What could Dickens mean by writing that book of *American Notes*? No man should write about the country under 5 years of experience, and as many of previous reading. A visit to the Tombs, to Laura Bridgman and the Blind Asylum, a description of Broadway—O Lord is that describing America?" (Thackeray in Nisbet, "The Mystery of *Martin Chuzzlewit,*" 212).

61. Sidney P. Moss, *Charles Dickens's Quarrel with America* (Troy, NY: Whitston, 1984), 64–65.

62. Dickens to Jonathan Chapman, February 22, 1842, in *Letters of Dickens,* 3:76.

63. Dickens, *American Notes,* 1: chap. 7.

64. Dickens to W. C. Macready, March 22, 1842, in *Letters of Dickens,* 3:156.

65. Dickens to Poe, March 6, 1842, in ibid., 3:105–6; and in Poe's letters.

66. Putnam, "Four Months with Charles Dickens."

67. "To the American People, A Memorial Sent to Dickens by Twelve British Authors," March 28, 1842, in *Letters of Dickens,* 3:621–22.

68. Dickens to W. C. Macready, April 1, 1842, in ibid., 3:175–76.

69. Dickens to Charles Sumner, March 13, 1842, in ibid, 3:127.

70. Dickens to Forster, April 26, 1842, in ibid., 3:207–8.

71. Dickens to Forster, May 3, 1842, in ibid., 3:233.

72. Ibid., 3:232.

73. Dickens to Thomas Beard, May 1, 1842, in ibid., 3:226.

74. On Timber Doodle, see Ackroyd, *Dickens*, 368.

75. Dickens to W. C. Macready, April 1, 1842, in *Letters of Dickens*, 3:175–76.

76. Mary Shelley, October 1, 1842, quoted in Moss, *Charles Dickens's Quarrel with America*, 79.

77. Dickens to Charles Sumner, July 31, 1842, in ibid., 3:296.

78. Charles Sumner quoted in ibid., 3:293. Sumner to Channing, June 23, 1842: "Dickens will write a series of graphic sketches on our country,— one on 'International Copyright;' another, I think, on 'Slavery,' with the first sentence from the Declaration of Independence for his motto."

79. Fanny Appleton (who was soon to marry Longfellow) wrote about the anticipated book: "This book will apparently be far from what is expected jocose & good natured, but is to lash our backs again about copyright & slavery. He meant, what would have been far wiser, only to introduce his American experiences to spice his future sketches of humanity, but his friends choose to expect a book about us which is very stupid of them, I think, for it is a thrice told tale & not in his line." Fanny Appleton quoted in ibid., 3:293.

80. Longfellow to Sumner, in Wagenknecht, "Dickens in Longfellow's Letters and Journals," 11.

81. Dickens to Jonathan Chapman, October 15, 1842, in *Letters of Dickens*, 3:345–46.

82. See chapter 14.

83. Dickens to Longfellow, December 29, 1842, in *Letters of Dickens*, 3:407.

84. The first person Macaulay asked to review it for the *Edinburgh Review* refused, replying, "I cannot praise it, and I will not cut it up." Napier to Macaulay in Nisbet, "The Mystery of *Martin Chuzzlewit*," 209.

85. [James Spedding], from a review in the *Edinburgh Review*, January 1843, and in Collins, *Dickens: The Critical Heritage*, 126–27. "The author of *Pickwick* will study the present as our historical novelists study the past—to find not what it is, but what he can make of it."

86. [Samuel Warren], from a review in *Blackwood's Magazine*, December 1842, and in Collins, *Dickens: The Critical Heritage*, 122.

87. Poe is quoted in *Letters of Dickens*, 3:348.

88. "The only consolation I can give you is that I do not believe any collection of detached pieces by an unknown writer, even though he were

an Englishman, would be at all likely to find a publisher in this metropolis just now." Dickens to Poe, November 27, 1842, in ibid., 3:385.

89. The abandoned introduction is reprinted with most modern editions and was first supplied by Forster in his *Life of Dickens*.

90. Ibid., but also discussed and quoted in Nisbet, "The Mystery of *Martin Chuzzlewit*," 202.

91. Dickens, *Martin Chuzzlewit*, chap. 33.

92. All quotations are from Charles Kent, *The Charles Dickens Dinner: An Authentic Record of the Public Banquet given to Mr. Charles Dickens . . . November 2, 1867* (London: Chapman and Hall, 1867). Dickens said more or less the same thing about America in a new preface to *Chuzzlewit*, written just before he left.

93. Moss, *Dickens's Quarrel with America*, 235, 285. At Longfellow's house, he scanned at the books on the poet's shelf and, seeing many of his own, murmured, "Ah, I see you read the good authors." Wagenknecht, "Dickens in Longfellow's Letters and Journals," 15.

94. Henry James, *The Notebooks of Henry James*, ed. F. O. Matthiessen and Kenneth B. Murdock (New York: Oxford University Press, 1947), 319; the entry is from either 1904 or 1905.

95. Twain saw Dickens in New York on December 31, 1867, and wrote about it on January 11, 1868, in a letter printed in the *Alta, California*, on February 5, 1868, which is quoted in Moss, *Charles Dickens's Quarrel with America*, 288.

96. The decline in Dickens's health over the course of the tour is abundantly reported. Sumner, for instance, found him "covered with mustard poultices and apparently voiceless." Ibid., 285.

97. Ever since Forster published the original ending in his biography of Dickens, in 1874, opinion has been decidedly mixed, with most critics siding with George Bernard Shaw, who wrote of *Great Expectations*, "Its beginning is unhappy, its middle is unhappy, and the conventionally happy ending is an outrage on it." George Bernard Shaw, introduction to *Great Expectations* (1937), in Michael Cotsell, *Critical Essays on Charles Dickens's Great Expectations* (Boston: G. K. Hall, 1990), 42.

98. "Those two American journeys especially transcend in tragic interest, to a thinking reader, most things one has seen in writing!" Carlyle to Forster, February 16, 1874, in *The Collected Letters of Thomas and Jane Welsh Carlyle*, ed. Ian M. Campbell et al. (Durham: Duke University Press), and at carlyleletters.org, 1: introduction.

99. Howells, *My Literary Passions*, 98–99.

100. Chesterton, *Dickens: A Critical Study*, 299.

101. Dickens, *Martin Chuzzlewit*, chap. 43.

102. Bret Harte, *Dickens in Camp* (San Francisco: J. Howell, 1922).

## 11. The Humbug

1. Edgar Allan Poe, "The Philosophy of Composition," *Graham's Magazine*, April 1846, and reprinted in *Essays and Reviews*. The authoritative edition of "The Raven" is in *Collected Works of Edgar Allan Poe*, ed. Thomas Ollive Mabbott (Cambridge: Harvard University Press, 1969), 1: Poems.

2. On "The Philosophy of Composition" as untruthful, see Mabbott's headnote, *Works of Poe*, 1:359.

3. The bread and molasses is quoted in Terence Whalen, *Poe and the Masses: The Political Economy of Literature in Antebellum America* (Princeton: Princeton University Press, 1999), 71. The begging for fifty cents in March of 1843 is in Dwight Thomas and David K. Jackson, *The Poe Log: A Documentary Life of Edgar Allan Poe, 1809–1849* (Boston: G. K. Hall, 1987), 404.

4. Poe to Frederick W. Thomas, May 4, 1845, in *The Letters of Edgar Allan Poe*, ed. John Ward Ostrom (Cambridge: Harvard University Press, 1948), 1:286. On "The Gold-bug" as Poe's "first genuine national success," see Benjamin F. Fisher, *Cambridge Introduction to Edgar Allan Poe* (Cambridge: Cambridge University Press, 2008), 7.

5. On Poe's great admiration for Coleridge, see, e.g., *Letters of Poe*, 1:257.

6. Poe, "Marginalia," *Southern Literary Messenger*, June 1849, and reprinted in *Essays and Reviews*, 1455.

7. For this account of Poe's death, see Ackroyd, *Poe: A Life Cut Short* (London: Chatto & Windus, 2008)

8. Poe to Jane E. Locke, May 19, 1848, *Letters of Poe*, 2:366. Poe's ethereality has proved durable. T. S. Eliot believed of Poe, "There can be few authors of such eminence who have drawn so little from their roots, who have been so isolated from any surroundings." Eliot, "From Poe to Valéry," in *The Recognition of Edgar Allan Poe*, ed. Eric Carlson (Ann Arbor: University of Michigan Press, 1970), 205–19. V. L. Parrington insisted that the "problem with Poe, fascinating as it is, lies quite outside the main current of American thought." Parrington quoted in Whalen, *Poe and the Masses*, 4. Edmund Wilson wrote that Poe endured "the darkness of solitary

confinement." Edmund Wilson, *The Shock of Recognition: The Development of Literature in the United States Recorded by the Men Who Made It* (New York: Octagon Books, 1943, 1975), 81.

9. "The Hungry Forties" is remarked upon in Sobel, *Panic on Wall Street*, 72. For more on the credit collapse, see Reginald Charles McGrane, *The Panic of 1837: Some Financial Problems of the Jacksonian Era* (New York: Russell and Russel, 1924, 1965), chap. 4, e.g., 93.

10. Poe to Joseph T. and Edwin Buckingham, May 4, 1833, in *Letters of Poe*, 1:53.

11. Ackroyd, *Poe*, 18.

12. Ibid., 19, 22, 23.

13. Ackroyd, *Poe*, 24.

14. "The death then of a beautiful woman is unquestionably the most poetical topic in the world, and equally is it beyond doubt that the lips best suited for such topic are those of a bereaved lover" ("The Philosophy of Composition"). For the supposition that Poe was referring to himself, by way of "poetical," see Fisher, *Cambridge Introduction to Edgar Allan Poe*.

15. On gold bugs and hum bugs, see Marc Shell, *Money, Language and Thought: Literary and Philosophic Economies from the Medieval to the Modern Era* (Baltimore: Johns Hopkins University Press, 1982), 12–13, and Poe to Dr. Thomas H. Chivers, September 27, 1842, in *Letters of Poe*, 1:215." Shell's first chapter (5–23) is a close reading of "The Gold-bug," placing it in the context of the debate about the gold standard. Shell's work has been influential. This is Whalen's approach, too. Whalen was able to rely on Thomas and Jackson's *Poe Log*, published in 1987. See also Terrence Whalen, "The Code for Gold: Edgar Allan Poe and Cryptography," *Representations* 46 (Spring 1994): 35–57; and Whalen, *Edgar Allan Poe and the Masses: The Political Economy of Literature in Antebellum America* (Princeton: Princeton University Press, 1999). Whalen explains his points of agreement and disagreement with Shell (*Poe and the Masses*, 216–17). A fair amount of work on the story deals with Poe's much-scrutinized puns (including "specie" and "bug"), e.g., Richard Hull, "Puns in 'The Gold-Bug': You Gotta Be Kidding," *Arizona Quarterly* 58 (Summer 2002): 1–48.

16. Sobel, *Panic on Wall Street*, 38.

17. Ibid., 47

18. "Marginalia," *Democratic Review*, November 1844, and reprinted in *Essays and Reviews*, 1318.

19. Ackroyd, *Poe*, 45.

20. Poe to Philip P. Cooke, September 21, 1839, in *Letters of Poe*, 1:117.

21. He was born in 1811, he said. He had traveled to Europe to fight in the Greek struggle for independence. He had written an autobiography under a nom-de-plume. None of these things is true. The best summary of this biographical dilemma is Ian Walker, "The Poe Legend," in *A Companion to Poe Studies*, ed. Eric W. Carlson (Westport, CT: Greenwood Press, 1996).

22. Ackroyd, *Poe*, 49.

23. Ibid., 61.

24. See Poe's letter about this in *Letters of Poe*, 1:57–58. For more on this question, see Mabbott, *Works of Poe*, 3: Tales, xxi.

25. The magazine's offices were just next door to the offices of the House of Ellis and Allan. Ackroyd, *Poe*, 67–68.

26. Poe to Maria Clemm, August 29, 1835, in *Letters of Poe*, 1:71. Virginia Clemm was born on November 5, 1822 (Thomas and Jackson, *Poe Log*, 52). Poe and Virginia were married on May 16, 1836. Cleland signed a bond saying that Virginia was twenty-one (*Poe Log*, 207). There is some possibility they were secretly married in October 1836 (171).

27. Whalen, *Poe and the Masses*, 66.

28. *New-Yorker*, April 29, 1837; Thomas and Jackson, *Poe Log*, 244.

29. On the timing of the Poes' arrival in New York, see Thomas and Jackson, *Poe Log*, 242.

30. McGrane, *Panic of 1837*, 18. For more on the housing bubble, see his chap. 2 and, e.g., 45.

31. Ibid., 50, 67, 72. On the factory closings, see 131.

32. Kenneth Silverman, *Edgar A. Poe: Mournful and Never-ending Remembrance* (New York: HarperCollins, 1991), 143.

33. Poe on Hawthorne, *Graham's Magazine*, April 1842, and in *Essays and Reviews*, 568; see also more of the same on 572.

34. Poe writes about this at length in "The Philosophy of Composition," but see also the editorial notes in Tales, 3:xviii–xix.

35. Whalen, *Poe and the Masses*, 9.

36. Poe to Thomas W. White, April 30, 1835, in *Letters of Poe*, 1:57–58.

37. Thomas and Jackson, *Poe Log*, 550.

38. James Kirke Paulding to Poe, March 3, 1836, in ibid., 193. "They desire me, however, to state to Mr. Poe that if he will lower himself a little to the ordinary comprehension of the generality of readers . . . they will make such arrangements with him as will be liberal and satisfactory."

39. Poe, "How to Write a Blackwood Article," 1838.

40. Poe to John P. Kennedy, February 11, 1836, in *Letters of Poe*, 1:84. "You are nearly, but not altogether right in relation to the satire of some of

my Tales. Most of them were *intended* for half banter, half-satire—although I might not have fully acknowledged this to be their aim even to myself."

41. Poe didn't much like writing anything long. Of his three other works of longer fiction, *Tales of the Folio Club* he divvied up and published as short stories; *The Journal of Julius Rodman* he serialized; and *Eureka* he called a prose poem.

42. Editorial note in Tales, 3:791. But note that Lowell published "The Tell-Tale Heart." See his letter to Poe, accepting it, December 1842, in Thomas and Jackson, *Poe Log*, 388.

43. Poe to Philip P. Cooke, September 21, 1839, in *Letters of Poe*, 1:119.

44. "Some Secrets of the Magazine Prison-House," *Broadway Journal*, February 15, 1845, and reprinted in *Essays and Reviews*, 1036.

45. Whalen, *Poe and the Masses*, 24.

46. Thomas and Jackson, *Poe Log*, 316. See also 311.

47. George Graham quoted in Whalen, *Poe and the Masses*, 72. For the argument that Poe was, chiefly, a journalist, see Sidney P. Moss, *Poe's Literary Battles: The Critic in the Context of His Literary Milieu* (Durham, NC: Duke University Press, 1963). Ackroyd demurs on this point in *Poe*, 90.

48. Edmund Wilson argued, in 1943, "His literary articles and lectures, in fact, surely constitute the most remarkable body of criticism ever produced in the United States." Poe had rather much the same opinion of himself. Wilson, *The Shock of Recognition*, 1:79.

49. Poe on Cooper, *Graham's Magazine*, November 1843, and in *Essays and Reviews*, 488–89. Poe on Dickens, *Graham's Magazine*, February 1842, and in *Essays and Reviews*, 244.

50. "The Literati of New York City," *Godey's Lady's Book*, various issues in 1846, and reprinted in *Essays and Reviews*, 1118.

51. Emerson is quoted in Wilson, *Shock of Recognition*, 81. Poe quoted in Moss, *Poe's Literary Battles*, 46–47; this is from 1836.

52. Poe on self-bepuffery is quoted in Thomas and Jackson, *Poe Log*, 394.

53. Poe on Theodore S. Fay, *Southern Literary Messenger*, December 1835, and in *Essays and Reviews*, 540. "The spirit of puffery" Poe wrote, is "an insult to the common sense." Quoted in Moss, *Poe's Literary Battles*, 35. He disliked "puffs anticipatory"; he felt "run down with puffs." "We are run down with puffs." Poe to J. Beauchamp Jones, August 8, 1839, in *Letters of Poe*, 1:113. "Editorial Miscellanies," *Broadway Journal*, September 20, 1845, and in *Essays and Reviews*, 1078.

54. Poe on Rufus Griswold, *Boston Miscellany*, November 1842, and in *Essays and Reviews*, 555.

55. Thomas and Jackson, *Poe Log*, 377.

56. Snodgrass in the *Saturday Visitor*, January 1842, in ibid., 356. POE-LEMICAL is from *Essays and Review*, 1081, with Poe's response.

57. Thomas and Jackson, *Poe Log*, 390.

58. On this point, see also Moss, *Poe's Literary Battles*, 246.

59. McGill, *American Literature and the Culture of Reprinting*, 184–85.

60. "Some Secrets of the Magazine Prison-House," *Broadway Journal*, February 15, 1845, and reprinted in *Essays and Reviews*, 1036.

61. Quoted in Whalen, *Poe and the Masses*, 72; Poe to Washington Irving, June 21, 1841, in *Letters of Poe*, 1:162; and Poe to Longfellow, June 22, 1841, in ibid., 1:166–68.

62. Poe to Frederick W. Thomas, July 4, 1841, in ibid., 1:172.

63. Poe to Frederick W. Thomas, June 26, 1841, in ibid., 1:170–71.

64. "A Few Words on Secret Writing," *Graham's Magazine*, July 1841, and in *Essays and Reviews*, 1277.

65. Poe to Richard Bolton, November 18, 1841, in *Letters of Poe*, 1:188.

66. Edgar Allan Poe, *In the Shadow of the Master: Class Tales by Edgar Allan Poe* (New York: William Morrow, 2009), headnote by Stephen King.

67. Thomas and Jackson, *Poe Log*, 358.

68. Ibid., 359.

69. Dickens, *American Notes*, chap. 3.

70. Thomas and Jackson, *Poe Log*, 361–63, 368 (on Poe's state of mind); Poe to Frederick W. Thomas, May 25, 1842, in *Letters of Poe*, 1:197. There are also hints that Poe was either fired or quit because he was drinking too heavily to do the work. See, e.g., *Poe Log*, 372–73. And, for an observation in September 1842 that Poe is drinking, see 380–81. For Poe claiming to be "straight as judges" in October 1842, see 382–83.

71. Graham quoted in Ackroyd, *Poe*, 90.

72. Dow in *Index* for June 23, 1842, quoted in Thomas and Jackson, *Poe Log*, 370.

73. Thomas and Jackson, *Poe Log*, 369, 384.

74. Poe to James Herron, early June 1842, in *Letters of Poe*, 1:198–99.

75. Poe to Joseph Evans Snodgrass, June 4, 1842, in ibid., 1:200–202.

76. Ackroyd, *Poe*, 100.

77. Poe to Dr. Thomas H. Chivers, September 27, 1842, in *Letters of Poe*, 1:215.

78. See Dow on Poe becoming drunk and abusive while in Washington in 1843, attempting to secure patronage, in Thomas and Jackson, *Poe Log*, 405. On Poe promising to join a temperance society, see 407.

79. Ibid., 404.

80. Ibid., 409.

81. Editorial note in Tales, 3:803–4, has Poe having the story "ready sometime in 1842"; the *Dollar Newspaper* contest was announced in April 1843; the story was published in June and July 1843.

82. On the other winners, see Thomas and Jackson, *Poe Log*, 416.

83. Poe had humor, it has been said; it was just never good humor. See also Ackroyd on this point, in *Poe*, 62.

84. Quoted in Shell, *Money, Language and Thought*, 9.

85. "The 'Gold Bug'—A Decided Humbug," *Daily Forum*, June 27, 1843; Thomas and Jackson, *Poe Log*, 419; on the reconciliation, see also 429.

86. On the popularity of "The Gold-bug" not relieving Poe's impecunious circumstances, see *Poe Log*, 393. In 1844, he bemoaned the "sad poverty & the thousand consequent contumelies & other ills which the condition of the mere Magazinist" had entailed upon him. Quoted in Whalen, *Poe and the Masses*, 21.

87. Ackroyd, *Poe*, 109.

88. Poe to Maria Clemm, April 7, 1844, from New York, in *Letters of Poe*, 1:252.

89. Poe to Dr. Thomas H. Chivers, November 15, 1845, in ibid., 1:302.

90. Poe to George Eveleth, January 4, 1848, in Arthur Hobson Quinn, *Edgar Allan Poe: A Critical Biography* (New York: D. Appleton, 1941), 347–48. "My enemies referred the insanity to the drink rather than the drink to the insanity."

91. Poe to Maria Clemm, July 7, 1849, in *Letters to Poe*, 2:452.

92. Quinn, *Edgar Allan Poe*, 643.

93. See Walker, "Poe Legend."

94. A good statement of this either-or problem is Stuart Levine, "The Poe Case," *American Quarterly* 17 (1962): 133–44.

95. James Russell Lowell, *A Fable for Critics* (1848); quoted in Walker, "Poe Legend," 21.

## 12. President Tom's Cabin

1. Harriet Beecher Stowe to Horace Mann, March 2, 1852, Harriet Beecher Stowe Papers, Massachusetts Historical Society.

2. Harry Stone, "Charles Dickens and Harriet Beecher Stowe," *Nineteenth-Century Fiction* 12 (1957): 200–201.

3. Dickens, *Martin Chuzzlewit*, chap. 21.

4. Thomas Moore, *Epistles, Odes, and Other Poems* (Philadelphia: John Watts, 1806), 209–10. See also Sidney P. Moss and Carolyn Moss, "The

Jefferson Miscegenation Legend in British Travel Books," *Journal of the Early Republic* (1987): 253–74.

5. Brown, *Clotel; Or, The President's Daughter*, 207.

6. Annette Gordon-Reed, *Thomas Jefferson and Sally Hemings: An American Controversy* (Charlottesville: University Press of Virginia, 1997) xxi.

7. Joseph Ellis, *American Sphinx: The Character of Thomas Jefferson* (New York: Knopf, 1997), 305.

8. Ibid., 25.

9. James Baldwin, "Everybody's Protest Novel," in *Notes of a Native Son* (Boston: Beacon, 1968).

10. Henry Randall to James Parton, June 1, 1868; Parton, "The Presidential Election of 1800," *Atlantic Monthly*, July 1873.

11. On Jefferson's comings and goings, see Winthrop D. Jordan, Review essay in *William and Mary Quarterly* 55 (1998): 318.

12. Gordon-Reed, *Jefferson and Hemings*, 101.

13. Gordon-Reed, *The Hemingses of Monticello: An American Family* (New York: Norton, 2008), 31.

14. Ibid., 31.

15. Ibid., 361.

16. Jefferson, *Notes on the State of Virginia*, 1782.

## 13. Pride of the Prairie

1. Harvey Lewis Carter, *"Dear Old Kit": The Historical Christopher Carson* (Norman: University of Oklahoma Press, 1968), 61–63, 65, 79, 90.

2. Hampton Sides, *Blood and Thunder: An Epic of the American West* (New York: Doubleday, 2006), 286.

3. Carter, *"Dear Old Kit,"* 85–86.

4. Ibid., 148–49, 15; DeWitt Peters, *Life and Adventures of Kit Carson . . . from Facts Narrated by Himself* (New York: R.W.C. Clark, 1858), v–vi.

5. Carter, *"Dear Old Kit,"* 28; Peters, *Kit Carson's Life and Adventures*, 17–18.

6. Blanche C. Grant, *Kit Carson's Story of His Own Life* (Taos, NM: n.p., 1926), 7.

7. Henry Nash Smith, *Virgin Land: The American West as Symbol and Myth* (1950; repr. Cambridge: Harvard University Press, 1978), 84–85.

8. Sides, *Blood and Thunder*, 5.

9. Charles E. Averill, *Kit Carson, The Prince of the Gold Hunters* (Boston: G. H. Williams, 1849), 80.

10. Carter, *"Dear Old Kit,"* 125–26; Sides, *Blood and Thunder*, 300–301.

11. R. C. Gordon-McCutchan, ed., *Kit Carson: Indian Fighter or Indian Killer?* (Niwot: University of Colorado Press, 1996), 6.

12. [Edward Ellis], *The Fighting Trapper: Or, Kit Carson to the Rescue* (New York: Frank Starr, 1874), 28.

13. Albert Johannsen, *The House of Beadle and Adams and its Dime and Nickel Novels: The Story of a Vanished Literature* (Norman: University of Oklahoma Press, 1950), 1:5.

14. Gordon-McCutchan, *Kit Carson*, 73–76, 85, xii.

15. Sides, *Blood and Thunder*, 7.

16. Ibid., 1.

17. Ibid., 142–43.

18. Ibid., 2.

19. Ibid., 290.

20. Ibid., 341–42, 347, 357, 340.

21. Ibid., 108–9, 136, 121, 219.

22. Ibid., 222.

23. Ibid., 66, 120.

24. Ibid., 39.

25. Ibid., 441.

26. Bill Brown, ed., *Reading the West: An Anthology of Dime Westerns* (Boston: Bedford, 1997), 2; W. H. Bishop, "Story-Paper Literature," *Atlantic Monthly* 44 (1879): 385.

27. Brown, *Reading the West*, 31.

28. Ibid., 20, 27; Bishop, "Story-Paper Literature," 384, 383.

29. William Everett, "Beadle's Dime Books," *North American Review* 24 (1864): 308, 306.

30. Brown, *Reading the West*, 34, 32, 14.

31. Sides, *Blood and Thunder*, 43–44.

32. Ibid., 292.

## 14. Longfellow's Ride

1. Assessments of Longfellow's popularity among his contemporaries are many, but remarks by Ruskin can be found in *Letters of Longfellow*, 3:1.

2. For a valuable discussion of Longfellow's career in the classroom, see Angela Sorby, *Schoolroom Poets: Childhood, Performance, and the Place of American Poetry, 1865–1917* (Durham: University of New Hampshire Press, 2005), chap. 1.

3. Berta Shaffer to Longfellow is reproduced in Christoph Irmscher, *Public Poet, Private Man: Henry Wadsworth Longfellow at 200* (Amherst: University of Massachusetts Press, 2009), 149–50. Longfellow's quite wonderful reply is reproduced on 151.

4. Lawrence Buell, introduction in *Henry Wadsworth Longfellow: Selected Poems* (New York: Penguin, 1988), vii.

5. "Feeble" is Arvin's favorite word, and he actually liked Longfellow. Newton Arvin, *Longfellow: His Life and Work* (Boston: Little, Brown, 1962).

6. Longfellow, "The New England Tragedies," prologue.

7. Helen F. Moore, "The Midnight Ride of William Dawes," *Century Magazine*, 1896.

8. Emerson quoted in Charles C. Calhoun, *Longfellow: A Rediscovered Life* (Boston: Beacon Press, 2004), 204.

9. Brooks and Mumford are cited in Arvin, *Longfellow*, 320–21.

10. For Pound, see Christoph Irmscher, *Longfellow Redux* (Urbana: University of Illinois Press, 2006), 52.

11. Arvin, *Longfellow*, 69.

12. Daniel Aaron, "The Legacy of Henry Wadsworth Longfellow," *Maine Historical Society Quarterly* 27 (1988): 59, 65; and "I wince a little every time a supercilious critic shoots an arrow into his all too vulnerable hide" (63).

13. Longfellow's correspondence with his mother is quoted in Virginia Jackson, "Longfellow's Tradition: Or, Picture-Writing a Nation," *Modern Language Quarterly* 59 (1998): 476–77.

14. Irmscher, *Longfellow Redux*, especially 53–54. See also Calhoun, *Longfellow*, 198–201. For another measure of Longfellow's popularity: "Between 1821 and 1882, Longfellow received more than 20,000 letters from nearly 7,000 different correspondents, and these didn't include over 1,300 requests for autographs and hundreds of birthday greetings" (Aaron, "Legacy of Longfellow," 59). See his diary entry for April 19, 1854: "At eleven o'clock, in No. 16. University Hall, delivered my Last Lecture; the last I shall ever deliver here or anywhere else. It was upon the last Canto of Dante's Inferno."

15. On this theme, and for its critique, see especially Irmscher, *Longfellow Redux*.

16. Ibid., 17. Irmscher's insight is that this is a legacy of Romanticism (75–76).

17. He continues, "or like throwing a ball of threads of many colors into the air, holding one end in your hand and letting it unroll itself to infinity." *Letters of Longfellow*, 3:19–20.

18. It is a photograph taken by Alexander Gardner in 1863, in Washington, DC. On Longfellow's politics, Hilen is suggestive: "Occasionally his letters reveal that Longfellow participated more actively than is generally suspected in the political dramas of his day" (*Letters of Longfellow*, 3:4). On the endless letters, Hilen points out that Longfellow sent Sumner at least 238 letters, and Sumner "became the correspondent most often in Longfellow's mind" (ibid., 3:9).

19. On Dickens and Longfellow, see Calhoun, *Longfellow*, 150–51; on Sumner's desolation, 52.

20. Irmscher, *Longfellow Redux*, 60.

21. Calhoun, *Longfellow*, 154–59.

22. When asked, in 1852, to write more about slavery, Longfellow declined: "I should feel less at liberty to decline, had I not already publicly made known my views on the subject of Slavery. But as I have already published 'Poems on Slavery,' . . . I think no one, who cares about the matter will be at any loss to discover my opinion on that subject" (Longfellow to Susan Farley Porter, June 8, 1852, in *Letters of Longfellow*, 3:348).

23. Longfellow to John Greenleaf Whittier, September 6, 1844, in ibid., 3:44.

24. Longfellow diary entry for October 26, 1848, in Samuel Longfellow, *The Life of Henry Wadsworth Longfellow* (Boston, 1893), 2:135.

25. Ibid., 4:3. Another good example is Longfellow to Sumner, April 21, 1857, with word of a book he thinks Sumner would like to read: "I have read as yet only one chapter—that on Slavery. It is very good; strong, direct, solid; with a fine page on the possible future of Africa" (ibid., 4:26). And also this: "Fanny send[s] kindest remembrances, and hopes you will soon have a chance to speak on the Fugitive Slave Law. I tell her to be patient. Neither the hour nor the man will fail" (Longfellow to Sumner, June 29, 1852, in ibid., 3:351).

26. Excerpts from Henry Wadsworth Longfellow's Account Books, transcribed from the original account books at the Houghton Library, Harvard University, by James M. Shea, director/museum curator, Longfellow National Historic Site, Cambridge, MA. Many thanks to Jim Shea for sharing his transcriptions with me.

27. Longfellow to Sumner, May 28, 1856, in *Letters of Longfellow*, 3:540.

28. Frederick J. Blue, "The Poet and the Reformer: Longfellow, Sumner, and the Bonds of Male Friendship, 1837–1874," *Journal of the Early Republic* 15 (1995): 273–97. Calhoun weighs in on the friendship as romantic (Calhoun, *Longfellow*, 135–37); and see also Longfellow's letter to Sumner, wishing they were in bed together (ibid., 153). For another discussion of the friendship, see Irmscher, *Public Poet*, 78–84, where the photograph is also discussed. Arvin only touches on this friendship but rightly observes that for much of the time, Sumner was essentially a lodger at Longfellow's house (Arvin, *Longfellow*, 52–53).

29. Longfellow to Sumner, November 5, 1857, in *Letters of Longfellow*, 4:55. And: "In the next No. of the 'Atlantic Monthly' look for a poem of mine entitled 'Sandalphon'" (Longfellow to Sumner, March 16, 1858, in ibid., 4:70.

30. Longfellow to Sumner, February 24, 1858, in ibid., 4:65.

31. George Sumner, *An Oration Delivered before the Municipal Authorities of the City of Boston* (Boston: Ticknor and Fields, 1859), 61–62.

32. Longfellow to Charles Sumner, August 4, 1859, in *Life of Longfellow*, 2:389.

33. Samuel Longfellow, *Life of Henry Wadsworth Longfellow, with Extracts from His Journals and Correspondence* (Boston: Houghton, Mifflin, 1886), 2:341–42.

34. Charles Sumner, *The Barbarism of Slavery* (New York: Young Men's Republican Union, 1863), 79. For an account of the speech's delivery and reception, see David Herbert Donald, *Charles Sumner and the Coming of the Civil War* (New York: Knopf, 1960), 352–57.

35. S. Longfellow, *Life of Longfellow*, 2:349, 352–54.

36. Ibid., 2:358.

37. On the image of the slave ship in abolitionist writing, see Marcus Wood, *Blind Memory: Visual Representations of Slavery in England and America, 1780–1865* (New York: Routledge, 2000).

38. As with Coleridge (whose poem on slave flight Longfellow would have read in Greek), the slave's race—"I would take wing with thee to fly / Through rugged Ocean's massy swell"—ends in a return to Africa, at death ("O DEATH, now leave the gates of dark, / And haste thee to a doom-bound folk"). Samuel Taylor Coleridge, "The Wretched Lot of the Slaves in the Islands of West India," in *Amazing Grace: An Anthology*

*of Poems about Slavery, 1660–1810,* ed. James G. Basker (New Haven: Yale University Press, 2002), 446–47.

39. James C. Austin, "J. T. Fields and the Revision of Longfellow's Poems: Unpublished Correspondence," *New England Quarterly* 24 (1951): 243.

40. Martin Luther King, Jr., "Where Do We Go from Here? (1967)," in *A Call to Conscience: The Landmark Speeches of Dr. Martin Luther King, Jr.*, ed. Clayborne Carson and Chris Shepherd (New York: IPM, 2001), 182.

41. "Text of President Ford's Address in Old North Church," *Boston Globe*, April 19, 1975.

42. Calhoun, *Longfellow*, ix.

43. Longfellow to Sumner, January 20, 1861, in *Letters of Longfellow*, 4:211.

44. S. Longfellow, *Life of Longfellow*, 2:361.

## 15. Rock, Paper, Scissors

1. *Maryland contested election —Harrison vs. Davis. Memorial of William G. Harrison, contesting the election of the Hon. H. Winter Davis, of the Fourth Congressional District of Maryland. February 9, 1860.* U.S. Congressional Serial Set. Vol. no. 1060, Session vol. no. 1. 36th Congress, 1st Session. H.Misc.Doc. 4, 139–40. Portions of this essay appeared, in a different form, in *The Whites of Their Eyes.*

2. Ibid., 154.

3. George W. McCrary, *A Treatise on the American Law of Elections* (Keokuk, IA: R.B. Ogden, 1875), 314.

4. David Grimsted, *American Mobbing, 1821–1861: Toward Civil War* (New York: Oxford University Press, 1986), 184. Richard Bensel, *The American Ballot Box in the Mid-Nineteenth Century* (Cambridge: Cambridge University Press, 2004), 11.

5. See, e.g., John Crowley, "Uses and Abuses of the Secret Ballot in the American Age of Reform," in *Cultures of Voting: The Hidden History of the Secret Ballot*, ed. Romain Bertrand et al. (London: Hurst; Paris: In association with Centre d'études et de recherches internationales, 2007), 43–68.

6. http://quickfacts.census.gov/qfd/states/00000.html. Alexander Keyssar, *The Right to Vote: The Contested History of Democracy in the United States* (New York: Basic Books, 2000).

7. To vote in England, John Milton wrote in 1660, was "to hold up a forrest of fingers, or to convey each man his bean or ballot into the box." John Milton, *Ready and Easy Way to Establish a Free Commonwealth* (1660), para. 213: "And this annual rotation of a Senat to consist of three hunderd, as is lately propounded , requires also another popular assembly upward of a thousand, with an answerable rotation. Which besides that it will be liable to all those inconveniencies found in the foresaid remedies, cannot but be troublesom and chargeable, both in thir motion and thir session, to the whole land; unweildie with thir own bulk, unable in so great a number to mature thir consultations as they ought, if any be allotted them, and that they meet not from so many parts remote to sit a whole year lieger in one place, only now and then to hold up a forrest of fingers , or to convey each man his bean or ballot into the box, without reason shewn or common deliberation."

8. For Pennsylvania, see Spencer Albright, *The American Ballot* (Washington, D.C.: American Council on Public Affairs, 1942), 16. On peas and beans in use in sixteenth- and seventeenth-century England, see Charles Gross, "The Early History of the Ballot in England," *American Historical Review* 3 (April 1898): 458; on voting with bullets, 459. On voting behavior more broadly, see Robert J. Dinkin, *Voting in Provincial America: A Study of Elections in the Thirteen Colonies, 1689–1776* (Westport, CT: Greenwood Press, 1977), chap. 6. Dinkin argues that voice voting was the most common method and details its workings (133–35).

9. Election Day was much like a carnival; it was also something of a spectacle. Robert J. Dinkin, *Election Day: A Documentary History* (Westport, CT: Greenwood Press, 2002), 1–27, 47–60.

10. Quoted in Dinkin, *Voting in Provincial America*, 135. On North Carolina paper voting, see 139.

11. John H. Wigmore, *The Australian Ballot System* (Boston: C. C. Soule, 1889), 26n1; Albright, *American Ballot*, 14–15.

12. On legislative elections in some Massachusetts towns still "voted by Kernels of Corn and Pease" even after Independence, see Robert J. Dinkin, *Voting in Revolutionary America: A Study of Elections in the Original Thirteen States* (Westport, CT: Greenwood Press, 1982), 102.

13. Hamilton, *Records of the Federal Convention of 1787*, 2:240–41. "Whether the electors should vote by ballot or *viva voce*, should assemble at this place or that place," Madison argued, "these and many other points would depend on the Legislatures" which might "mould their regulations to favor the candidates they wished to succeed."

14. Madison, *Debates Concerning the Method of Selecting the Executive*, 1787. http://www.law.umkc.edu/faculty/projects/ftrials/conlaw/elector1787 .html.

15. Douglas Campbell, "The Origin of American Institutions, as Illustrated in the History of the Written Ballot," *Papers of the American Historical Association* 4 (1891): 179. And yet, L. E. Fredman says, "All but one of the new state constitutions of the era of the Revolution required ballot papers." Fredman, *The Australian Ballot: The Story of an American Reform* (Lansing: Michigan State University Press, 1968), 20.

16. Dinkin, *Voting in Revolutionary America*, 102.

17. See, broadly, Keyssar, *Right to Vote*; and Wilentz, *Rise of American Democracy*.

18. An 1848 Free Soil Party ticket is reproduced at "Vote: The Machinery of Democracy," http://americanhistory.si.edu/vote/paperballots.html.

19. *Henshaw v. Foster et al.*, 26 Mass. 312 (1830).

20. On knifing, see Fredman, *Australian Ballot*, 22, 28; Bensel, *American Ballot Box*, 15.

21. William M. Ivins, *Machine Politics and Money in Elections in New York City* (New York: Harper, 1887), 56–57, 63–64.

22. Frank O'Gorman, "The Secret Ballot in Nineteenth-Century Britain," in *Cultures of Voting*, 22–23.

23. Roy G. Saltman, *The History and Politics of Voting Technology* (New York: Penguin, 2006), 64, 74; Fredman, *Australian Ballot*, 26.

24. Michael Brunet, "The Secret Ballot Issue in Massachusetts Politics from 1851 to 1853," *New England Quarterly* 25 (September 1952): 354–62.

25. *Maryland contested election*, 74.

26. Fredman, *Australian Ballot*, 8.

27. Ibid., 11; Albright, *American Ballot*, 30.

28. For more on American attempts to defeat the Tasmanian Dodge, see Fredman, *Australian Ballot*, 50–51.

29. Mill, "Thoughts on Parlimentary Reform" (1859) and "Considerations on Representative Government" (1861). For a recent critique, see Annabelle Lever, "Mill and the Secret Ballot: Beyond Coercion and Corruption," *Utilitas* 19 (September 2007): 354–78.

30. The most useful account is O'Gorman, "Secret Ballot," 16–42. On the persistence of opposition: "As many contemporaries continued to argue down to the passage of the 1872 Act, legitimate political action was the consequence not of secrecy and concealment but of manly honesty and public debate" (19). On why the act passed in 1872, see especially 29–31.

31. See the concise summary of the investigation in Saltman, *History and Politics of Voting Technology*, 74–75.

32. Henry George, "Bribery in Elections," *Overland Monthly* 7 (December 1871): 497–504.

33. Saltman, *History and Politics of Voting Technology*, 91–92, 84. Confidence fell further after the botched presidential election of 1876, in which the Democrat, Samuel Tilden, won the popular vote but lost the election to the Republican, Rutherford B. Hayes. To a recount in Florida—it initially appeared that Tilden had won that state by fewer than 100 votes—one member of the Republican National Committee carried a suitcase stuffed with $10,000 in small bills.

34. Henry George, "Money in Elections," *North American Review* 136 (March 1883): 211.

35. Ivins, *Machine Politics*, especially 63, 77.

36. Fredman, *Australian Ballot*, 32–33.

37. December 13, 1888, and quoted in Wigmore, *Australian Ballot System*, 23–24; see also Fredman, *Australian Ballot*, ix.

38. Fredman, *Australian Ballot*, 42–43.

39. Herbert J. Bass, *'I Am a Democrat': The Political Career of David Bennett Hill* (Syracuse: Syracuse University Press, 1961), 149; *New York Herald*, January 17, February 9, 1890; and *New York Times*, March 4, 29, 1890. See also the illustration of Hill wielding the ballot in *Harper's Weekly*, June 16, 1888.

40. Fredman, *Australian Ballot*, 53–55.

41. For a state-of-the-union, see Philip Loring Allen, "Ballot Laws and Their Workings," *Political Science Quarterly* 21 (March 1906): 38–58. On the early consequences and the 90 percent figure, see Jerrold G. Rusk, "The Effect of the Australian Ballot Reform on Split Ticket Voting: 1876–1908," *American Political Science Review* 64 (December 1970): 1220–38.

42. Full text, plus illustration, reprinted in Wigmore, *The Australian Ballot System* (1889).

43. Crowley, "Uses and Abuses," 59.

44. "Is a Vote by Machine a Constitutional Ballot?" *Michigan Law Review* 3 (June 1906): 648–50. In 1905, for instance, a Detroit election official refused to allow the installation of a voting machine in his district. The case, heard by the state's Supreme Court, turned, like earlier challenges to printed ballots, on the definition of a "ballot"; the courts decided in favor of machines. See *People ex rel City of Detroit v. Board of Inspectors of Elections* (1905).

45. See, e.g., Aviel Rubin, *Brave New Ballot: The Battle to Safeguard Democracy in the Age of Electronic Voting* (New York: Morgan Road Books, 2006).

## 16. Objection

1. All quotations from Darrow's argument in *Wisconsin v. Kidd* are taken from Clarence Darrow, *The Woodworkers' Conspiracy Case* (Chicago: Campbell Printers, 1898). On Paine Lumber, see also Michael J. Goc, *Land Rich Enough: An Illustrated History of Oshkosh and Winnebago County* (Northridge, CA: Windsor Publications, 1988), 29. On Paine's arrival from Canisteo, see *Oshkosh: One Hundred Years a City* (Oshkosh: Oshkosh Centennial, 1938), 15, 238–40. He came to survey in 1853, the year the city was incorporated, and came back with all his machinery and his sons two years later. An exhaustively detailed account of the strike is Virginia Glenn Crane, *The Oshkosh Woodworkers' Strike of 1898: A Wisconsin Community in Crisis* (privately printed, 1998).

2. Goc, *Land Rich Enough*, 72.

3. Nell Irvin Painter, *Standing at Armageddon: The United States, 1877–1919* (New York: Norton, 1987), 22.

4. "Morris's Skull in Court," *Milwaukee Sentinel*, December 7, 1898.

5. "Labor Troubles the Oshkosh Strike," *Commercial Appeal*, June 30, 1898; "Troops Face Oshkosh Mob," *Wisconsin State Register*, July 2, 1898; "Both Sides Defiant," *Milwaukee Sentinel*, July 8, 1898; "Kidd Case at Oshkosh," *Milwaukee Journal*, October 14, 1898, http://www.oshkoshdoor.com/history.html. Also see Virginia Glenn Crane, "'The Very Pictures of Anarchy': Women in the Oshkosh Woodworkers' Strike of 1898," *Wisconsin Magazine of History* 84 (2001): 44–59. A bit more about the history of Paine Lumber can be found in William Dawes and Clara Dawes, *History of Oshkosh* (Oshkosh, WI: Service Print Shop, 1938), 27. According to the Dawes, Darrow returned to Oshkosh shortly after the trial and gave a Democratic campaign speech in the Opera House (59).

6. "Acquittal for Kidd," *Milwaukee Sentinel*, November 3, 1898; *State of Wisconsin v. Thomas I. Kidd, 1898*, Municipal Court for City of Oshkosh and Winnebago County, Wisconsin, Criminal Docket, vol. 1, file no. A 407, Oshkosh Public Library; Crane, *Oshkosh Woodworkers' Strike*, chaps. 24–27.

7. "Kidd's Trial Is Begun," *Milwaukee Sentinel*, October 15, 1898.

8. Darrow, *Woodworkers' Case*, 12.

9. Andrew E. Kersten, *Clarence Darrow: American Iconoclast* (New York: Hill and Wang, 2011), xi. He also calls Darrow a "flip-flopper" (ix).

10. John A. Farrell, *Clarence Darrow: Attorney for the Damned* (New York: Doubleday, 2011), 8.

11. Richard J. Jensen, *Clarence Darrow: The Creation of an American Myth* (New York: Greenwood Press, 1992), 3.

12. Farrell, *Clarence Darrow*, 13.

13. The day the Scopes trial began, Darrow professed himself bewildered: "Can it be possible that this trial is taking place in the twentieth century?" Irving Stone, *Clarence Darrow for the Defense* (Garden City, NY: Doubleday, Doran, 1941), 453.

14. Clarence Darrow, *The Story of My Life* (New York: Charles Scribner's Sons, 1932), 249, 276.

15. Ibid., 75.

16. Edward J. Larson and Jack Marshall, introduction in *The Essential Words and Writings of Clarence Darrow* (New York: Modern Library, 2007), xvii.

17. Darrow, *Story of My Life*, 232.

18. Ibid., 32.

19. Stone, *Clarence Darrow*, 80.

20. Darrow, quoted in Farrell, *Clarence Darrow*, 290.

21. "I sometimes think that pessimism is my dope." Clarence Darrow, "Is Life Worth Living?" (1917), in *Essential Words and Writings*, 107.

22. Darrow, *Story of My Life*, 54.

23. Ibid., 1.

24. Kersten, *Clarence Darrow*, xii.

25. Stone, *Clarence Darrow*, 1, 470.

26. Clarence Darrow, *Farmington* (1904; repr. New York: Charles Scribner's Sons, 1932), 171. "I happen to have born of an abolitionist father and mother," he saw fit to mention, in his closing argument in *Wisconsin v. Kidd* (Darrow, *Woodworkers' Case*, 71).

27. Darrow, *Story of My Life*, 14, 32.

28. *Essential Words and Writings*, xvii.

29. Darrow, quoted in Farrell, *Clarence Darrow*, 23.

30. Darrow, *Story of My Life*, 28–29.

31. Darrow, in a letter, quoted in Stone, *Clarence Darrow*, 18.

32. "Most men never have but one or two ideas, anyhow, and to these they hang like grim death." Darrow, *Story of My Life*, 234.

33. Painter, *Standing at Armageddon*, xx.

34. Darrow, *Story of My Life*, 52.

35. Ibid., 69.

36. Kersten, *Clarence Darrow*, 62.

37. Painter, *Standing at Armageddon*, 39, 121–25. "Eugene Debs was sent to jail in Woodstock, Ill., for trying to help his fellow man," Darrow wrote. He wasn't the first; he wouldn't be the last. Darrow shrugged. "He really got off easy." Darrow, *Story of My Life*, 67.

38. Farrell, *Clarence Darrow*, 70.

39. Jensen, *Clarence Darrow*, 38.

40. Goc, *Land Rich Enough*, 46–47.

41. "Labor Unions Watch Trial of T. I. Kidd," *Oshkosh Daily Northwestern*, October 14, 1898. Second largest city and paper of record: Goc, *Land Rich Enough*, 53, 57. See also "Great Interest in It," *Oshkosh Daily Northwestern*, October 14, 1898; and "Kidd's Trial Is Begun," *Milwaukee Sentinel*, October 15, 1898.

42. Darrow, *Argument of Clarence Darrow*.

43. Jury selection ran from October 10 to October 13.

44. "He knows right from wrong, although he seldom finds anything right. He believes in John Calvin and eternal punishment. Get rid of him with the fewest possible words before he contaminates the others; unless you and your clients are Presbyterians you probably are a bad lot, and even though you may be a Presbyterian, your client most likely is guilty." Darrow, "How to Pick a Jury" (1936), in *Essential Words and Writings*.

45. "Labor Unions Watch Trial of T. I. Kidd." Here's how this went: In this municipal court, you had a right to strike six jurors without cause. Darrow argued that he should be able to strike eighteen, because he had three clients. Hoss ruled against him (Crane, *Oshkosh Woodworkers' Strike*, 439).

46. "State Is After Kidd," *Oshkosh Times*, October 22, 1898. See also "Dealt with Pickets," *Oshkosh Times*, October 22, 1898.

47. Darrow, *Woodworkers' Case*, 45, 19. Paine had also filed a civil suit against Kidd: "Secretary Kidd was also subsequently served with papers in a civil suit for the Paine Lumber company" ("Great Interest in It").

48. Darrow, *Woodworkers' Case*, 12.

49. Ibid., 30. The prolabor *Times* used a subhead, "Darrow's Kindergarten," when reporting Darrow's examination of boys who worked at the mill. "Boys on the Stand," *Oshkosh Times*, October 29, 1898.

50. Farrell, *Clarence Darrow*, 435.

51. "Striker Pickets as Witnesses," October 19, 1898; "New Line of Evidence," October 22, 1898; "State Finished Case," October 25, 1898, *Oshkosh Daily Northwestern*. The grounds for this motion are my supposition.

52. "Advised No Violence," *Oshkosh Daily Northwestern*, October 25, 1898.

53. Darrow, *Woodworkers' Case*, 26.

54. Ibid., 33.

55. "The Testimony Closed," *Oshkosh Daily Northwestern*, October 28, 1898. On Darrow's thwarted defense: "The defense had given out at the beginning of the trial that it would prove conspiracy on the part of the mill men but the testimony which they claimed would do this was ruled out by the court." The *Times* also referred to "frequent passages at arms between the attorneys" ("Dealt with Pickets").

56. Darrow, "How to Pick a Jury." The courtroom was packed: "The flow of oratory is being absorbed by large crowds which fill every available seat in the court room" ("Oratory on Tap," *Oshkosh Daily Northwestern*, October 29, 1898).

57. Farrell, *Clarence Darrow*, 6–8.

58. Darrow, *Woodworkers' Case*, 20–21.

59. Ibid., 9, 23, 12.

60. Ibid., 51, 34, 41, 55–56, 44.

61. Ibid., 71.

62. Ibid., 72.

63. Ibid., 80. Goss's charge to the jury is reprinted in "Decisions of Courts Affecting Labor," *Bulletin of the Department of Labor* no. 23 (1899): 575–79. It's brief and fair.

64. Darrow, *Woodworkers' Case*, 4.

65. He offered, in that closing argument, a creed: "I believe that the world is filled with wrong." Ibid., 75. It's an interesting counter to Dickens's creed: "I believe in the existence of beautiful things."

66. Darrow, Anthracite Miners (1903), in *Attorney for the Damned*, 341. On the interruption, etc., see 333.

67. Farrell, *Clarence Darrow*, 259, 240, 278.

68. Darrow in Kersten, *Clarence Darrow*, 195.

69. Darrow, *Woodworkers' Case*, 79.

## 17. Chan the Man

1. Earl Derr Biggers, *The House Without a Key* (1925) in *Charlie Chan: Five Complete Novels* (New York: Avenel Books, 1981), 37–40.

2. Yunte Huang, *Charlie Chan: The Untold Story of the Honorable Detective and His Rendezvous with American History* (New York: Norton, 2010), 172–73.

3. Numbers can be found in Howard M. Berlin, *The Charlie Chan Film Encyclopedia* (Jefferson, NC: McFarland, 2000). But a better discussion of each Chan iteration is in Ken Hanke, *Charlie Chan at the Movies: History, Filmography, and Criticism* (Jefferson, NC: McFarland, 1989).

4. Chin, "The Sons of Chan," and Jen, "The Asian Illusion," as quoted in Huang, *Charlie Chan*, 279–82.

5. Jessica Hagedorn, ed., *Charlie Chan Is Dead: An Anthology of Contemporary Asian-American Fiction* (New York: Penguin, 1993).

6. *Charlie Chan's Secret* (20th Century Fox, 1936).

7. Huang, *Charlie Chan*, 284.

8. Ibid., 172–73.

9. Ibid., chap. 1.

10. Ibid., chaps. 2–5. Chinese population of Hawaii c. 1900: 57; breakdown of the HPD: 49.

11. Ibid., chap. 8, and 207–8.

12. Ibid., 61. Becoming a detective: 68. Crime-busting squad: 70.

13. Ibid., 66. Death penalty: 74.

14. Ibid., chap. 13.

15. Ibid., 109.

16. Ibid., 147.

17. Ibid., 148, 156.

18. Ibid., 116–17.

19. Ibid., 81, 83, chap. 10, 284, and 161.

20. See also Hanke, *Charlie Chan at the Movies*.

21. Huang, *Charlie Chan*, 158, 171, 180–82.

22. Stephen D. Youngkin, *The Lost One: A Life of Peter Lorre* (Louisville: University of Kentucky Press, 2005), 157. Lorre was concerned with the figure because of the comparison with the wages of Mr. Moto.

23. Hanke, *Charlie Chan at the Movies*, xiii–xv, 4.

24. Huang, *Charlie Chan*, chap. 22; "Charlie Chan at It Again," *New York Times*, June 12, 1931.

## 18. The Uprooted

1. The transcript is in the Library of Congress, http://memory.loc.gov/wpaintro/manbar.html.

2. See especially Ann Banks, ed., *First-Person America* (New York: Knopf, 1980); Monty Noam Penkower, *The Federal Writers' Project: A Study*

*in Government Patronage of the Arts* (Urbana: University of Illinois Press, 1977); Jerre Mangione, *The Dream and the Deal: The Federal Writers' Project, 1925–1943* (Philadelphia: University of Pennsylvania Press, 1983); Jerrold Hirsch, *Portrait of America: A Cultural History of the Federal Writers' Project* (Chapel Hill: University of North Carolina Press, 2003); and David A. Taylor, *Soul of a People: The WPA Writers' Project Uncovers Depression America* (New York: Wiley, 2009). For a short but useful overview, see http://lcweb2.loc.gov/ammem/wpaintro/intro02.html. On Ellison, see Mangione, *The Dream and the Deal*, 255–57. On the numbers, see Taylor, *Soul of a People*, 6, 12. That interviewers were paid $20 a week can be found in Banks, *First-Person America*, xiii.

3. Federal Writers' Project, *These Are Our Lives, as Told by the People and Written by Members of the Federal Writers' Project of the Works Progress Administration in North Carolina, Tennessee and Georgia* (Chapel Hill: University of North Carolina Press, 1939). On 800 volumes: Morris Dickstein, *Dancing in the Dark: A Cultural History of the Great Depression* (New York: Norton, 2009), 447.

4. Ralph Ellison, *The Invisible Man* (New York: Modern Library, 1994), 248–50. On Ellison's FWP work, see Arnold Rampersad, *Ralph Ellison: A Biography* (New York: Knopf, 2007), 115–16. Ellison conducted interviews but also did a lot of archival work, especially in tracing the history of blacks in New York (compiling a report, for instance, on the 1741 slave revolt). "Once you touched the history of blacks in New York," Ellison told Banks, "you were deep into American history" (Banks, *First-Person America*, xx).

5. A summary of Jim Crow laws is in Isabel Wilkerson, *The Warmth of Other Suns: The Epic Story of America's Great Migration* (New York: Random House, 2010), 48–51.

6. Ibid., 11–12.

7. Wilkerson makes this WPA comparison herself (ibid., 670).

8. Botkin, and his predecessor, John Lomax, sent writers out to interview them. (Botkin, who coined the term "folk-say," trained his staff to write talk down right.) Botkin wrote of the ex-slave narratives, "They have the forthrightness, tang and tone of people talking, the immediacy and concreteness of the participant and the eyewitness, and the salty irony and mother wit which, like the gift of memory, are kept alive by the bookless" (Botkin quoted in Mangione, *Dream and the Deal*, 265). Ellison later said, about writing down speech, "I tried to use my ear for dialogue to given an impression of just how the people sounded. I developed a technique of transcribing that captured the idiom rather than trying to convey

the dialect through misspellings" (Ellison as interviewed by Banks, *First-Person America*, xx).

9. Benjamin A. Botkin, ed., *Lay My Burden Down: A Folk History of Slavery* (Chicago: University of Chicago Press, 1945), ix–xiv.

10. Wright in *First Person America*, xvii, from an interview Banks conducted in 1977.

11. Wilkerson, "Notes on Methodology," in *Warmth of Other Sons*, appendix.

12. On the Chicago School, see James B. McKee, *Sociology and the Race Problem: The Failure of a Perspective* (Urbana: University of Illinois Press, 1993), especially chap. 3.

13. "The sand of our simple folk lives run out on the cold city pavements." Richard Wright, *12 Million Black Voices* (1941; repr. New York: Arno Press, 1969), 93, 136.

14. Terkel always said he was a "guerilla journalist." His work was controversial and especially raised hackles when he won a Pulitzer Prize for Nonfiction in 1985. "Sure it's oral, but is it history?" one critic asked. "There is no real analysis or interpretation, which is what a historian is supposed to do," the historian Robert Remini observed. "He's more like a chronicler than a historian" (John Blades, "Prize-winner," *Chicago Tribune*, April 26, 1985).

15. Wilkerson, *Warmth of Other Sons*, 26, 29, 31, 26–27, 37, 45–46, 40.

16. Ibid., 26, 33, 35, 33, 112, 196–97, 113, 116–19.

17. Ibid., 145–47, 171–73.

18. Ibid., 196–97, 217–18, 226, 237, 278.

19. Ibid., 301–2, 374, 330–31, 334, 373–75, 414–15.

20. Ibid., 477–78, 488–89.

21. Ibid., 553, 579–81.

22. Wright, *12 Million Black Voices*, 43.

23. Leo Gurley, as taken down by Ellison and reprinted in Banks, *First-Person America*, 244.

24. A very good Chicago study is Arnold R. Hirsch, *Making the Second Ghetto: Race and Housing in Chicago, 1940–1960* (Cambridge: Cambridge University Press, 1983).

25. Wilkerson, *Warmth of Other Sons*, 668.

26. Wright, *12 Million Black Voices*, 136. And (more of Wilkerson echoing Wright): "the courts and the morgues become crowded with our lost children" (136).

27. Wilkerson, *Warmth of Other Sons*, 664, 579.

28. Ibid., 633–34, 579, 648–49, 655.

## 19. Rap Sheet

1. Dave Collins, "Lawmakers Suggest Reforms in Wake of Cheshire Killings," AP, September 6, 2007. More on the suspects' background can be found in various places, including Stacey Stowe and Alison Leigh Cowan, "Earlier Burglaries," *New York Times*, July 27, 2007. Komisarjevsky's criminal record is detailed at http://www.wfsb.com/news/13745324/detail.html. Hayes's record is at http://www.wfsb.com/news/13745529/detail.html.

2. On the then anticipated single trial, see http://www.wtnh.com/dpp/news/crime/news_ap_new_haven_one_trial_sought_for_cheshire_suspects_200909030810.

3. A cultural history is Jean Murley, *The Rise of True Crime: Twentieth-Century Murder and American Popular Culture* (Westport, CT: Praeger, 2008). See also, e.g., Karen Haltunen, *Murder Most Foul: The Killer and the American Gothic Imagination* (Cambridge: Harvard University Press, 1998).

4. For an interesting if brief statement on this point, see Eric H. Monkkonen, *Crime, Justice, History* (Columbus: Ohio State University Press, 2002), chap. 5: "The Puzzle of Murder Statistics: A Search for Cause and Effect," 72–74.

5. Rates in Randolph Roth, *American Homicide* (Cambridge: Harvard University Press, 2009), 4–5; and Stuart Banner, *The Death Penalty: An American History* (Cambridge: Harvard University Press, 2002), 300–301. Figures from the World Health Organization from 1960 to 1991 are available in Gary LaFree, *Losing Legitimacy: Street Crime and the Decline of Social Institutions in America* (Boulder, CO: Westview Press, 1998), table 2.1, p. 29.

6. The best summary of Monkkonen's work is Eric Monkkonen, "Homicide: Explaining America's Exceptionalism," *American Historical Review* (February 2006): 76–94. For his take on the rise of historical homicide studies, see 82.

7. A good discussion of this is Eric H. Monkkonen, "Estimating the Accuracy of Historic Homicide Rates," *Social Science History* 25 (2001): 53–66.

8. On the scope, and 1300, see Petrus Spierenburg, *A History of Murder: Personal Violence in Europe from the Middle Ages to the Present* (Cambridge, England: Polity, 2008), 2. Also, see his introduction for a very interesting discussion of the nature of the data.

9. See ibid., and also Petrus Spierenburg, "Democracy Came Too Early: A Tentative Explanation for the Problem of American Homicide," *AHR* (2006): 104–14.

10. Some of the current scholarship is reported in Monkkonen, "Homicide"; but see, especially, Spierenburg, *History of Murder*. Also see various debates about whether to exclude Russia as a special case, as this figure does.

11. Most of the numbers are from Roth, *American Homicide*. The 2008 number is from the UCR 9/15/09 release: http://www.fbi.gov/ucr/cius2008/offenses/violent_crime/murder_homicide.html.

12. See http://www.fbi.gov/ucr/cius2008/offenses/expanded_information/data/shrtable_07.html.

13. Spierenberg, "Democracy Came Too Early." Roth discusses this literature in *American Homicide*, 12. For a modern take on the culture of honor thesis (which has nineteenth-century antecedents, including *Homicide, North and South* [1888]), see Richard E. Nesbit, *Culture of Honor: The Psychology of Violence in the New South* (Boulder, CO: Westview Press, 1996).

14. Monkkonen, "Homicide"

15. For Monkkonen's take on the rise of historical homicide studies, see ibid., 82.

16. See the database's website and, better, Roth's appendices on sources and methods, in *American Homicide*. A useful website on the UCR is http://www.fbi.gov/ucr/cius2008/about/about_ucr.html.

17. Roth, *American Homicide*, 14–16. For an important comparison, see, e.g., Monkkonen, "Homicide over the Centuries," in *Crime, Justice, History*, 78–84. On the problem of infanticide and the data, see Spierenberg, *History of Murder*, 5.

18. LaFree discussed the literature on this subject in *Losing Legitimacy*, 42–47.

19. Ibid. See also Roth, *American Homicide*, 450–51, tables 9.4 and 9.5.

20. LaFree discussed these data in *Losing Legitimacy*, chap. 6.

21. Roth, *American Homicide*, 18.

22. Ibid., 38, fig. 1.2.

23. Roth, *American Homicide*, 472. LaFree uses presidential approval ratings.

24. *New York Times*, September 14, 2009, http://www.nytimes.com/2009/09/15/us/15crime.html?_r=1&scp=1&sq=FBI%20crime&st=cse.

25. Mark A. R. Kleiman, *When Brute Force Fails: How to Have Less Crime and Less Punishment* (Princeton: Princeton University Press, 2009), 23; Roth, *American Homicide*, 5.

26. There has been much discussion of the origins and consequences of California's signal legislation; see, e.g., Franklin E. Zimring, Gordon Hawkins, and Sam Kamin, *Punishment and Democracy: Three Strikes and You're Out in California* (New York: Oxford University Press, 2001); and, for a discussion of populist penal codes, Gary LaFree, "Too Much Democracy or Too Much Crime? Lessons from California's Three-Strikes Law," *Law and Social Inquiry* 27 (2002): 875–902.

27. Amanda Cuda, "Home Invasion Led to Legal Greater Penalties," *Connecticut Post Online*, July 22, 2008. On the three-strikes efforts, see Frank Juliano, "3 Strikes Law Gaining Support," *Connecticut Post Online*, October 16, 2008.

28. Kleiman, *When Brute Force Fails*, 1.

29. Kleiman's incarceration figures for 1974–2008 are in ibid., 14–15.

30. See http://www.threestrikesnow.com/.

31. Connecticut's death row inmates: http://www.courant.com/news/connecticut/hc-deathrow-pg,0,871806.photogallery?index=hc-peeler.

32. Rell's veto: http://www.cnadp.org/10June2009RellVetoStatement.pdf.

33. Robert Asher, Lawrence B. Goodheart, and Alan Rogers, eds., *Murder on Trial, 1620–2002* (Albany: State University of New York Press, 2005).

34. Noah Hobart, *Excessive Wickedness, the Way to an Untimely Death* (New Haven, 1768), i–ii. Banner comments on these three-strikes laws in *The Death Penalty* (6): "Burglary and robbery . . . were not capital crimes under the initial criminal statues of Connecticut, Massachusetts, Plymouth, or Pennsylvania, and were capital only in the third offense in the initial codes of New York, New Hampshire, and New Haven. Arson was not a capital crime in early Connecticut, MA, NY, or PA."

35. *Connecticut Courant*, September 22, 1768. The question itself is straight from Beccaria, *Of Crimes and Punishments* (1764), chap. 16.

36. On the American editions, see Banner, *Death Penalty*, and Alan Rogers, *Murder and the Death Penalty in Massachusetts* (Amherst: University of Massachusetts Press, 2008).

37. Banner, *Death Penalty*, 101.

38. *Report of the Joint Select Committee on that part of the Governor's Message relating to Capital Punishment together with a Bill in form for Its Abolishment* (New Haven, 1842); and *Report of the Joint Select Committee on so much of the Governor's Message as relates to Capital Punishment* (New Haven, 1850). Banner, *Death Penalty*, 222.

39. On the international history of the abolition of capital punishment, see Banner, *Death Penalty*, 300–301. Banner argues that the United States failed to abolish capital punishment in the 1960s and 1970s, thereby falling out of step with the world's affluent democracies, because the nation, as a whole, was experiencing an elevated murder rate, the same elevated murder rate that has led, in the decades since, to the sentencing guidelines industry responsible for the nation's rate of incarceration.

40. Louis J. Palmer, Jr., *Encyclopedia of Capital Punishment in the United States*, 2d edition (Jefferson, NC: McFarland, 2008), 124–25.

41. *A Brief Narrative of the Life and Confessions of Barnett Davenport* (Hartford? 1780).

## 20. To Wit

1. Abraham Lincoln, First Inaugural Address, in Robert Vincent Remini and Terry Golway, eds., *Fellow Citizens: The Penguin Book of U.S. Presidential Inaugural Addresses* (New York: Penguin Books, 2008). With the exception of Barack Obama's 2009 inaugural address, all quotations to inaugural addresses quoted in this chapter are taken from this edition, but since these addresses are easily available online, citations are not given in the notes.

2. James Garfield, *The Diary of James A. Garfield*, ed. Harry James Brown and Frederick D. Williams (Lansing: Michigan State University Press, 1981), 4:529.

3. Ted Sorensen is quoted in Robert Schlesinger, *White House Ghosts: Presidents and Their Speechwriters* (New York: Simon and Schuster, 2008), 105; inaugural address of John F. Kennedy,

4. Nixon is quoted in Remini and Golway, *Fellow Citizens*, 397–98.

5. Arthur Schlesinger, Jr., "The Inaugural Addresses: Panorama of American History," in *The Chief Executive: Inaugural Addresses of the Presidents of the United States from George Washington to Lyndon B. Johnson* (New York: Crown, 1965), vii. See also Ted Widmer, "So Help Me God," *American Scholar* 75 (2005): 29–42; Edward Chester, "Beyond the Rhetoric: A New Look at Presidential Inaugural Addresses," *Presidential Studies Quarterly* 10 (1980): 571–81; David Ericson, "Presidential Inaugural Addresses and American Political Culture," *Presidential Studies Quarterly* 27 (1997): 727–44; Michael J. Korzi, "The President and the Public: Inaugural Addresses in American History," *Congress and the Presidency* 31 (2004): 21–52; and Cynthia Toolin, "American Civil Religion from 1789 to 1981: A Content Analysis of Presidential Inaugural Addresses," *Review of Religious Research* 25 (1983): 39–48.

6. Inaugural addresses of James Buchanan, Ulysses S. Grant, Theodore Roosevelt, Dwight D. Eisenhower, George H. W. Bush, Jimmy Carter, and Warren G. Harding.

7. Schlesinger, *White House Ghosts*, 105.

8. The first: Thomas Hudson McKee, *Presidential Inaugurations: From George Washington, 1789, to Grover Cleveland, 1893* (Washington, DC: Statistical Publishing Company, 1893).

9. Karlyn Kohrs Campbell and Kathleen Hall Jamieson, *Presidents Creating the Presidency: Deeds Done in Words* (Chicago: University of Chicago Press, 2008), 31.

10. Inaugural addresses of William J. Clinton and Theodore Roosevelt.

11. Hereafter, all references to Garfield's reading notes are taken from his *Diary* and are easily located therein by date, but discussion of his inaugural addresses appears on 4: 511–12, 514–15, 519, 521, 525, 529, 534–35, 541–42, 544–46, 548, 550, 552, 554.

12. Paul F. Boller, Jr., *Presidential Inaugurations* (New York: Harcourt, 2001), 12–13.

13. The best account of the early history of the address is the introduction to Rimini and Golway, *Fellow Citizens*.

14. Ibid., 47–48, 59. See also Boller, *Presidential Inaugurations*, 61–62.

15. On Washington's drafts, see Boller, *Presidential Inaugurations*, 4; and Jeffrey K. Tulis, *The Rhetorical Presidency* (Princeton: Princeton University Press, 1987), 48–50.

16. Webster is quoted in Boller, *Presidential Inaugurations*, 141.

17. Ibid., 145–46; inaugural address of Abraham Lincoln.

18. Campbell and Jamieson, *Presidents Creating the Presidency*, 17.

19. Schlesinger, *White House Ghosts*, 269.

20. Ibid., 312–13.

21. Ibid., 403.

22. Campbell and Jamieson, *Presidents Creating the Presidency*, introduction.

23. Tulis, *Rhetorical Presidency*, 48–51.

24. Ibid., 174–78. See also Richard Ellis, ed., *Speaking to the People: The Rhetorical Presidency in Historical Perspective* (Amherst: University of Massachusetts Press, 1998).

25. Elvin T. Lim, *The Anti-Intellectual Presidency: The Decline of Presidential Rhetoric from George Washington to George W. Bush* (New York: Oxford University Press, 2008).

26. Ibid., 64–65.

27. Ibid., chap. 3.

28. Strunk and White, *Elements of Style*; George Orwell, "Politics and the English Language"; H. L. Mencken, "Gamalielese," in *On Politics: A Carnival of Buncombe*, ed. Malcolm Moos (Baltimore: John Hopkins University Press, 1956), 42.

29. Inaugural address of Barack Obama, available at http://www.nytimes.com/2009/01/20/us/politics/20text-obama.html?pagewanted=all.

30. Inaugural addresses of James Garfield, George Washington, John Adams, Thomas Jefferson, Andrew Jackson, and James K. Polk.

31. Inaugural addresses of James Monroe, Martin Van Buren, William Henry Harrison, Franklin Pierce, and Abraham Lincoln.

32. Inaugural addresses of Garfield, William McKinley, and William Taft.

33. Inaugural addresses of Woodrow Wilson, Franklin Delano Roosevelt, Harry S. Truman, and Dwight Eisenhower.

34. Inaugural addresses of Harrison, Ronald Reagan, and George Bush.

35. Inaugural address of Garfield, Reagan, and Clinton; Barack Obama, speech, March 2008, transcript available at http://www.cbsnews.com/2100-250_162-3947908.html.

36. Inaugural address of Garfield.

# INDEX

244, 383n13; inaugural addresses
of, 307; on Marshall's biography of
Washington, 138; speechwriting for
Washington of, 134, 135, 310; on
Washington, 353n41
Making-Out-Road, 210
Mallery, Caleb, 303
manifest destiny, 218–19
Mann, Horace, 197
Manning, William, 77, 328n12, 329n16
*Man of the People: The Maverick Life
and Career of John McCain* (Alex-
ander), 158
Manuelito (Navajo), 215–16
*A Map of Virginia* (Smith), 18
Mark (slave), 235
"Marrying for Money," 193
Marshall, John, 132, 137–38, 140,
350n1, 353nn30–31, 353nn37–38
Marshall, Thurgood, 84, 86
*Martin Chuzzlewit* (Dickens), 162, 175,
197–98, 258, 362n9, 370n92
Marx, Karl, 83
Massachusetts Bay Colony, 34
Massasoit, 34, 37
Mather, Cotton, 33, 95, 231
Mather, Increase, 37, 231
*Mayflower: A Story of Courage, Com-
munity, and War* (Philbrick), 34–36,
38–41
McCain, John, 157–58
McKinley, William, 156, 251, 313, 317
McNamara brothers (John J. and James
B.), 267
Mechanics and Apprentices Library,
106
Meese, Edwin, III, 84, 86
Melville, Herman, 143–45, 230,
357nn59–62
*The Memoirs of Fanny Hill* (Cleland),
164
Mencken, H. L., 305
Metacom, 34
"Metzengerstein" (Poe), 183
Mexican War, 209, 214–16, 218–19
*Middletown: A Study in Modern Ameri-
can Culture* (Lynd and Lynd), 81

Mill, James, 247
Mill, John Stuart, 249
Miller, Perry, 42, 63
Milton, John, 383n7
Minerva Winterslip (character),
268–69
mobility, 295
*Moby Dick* (Melville), 144, 357nn60–61
Moley, Raymond, 311
Monkkonen, Eric, 293, 295–96
Monroe, James, 125; as ambassador,
66, 148; inaugural address of, 307,
309, 316
Monroe Doctrine, 149
*The Monthly Epitome*, 165, 365n39
*The Monthly Review*, 164–65
Moore, Thomas, 197–98
Morgan, Edmund, 20, 36
Morison, Samuel Eliot, 27, 31–43,
328n12; Beck's attack on, 331n33;
charge of Communism against,
43; history of Bradford by, 36–37,
42–43; on history writing, 40–43;
scholarly approach of, 35–36, 43
Morris, Jimmie, 254–55, 262, 265
Morton, Samuel, 216
The Mount Vernon Statement, 84–85
Moynihan, Daniel Patrick, 283
"MS in a Bottle" (Poe), 183
Mumford, Lewis, 223
murder, 291–92; capital punishment
for, 291–92, 300–303, 396n39; the
civilizing process and, 294–96;
documentary record of, 293–94;
European rates of, 294, 394n10;
FBI's Uniform Crime Reports
of, 296, 299–300; mandatory
penalties for, 299; proportional
punishment for, 301–2; role of
guns in, 295; Roth's investigation
of, 293–99; U.S. rates of, 293–98,
396n39
"The Murders in the Rue Morgue"
(Poe), 191–92, 193
Murray, James, 128
"The Mystery of Marie Roget" (Poe),
192–93